World Class

EXPANDING ENGLISH FLUENCY

NATIONAL GEOGRAPHIC LEARNING | CENGAGE Learning®

Australia • Brazil • Japan • Korea • Mexico • Singapore • Spain • United Kingdom • United States

1

World Class

TEACHER'S EDITION

NANCY DOUGLAS | JAMES R. MORGAN

NATIONAL GEOGRAPHIC LEARNING | CENGAGE Learning

Australia • Brazil • Japan • Korea • Mexico • Singapore • Spain • United Kingdom • United States

World Class 1 Teacher's Edition

Nancy Douglas and James R. Morgan

Publisher: Sherrise Roehr

Managing Editor: Sarah Thérèse Kenney

Development Editor: Michael Poor

Senior Technology Project Manager: Scott Rule

Technology Project Manager: Chris Conroy

Director of Global Marketing: Ian Martin

Senior Product Marketing Manager: Katie Kelley

Director, Content and Media Production: Michael Burggren

Content Project Manager: Andrea Bobotas

Print Buyer: Mary Beth Hennebury

Cover Designer: Cenveo Publisher Services

Cover Image: Jeff Curtes

Compositor: Cenveo Publisher Services

ISBN-13: 978-1-133-56578-9

National Geographic Learning
20 Channel Center Street
Boston, MA 02210
USA

Cengage Learning is a leading provider of customized learning solutions with office locations around the globe, including Singapore, the United Kingdom, Australia, Mexico, Brazil and Japan.

Cengage Learning products are represented in Canada by Nelson Education, Ltd.

Visit National Geographic Learning online at **ngl.cengage.com**

Visit our corporate website at **www.cengage.com**

Printed in Canada
1 2 3 4 5 6 7 8 9 10 15 14 13 12

Contents

World Class Series Overview

World Class has everything teachers and students need to help learners expand their overall fluency!

Student Books help high-intermediate and advanced learners develop fluency through a range of interesting, engaging activities. Featuring twelve thematically-based units, learners build their listening, speaking, reading, and writing skills toward a larger investigation of the themes. Each unit ends with the "Expanding Your Fluency" section, a communicative task in which they can apply what they've learned.

Each Student Book comes with a choice of a **Student CD-ROM** or an **Online Workbook***, both of which contain:

- 12 authentic video clips, including feature stories, PSAs, and National Geographic documentaries.
- Video activities to consolidate and reinforce language introduced in the Student Book
- Additional and automatically graded comprehension exercises—giving students instant feedback—and saving teachers and instructors valuable time.
- Audio clips from the Student Book, including model dialogues, listening activities, and pronunciation.

*Powered by *MyELT*, the Online Workbooks have both teacher-led and self- study options.

Workbooks provide additional practice for students to develop language skills presented in the student book. In addition, the Workbook exercises ensure students' fulfillment of the Outcomes that are expected upon completion of each Student Book unit. Students have the opportunity to self-assess their ability to meet the four unit Outcomes on a scale of 1–5. The Workbook also features four Review sections, 12 end-of-book class surveys, and four vocabulary and grammar crossword puzzles for additional practice.

Teacher's Editions have an easy-to-use wrap around design that presents not only teaching and classroom management suggestions but also additional information about the content of the Student Books. Each strand includes pacing suggestions and an Extension activity for further investigation of skills. Teachers are also given options to have their students do more research on topics presented in each unit through Internet Activities.

Presentation Tool CD-ROMs Bring a new dimension to the language learning classroom, making instruction clearer and learning simpler. The CD-ROMs feature interactive activities from the Student Book and Workbook, as well as audio and video clips and can be used with an interactive whiteboard or computer projection.

Online Lesson Planners allow teachers to create and customize lesson plans for their classes, then save and share them in abroad range of formats.

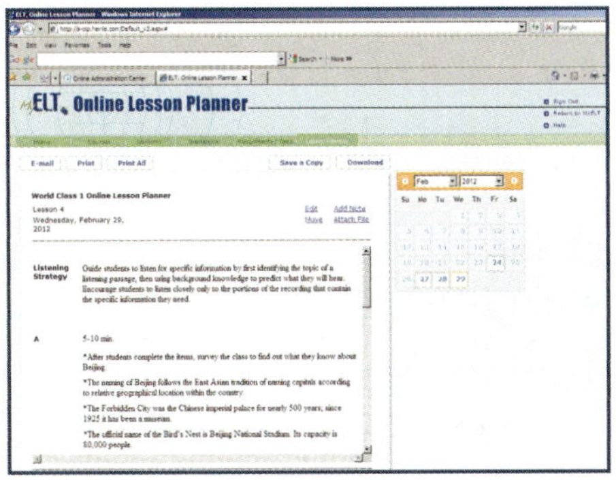

A **Classroom DVD** contains authentic videos, including feature stories, PSAs, and National Geographic documentaries for use in the classroom. Each Classroom DVD is 45 minutes long and has been carefully graded for learners of English at the upper-intermediate and advanced levels.

- A "Video" page is part of each unit, giving students the opportunity to interact meaningfully with the videos.
- Two additional practice exercises related to the videos are incorporated in each unit of the Workbook.
- Videos are embedded in the Online Workbooks so that students can watch as they complete practice exercises.

The **Classroom Audio CD** contains all listening activities from the student book. In addition, several activities from the Student' Book's Pronunciation Appendix are recorded on the CD for students to hear the distinct aural features of spoken English.

The **Assessment CD-ROM with Exam*View*®** is a test generating software with a data bank of readymade test questions designed to allow teachers to administer class assessments quickly and conveniently.

Teaching a Unit of World Class

Overview

World Class engages students with compelling National Geographic content, including photographs, readings, and videos, to bring the world close to home while helping them expand their English fluency. Each twelve-page unit opens with a striking thematic image and is followed by skill-building content and exercises that offer practice in vocabulary, grammar, listening, speaking, reading, and writing. Additionally, each unit includes a page of video-related content tied to the **World Class** Video Program.

The order of the skills strands in each unit varies depending on the culminating task. This is part of the methodology of the series. Each unit of **World Class** begins with an opener, followed by vocabulary and grammar pages that give students the tools they need to discuss the unit theme. Beyond these pages and before the final "Expanding Your Fluency" page, the order of the speaking, reading, video, and writing strands is flexible. Each unit also has skill-building strategies that are incorporated on an as-needed basis. Rather than prescribing a regimented order or quota, this flexible structure allows the strands to build toward a larger investigation of the theme and outcomes in the way that best serves each unit.

World Class Components

Student Book
DVD
Teacher's Edition
Workbook
Audio CD
CD-ROM with additional Workbook Practice
Online Workbook with embedded Video
Interactive Presentation Tool
Online Lesson Planner

Unit Opener

Each unit begins with a two-page spread of striking images related to the unit theme. The images both illustrate the theme and help initiate discussions about the topics that students will explore in the unit. Three warm-up questions are designed to be answered individually or as a class. The opener also introduces the four Unit Outcomes that will be addressed once students have successfully completed the unit.

In this Teacher's Edition, a Unit Overview is provided to give supporting information that may be useful in discussing the unit theme. Teachers are given three additional questions to ask students as a preview to the unit. A photo caption explains the subject and location (when applicable) of the opener image. Throughout the lesson notes, Background Information features provide additional facts about the topic of a listening passage, reading, or video.

Vocabulary

The Corpus of Contemporary American English (COCA) was used to identify the majority of the target vocabulary in the course. These items, which are related to the unit theme, are introduced and defined in the Word Bank feature on the Vocabulary page. Notes on usage and collocations appear in boxes near the Word Bank; different parts of speech for target vocabulary are listed in the Language Summary beginning on page 152 of the Student Book.

In exercises on the page, students move from guided to open-ended discourse-level practice of the target language. Exercises are contextualized in real-life scenarios and events, often inspired by National Geographic.

The notes in this Teacher's Edition provide additional information on word forms or common collocations. Sometimes, other common uses of the words in the Word Bank may be defined. Language Notes may point out additional words or features to explain to students. An optional Extension exercise provides more practice with the target vocabulary.

Grammar

Each **World Class** unit presents one grammar point that is revisited throughout the unit. Some grammar pages review and synthesize concepts (such as contrasting uses of future forms) and are designated with a review icon. Other units introduce new forms appropriate for upper-intermediate and advanced-level learners (such as reported speech).

At the upper levels, it is not uncommon to find that many students have had exposure to a number of grammatical forms; nevertheless, they still need practice using both new and familiar structures in meaningful contexts to build fluency and to broaden their awareness of how this language in used in everyday spoken and written English. To that end, each target structure has been selected so that it fits with the communicative goal of a given unit. On every grammar page, students are given the opportunity to use the target structure in context, beginning with more controlled practice and followed by more open-ended, communicative production of the language. Learners then continue to encounter the structure elsewhere in the unit as it is recycled throughout. The Grammar Summaries beginning on page 158 of the Student Book expand on the structures presented in the units.

The notes in this Teacher's Edition provide additional examples, rules, or usage notes when appropriate. The optional Extension exercise provides additional practice with the grammar point, usually involving more open-ended production.

Listening

After doing a warm-up exercise to introduce the subject of the Listening page, students listen to a recording and complete a series of written exercises. These exercises focus on the development of key skills such as listening for the gist and details, inferring information, note taking, or using visuals to aid in listening. A post-listening task helps students to explore and personalize what they've heard.

Occasionally, a Word Bank is provided to help students preview new vocabulary they will hear. In addition, a Listening Strategy may be included to guide students to listen for nuances in spoken English.

This Teacher's Edition provides background information and language notes to explain in further detail the content of the listening text. An optional Extension exercise suggests an approach for teachers to give students additional listening practice. Additionally, scripts for each audio recording are available in the back of this Teacher's Edition, beginning on page T-167.

Connections

The Connections page provides an opportunity for students to synthesize what they have learned so far in the unit through personalized communication. The exercises encourage students to think in depth about the theme and to relate it to their own lives or experience. Grammar and vocabulary are recycled and elicited in student communication. This practice does not focus on right or wrong answers, but personalized, communicative discourse involving the unit theme and structures.

In this Teacher's Edition, an optional Extension exercise expands upon the communicative goals of the Connections page with the aim of exploring the theme in another way.

Reading

The Reading strand of each unit occupies a two-page spread. Reading texts usually feature authentic National Geographic content and represent a variety of genres, including articles, profiles, and interviews. The practice follows a carefully structured pre-, while-, and post-reading sequence. The first exercise invites students to preview and make predictions about the text by reading titles, looking at pictures, or scanning. Subsequent exercises focus on identifying the main ideas and supporting details of the reading, and getting students to analyze the text critically. Occasionally, a Reading Strategy is provided to help students approach the reading in a specific, prescribed way.

This Teacher's Edition provides background information on the reading content, including culture notes, factual information about the topic, and unique language features. Notes in the Teacher's Edition also address genre, rhetorical modes, signpost questions, and reader expectations. An optional Extension exercise provides an additional opportunity to work with different elements of the text. Finally, suggestions are offered to have students further practice the Reading Strategy or to research a related topic beyond the reading.

Video

Each unit of **World Class** references a video in the World Class Video Program that is tied to the theme of the unit. These compelling videos come from a variety of contemporary, authentic sources, and include news stories, animated pieces, public service announcements, and National Geographic features and documentaries. The Video page often includes a Word Bank of terms mentioned in the video that students might not be familiar with. Like the Reading page, the Video page follows a carefully structured pre-, while-, and post-viewing sequence. The first exercise is intended to preview the video before students watch it. For the exercises that follow, students watch the video, first to note general themes and main ideas, and then to identify specific information. The activity concludes with an exercise that asks students to summarize, explain, or apply the information they learned in the video.

This Teacher's Edition provides background information and language notes relating to the video. An optional Extension exercise encourages students to explore the video's topic further.

Speaking

The Speaking page serves either as one of the skill-building strands in the unit or as its culminating task. In either function, it always directs students to engage in conversations in pairs or small groups. The page focuses on consolidating the vocabulary, structures, and content of the unit in a step-by-step, interactive task or project. Learners are challenged to use their critical thinking skills and to extend language learned in the unit to new situations.

The page sometimes includes a Speaking Strategy, such as responding to interview questions, reaching a compromise, speaking from an outline, or refuting an idea. These are high-frequency, need-to-know expressions that will enable learners to complete the task and communicate in English in a variety of different contexts outside the classroom.

The Teacher's Edition always includes a rubric to help the instructor assess students' performance in the speaking task. An optional Extension exercise gives students more practice in speaking on related topics.

Writing

The Writing assignment serves either as one of the skill-building strands in the unit or as its culminating task. In either function, the writing addresses a variety of rhetorical styles and incorporates the theme, vocabulary, and grammatical structures that students have already practiced in the unit. A Writing Strategy is often provided to help students focus on a particular aspect of their writing within a given genre. A writing model is provided as a prompt; students are asked to analyze it and use it to guide their own writing. In the final activity, students exchange papers and provide one another with feedback.

This Teacher's Edition provides a rubric to help the teacher assess students' writing. An optional Extension exercise gives students more opportunity to practice writing or expand upon the writing theme.

Culminating Task

The page before Expanding Your Fluency always features the unit's culminating task, be it Writing or Speaking. Every section of the unit leads up to this page, scaffolding students' skills to complete a deeper investigation of the unit theme using the target structures. This culminating sequence of activities calls on students to put their critical thinking skills to use in a communicative, discourse-level task, all the while making sure they have enough support to complete the task successfully.

Expanding Your Fluency

This optional section is a final "wind down" to the unit. Students expand their fluency through exercises that involve vocabulary building, review, or personalized communication. The page allows students to see the ways in which they can use their knowledge from the unit to think about and discuss related issues. It also encourages students to assess their own learning throughout the unit. Students can reflect on their achievement of the prescribed outcomes of the unit, which were first presented on the Unit Opener, by rating themselves on each one in the "Check What You Know" rubric.

This Teacher's Edition provides a reference to the exercise where each outcome was met. This allows teachers to direct students back to sections of the unit that may have been challenging. An Extension exercise is provided as a final opportunity for students to expand their English fluency in the unit.

Also Available for Your Convenience

- **Pronunciation Appendix**, pages 144–151 of the Student Book. Highlights nuances in pronouncing American English and includes audio recordings and exercises to help students refine their aural comprehension skills.
- **Language Summaries,** pages 152–157 of the Student Book. Consolidates the Vocabulary learned in the Student Book. Terms are listed alphabetically by unit, along with their meanings and related words.
- **Grammar Summaries,** pages 158–163 of the Student Book. Consolidates the Grammar topics covered in the Student Book.
- **Audio Scripts,** pages T167–T178 of the Teacher's Edition. Includes scripts for all audio recordings in the **World Class** Student Book.
- **Workbook Answer Key,** pages T179–T190 of the Teacher's Edition. Includes answers to help teachers assess students' Workbook practice.
- **Video Scripts,** pages T191–T202 of the Teacher's Edition. Includes transcripts of all twelve videos for this level that are included on the DVD.

1

World Class

EXPANDING ENGLISH FLUENCY

NATIONAL GEOGRAPHIC LEARNING | CENGAGE Learning®

Australia • Brazil • Japan • Korea • Mexico • Singapore • Spain • United Kingdom • United States

NATIONAL GEOGRAPHIC LEARNING | CENGAGE Learning

World Class: Expanding English Fluency
Student Edition

Nancy Douglas and James R. Morgan

Publisher: Sherrise Roehr

Managing Editor: Sarah Thérèse Kenney

Development Editors: Michael Poor, Michael Tom

Senior Technology Product Manager: Scott Rule

Technology Project Manager: Chris Conroy

Director of Global Marketing: Ian Martin

Senior Product Marketing Manager: Katie Kelley

Director, Content and Media Production: Michael Burggren

Content Project Manager: Andrea Bobotas

Print Buyer: Mary Beth Hennebury

Cover Designer: Cenveo Publisher Services

Cover Image: Jeff Curtes

Compositor: Cenveo Publisher Services

Student Book + Student CD-ROM ISBN: 978-1-133-31081-5

Student Book + Online Workbook ISBN: 978-1-285-06309-6

National Geographic Learning
20 Channel Center Street
Boston, MA 02210
USA

Cengage Learning is a leading provider of customized learning solutions with office locations around the globe, including Singapore, the United Kingdom, Australia, Mexico, Brazil and Japan.

Cengage Learning products are represented in Canada by Nelson Education, Ltd.

Visit National Geographic Learning online at **ngl.cengage.com**

Visit our corporate website at **www.cengage.com**

Printed in Canada
1 2 3 4 5 6 7 8 9 10 15 14 13 12

Acknowledgements

The authors and editorial team would like to thank the many dedicated instructors who took the time to review World Class. *Their feedback was invaluable during the development of this program.*

UNITED STATES Touria Ghaffari, EC New York, New York, New York**; Olga Gusak,** Computer Systems Institute, Skokie, Illinois**; William Jex,** American Language Institute, New York University, New York, New York**; Bridget McDonald,** Independent Learning Services, Boston, Massachusetts**; Saida Pagan,** North Valley OC, Mission Hills, California**; Tara Tarpey,** American Language Institute, New York University, New York, New York

LATIN AMERICA Luiz Otávio Barros, Associação Alumni, Brazil; **Clarissa Bezerra,** Casa Thomas Jefferson, Brazil**; Isabela Villas Boas,** Casa Thomas Jefferson, Brazil**; Tatiane C. de Carvalho,** Cultura Britânica e Americana, Brazil**; Rafael Reis Carpanez,** Cultura Inglesa, Brazil**; Janette Carvalhinho de Oliveira,** Centro de Linguas - UFES, Brazil**; Samara Camilo Tomé Costa,** IBEU, Brazil**; Frank Couto,** Casa Thomas Jefferson, Brazil**; Denise Santos da Silva,** Associação Cultural Estados Unidos, Brazil**; Marilena Fernandes,** Associação Alumni, Brazil**; Vanessa Ferreira,** Associação Cultural Brasil Estados Unidos, Brazil**; Marcia Ferreira,** CCBEU Franca, Brazil**; Maria Regina Filgueiras,** College Language Center, Brazil**; Maria Righini,** Associação Cultura Inglesa, Brazil**; Bebeth Silva Costa,** Betina's English Course, Brazil**; Domingos Sávio Siqueira,** Federal University of Bahia, Brazil**; Joyce von Söhsten,** English by Joyce von Söhsten, Brazil**; Doris Flores,** Universidad Santo Tomas, Chile**; Sandra Herrera,** Inacap Apoquindo, Chile**; Jair Ayala Zarate,** La Salle University, Colombia; **Rosario Mena,** Instituto Cultural Dominico Americano, Dominican Republic**; Raúl Billini,** Language Program Administration, Dominican Republic**; Rosa Vásquez,** John F. Kennedy Institute of Languages, INC., Dominican Republic**; Elizabeth Ortiz,** COPEI-COPOL English Institute, Ecuador**; José Alonso Gaxiola Soto,** Universidad Autonoma de Sinaloa, Mexico**; María Elena Mesías Ratto,** Universidad de San Martín de Porres, Peru

EUROPE AND THE MIDDLE EAST Juan Irigoyen, International Institute, Spain**; Nashwa Nashaat Sobhy,** San Jorge University, Spain; **Barbara Van der Veer,** International Institute, Spain **Deborah Wilson,** American University of Sharjah, United Arab Emirates

ASIA Michael Lay, American Intercon Institute, Cambodia**; Kirkland Arizona Kenney,** Beijing New Oriental School, China**; Isao Akama,** Waseda University, Japan**; Benjamin Bailey,** University of Shizuoka, Japan**; James Baldwin,** Toyko University of Agriculture and Technology, Japan**; Jonathan deHaan,** University of Shizuoka, Japan**; Todd Enslen,** Tohoku University, Japan**; Peter Gray,** Hokusei Gakuen University, Japan**; Linda Hausman,** Gakushuin University, Japan**; Mauro Lo Dico,** Nanzan University, Japan**; Nobue Mori,** Kumamoto Gakuen University, Japan**; Yuri Nishio,** Gifu Pharmaceutical University, Japan**; Geraldine Norris,** The Prefectual University of Shizuoka, Japan**; Christopher Piper,** Takushoku University, Japan**; Michael Radcliffe,** Yokohama City University, Japan**; Jean-Pierre Richard,** Kanagawa University, Sophia University, Japan; **Greg Rouault,** Konan University, Hirao School of Management, Japan; **Stephen Ryan,** Yamagata University, Japan; **Gregory Strong,** Aoyama Gakuin University, Japan; **Michael Yasui,** Tokyo Metropolitan University, Japan; **Sun Mi Ma,** Ajou University, Korea; **Palarak Chaiyo,** Rajamangala University of Technology Suvarnabhumi, Thailand; **Krishna Kosashunhanan,** Thai-Nichai Institute of Technology, Thailand; **Jonee de Leon,** Universal English Center, Vietnam**; Ai Nguyen Huynh Thi,** VUS, Vietnam

We would also like to extend a special thank-you to Yeny Kim for her many insights. Her thoughtful contributions were a great asset and will be felt by students and teachers alike.

READING	WRITING	SPEAKING	VIDEO
Cleopatra: The Search for the Last Queen of Egypt	Write a personal statement as part of an application **Strategy:** Writing a personal statement	Interview to be a cultural ambassador **Strategy:** Responding to questions	*The Human Family Tree*
Traveling Troubadour: An interview with singer Jason Mraz	Write a descriptive paragraph about a place **Strategy:** Create a mental image	Create a bucket list of things you want to do **Strategy:** Making suggestions and giving advice	*Barcelona's Street Life*
Plugging Into the Sun: Why don't we use solar energy more? **Strategy:** Identifying key details	Write a persuasive paragraph that presents and justifies your point of view **Strategy:** Being persuasive	Persuade an audience to make a change	*We Need to Be Leaders Ourselves*
Hip Hop Goes Home: A struggling rapper in Africa	Write a profile of a person that you admire **Strategy:** Paraphrasing	Analyzing a music contract **Strategy:** Talking pros and cons	*Songs under a Big Sky* (excerpt): Profile of Irish singer Iarla Ó Lionáird
Everest's Deadliest Day: Two teams compete to reach the summit first – with deadly results	Write a set of instructions describing how to do something **Strategy:** Explaining the steps in a process	Discuss a difficult environmental issue **Strategy:** Reaching a compromise	*Surviving Deadly Everest*
Every Shoe Tells a Story: They say a lot about us, even when we're not wearing them	Present and defend and argument **Strategy:** Making a successful argument	Give your opinions in a shopping and fashion survey **Strategy:** Reacting to someone else's point of view	*How to Spot a Fake Louis Vuitton Bag*

READING	WRITING	SPEAKING	VIDEO
One Foot on The Gas: Children of immigrants discover American car culture	Write a letter of complaint	Consider the facts in an immigration case **Strategy:** Presenting facts and announcing a decision	*Capital Bikeshare*
Nowhere to Hide: What happens when our private lives become public	Give an opinion on an event **Strategy:** Writing an effective online post	Evaluate different surveillance practices	*Protecting reputations online*
Orphan Elephants: A center in Kenya rescues, rehabilitates and researches baby elephants	Write an informational brochure **Strategy:** Getting the reader's attention	Debate what to do about three animals at risk	*Great Migrations* (excerpt)
The Teenage Brain: Why teenagers act the way they do **Strategy:** Recognizing cause and effect	Use cause and effect to explain a decision you'd make **Strategy:** Showing cause and effect	Analyze how you handle peer pressure	*Moral Dilemma* (excerpt): **Pronunciation:** Thought groups
Storm Chasers: Scientists risk their lives to gather data about tornadoes **Strategy:** Making inferences	Describe a time weather impacted your life **Strategy:** Include figurative language	Which weather story is false?	*Sinking England*
The Spirit of Kung Fu: A Shaolin master faces the world of kung fu	Write about important qualities **Strategy:** Writing a timed essay	Present an activity **Strategy:** Speaking from an outline	Alain Robert, "*The French Spiderman*"

World Class 1 Student Book Walkthrough

Explore a Unit

The first half of each unit leads students through guided and communicative practice to master target structures.

2 The World Awaits

Unit Outcomes

Clearly stated **Unit Outcomes** provide a roadmap of learning for the student.

Stunning images and thought-provoking questions encourage learners to **think critically** about the unit theme.

Relevant, high frequency vocabulary is practiced in contextualized exercises.

Pronunciation boxes offer support and tips as well as cross reference to full explanation and practice in the appendix.

The **Grammar** section allows learners to refine their grammar skills and practice the grammar through first controlled and then open-ended activities.

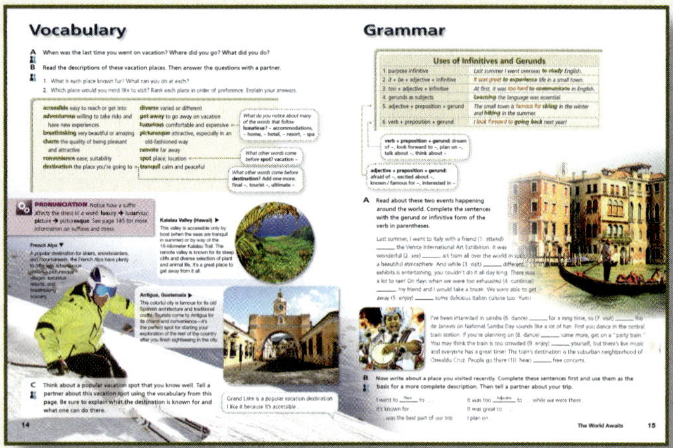
Vocabulary

Grammar

Uses of Infinitives and Gerunds

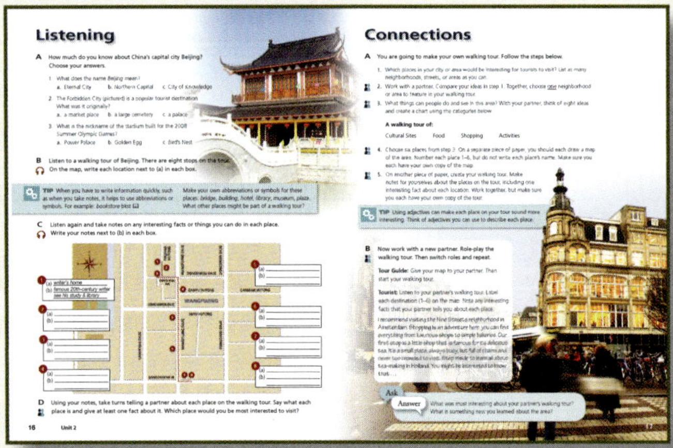
Listening

Connections

Listening activities encourage learners to listen for and consolidate key information, reinforcing the language, and allowing learners to personalize and think critically about the information they hear.

The **Connections** section allows learners to synthesize the vocabulary and grammar they have learned through personalized communication.

The second half of the unit focuses on skill-building and communication. The strands build on one another with a final communicative task before Expanding Your Fluency. For this reason, the order of strands may vary from unit to unit.

Learners navigate **interesting and relevant readings** from National Geographic through pre-, while-, and post-reading activities,helping them to comprehend the main idea and key details of the passage.

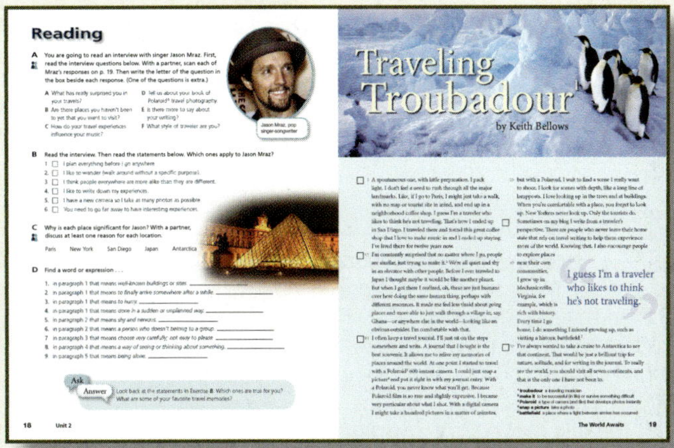
Reading

Traveling Troubadour

by Keith Bellows

I guess I'm a traveler who likes to think he's not traveling.

Learners are encouraged to perform **Speaking** tasks in pairs and groups. Where appropriate, **strategies** are provided to ensure students' successful communication.

The **Video** section brings the world into the classroom with authentic clips, including news stories, PSAs, and National Geographic documentaries.

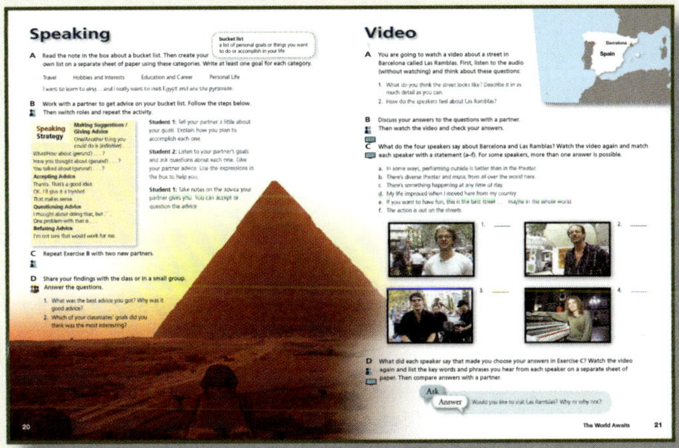
Speaking

Video

The **Writing** section includes writing models to prompt learners to complete a functional piece of writing and also serves as a culminating activity in many units.

The **Expanding Your Fluency** section allows learners to apply the language they have learned throughout the unit in real-world tasks and offers self-assessment checks.

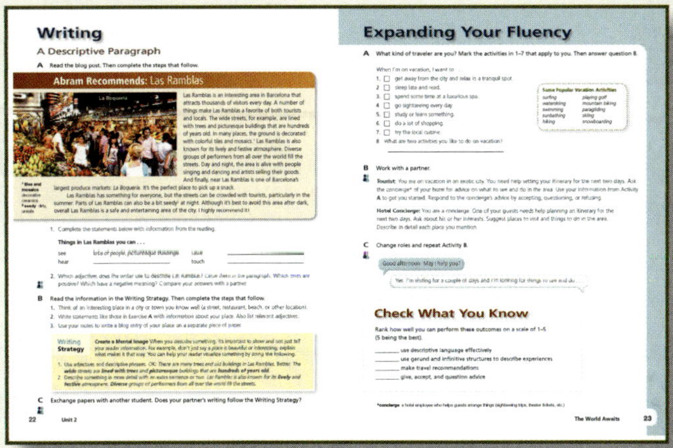
Writing

A Descriptive Paragraph

Abram Recommends: Las Ramblas

Expanding Your Fluency

Check What You Know

Unit 1
Who We Are

Unit Overview

- Unit 1 is about personal identity. Students will learn how genealogy, history, and culture help define who they are.
- The global population is currently estimated at seven billion people, 60% of which live in Asia. Despite immense diversity in human cultures, languages, customs, and traits, genetic studies indicate that humans are more similar than they are different.
- Ask students what they think is meant by the unit title, "Who We Are." Inform them that "We" refers to all humans and that the title conveys the concepts of personal and human identity.
- Preview the unit by asking students the following questions:

1. Who is the world's most typical person? Prompt students to guess at age, nationality, native language, and gender.
2. How are people all over the world alike? How are they different?
3. What factors make us who we are?

Photo Caption

The individuals in this collage represent the diversity of the people on the planet in terms of ethnicity—African, Asian, Caucasian, and Hispanic; age—youth, adult, and older; and gender—male and female.

1 Who We Are

VOCABULARY	GRAMMAR	LISTENING	VIDEO
Who is the world's most typical human?	Review of past tenses	New Family Tree Web site **Pronunciation:** Rising and falling intonation	*The Human Family Tree*

1 Look at the four photos. Who are these people? Describe each person in as much detail as you can.

2 Where do you think these people come from? Tell a story about one of them.

3 Do you think you have anything in common with the people in the photos? Why or why not?

Unit Outcomes

In this unit, you will learn to:

- use past tenses to ask and answer questions about memorable life events
- summarize the key outcomes of a study
- explain and evaluate qualifications
- handle challenging questions

1

5-10 min. **Warm-Up Questions**
Extension: 10-15 min.

Background Information

During the twentieth century, the world saw the greatest increase in its population in human history. The global population is currently estimated at seven billion people and is projected to reach ten billion by the year 2050. China, India, and the United States are the most populous countries in the world (the first two account for 37% of the world's population).

Warm-Up Questions

- Read the unit title aloud and invite students to look at the photos. Ask them to guess the theme of the unit.
- Read Question 1 aloud. Guide the class in describing in detail each person pictured. Alternatively, have pairs of students take turns describing the people.
- Divide the class into four groups; assign a photo to each one. Tell them that the person's story should be simple and believable, yet interesting. Then have each group tell their story to the class.
- Ask students to think of three words that best describe themselves. Then go through Question 3 as a class.

Extension

Write the following on the board: *nationality, language, physical characteristics, education, personality, character, family history, peer group, religion, profession/occupation*. In small groups, have students discuss which aspects of identity as described by these words are most influential in defining who a person is.

READING	WRITING	SPEAKING	OUTCOMES
Cleopatra: The Search for the Last Queen of Egypt	Write a personal statement as part of an application **Strategy:** Writing a personal statement	Interview to be a cultural ambassador **Strategy:** Responding to questions	• use past tenses to ask and answer questions about memorable life events • summarize the key outcomes of a study • explain and evaluate qualifications • handle challenging questions

Vocabulary

15-20 min. **A**
10-15 min. **B**
15-20 min. **C**
Extension: 10 min.

A Survey the class to find out if there is a consensus on the description of the school's most typical student.

Language Notes

- Provide an additional collocation for *average: on ~* Point out that *statistics* usually appears in the plural.
- Remind students that a *trait* can refer to personal nature or to physical qualities.

B
- After students make their guesses, give the correct answers. Ask students how they did.
- Provide statistics to support these traits of the most typical human: 13% of people in the world speak Mandarin as their first language; the ratio of males to females is 1.01 to 1; the average age is 28; the world has about five billion cell phone subscribers; the income of the most typical human is under US$12,000 annually; 51% live in urban environments.

Answers: 1. speaks Chinese; 2. is male; 3. is 21–30; 4. has a cell phone; 5. doesn't have a bank account; 6. lives in a big city

C
- To create the "most typical face" photo, the Chinese Academy of Sciences used 190,000 photos of 28-year-old Han Chinese men to create a single composite image. Then a digital artist re-created the photo using 7,000 human figures, each one representing one million people, to depict the world's population of 7 billion. Students can see the image at http://ngm.nationalgeographic.com/2011/03/age-of-man/face-interactive.

Answer: top left (Chinese male)

Photo Caption

The crowd in this photo is in Times Square in New York City on New Year's Eve, 2007. People have gathered in Times Square to celebrate New Year's for over one hundred years. The celebration culminates with the "ball drop" at 11:59 p.m., when a giant crystal ball atop a flagpole begins its 77-foot (23 m) descent and lights up at exactly midnight. Over one million people gather in Times Square each year to take part in the festivities.

Vocabulary

A Describe the most typical person at your school. Do you fit the description of the "most typical person"? Why or why not? Tell a partner.

The typical person in this school is between 19 and 22 years old, has dark hair . . .

ambitious needing exceptional effort and resources to be carried out successfully; the desire to achieve something exceptional
average the normal amount or quality for a group of things or people
come up with to suggest or think of an idea or plan
determine to find out or to confirm certain information
set out to start trying to do something
statistics numerical facts that are gathered through analyzing information
trait a particular characteristic a person has
typical showing the most usual characteristics of a person or thing

average *~ year, ~ day, ~ income, above/below ~*

typical *~ day, ~ student, ~ pattern, ~ behavior*

B On our planet of seven billion people, who is the most typical human? In an ambitious effort, scientists set out to list the traits of the most typical human being. Guess what they found.

According to statistics, the average person . . .

1. speaks Spanish / English / Chinese / French.
2. is male / female.
3. is under 20 / 21–30 / over 30.
4. has / doesn't have a cell phone.
5. has / doesn't have a bank account.
6. lives in a big city / in a small suburb / in the country.

C To determine what the average human being on Earth looks like, scientists then collected photos of 190,000 of the world's most typical people. After combining the photos electronically, the scientists came up with a face that looked like one of the photos on the unit opener. In pairs, discuss: Which photo is it?

Ask Answer How similar are you to the world's most typical person? Explain your answer with examples.

Extension

Have students recall their description from Exercise **A** of the "most typical person" at their school. Ask them to compare and contrast that type of person with the "most typical human" they learned about in Exercise **B**. Have them write a paragraph about this comparison.

Grammar

A What do we know about Dan's living situation? Match each sentence (1–4) with an explanation (a–c). Use the chart to help you. Explain your answers to a partner.

1. Dan lived in Europe for two years.
2. Dan was living in Europe at the time.
3. Dan has lived in Europe since 2010.
4. Dan has been living in Europe for two years.

a. Dan lives in Europe now.
b. Dan doesn't live in Europe anymore.
c. Dan may or may not live in Europe now.

TIP Use *for* (+ a period of time) and *since* (+ a specific point in time) with the perfect tenses to describe "time up to now." Use *for* (but not *since*) with the simple past tense for a time period that has come to an end.

Review of Past Tenses	
simple past: Use for actions completed in the past at a specific time (sometimes inferred). Use time expressions like *a year ago, earlier today, last summer,* and *the other day*.	We **graduated** together. He **worked** there for a year.
past continuous: Use for ongoing past actions that may or may not be completed. Use with the simple past to describe what was going on when the action in the simple past occurred.	I **was working** all day yesterday. We **were studying** in college when we rented that apartment.
present perfect: Use for actions begun in the past and continuing up to now and for actions in the past that relate to the present. Use time expressions like *lately, recently, up to now, during the last two months,* and *this week*.	**I've worked** here for a year. **Have** you ever **studied** Portuguese?
present perfect continuous: Use to emphasize the length of an event. In spoken English the verb *to be* is almost always a contraction.	Recently, **I've been working** too much. She**'s been waiting** for an hour!

B Read about Liam. Complete each sentence with the correct past form of the verb in parentheses.

During and after college He (1. live) __________ in the dorms while he (2. attend) __________ college. After graduation, he (3. move) __________ back in with his parents for a year to save money. He (4. live) __________ there ever since.

Occupation He (5. start) __________ a small business with two other people when he (6. be) __________ 24. It (7. close) __________ a year ago. Since then, he (8. work) __________ for a large tech company.

Health He never (9. smoke) __________ in his life. Last year, he (10. run) __________ in his first marathon.

Relationships He (11. meet) __________ his wife two years ago. They (12. talk) __________ about having a baby in the next year.

C Now ask your partner three questions about Liam.

> Where did he live while he was attending college?

D Now it's your turn! In pairs, tell each other a little bit about yourselves, using the same categories and model language in Activity **B**.

Grammar

15 min. **A**
10-15 min. **B**
5-10 min. **C**
10-15 min. **D**
Extension: 15-20 min.

A
- Go through the chart as a class. For each use, give additional examples from your own life. Elicit student responses by asking about their studies.
- Go over the answers to Exercise **A** as a class.
- Read through the Tip as a class. On the board, create a simple timeline showing the last ten years. Mark visual representations of Dan's living situation for items 1–4 (e.g., for item 1, block off a two-year period).

Answers: 1. b; 2. c; 3. a; 4. a

B For extra practice, ask students these discussion questions related to Liam's information:

1. Where did you live while you were going to college?
2. Do many people your age smoke these days? Have you ever smoked?
3. Have you ever run in a marathon?
4. If you have a girlfriend or a boyfriend, how did you meet her or him? How long have you been dating?

Answers: 1. lived; 2. was attending; 3. moved; 4. 's lived; 's been living; 5. started; 6. was; 7. closed; 8. 's been working; 9. has smoked; 10. ran; 11. met; 12. 've talked; 've been talking

C **Outcome:** Upon completing this exercise, students will have met the Outcome ***use past tenses to ask and answer questions about memorable life events.***

Extension

Tell students to write eight sentences describing key moments or information about their lives using the past tenses in the chart on this page. Five of the sentences should be true and three should be false. In small groups, have students take turns reading their sentences aloud. Their classmates should guess which statements are true and which are false.

Listening

10 min. **A**
10-15 min. **B**
10-15 min. **C**
10-15 min. **D**
Extension: 15-20 min.

Background Information

This audio recording consists of an advertisement for a fictitious Web site where family members can share memories, photos, and other information, thus creating a sort of "living family tree."

A
- Model the activity by talking about your own family.
- If students are not comfortable talking about their families, encourage them to talk about another family they know.
- Ask for volunteers to share facts about their family histories.

B
- Have a volunteer read the Tip aloud. Ask students to predict what information they would expect to hear in an ad for a Web site. After playing the audio, have students identify the repeated words and ideas that they hear.
- Some repeated words and ideas: *they* (in reference to the other "boring" Web sites on the market); *you can* (to emphasize the self-directed nature of the Web site and its usefulness); *a place where* (to emphasize how the Web site can keep memories centrally located).
- Play the audio recording of the advertisement one or more times. **Audio CD Track 2**

Answers: lets you upload photos and video; allows members to share and tell stories; enables you to share memories with your relatives

C Play the audio recording that explains how the Web site works. **Audio CD Track 3**

Answers: a. 2, b. 4, c. 1, d. *blank*, e. 3, f. 5

D Play the audio recording of the explanation again. Pause the recording after each target question to allow students time to write. **Audio CD Track 4**

Answers: 1. meet Dad; 2. best friend when you were growing up; 3. subject in school; 4. been in love; 5. makes you smile

Listening

generation the period of time (about thirty years) it takes for children to grow up and have their own families

preserve to save or protect something for the future

A Look at the illustration. Answer the questions with a partner.

1. What do you know about your family tree? Tell your partner two facts.
2. How did you learn that information? How has your family history been preserved?

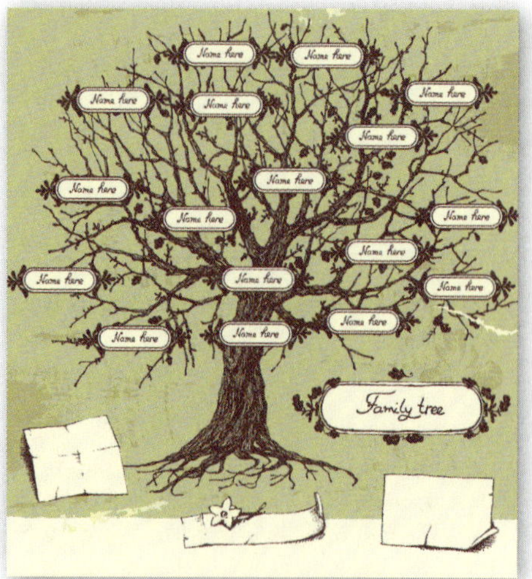

A family tree is a diagram that shows family members and their relationships over several generations. Typically, the older generations are at the top of the tree and the youngest relatives are at the bottom.

B Listen to an advertisement for a Web site. Mark all of the statements that are true.

New Family Tree . . .

- ☐ focuses on family statistics and research.
- ☐ lets you upload photos and video.
- ☐ connects you with families all over the world.
- ☐ allows members to share and tell stories.
- ☐ enables you to share memories with your relatives.

TIP Listen for words or ideas that are repeated. Repeated information often means that it is important and you should pay attention.

C How does the site work? Listen and number the steps in the correct order. One step is extra.

_____ a. choose a question
_____ b. send the question to someone
_____ c. log in
_____ d. pay a membership fee
_____ e. write an answer to the question
_____ f. read the answer to the question

PRONUNCIATION Notice that the pitch of your voice should drop at the end of these questions. See page 144 for more information on intonation.

D What kinds of questions can you answer on the site? Listen again and complete the sample questions below. Then choose one and ask your partner about it.

1. How did you ____________________?
2. Who was your ____________________?
3. What's your favorite ____________________?
4. Have you ever ____________________?
5. What is a memory from your childhood that ____________________?

Extension

Have students draw a simple family tree and share it with the class. Encourage them to start by drawing boxes for themselves and immediate family members before going on to chart the extended family and previous generations. Model how to connect the boxes: spouses are joined with dashed lines, a solid line that descends from that indicates their children, and so forth. If students are not comfortable sharing information about their families, tell them to make a fictitious family tree or one of a famous family.

Video

A You are going to watch the video *The Human Family Tree*. Complete the sentences with the correct options.

ancestors	determine	generations	setting out

Scientists are (1) ______ to answer some questions. On a single street in New York City, they are collecting DNA samples from people from all over the world including Thailand, Ecuador, Africa, and the Caribbean. They are trying to use the DNA to come up with some answers about the past. Will the scientists be able to use the samples to trace back each person's (2) ______ many (3) ______ and (4) ______ where they came from? And will they learn anything about the "human family tree"?

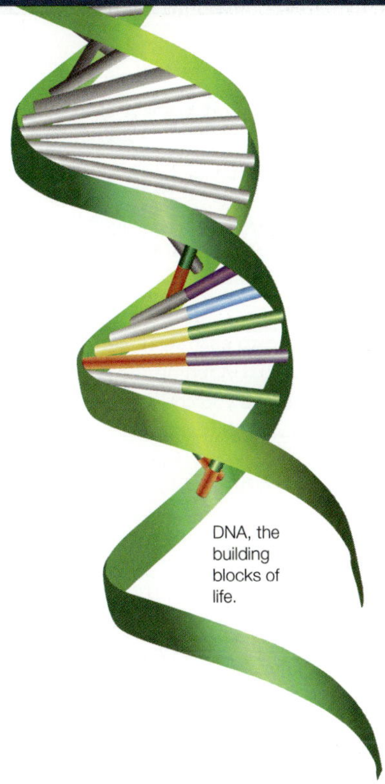

DNA, the building blocks of life.

B Answer these questions with a partner.

1. Why are the scientists doing DNA tests in New York City?
2. What do you think they will learn about the "human family tree"?

C Watch the video. Decide if each statement is true or false. Then, correct the false sentences to make them true. Explain your answers to a partner.

1.	A key human question is: "Where are my ancestors?"	True	False
2.	Typically, we can trace our family tree back one or two generations.	True	False
3.	DNA testing takes us back up to twelve generations.	True	False
4.	We each carry a kind of genetic historic document inside us.	True	False
5.	Our ancestors adapted to different cultures.	True	False
6.	At the genetic level, we are basically identical.	True	False

VIDEO GLOSSARY

adapt to change your ideas or behavior to suit a different situation

genetics the study of how certain characteristics (e.g., eye color, hair color, and skin color) are passed from one generation to the next by our genes

identical exactly the same

D Summarize the video in your own words. Use these questions to help you.

What was happening?
Who was leading the study, and why did they do it?
What did they discover?
What were people hoping to find out?

Ask Answer Would you be interested in participating in this study? Why or why not?

Internet Activity

Tell students they are going to explore how key events in human history have left marks on our genetic makeup. Have them use the "Atlas of Human History" feature on the Genographic Project's Web site (https://genographic.nationalgeographic.com/genographic/lan/en/globe.html#). Students should pick one point on the globe that is close to their geographic center and one point that is far away. Tell students to briefly summarize the historical information in their own words and guess how these key events in history might have affected their own genetic makeup.

Video

5-10 min. **A**
5-10 min. **B**
15 min. **C**
15-20 min. **D**
Extension: 20 min.

Background Information

Spencer Wells is an American geneticist and anthropologist and Explorer-in-Residence at National Geographic. He leads The Genographic Project, a genetic anthropology study, launched in 2005.

Before You Watch

A
- Tell students that they're going to learn about a scientific study that uses genetic markers to create a "human family tree."
- Have students read the paragraph once before filling in the blanks.

Answers: 1. setting out; 2. ancestors; 3. generations; 4. determine

Language Notes

- *DNA* stands for "**d**eoxyribo**n**ucleic **a**cid."
- Point out the uses of *gonna* and *'cause* in the video. Remind students that relaxed pronunciation and word reductions are common features of informal speech.

C
- Read the statements aloud and have the class predict the answers orally.
- Play the video more than once if needed.

Answers: 1. False: A key human question is: "Who are my ancestors?" 2. False: Typically we can trace our family tree back four or five generations. 3. False: DNA testing takes us back many thousands of generations. 4. True. 5. False: Our ancestors adapted to different climates. 6. True

D **Outcome:** Upon completing this exercise, students will have met the Outcome ***summarize the key outcomes of a study***.

Extension

Direct students to watch an online episode of the English-language television show *Who Do You Think You Are?* in which celebrities trace their genealogies (http://www.nbc.com/who-do-you-think-you-are). Tell them to take notes on the most interesting information that people unearthed during their genealogical studies. In class, have pairs of students share what they learned.

Reading

10 min. **A**
5-10 min. **B**
5 min. **C**
5-10 min. **D**
5 min. **E**
15 min. **F**
Extension: 15-20 min.

Purpose for Reading

Remind students that they have been exploring the topic of identity in this unit: Who is the most typical human? Who am I? What's my background? Who were my ancestors? In this reading, they are going to read and talk about a famous person from history to answer the question: Who was she really?

A Have partners share their lists with the class. Write their ideas on the board. Then have them read the article.

B Have students read the article a second time before answering the questions.

Answers: 1. F; 2. T; 3. T; 4. P; 5. T; 6. P; 7. F; 8. P

C
- If necessary, inform students that *BCE* is an acronym that stands for "Before the Common Era."
- Remind students that scanning, or moving one's eyes quickly down the page, is a useful way to find specific words or phrases within a text.

Answers: *69 BCE* is the year she was born; *4* is the number of children she had; *18* is the age when she became queen; *22* is the year her son with Caesar was born; *44 BCE* is the year Caesar died; later she met Marc Antony; *30 BCE* is the year Rome invaded Egypt and Cleopatra died; *39* is her age when she died; *20,000* is the number of objects found in the Mediterranean; many probably existed during Cleopatra's lifetime

D Remind students to use their own words when they summarize.

F
- Before dividing the class into groups, start a discussion about TV talk shows, especially those that regularly feature interviews with athletes and celebrities. See if students can name any that are popular in their country.

continued on page 7

Reading

Cleopatra's kingdom at greatest extent, 34–31 B.C.

A Read the title of the passage and look at the photos. With a partner, make a list of everything you know about Cleopatra. Then read the passage. How many of your ideas were mentioned in the article?

B Next to each statement, write the correct letter (*T, F,* or *P*). Underline the information in the passage that helped you choose your answers.

T = definitely true **P** = possible, but not 100% certain
F = definitely false

Cleopatra . . .

_____ 1. was Egypt's first queen.
_____ 2. was Greek.
_____ 3. was well-educated.
_____ 4. was a beautiful woman.
_____ 5. had four children.
_____ 6. was killed by a snake.
_____ 7. was honored by the Romans after her death.
_____ 8. is buried near the city of Alexandria.

C Why are these numbers and dates important to Cleopatra's life and the search for her? Write your answers on another piece of paper.

69 BCE 4 18 22 44 BCE 30 BCE 39 20,000

D Use the information in Exercises **B** and **C** to summarize Cleopatra's life.

E Make a list of 4–6 ages, numbers, and dates that are important in your life. Use them to tell a partner about "who you are."

F It's time to step out of your own identity and into someone else's. Get into a small group of 3–5 people. One person is a TV talk show host who interviews popular celebrities. The others are today's guests on the show; you can choose from Cleopatra, her brother Ptolemy, Julius Caesar, and Marc Antony. You are going to create a 2–3 minute role-play.

- First, come up with 5–6 interesting questions to ask the show's guests. Decide how each guest would respond. Use information from the reading and your imaginations to help you.
- Present your role-play to another group.

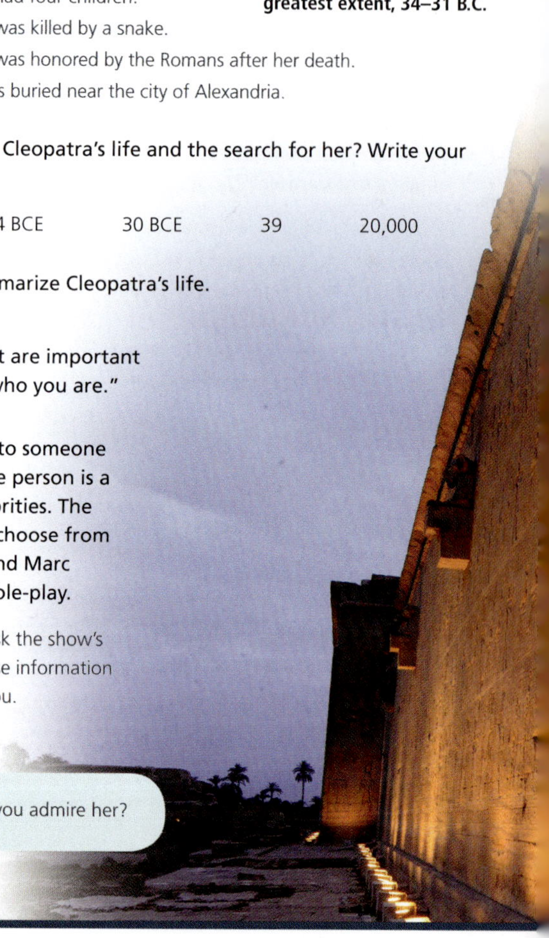

Ask Answer What do you think of Cleopatra? Do you admire her?

6 **Unit 1**

Extension

In pairs, have students think of another historical figure about whom there exists much speculation and legend. If they have trouble coming up with someone, you may suggest any of the following: King Arthur, Confucious, Genghis Khan, Montezuma, Rasputin, Joan of Arc. Have them compare and contrast that person with Cleopatra.

CLEOPATRA

• THE SEARCH FOR THE LAST QUEEN OF EGYPT •

The deadly snake sat in its case. "Bring me the basket!" Cleopatra ordered her servants. Roman soldiers were invading[1] her country, and the queen of Egypt would rather die than live as a prisoner. Cleopatra picked up the snake and let it bite her. Within minutes, she was dead.

This story has been told for centuries. But did it really happen? Like so much about Cleopatra, no one knows for sure.

Teen Queen

We know little about Cleopatra, but some information about her has survived. We know, for example, that she was born in 69 BCE to a Greek family who ruled Egypt for nearly three hundred years. Growing up in Alexandria, Cleopatra studied science and math. She also learned to speak several languages, including Greek, Latin, and Egyptian.

By the time she became queen at age 18, Egypt—one of the world's richest nations—was in trouble. The Roman Empire was planning to invade. Cleopatra was also at war with her younger brother, Ptolemy. To stop him, Cleopatra persuaded[2] the Roman general Julius Caesar to help her. With Caesar's help, Cleopatra defeated[3] her brother. Caesar also helped Cleopatra preserve Egypt's independence from Rome.

The partners soon became a couple, and at age 22, Cleopatra had a son. After Caesar's death in 44 BCE, Cleopatra met another powerful Roman, Marc Antony. The pair eventually had three children, and for years they fought to stop Rome from invading Egypt. In the summer of 30 BCE, though, Rome won. Rather than accept defeat, Marc Antony and Cleopatra killed themselves. Cleopatra—Egypt's last pharaoh (ruler)—was 39 years old.

Erasing the Past

After Cleopatra died, the Romans invented negative stories about her and destroyed art with her image on it. They didn't want Egyptians to remember their former queen. Over time, earthquakes also destroyed buildings, and the sea around Alexandria rose. Within a few hundred years, most of Cleopatra's world was buried[4] under water. As a result, we know very little about how Cleopatra lived or exactly how she died. Although stories often describe her as beautiful, we don't really know what she looked like.

The Search Begins

But this may be changing. Today, archaeologists[5] have started searching the Mediterranean near Alexandria, Cleopatra's home. So far, they've brought up 20,000 objects from the sea. Many probably existed during Cleopatra's lifetime.

On land nearby, other archaeologists have discovered new tombs, and there are signs that someone important may be buried there. "My dream is to find a statue of Cleopatra," says one explorer. So far, however, neither search has located Cleopatra—yet.

Cleopatra (left) in one of the few images that still exists of her.

[1] **invading** entering a country by force with an army
[2] **persuade** to cause someone to do something by giving good reasons for doing it
[3] **defeat** to win a victory over someone in a battle or game
[4] **buried** under the ground and covered with earth
[5] **archaeologists** scientists who study people and societies of the past

Beyond the Reading

Have students use the Internet to learn more about the maritime archaeology underway near Alexandria, led by Franck Goddio (suggested sites: www.nationalgeographic.com; www.archaeology.org; www.underwaterdiscovery.org). Ask them to prepare a poster about the archaeological findings and what clues they give about Cleopatra's life and times. Encourage them to include visuals.

Reading *continued*

F
- To get students started, brainstorm a few questions the host could ask his or her guests. For example, from the reading they know that Cleopatra had a relationship with Julius Caesar. Questions about this could include: How long were you and Caesar together? How exactly did you meet? Cleopatra, did you really love Caesar or did you just use him to protect your country? Caesar, how did you feel about Cleopatra? The students playing Cleopatra and Caesar should respond in character and can even ask each other questions.
- Have students jot down ideas on note cards. They can use the notes during the role-play, but encourage them to be creative and spontaneous in their answers.
- Have one or two groups present their role-play to the whole class.

Background Information

- Cleopatra's (69 BCE–August 12, 30 BCE) full name was Cleopatra VII Philopator. She belonged to the Ptolemaic dynasty, a Greek royal family that ruled Egypt from 305 to 30 BCE. All male rulers (such as Cleopatra's brother) took the name Ptolemy; all female rulers took the names Cleopatra, Berenice, or Arsinoe. Ptolemaic pharaohs often ruled together with their wives; Cleopatra did so with her father, each of her brothers, and then her son (with Caesar).
- Gaius Julius Caesar (100 BCE–44 BCE) was a Roman general and statesman. He was famously assassinated in March 44 BCE, by a group of senators led by Marcus Junius Brutus.
- Marc Antony (83 BCE–30 BCE) was a Roman politician and general. He was loyal to Julius Caesar; after Caesar's assassination, Antony aligned with Caesar's son, Octavian, but this alliance eventually broke down. Octavian invaded Egypt and Antony committed suicide after losing a decisive battle.
- Alexandria was founded in 331 BCE by the Greek king Alexander the Great. Due to its strategic location, it grew rapidly into the largest city in the world and was home to people of diverse backgrounds, including Greek, Egyptian, and Jewish.

Photo Caption

This bas relief of Cleopatra (left) in Dendera, Egypt, is the only known portrait of her at the time she lived. She is depicted with her son (right) by Julius Caesar.

Connections

15-20 min. A
10-15 min. B
15-20 min. C
Extension: 10-15 min.

A Clarify the meaning of the word *ambassador*: someone who lives in a foreign country and represents his or her own country's interests there.

Sample Answers:

What a cultural ambassador does: A cultural ambassador travels and talks to people about his or her country and customs.

Possible traits of a good ambassador: confident, dedicated, enthusiastic, friendly, hard-working, knowledgeable, motivated, outgoing

B Students will use the questions in Section 5 to write a personal statement in the Writing section on the next page.

Connections

A Read the ad. Then discuss with a partner: What does a cultural ambassador do? What personality traits should a good cultural ambassador have?

Be a cultural ambassador in Australia!

Australia Cultural Exchange (ACEX) is a three-month program for people who want to improve their English, learn about another culture, and teach others about their own. Individuals in the program act as cultural ambassadors. As a representative of your country, you will travel around Australia and visit local schools. You'll talk to others about your country and customs. For more information and to fill out your application, visit www.ACEX.au.ng.

B You are applying for this position. Complete Sections 1–4 (not 5) of the application.

AUSTRALIA CULTURAL EXCHANGE

SECTION 1: STUDENT INFORMATION

Name (first, middle, last) ____

Date of birth ____ E-mail address ____

City ____ State/Territory ____ Country ____

SECTION 2: EDUCATION

School	Location	Dates attended	Major

SECTION 3: LANGUAGES AND TRAVEL EXPERIENCE

Languages you speak ____ Years studied ____

Travel experience (domestic or international) ____

SECTION 4: ACTIVITIES

Please list any activities that you participate in: work, sports, music, etc.

Activity	Years/months doing it	Hours each week	Awards won

SECTION 5: PERSONAL STATEMENT

Why do you want to be a cultural ambassador? Why would you be a good one? Explain which personal traits, education, skills, and experience you have.

C Take turns. Tell a partner at least one thing about yourself from each of the first four sections of the application. Then join another pair of students and introduce your partner to them.

Extension

Tell students to imagine that they earned the position as cultural ambassador with ACEX. Have them prepare notes about what they would say during a visit to an Australian school, including introducing themselves, talking about their background, sharing information about their country's culture and customs. Then, in small groups, have students take turns role-playing the school visit; their partners will be Australian students who will ask follow-up questions.

Writing

A Personal Statement

Writing Strategy

Writing a Personal Statement
Before you write, read the information about the school or company. What qualities are they looking for in an applicant? Next, write down the facts about your personal experience. Finally, write your statement and show how your background makes you the kind of person they are seeking. Pay attention to the use of past tenses.

A Read one student's personal statement and answer the questions.

I want to be a cultural ambassador because I'm interested in learning more about Australia. I also want to teach others about my country, Brazil. I believe that my background and experience have prepared me to participate in the ACEX program in different ways.

To be a good cultural ambassador, a person should be knowledgeable about his culture. I think I am. For example, I've been studying capoeira for the last three years. Capoeira is a Brazilian art form that combines dance and martial arts. I practice for eight hours a week, and I love it. Once I performed for a group of tourists. After the performance, they asked many questions about capoeira and Brazil. I enjoyed telling them about both in English.

I've always liked learning about other cultures, too. I majored in English, and I also speak some Spanish. I have never traveled outside Brazil, but I've met many people from all over the world here in Sao Paulo. I believe this experience has also prepared me to participate in this program.

I am ready to set out on a big adventure—to be a cultural ambassador in Australia. I think it's important to learn about other countries' customs and to share your own with the rest of the world. I hope that you will consider my application!

First paragraph: Explain why you are applying.

Last paragraph: Restate your interest in the position.

TIP Be sure to define any words (e.g., *capoeira*) that are unfamiliar to your reader.

Capoeira dancer

1. Did the applicant answer both questions asked in Section 5 of the application on page 8?
2. Would he be a good cultural ambassador? Why or why not?

B Now write your own personal statement.

- Reread Sections 1–4 of your application on page 8. What information is important to include in your statement?
- Look back at your list of traits in Exercise **A** on page 8. Which ones describe you? Include them in your statement.

C Exchange papers with another student. Read your partner's statement. Does it . . .

- answer both questions asked in Section 5 of the application?
- follow the Writing Strategy?

9

Writing

15-20 min. A
20-25 min. B
5-10 min. C
Extension: 15-20 min.

Purpose of Writing

The purpose of this personal statement is to describe one's background information, personal experience, and qualifications for an application.

A Have students read the prompt in Section 5 of the application on the previous page. After they read the sample statement, ask students if the applicant answered the questions in Section 5. Have them explain where in the sample the applicant explains why he wants to be a cultural ambassador and why he would be a good one.

B After students finish writing their personal statements, tell them to make sure they've answered the two questions in the prompt (Why do you want to be a cultural ambassador? Why would you be a good one?).

Outcome: Upon completing this exercise, students will have met the Outcome *explain and evaluate qualifications*.

Extension

Collect students' personal statements, shuffle them, and read them aloud, without naming the student. Have the class guess the student's identity based on the description.

Rubric	Very Good	Satisfactory	Needs Improvement
Content			
Use of descriptive language			
Use of grammar			
Organization			

Speaking

10-25 min. **A**
15 min. **B**
15 min. **C**
Extension: 20 min.

A • Remind students that the questions here should focus on learning about the applicant's background and character as well as his or her education, skills, and activities. Emphasize the importance of asking questions that elicit information that is listed in the application; also stress the value of follow-up questions that get the applicant to explain an answer in more detail.

• Have students come up with one more follow-up question. Remind students that the goal is not just to ask any question, but one that (a) is derived from the applicant's responses, and (b) helps them to learn more about the applicant's ability to be a good cultural ambassador.

B After the interview, you can encourage both the interviewer and the applicant to reflect on how the interview went by following up with questions like these:

Interviewer: Did the applicant . . .
Applicant: Did I . . .

1. speak at a normal speed?
2. hesitate much?
3. answer the questions clearly and in enough detail?
4. show enthusiasm and interest in the program?

C If possible, have students make video recordings of their interviews.

Outcome: Upon completing this exercise, students will have met the Outcome ***handle challenging questions***.

Speaking

A Imagine that you work for the ACEX program. You are going to interview people who have applied to be cultural ambassadors in Australia. Read the questions below. Then look back at the application on page 8 and write six additional interview questions on a separate piece of paper. Remember: you want to learn about the applicant's background, education, skills, and activities in as much detail as you can. You also want to know why the person wants to be a cultural ambassador.

1. Tell me a little about yourself. Where are you from? Have you ever lived or traveled anywhere else?
2. What are your hobbies? How long have you been [doing that hobby]? Why did you decide to do it?

TIP Here are some useful prompts to help formulate additional questions.

- Tell me more about . . .
- Why did you decide to . . .
- What did you learn from . . .
- Why is ____ important to you?
- Have you ever . . .

B Work in pairs. One of you will interview the other, using your questions from Exercise **A**. Take notes on your partner's responses. Use the expressions in the Speaking Strategy to help you.

So, tell me: Why do you want to be a cultural ambassador?

Great question. I guess the main reason is . . .

C Switch roles and repeat Exercise **B**.

Ask

Answer

Do you want to be a cultural ambassador? If so, to which country?

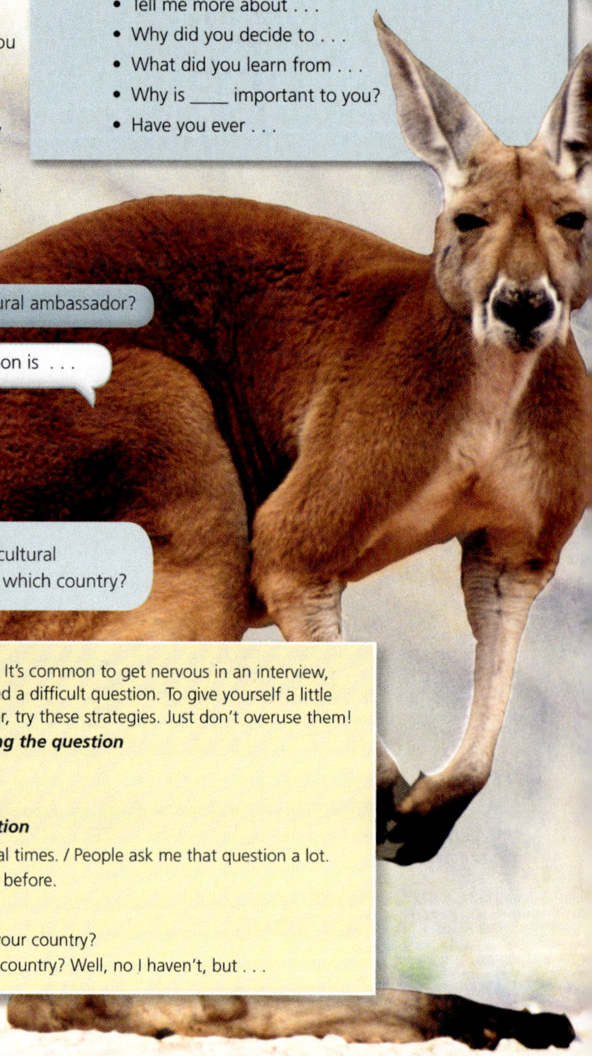

Speaking Strategy

Responding to questions It's common to get nervous in an interview, especially when you're asked a difficult question. To give yourself a little time to prepare your answer, try these strategies. Just don't overuse them!

Complimenting the interviewer for asking the question
(That's a) good / great question.
I'm glad you asked (me) that (question).

Showing your experience with the question
Actually, I've been asked that question several times. / People ask me that question a lot.
That's interesting. I've never been asked that before.

Repeating the question
Interviewer: Have you ever traveled outside your country?
Interviewee: Have I ever traveled outside my country? Well, no I haven't, but . . .

10

Extension

Add humor to the unit by asking pairs of students to write the dialogue for two interviews: one that goes very well for a very polished applicant and one in which an overly nervous applicant does poorly. Have the pairs role-play the interviews for other pairs of students, who will evaluate at which points the interviews went well or not and why.

Rubric	Very Good	Satisfactory	Needs Improvement
Ability to sustain a conversation			
Use of vocabulary			
Use of grammar			
Pronunciation and fluency			

Expanding Your Fluency

Before You Play

- Work in a group of four. Complete the questions on the game board.
- Take ten small pieces of paper. Write *T* (true) on five pieces and *F* (false) on the other five. Shuffle the papers and place them face down in a deck.
- Put your markers on START.

Playing the Game

Flip a coin. Heads = move one square. Tails = move two squares. Read the question on that square.

- Turn over a piece of paper; don't show your group. If the paper says *T*, answer the question truthfully. If it says *F*, make up an answer. Return the paper to the bottom of the deck.
- Each person will ask you one follow-up question to determine if you are telling the truth.
- Finally, each person guesses if it's the truth or not. If most people guess correctly, you stay where you are. If most people guess incorrectly, you move forward one space. The first player to reach FINISH is the winner!

➔ 10. Have you ever (be) _______ out of the country?	11. What were you (think) _______ about when you (wake) _______ up this morning?	12. What book are you reading now and how long have you (read) _______ it?	13. Have you ever (meet) _______ a famous person? Who?	**FINISH**
↑ 9. When was the last time you (get) _______ angry?	← 8. Have you ever (buy) _______ anything expensive?	7. What (do) _______ you do on your last day off?	6. How many times have you (move) _______ in your life?	← 5. What were you (do) _______ between 6:00 and 8:00 p.m. last night?
START ➔	1. When was the last time you (eat) _______ something you didn't like?	2. Have you ever (visit) _______ relatives in another city?	➔ 3. Who were you (sit) _______ next to in class yesterday?	↑ 4. How long have you (study) _______ English?

Check What You Know

Rank how well you can perform these outcomes on a scale of 1–5 (5 being the best).

_______ use past tenses to ask and answer questions about memorable life events
_______ summarize the key outcomes of a study
_______ explain and evaluate qualifications
_______ handle challenging questions

Extension

In small groups, have students create a similar game board with their own questions. Have them exchange boards with another group, who will check the grammar and spelling of the questions, then play the game.

Expanding Your Fluency

15-20 min. **Before You Play**
25-35 min. **Playing the Game**
Extension: 20 min.

Before You Play

If needed, have students review the chart on page 3 before filling in the blanks.

Answers: 1. ate; 2. visited; 3. sitting; 4. been studying / studied; 5. doing; 6. moved; 7. did; 8. bought; 9. got; 10. been; 11. thinking / woke; 12. been reading; 13. met

Playing the Game

- Encourage students to answer the questions with complete sentences.
- If students need help coming up with follow-up questions to ask, suggest the following ideas: 1. *What did you eat?* 2. *Where do your relatives live?* 3. *What was he or she wearing?* 4. *What year did you take your first class?* 5. *Who was with you at the time?* 6. *Where was the last place you lived?* 7. *What did you do after that?* 8. *What did you buy?* 9. *What made you mad?* 10. *What is the farthest place you have traveled?* 11. *What made you think about that?* 12. *What book was the last book you read before that?* 13. *What did you say to this person?*
- When the game is finished, survey the class about their experiences playing the game. Ask them how they were able to tell if someone was telling the truth or not. Find out who in the class was the best at making up answers (that is, fooling classmates into believing that they told the truth).

Check What You Know

Refer students back to the exercises in the unit where each Outcome is addressed.

- *use past tenses to ask and answer questions about memorable life events:* Grammar, Exercise **C**, page 3
- *summarize the key outcomes of a study:* Video, Exercise **D**, page 5
- *explain and evaluate qualifications:* Writing, Exercise **B**, page 9
- *handle challenging questions:* Speaking, Exercise **C**, page 10

Unit 2
The World Awaits

Unit Overview

- Unit 2 is about travel and tourism. From Beijing to Barcelona, students will learn about the unique characteristics of various places throughout the world.
- Travel and tourism is an industry that has grown steadily over the past sixty years. In 1950, according to the World Tourism Organization, there were twenty-five million international arrivals. In 2012, that number exceeded one billion. More than half of all tourist arrivals worldwide happen in Europe.
- Ask students what they think is meant by the unit title, "The World Awaits." Inform them, if necessary, that it is an expression that means the world is a place waiting to be explored, and there is a lot to learn about different places and cultures.
- Preview the unit by asking students the following questions:

1. What types of places do you like?
2. What activities do you like to do?
3. What is on your list of things to do during your lifetime?

Photo Caption

This image is of the Greek island of Symi, located in the southeast Aegean Sea, near the coast of Turkey. Symi is just one of the 162 Dodecanese Islands; *Dodecanese* means "twelve islands," referring to the largest dozen islands in the group. The quiet charm of Symi, whose population is only 2,500, draws tourists from all over the world, particularly from England and Italy. Symi's attractions include beautifully restored historical buildings, the Panormitis Monastery, and isolated beaches, some of which are only accessible by boat.

2 The World Awaits

VOCABULARY	GRAMMAR	LISTENING	READING
Popular vacation destinations **Pronunciation:** Stress changes with prefixes and suffixes	Uses of infinitives and gerunds	A walking tour of Beijing	*Traveling Troubadour:* An Interview with Singer Jason Mraz

1 Where do you think this photo was taken? What do you think people do there? Describe the photo in as much detail as you can.

2 Describe your ideal vacation. Where would you go? What would you do? Who would you go with?

3 What are some popular sites that tourists like to visit in your city or country? Have you ever been to any of these places?

Unit Outcomes

In this unit, you will learn to:

- use descriptive language effectively
- use gerund and infinitive structures to describe experiences
- make travel recommendations
- give, accept, and question advice

13

5-10 min. **Warm-Up Questions**
Extension: 10-15 min.

Background Information

For millennia, people with the means to travel have visited distant lands to experience different cultures, cuisines, and languages. For 2010, the most visited countries were France, the United States, China, Spain, Italy, the United Kingdom, Turkey, Germany, Malaysia, and Mexico. Countries whose main industry is tourism, such as Spain and New Zealand, find themselves more vulnerable to global economic downturns.

Warm-Up Questions

- Read the unit title aloud and invite students to look at the photo. Ask them to guess the theme of the unit.
- Read through Question 1 as a class. Ask several students to guess where this place is and what people do there. Work as a class to describe the photo in detail.
- Have students work with a partner to answer Question 2. Ask a few students to report back about their partner's ideal vacation.
- Ask students if they think your city or region is a good place for a vacation. Then go through Question 3 as a class.

Extension

Have students work in pairs. Ask them to think about what they prefer in a tourist destination and to rank the following factors in order of importance: local culture, cuisine, architecture, music, relaxation opportunities, language, sports / activities, history. Then have them choose a country or city to visit and explain how their preferences are reflected in that choice.

SPEAKING	VIDEO	WRITING	OUTCOMES
Create a bucket list of things you want to do **Strategy:** Making suggestions and giving advice	*Barcelona's Street Life*	Write a descriptive paragraph about a place **Strategy:** Create a mental image	• use descriptive language effectively • use gerund and infinitive structures to describe experiences • make travel recommendations • give, accept, and question advice

Vocabulary

5-10 min. **A**
25-30 min. **B**
10-15 min. **C**
Extension: 10 min.

B
- Have students read the descriptions individually.
- Explain the difference between *destination* (the place you're going to) and *destiny* (a predetermined course of events); these words may be easily confused by speakers of Romance languages.
- The answers for boxed questions on collocations with destination and spot are found in the place descriptions for French Alps and Antigua.

Answers: *French Alps:* It's known for its picturesque villages, luxurious resorts, and breathtaking scenery. You can go skiing, snowboarding, and mountain climbing there. *Kalalau Valley:* It's known for steep cliffs and diverse plant and animal life. It's also difficult to get to. You can get away from it all there. *Antigua, Guatemala:* It's known for its old Spanish architecture and traditional crafts. You can go sightseeing there before exploring the rest of the country.

Word Bank Answers:
destination: popular ~
luxurious: They are places or locations.
spot: perfect ~

C
- Allow students to describe a place that they have not visited personally.
- Before pairing students, allow them to jot down some notes about their chosen vacation spot.
- Be sure that students take turns talking about their vacation spot.

Vocabulary

A When was the last time you went on vacation? Where did you go? What did you do?

B Read the descriptions of these vacation places. Then answer the questions with a partner.

1. What is each place known for? What can you do at each?
2. Which place would you most like to visit? Rank each place in order of preference. Explain your answers.

accessible easy to reach or get into
adventurous willing to take risks and have new experiences
breathtaking very beautiful or amazing
charm the quality of being pleasant and attractive
convenience ease; suitability
destination the place you're going to
diverse varied or different
get away to go away on vacation
luxurious comfortable and expensive
picturesque attractive, especially in an old-fashioned way
remote far away
spot place; location
tranquil calm and peaceful

What do you notice about many of the words that follow **luxurious**? ~ accommodations, ~ home, ~ hotel, ~ resort, ~ spa

What other words come before **spot**? vacation ~

What other words come before **destination**? Add one more. final ~, tourist ~, ultimate ~

PRONUNCIATION Notice how a suffix affects the stress in a word: **lux**ury ➔ lux**ur**ious; **pic**ture ➔ pictur**esque**. See page 145 for more information on suffixes and stress.

Kalalau Valley (Hawaii) ▶
This valley is accessible only by boat (when the seas are tranquil in summer) or by way of the 18-kilometer Kalalau Trail. The remote valley is known for its steep cliffs and diverse selection of plant and animal life. It's a great place to get away from it all.

French Alps ▼
A popular destination for skiers, snowboarders, and mountaineers, the French Alps have plenty to offer less adventurous visitors—picturesque villages, luxurious resorts, and breathtaking scenery.

Antigua, Guatemala ▶
This colorful city is famous for its old Spanish architecture and traditional crafts. Tourists come to Antigua for its charm and convenience—it's the perfect spot for starting your exploration of the rest of the country after you finish sightseeing in the city.

C Think about a popular vacation spot that you know well. Tell a partner about this vacation spot using the vocabulary from this page. Be sure to explain what the destination is known for and what one can do there.

Grand Lake is a popular vacation destinatic
I like it because it's accessible . . .

14

Extension

Divide the class into groups of three or four. One student is unsure about where to go on vacation; the other group members each want to go to a different location. Tell the undecided students to jot down their travel preferences while the other students each pick a location and compose a list of its most appealing features. Then, in groups, have the students try to convince their classmate to choose their preferred destination; the undecided student will accept or reject the destinations and explain why.

Grammar

Uses of Infinitives and Gerunds	
1. purpose infinitive	*Last summer I went overseas **to study** English.*
2. *it* + *be* + adjective + infinitive	*It was great **to experience** life in a small town.*
3. *too* + adjective + infinitive	*At first, it was too hard **to communicate** in English.*
4. gerunds as subjects	***Learning** the language was essential.*
5. adjective + preposition + gerund	*The small town is famous for **skiing** in the winter and **hiking** in the summer.*
6. verb + preposition + gerund	*I look forward to **going back** next year!*

verb + preposition + gerund: dream of ~, look forward to ~, plan on ~, talk about ~, think about ~

adjective + preposition + gerund: afraid of ~, excited about ~, known / famous for ~, interested in ~

A Read about these two events happening around the world. Complete the sentences with the gerund or infinitive form of the verb in parentheses.

Last summer, I went to Italy with a friend (1. attend) ______ the Venice International Art Exhibition. It was wonderful (2. see) ______ art from all over the world in such a beautiful atmosphere. And while (3. visit) ______ different exhibits is entertaining, you couldn't do it all day long. There was a lot to see! On days when we were too exhausted (4. continue) ______, my friend and I would take a break. We were able to get away (5. enjoy) ______ some delicious Italian cuisine too. Yum!

I've been interested in samba (6. dance) ______ for a long time, so (7. visit) ______ Rio de Janeiro on National Samba Day sounds like a lot of fun. First you dance in the central train station. If you're planning on (8. dance) ______ some more, get on a "party train." You may think the train is too crowded (9. enjoy) ______ yourself, but there's live music and everyone has a great time! The train's destination is the suburban neighborhood of Oswaldo Cruz. People go there (10. hear) ______ free concerts.

B Now write about a place you visited recently. Complete these sentences first and use them as the basis for a more complete description. Then tell a partner about your trip.

I went to ______ (Place) to . . .	It was too ______ (Adjective) to . . . while we were there.
It's known for . . .	It was great to . . .
. . . was the best part of our trip.	I plan on . . .

Extension

Ask students to write about a trip to a well-known destination using the cues in Exercise **B** but without mentioning the name of the place. In small groups, have them take turns reading their descriptions aloud for their classmates to guess.

Grammar

10-15 min. **A**
30-40 min. **B**
Extension: 10-20 min.

A
- Go through the chart as a class. For each use, give additional examples. Elicit student responses by asking them about their academic and / or travel experiences. For items 5 and 6, use the additional boxed phrases to ask students about their weekend plans and personal interests.
- Remind students that gerunds are nouns formed from verbs by adding *-ing*.
- Tell students to read through each paragraph once. Then have them reread the paragraphs and fill in the blanks.

Answers: 1. to attend; 2. to see; 3. visiting; 4. to continue; 5. to enjoy; 6. dancing; 7. visiting; 8. dancing; 9. to enjoy; 10. to hear

B
- If students have not taken a trip recently, have them choose one of the destinations featured on these pages and write about an imaginary trip.
- Encourage students to use at least three words from the word bank on page 14.

Outcome: Upon completing this exercise, students will have met the Outcome *use gerund and infinitive structures to describe experiences*.

Photo Captions

The top image is of a gondola (boat) on one of the canals in the city of Venice in Northern Italy. Venice is made up of several islands that are separated by waterways and connected by bridges. Gondola rides give tourists breathtaking views of the old city.

The bottom image is of a dancer in one of Rio de Janeiro's numerous Samba Schools, or dance clubs. Many Samba Schools represent neighborhoods in Rio, and members often practice dancing outside all year to prepare for the Carnival parade in February.

Listening

5-10 min. **A**
15-20 min. **B**
10-15 min. **C**
10 min. **D**
Extension: 15-20 min.

Listening Strategy

Guide students to listen for specific information by following these steps: First, identify the topic of a listening passage. Then use background knowledge to predict what they will hear. Encourage students to listen closely only to the parts of the recording that contain the information they need.

A
- The naming of Beijing follows the East Asian tradition of naming capitals according to relative geographical location within the country.
- The Forbidden City was the Chinese imperial palace for nearly five hundred years; since 1925 it has been a museum.
- The official name of the Bird's Nest is Beijing National Stadium. Its capacity is 80,000 people.

Answers: 1. b; 2. c; 3 c

B
- Tell students that they are going to hear a walking tour of the city of Beijing. Draw attention to the map. Explain that they do not have to write the complete name of each site.
- Point out that they only need to fill in the locations next to (a), and that the first item is already completed.
- Play the audio recording one or more times. **Audio CD Track 4**

Answers: 2. alley; 3. massage center; 4. church / cathedral; 5. bookstore; 6. Snack Street; 7. shopping mall; 8. hotel

C Play the audio recording again. Pause briefly after each section to allow students time to jot down notes. **Audio CD Track 4**

Sample Answers: 2. see beautiful homes; 3. traditionally done by the blind; 4. 17th century, destroyed three times, see skateboarders; 5. largest supply of foreign language materials, buy books; 6. eat Chinese food / noodles; 7. Chinese and foreign brands, shop, eat, and drink; 8. take photos

D If you have a large class, this exercise may be done in groups of four.

Listening

A How much do you know about China's capital city Beijing? Choose your answers.

1. What does the name *Beijing* mean?
   a. Eternal City b. Northern Capital c. City of Knowledge
2. The Forbidden City (pictured) is a popular tourist destination. What was it originally?
   a. a market place b. a large cemetery c. a palace
3. What is the nickname of the stadium built for the 2008 Summer Olympic Games?
   a. Power Palace b. Golden Egg c. Bird's Nest

B Listen to a walking tour of Beijing. There are eight stops on the tour. On the map, write each location next to (a) in each box.

TIP When you have to write information quickly, such as when you take notes, it helps to use abbreviations or symbols. For example: *bookstore* bkst 📖

Make your own abbreviations or symbols for these places: *bridge, building, hotel, library, museum, plaza*. What other places might be part of a walking tour?

C Listen again and take notes on any interesting facts or things you can do in each place. Write your notes next to (b) in each box.

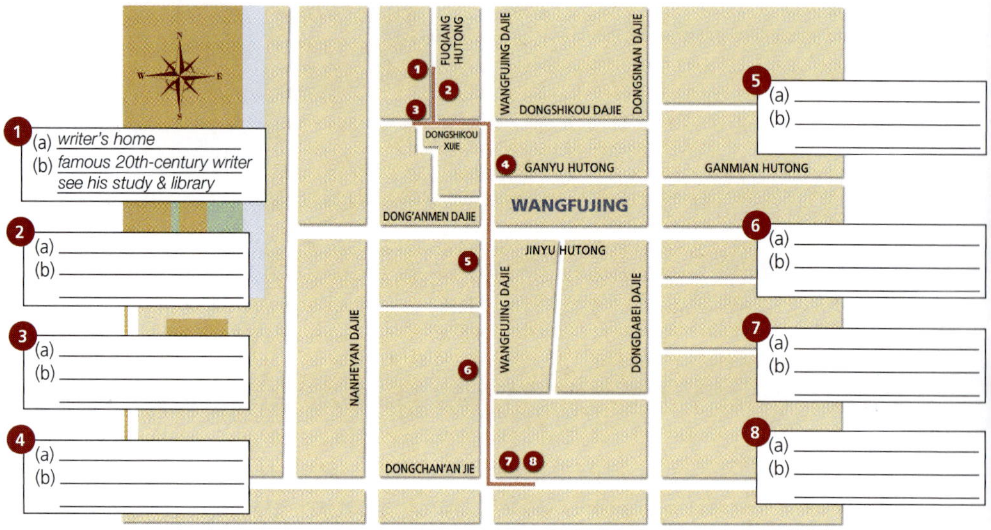

D Using your notes, take turns telling a partner about each place on the walking tour. Say what each place is and give at least one fact about it. Which place would you be most interested to visit?

Extension

Have students use their completed maps from Exercise **C** to play a game. In pairs or small groups, students take turns describing one of the locations to their classmate(s), who may not consult the map. The classmate has to identify the location. Tell students to be vague enough in their descriptions so that they don't give away the location too easily (e.g., for item 1, "You can read about his life and view his study and library.").

Connections

A You are going to make your own walking tour. Follow the steps below.

1. Which places in your city or area would be interesting for tourists to visit? List as many neighborhoods, streets, or areas as you can.
2. Work with a partner. Compare your ideas in step 1. Together, choose one neighborhood or area to feature in your walking tour.
3. What things can people do and see in this area? With your partner, think of eight ideas and create a chart using the categories below.

   A walking tour of:

   Cultural Sites   Food   Shopping   Activities

4. Choose six places from step 3. On a separate piece of paper, you should each draw a map of the area. Number each place 1–6, but do not write each place's name. Make sure you each have your own copy of the map.
5. On another piece of paper, create your walking tour. Make notes for yourselves about the places on the tour, including one interesting fact about each location. Work together, but make sure you each have your own copy of the tour.

TIP Using adjectives can make each place on your tour sound more interesting. Think of adjectives you can use to describe each place.

B Now work with a new partner. Role-play the walking tour. Then switch roles and repeat.

Tour Guide: Give your map to your partner. Then start your walking tour.

Tourist: Listen to your partner's walking tour. Label each destination (1–6) on the map. Note any interesting facts that your partner tells you about each place.

I recommend visiting the Nine Streets neighborhood in Amsterdam. Shopping is an adventure here: you can find everything from luxurious shops to simple bakeries. Our first stop is a little shop that is famous for its delicious tea. It's a small place, always busy, but full of charm and never too crowded to visit. Step inside to learn all about tea-making in Holland. You might be interested to know that . . .

Ask Answer What was most interesting about your partner's walking tour? What is something new you learned about the area?

17

Connections

35-45 min. **A**
5-10 min. **B**
Extension: 10-15 min.

A
- For step 3, ask students to include at least two places per category, if possible.
- For step 4, have students use the map on page 16 as a model.
- For step 5, tell students to write key words rather than a script of everything that they're going to say. The key words will allow them to "give the tour" to someone else.

B
- Before forming new pairs, allow students time to practice their tours individually.
- If possible, have the tour "guides" bring in a photo or other visual for each site on the tour. If time and space allows, have the guides post their visuals at various points in the classroom. Instruct the pairs to walk together and stop at each image, thus simulating a tour.
- Encourage the "tourist" in each pair to make comments or ask questions about each place.
- Have students record their walking tours and share the recordings in the class.

Extension

Assign one pair of students to create a walking tour of the area near your school or campus. Have those students lead the whole class on a walking tour of the surrounding area. Encourage the "tourists" to ask their guides questions during the tour.

Photo Caption

This image is of Amsterdam, the capital of the Netherlands and its largest city. Pictured is one of Amsterdam's *Negen Straatjes,* or Nine Streets, a shopping district in the city's center. The Nine Streets neighborhood is known for its fashionable clothing stores. Many of the retail shops in Nine Streets are privately owned, setting it apart from other more commercial shopping districts in the city.

Internet Activity

Tell students to imagine that they are going to travel to a new city next weekend and they need to pick a destination. Have students take virtual walking tours of two different cities (e.g., http://www.virtuar.com/virtour/). Then, based on the tours, ask students to write a paragraph comparing the two cities. They should use the vocabulary and grammar presented on pages 14 and 15 and state which destination they chose for their trip and why.

Reading

5-10 min. **A**
15-20 min. **B**
10-15 min. **C**
10 min. **D**
Extension: 20 min.

A Remind students that, when scanning the text, they should not read every word.

Answer: The extra question is C, "How do your travel experiences influence your music?" The placement of the other questions in the interview is given on page 19.

B
- Encourage students to read the interview once before they read the statements. Have them read the interview a second time before identifying which statements belong to Jason Mraz.
- Encourage students to find information in the interview to support their answers.

Answers: *Checked:* 2, 3, 4

C

Answers: He mentions *Paris* to talk about how he likes to wander with no particular destination in mind. He mentions *New York* as a place where the locals "never look up." They don't appreciate the atmosphere / environment. He mentions *San Diego* because he visited the city and ended up staying there. He lives there now. He mentions *Japan* to explain that people are basically the same anywhere you go. He mentions *Antarctica* because he wants to go there. It's the only continent he hasn't visited.

Photo Caption

The Louvre (French: *Musée du Louvre*) is the most visited art museum in the world, with more than eight million visitors annually, as well as one of the largest. Its main entrance, completed in 1989, is enclosed within a large glass-and-metal pyramid. Inside, visitors can observe 35,000 works of art, including the *Mona Lisa*.

D You may want to have students complete this exercise in pairs.

Answers: 1. landmarks; 2. end up; 3. rush; 4. spontaneous; 5. timid; 6. outsider; 7. particular; 8. perspective; 9. solitude

Reading

Jason Mraz, pop singer-songwriter

A You are going to read an interview with singer Jason Mraz. First, read the interview questions below. With a partner, scan each of Mraz's responses on p. 19. Then write the letter of the question in the box beside each response. (One of the questions is extra.)

A What has really surprised you in your travels?
B Are there places you haven't been to yet that you want to visit?
C How do your travel experiences influence your music?
D Tell us about your book of Polaroid® travel photography.
E Is there more to say about your writing?
F What style of traveler are you?

B Read the interview. Then read the statements below. Which ones apply to Jason Mraz?

1. ☐ I plan everything before I go anywhere.
2. ☐ I like to wander (walk around without a specific purpose).
3. ☐ I think people everywhere are more alike than they are different.
4. ☐ I like to write down my experiences.
5. ☐ I have a new camera so I take as many photos as possible.
6. ☐ You need to go far away to have interesting experiences.

C Why is each place significant for Jason? With a partner, discuss at least one reason for each location.

Paris New York San Diego Japan Antarctica

D Find a word or expression . . .

1. in paragraph 1 that means *well-known buildings or sites.* ______________
2. in paragraph 1 that means *to finally arrive somewhere after a while.* ______________
3. in paragraph 1 that means *to hurry.* ______________
4. in paragraph 1 that means *done in a sudden or unplanned way.* ______________
5. in paragraph 2 that means *shy and nervous.* ______________
6. in paragraph 2 that means *a person who doesn't belong to a group.* ______________
7. in paragraph 3 that means *choose very carefully; not easy to please.* ______________
8. in paragraph 4 that means *a way of seeing or thinking about something.* ______________
9. in paragraph 5 that means *being alone.* ______________

Ask Answer Look back at the statements in Exercise **B**. Which ones are true for you? What are some of your favorite travel memories?

Extension

Have students copy the statements from Exercise **B** on a sheet of paper and ask them to write their initials next to the statements that apply to them. Then have students circulate around the room to try to find their ideal travel companion (someone who agrees with the same or nearly all of the same statements).

Traveling Troubadour[1]

by Keith Bellows

A spontaneous one, with little preparation. I pack light. I don't feel a need to rush through all the major landmarks. Like, if I go to Paris, I might just take a walk, with no map or tourist site in mind, and end up in a neighborhood coffee shop. I guess I'm a traveler who likes to think he's not traveling. That's how I ended up in San Diego. I traveled there and found this great coffee shop that I love to make music in and I ended up staying. I've lived there for twelve years now.

I'm constantly surprised that no matter where I go, people are similar, just trying to make it.[2] We're all quiet and shy in an elevator with other people. Before I ever traveled to Japan I thought maybe it would be like another planet. But when I got there I realized, oh, these are just humans over here doing the same human thing, perhaps with different resources. It made me feel less timid about going places and more able to just walk through a village in, say, Ghana—or anywhere else in the world—looking like an obvious outsider. I'm comfortable with that.

I often keep a travel journal. I'll just sit on the steps somewhere and write. A journal that I bought is the best souvenir. It allows me to relive my memories of places around the world. At one point I started to travel with a Polaroid[3] 600 instant camera. I could just snap a picture[4] and put it right in with my journal entry. With a Polaroid, you never know what you'll get. Because Polaroid film is so rare and slightly expensive, I became very particular about what I shot. With a digital camera I might take a hundred pictures in a matter of minutes, but with a Polaroid, I wait to find a scene I really want to shoot. I look for scenes with depth, like a long line of lampposts. I love looking up in the trees and at buildings. When you're comfortable with a place, you forget to look up. New Yorkers never look up. Only the tourists do.

Sometimes on my blog I write from a traveler's perspective. There are people who never leave their home state that rely on travel writing to help them experience more of the world. Knowing that, I also encourage people to explore places near their own communities. I grew up in Mechanicsville, Virginia, for example, which is rich with history. Every time I go home, I do something I missed growing up, such as visiting a historic battlefield.[5]

> "I guess I'm a traveler who likes to think he's not traveling."

I've always wanted to take a cruise to Antarctica to see that continent. That would be just a brilliant trip for nature, solitude, and for writing in the journal. To really see the world, you should visit all seven continents, and that is the only one I have not been to.

[1] **troubadour** a traveling musician
[2] **make it** to be successful (in life) or survive something difficult
[3] **Polaroid** a type of camera (and film) that develops photos instantly
[4] **snap a picture** take a photo
[5] **battlefield** a place where a fight between armies has occurred

Background Information

- Jason Thomas Mraz (b. 1977) started playing guitar at age 18. His first studio album, *Waiting for My Rocket to Come*, was released in 2002, followed by *Mr. A–Z* in 2005 and the highly successful *We Sing. We Dance. We Steal Things.* in 2008. Mraz's most recent album is 2012's *Love is a Four Letter Word*. His songs blend elements of pop, reggae, folk, jazz, rock, and hip-hop.
- Mechanicsville, Virginia, is a small city of about 35,000 residents just outside of Richmond. There were several battles in the area during the American Civil War (1861–1865), including one in Mechanicsville in June 1862.

Language Notes

- *like* = for example; Speakers also use *like* to give themselves time to think as they are talking. Students also hear this expression in the Video section on page 21.
- Point out the phrase *no matter where* in Line 10. Teach the expression *no matter where / how / what / etc.* Have students listen for this expression in the video as well.

A

Placement of interview questions:
Paragraph 1: F, What style of traveler are you?
Paragraph 2: A, What has really surprised you in your travels?
Paragraph 3: D, Tell us about your book of Polaroid® travel photography.
Paragraph 4: E, Is there more to say about your writing?
Paragraph 5: B, Are there places you haven't been to yet that you want to visit?

Beyond the Reading

Direct students to watch the video for Jason Mraz's song "93 Million Miles" on YouTube at http://www.youtube.com/watch?v=u5WiqJFq2-o. Have them read the lyrics on the screen and take notes. Then have them discuss the song with a partner and answer this question: *How does the song relate to what Jason Mraz says in this interview about traveling?*

Speaking

10-15 min. A 10 min. B 15-20 min. C 5-10 min. D Extension: 10 min.

A • Explain that the phrase *bucket list* comes from the idiomatic expression *to kick the bucket*, meaning "to die."
- This phrase was widely popularized by the 2007 Hollywood film *The Bucket List*, starring Jack Nicholson and Morgan Freeman.
- Suggest that students complete their lists as homework.

B • Read through the expressions in the strategy box.
- Refer students to the "Uses of Infinitives and Gerunds" box on page 15.
- Model making suggestions and accepting advice. Ask a student what he / she would like to do before the end of the year. Then make some suggestions and encourage the student to respond using the expressions from the strategy box.

Outcomes: Upon completing this exercise, students will have met the Outcomes ***make travel recommendations*** and ***give, accept, and question advice.***

Extension

After completing Exercise **D**, pair together students who have identical or similar items on their bucket lists. Have them compare the advice that they received and select the best way to complete their goal.

Photo Caption

This image shows part of the Giza Necropolis (city of the dead) near Cairo, Egypt, at sunset. One of the most visited tourist destinations in the world, Giza includes three large pyramids and the massive stone sculpture known as The Sphinx. In this image, The Sphinx is in the foreground, while in the background sits the Great Pyramid of Khufu—the only one of the Seven Wonders of the Ancient World that still exists.

Speaking

bucket list
a list of personal goals or things you want to do or accomplish in your life

A Read the note in the box about a bucket list. Then create your own list on a separate sheet of paper using these categories. Write at least one goal for each category.

Travel   Hobbies and Interests   Education and Career   Personal Life

I want to learn to sing. . . and I really want to visit Egypt and see the pyramids.

B Work with a partner to get advice on your bucket list. Follow the steps below. Then switch roles and repeat the activity.

Speaking Strategy

Making Suggestions / Giving Advice
One/Another thing you could do is (*infinitive*) . . .
What/How about (*gerund*) . . . ?
Have you thought about (*gerund*) . . . ?
You talked about (*gerund*) . . . ?

Accepting Advice
Thanks. That's a good idea.
OK, I'll give it a try/shot.
That makes sense.

Questioning Advice
I thought about doing that, but . . .
One problem with that is . . .

Refusing Advice
I'm not sure that would work for me.

Student 1: Tell your partner a little about your goals. Explain how you plan to accomplish each one.

Student 2: Listen to your partner's goals and ask questions about each one. Give your partner advice. Use the expressions in the box to help you.

Student 1: Take notes on the advice your partner gives you. You can accept or question the advice.

C Repeat Exercise **B** with two new partners.

D Share your findings with the class or in a small group. Answer the questions.

1. What was the best advice you got? Why was it good advice?
2. Which of your classmates' goals did you think was the most interesting?

20

Rubric	Very Good	Satisfactory	Needs Improvement
Ability to sustain a conversation			
Use of vocabulary			
Use of grammar			
Pronunciation and fluency			

Video

A You are going to watch a video about a street in Barcelona called Las Ramblas. First, listen to the audio (without watching) and think about these questions:

1. What do you think the street looks like? Describe it in as much detail as you can.
2. How do the speakers feel about Las Ramblas?

B Discuss your answers to the questions with a partner. Then watch the video and check your answers.

C What do the four speakers say about Barcelona and Las Ramblas? Watch the video again and match each speaker with a statement (a–f). For some speakers, more than one answer is possible.

a. In some ways, performing outside is better than in the theater.
b. There's diverse theater and music from all over the world here.
c. There's something happening at any time of day.
d. My life improved when I moved here from my country.
e. If you want to have fun, this is the best street . . . maybe in the whole world.
f. The action is out on the streets.

1. ______

2. ______

3. ______

4. ______

D What did each speaker say that made you choose your answers in Exercise **C**? Watch the video again and list the key words and phrases you hear from each speaker on a separate sheet of paper. Then compare answers with a partner.

Ask Answer Would you like to visit Las Ramblas? Why or why not?

Video

5-10 min. **A**
5-10 min. **B**
15 min. **C**
15-20 min. **D**
Extension: 15-20 min.

Before You Watch

A Read the two questions aloud for the class. Encourage students to form a mental image of Las Ramblas as they listen to the audio. Ask them what they see in their mind's eye.

Language Notes

Point out the use of filler words by various speakers in the video: *like, I don't know, I mean*. Remind students that these words are common in everyday speech and do not carry meaning but rather give the speaker time to think.

C
- Have students look at the photos and predict which speaker says each statement. Then play the video.
- Allow students to watch the video more than once if needed.

Answers: *Speaker 1:* c, f; *Speaker 2:* c, d; *Speaker 3:* b; *Speaker 4:* a, e

D Pause the video after each speaker to give students time to write their responses.

Answers: *Speaker 1 says:* ". . . any time you go out of your house, there's always something going on. You can always find a friend on the street." *Speaker 2 says:* "You can go out on the street at night; it's always lively. . . . Every hour a day there is life. I came here and I felt somehow better than in Amsterdam . . . more alive." *Speaker 3 says:* ". . . in the Ramblas you can find, I don't know, theater, music, from Argentina, from Spain, from Africa, from all the world." *Speaker 4 says:* "Things that on the street happen, never will happen in a theater. For example, if we play, and like, ten to fifteen people start to dance . . . then you think . . . this is beautiful. . . ." "The Ramblas is *the* street in Barcelona, and I think in Europe, and maybe in the world that, like, you're going to be entertained. No matter how . . ."

Extension

Ask students to think of a popular street in their city or a place they have visited. Then have them make a chart in which they compare that street to Las Ramblas. They should write down similarities and differences between the streets. Then ask for volunteers to explain their charts to the class.

Writing

15-20 min. A
20-25 min. B
5-10 min. C
Extension: 10-15 min.

Purpose of Writing

The purpose of this blog is to describe a place and to persuade others to visit it.

A After students complete step 2, tell them to close their eyes and visualize Las Ramblas as you read the passage aloud. You could also show parts of *Barcelona's Street Life* (with the sound off) from the Video section on page 21 and ask students if the description in this blog matches what they see in the video.

Possible Answers: 1. *see: lots of people, picturesque buildings*, streets lined with trees, tiles, and mosaics on the ground, performers from all over the world; *hear*: people singing, musicians playing music; *taste*: food from La Boqueria; *touch:* artists' goods, produce from the market; 2. *positive:* interesting, lined with trees, picturesque, colorful, lively, festive, alive, perfect, yummy, safe, entertaining; *negative:* overrun with tourists, crowded, seedy; *neutral:* wide, diverse, largest

Extension

Print out or project the photos of Las Ramblas from the Web site http://www.barcelona-tourist-guide.com/en/albums-en/ramblas/. Have students work with a partner to match each description in paragraph 1 of Abram's blog to the appropriate photo (not all photos will be used).

B
- For step 2, work with students to brainstorm ideas. Encourage them to go beyond simple adjectives like *beautiful, old*, and *interesting*, and to use words and phrases that evoke more of an image.
- To help students visualize the location, you may want to ask them to find a photo of their chosen place online or to sketch a picture of it before they write.

Outcome: Upon completing this exercise, students will have met the Outcome *use descriptive language effectively.*

Writing

A Descriptive Paragraph

A Read the blog post. Then complete the steps that follow.

Abram Recommends: Las Ramblas

Las Ramblas is an interesting area in Barcelona that attracts thousands of visitors every day. A number of things make Las Ramblas a favorite of both tourists and locals. The wide streets, for example, are lined with trees and picturesque buildings that are hundreds of years old. In many places, the ground is decorated with colorful tiles and mosaics.[1] Las Ramblas is also known for its lively and festive atmosphere. Diverse groups of performers from all over the world fill the streets. Day and night, the area is alive with people singing and dancing and artists selling their goods. And finally, near Las Ramblas is one of Barcelona's largest produce markets: *La Boqueria*. It's the perfect place to pick up a snack.

Las Ramblas has something for everyone, but the streets can be crowded with tourists, particularly in the summer. Parts of Las Ramblas can also be a bit seedy[2] at night. Although it's best to avoid this area after dark, overall Las Ramblas is a safe and entertaining area of the city. I highly recommend it!

[1] **tiles and mosaics** decorative ceramics
[2] **seedy** dirty, unsafe

1. Complete the statements below with information from the reading.

Things in Las Ramblas you can . . .

see	*lots of people, picturesque buildings*	taste	________
hear	________	touch	________

2. Which adjectives does the writer use to describe Las Ramblas? Circle them in the paragraph. Which ones are positive? Which have a negative meaning? Compare your answers with a partner.

B Read the information in the Writing Strategy. Then complete the steps that follow.

1. Think of an interesting place in a city or town you know well (a street, restaurant, beach, or other location).
2. Write statements like those in Exercise **A** with information about your place. Also list relevant adjectives.
3. Use your notes to write a blog entry of your place on a separate piece of paper.

Writing Strategy

Create a Mental Image When you describe something, it's important to *show* and not just *tell* your reader information. For example, don't just say a place is beautiful or interesting; explain what makes it that way. You can help your reader visualize something by doing the following:

1. Use adjectives and descriptive phrases. OK: *There are many trees and old buildings in Las Ramblas.* Better: *The **wide** streets are **lined with trees** and **picturesque** buildings that are **hundreds of years old.***
2. Describe something in more detail with an extra sentence or two. *Las Ramblas is also known for its **lively** and **festive** atmosphere. **Diverse** groups of performers from all over the world fill the streets.*

C Exchange papers with another student. Does your partner's writing follow the Writing Strategy?

22 Unit 2

Rubric	Very Good	Satisfactory	Needs Improvement
Content			
Use of descriptive language			
Use of grammar			
Organization			

Expanding Your Fluency

A What kind of traveler are you? Mark the activities in 1–7 that apply to you. Then answer question 8.

When I'm on vacation, I want to . . .

1. ☐ get away from the city and relax in a tranquil spot.
2. ☐ sleep late and read.
3. ☐ spend some time at a luxurious spa.
4. ☐ go sightseeing every day.
5. ☐ study or learn something.
6. ☐ do a lot of shopping.
7. ☐ try the local cuisine.
8. What are two activities you like to do on vacation?

____

Some Popular Vacation Activities

surfing	*playing golf*
waterskiing	*mountain biking*
swimming	*paragliding*
sunbathing	*skiing*
hiking	*snowboarding*

B Work with a partner.

Tourist: You are on vacation in an exotic city. You need help setting your itinerary for the next two days. Ask the concierge* of your hotel for advice on what to see and do in the area. Use your information from Activity **A** to get you started. Respond to the concierge's advice by accepting, questioning, or refusing.

Hotel Concierge: You are a concierge. One of your guests needs help planning an itinerary for the next two days. Ask about his or her interests. Suggest places to visit and things to do in the area. Describe in detail each place you mention.

C Change roles and repeat Activity **B**.

Good afternoon. May I help you?

Yes. I'm visiting for a couple of days and I'm looking for things to see and do . . .

Check What You Know

Rank how well you can perform these outcomes on a scale of 1–5 (5 being the best).

________ use descriptive language effectively
________ use gerund and infinitive structures to describe experiences
________ make travel recommendations
________ give, accept, and question advice

***concierge** a hotel employee who helps guests arrange things (sightseeing trips, theater tickets, etc.)

Expanding Your Fluency

10-15 min. A
15-20 min. B
15-20 min. C
Extension: 15-20 min.

A For item 8, students can use ideas from the box or come up with their own.

B
- The hotel setting can be in the students' city or country. In this situation, it might be a good idea to have student 1 pretend to be a foreign guest whose native language is different from the concierge's, in which case the two might use English to communicate.
- It may be helpful to specify the season / time of year, as this would affect the activities available in some locations.
- Have students review the expressions from the Speaking Strategy box on page 20.

C Ask for volunteers to role-play their conversations for the class.

Check What You Know

Refer students back to the exercises in the unit where each Outcome is addressed.

- *use descriptive language effectively:* Writing, Exercise **B**, page 22
- *use gerund and infinitive structures to describe experiences:* Grammar, Exercise **B**, page 15
- *make travel recommendations:* Speaking, Exercise **B**, page 20
- *give, accept, and question advice:* Speaking, Exercise **B**, page 20

Extension

After completing Exercise **C**, have students write a journal entry detailing their first two days of the vacation. Have them exchange papers with a partner who will check their writing for accuracy.

Unit 3
The Great Energy Challenge

Unit Overview

- Unit 3 is about energy sources and consumption. Students will learn about sustainable sources of energy and ways to reduce their consumption.
- As the world population continues to grow, so does the demand for energy. Fossil fuels represent about 85% of the world's energy sources, but growing concern over global warming has many countries investing in "greener" energy production, such as solar power.
- Ask students what they think is meant by the unit title, "The Great Energy Challenge."
- Preview the unit by asking students the following questions:

1. What are three things you've used today that require energy?
2. What is something you use that consumes energy that you think you could live without?
3. Do you think the efforts to use more renewable energy sources will be enough to help the future of the planet? Explain your answer.

Photo Caption

This image is of the Golden Gate Bridge at night spanning San Francisco Bay, with the city of San Francisco, California, in the background. The Golden Gate Bridge is considered one of the modern "Wonders of the World"; at 1.7 miles (2.7 km) in length, it connects San Francisco with Marin County, California.

San Francisco is the 13th largest city in the United States, but ranks second behind New York City in population density, with over 17,000 people per square mile. Like many large cities, San Francisco has a high need for energy. The state of California is one of the leaders in the U.S. in using renewable energy sources like wind, solar, and hydroelectric.

VOCABULARY	GRAMMAR	LISTENING	READING
An energy quiz **Pronunciation:** Heteronyms and stress shift	Review of future forms	The family energy challenge	*Plugging Into the Sun:* Why don't we use solar energy more? **Strategy:** Identifying key details

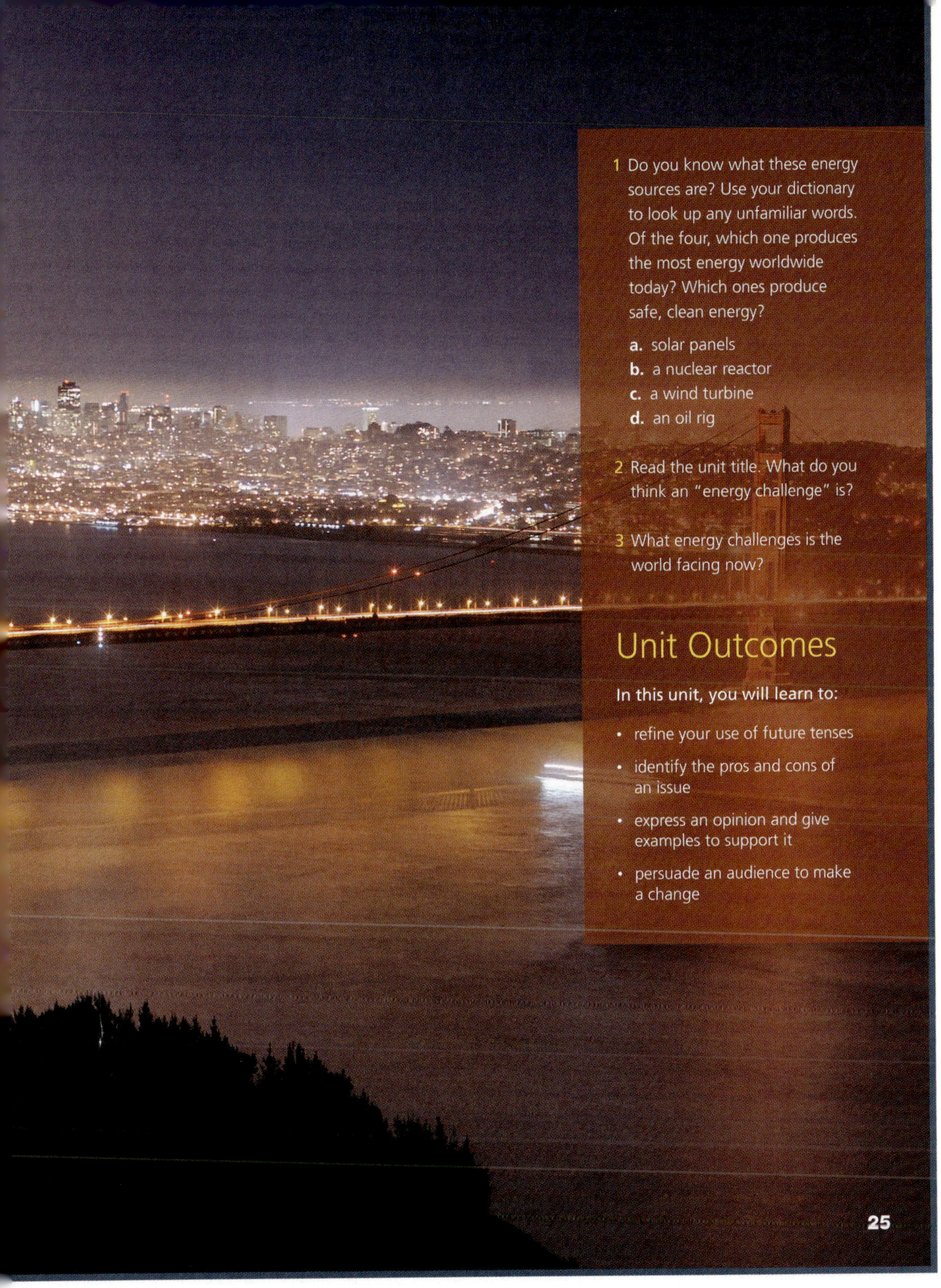

1 Do you know what these energy sources are? Use your dictionary to look up any unfamiliar words. Of the four, which one produces the most energy worldwide today? Which ones produce safe, clean energy?

a. solar panels
b. a nuclear reactor
c. a wind turbine
d. an oil rig

2 Read the unit title. What do you think an "energy challenge" is?

3 What energy challenges is the world facing now?

Unit Outcomes

In this unit, you will learn to:

- refine your use of future tenses
- identify the pros and cons of an issue
- express an opinion and give examples to support it
- persuade an audience to make a change

25

5-10 min. **Warm-Up Questions**
Extension: 15-20 min.

Background Information

Since 1990, the world population has grown by 27% and the average use of energy per person by 10%. The vast majority of the energy that we use comes from oil, gas, and coal, which has an enormous environmental impact and contributes to global warming. Concerns about pollution and climate change, high cost, and also the understanding that fossil fuels will one day run out, are all factors that are driving governments and individuals to seek out clean, sustainable energy sources.

Warm-Up Questions

- Read the unit title aloud and invite students to look at the photo. Ask them to guess the theme of the unit.
- Read Question 1 aloud. Work as a class to come up with a brief description for each energy source; write them on the board.
- Have students work in pairs to answer Questions 2 and 3. Then survey the class to find out what energy challenges students rate as most critical.

Extension

Write these energy sources on the board: *biomass, coal, gas, geothermal, hydro, nuclear, oil, solar, wind*. In groups, have students briefly define each energy source. Check answers and, correcting the information as needed, write the definitions on the board. Then have the groups categorize the sources as nonrenewable or sustainable.

VIDEO	WRITING	SPEAKING	OUTCOMES
We Need to Be Leaders Ourselves	Write a persuasive paragraph that presents and justifies your point of view **Strategy:** Being persuasive	Persuade an audience to make a change	• refine your use of future tenses • identify the pros and cons of an issue • express an opinion and give examples to support it • persuade an audience to make a change

Vocabulary

20-25 min. A
10-15 min. B
10-15 min. C
Extension: 10 min.

Language Notes

- Provide an additional definition for *supply*: n. The amount of something that is available to be used.
- Help students differentiate the pronunciation of the vocabulary word *project* (pro-JECT), which is a verb, and *project* (PRAH-ject), which is a noun.

A
- Read through the energy statistics as a class.
- Remind students that hydro power is derived from the energy of moving water.
- Fossil fuels (oil, gas, coal) were formed hundreds of millions of years ago from the remains of prehistoric organisms.
- Go over the statistic about nuclear power in France. Ask students what the advantages and disadvantages are when a country relies mainly on one source of energy.

B
- For more of a challenge, have students cover up the prompts in the Word Partnership box with a piece of paper; instead, tell them to consult the word bank to find three verbs and one noun that *energy* can be used with.
- After checking answers, have students use each word partner in a sentence.

Answers: generate; run; supply; source

C If necessary, remind students that they do not have to know the answers to these questions. Instead they should either guess or offer their opinions as they discuss them with a partner.

Vocabulary

consume to use, especially in large amounts
eliminate to remove something entirely
entire the whole of something
generate to make or produce
project to predict
rely on to depend on or use
residents the people who live in a certain place (house, neighborhood, city, etc.)
reverse to cause something to move in the opposite direction
run out to use something (up) completely
source the origin or starting place of something
supply to give an amount; provide
sustainable long-lasting or good for the environment

***reverse** the effects (of something), ~ a decision, ~ the order, Put your car in ~.*

PRONUNCIATION Notice that these two words are different. *We're launching the **PROject** next year. They **proJECT** a 10 percent increase by 2020.* For more information on heteronyms and stress shift, see page 146.

A Read the energy statistics. Use the word bank to help you. Did any of the information surprise you? Why?

Did you know?

- Hydro power could generate 20 percent of the energy that developed nations need.
- Wind power could supply forty times more energy than we consume now.
- One hour of sunlight can supply the world with enough energy for an entire year. Using solar energy (instead of fossil fuels) could also help reverse the effects of global warming.
- Coal, the largest source of electric power today, can be mined in a third of the world's countries.
- Experts project that natural gas will produce 26 percent of the world's energy by 2020.
- Oil powers our lives, but using oil is not sustainable and experts predict it will run out in the next century.
- Residents of France rely on nuclear power; 78 percent of the country's electricity comes from this energy source, more than any other nation in the world.

***global warming** an increase in Earth's temperature caused by burning **fossil fuels** (oil, gas, and coal)*

B Which words from the list go with *energy*? Complete the Word Partnership box.

Word Partnership
Use *energy* with:
v: consume, g_______,
r____ out (of),
s_______ *energy*
n: *energy* s_________

C Discuss these questions with a partner.

1. Which energy sources does your country rely on the most?
2. Are there energy sources we should eliminate from our day-to-day lives?
3. Do you believe that oil will eventually run out completely? Why or why not?
4. What is one thing you or your community can do to consume less energy?
5. Do you think we can reverse the effects of global warming? Why or why not?

26

Extension

Ask students to write six true/false statements about the energy facts in the *Did you know?* box. Have students exchange papers with a partner and complete the activity.

Grammar

A Choose the best answer(s) for items 1–4. More than one option may be possible. Then explain your answers to a partner.

1. **A:** Do you want to see a movie? **B:** I can't. _________ this evening.
   a. I'm studying   b. I'll study   c. I'm going to study
2. Experts think the cost of solar power _____ decrease in the future.
   a. is going to   b. will
3. a. I'll text you when I get a break.   b. I'll text you when I'll get a break.
4. At this time tomorrow, ____ to Asia.
   a. I'll travel   b. I'll be traveling

Review of Future Forms	
definite plans	**I'm going to take** the TOEFL next Saturday. **I'm taking** the TOEFL next Saturday.
predictions	By 2040, there **are going to be** over 8 billion people on Earth. By 2040, there **will be** over 8 billion people on Earth.
promises	**I'll call** you tonight after I get home. I **won't** forget.
ongoing future actions	Within ten years, Germany **will be using** less oil and more renewable sources.

B Complete this quiz with an appropriate future form of the verb in parentheses. Then ask and answer the questions with a partner.

1. Which country ________ (consume) the most energy in the near future?
   a. China   b. India   c. the United States
2. Which country ________ (have) the largest per person energy consumption this year?
   a. Canada   b. Russia   c. South Africa
3. What country ________ (continue) to generate the most geothermal energy?
   a. Iceland   b. Costa Rica   c. the United States
4. Which country ________ (run) 50 percent of their cars on ethanol (fuel made from corn) in the future?
   a. Mexico   b. Brazil   c. Japan
5. Global energy demand will ________ (increase) as the population ________ (increases). How much of that increase _________ (come) from the richest countries in the world?
   a. 7 percent   b. 17 percent   c. 27 percent

C Discuss these predictions with a partner. Do you agree with the statements?

In the future . . .

Fewer people will be driving gas-powered cars.
More people will rely on nuclear energy.
My country is going to be oil independent.
Your own idea: ___________________________

Internet Activity

Have students use www.grammarbank.com for extra practice of future forms. This Web site provides simple grammar explanations with visuals, exercises and practice quizzes, a grammar help forum, games, vocabulary sections, and more.

Grammar

15-20 min. A
15-20 min. B
10-15 min. C
Extension: 10-15 min.

A Go over the chart as a class. For each use, give additional examples that deal with future events in your class. Then, ask students questions about their plans, predictions, promises, and future actions.

Answers: 1. a or c; 2. a or b; 3. a; 4. b

B
- Have students fill in the blanks with the correct verb form. Check the answers as a class; have volunteers match each verb form to its use listed in the chart on this page.
- Then have students form pairs and do the quiz.
- Check answers as a class. Ask students if there are any answers that were surprising to them.

Answers: *Verb forms:* 1. will be consuming; 2. will have / is going to have; 3. is going to continue / will continue; 4. will be running; 5. will increase; will come; *Quiz:* 1. a; 2. b; 3. c; 4. b; 5. a

Outcome: Upon completing this activity, students will have met the Outcome ***refine your use of future tenses.***

C
- After students discuss the predictions in pairs, survey the class to see if there is a consensus of opinion on each item.
- Have volunteers share their own predictions with the class. Then ask the class to state whether or not they agree and why.

Extension

On their own, have students write four sentences that use each of the future forms they learned on this page and four different vocabulary words from page 26. When they have finished, instruct them to switch their papers with a partner and correct any errors they find.

Listening

5-10 min. A
10 min. B
10-15 min. C
15-20 min. D
Extension: 15 min.

Background Information

This audio recording consists of a portion of an episode of a TV program that deals with ways to protect our planet; three people are interviewed about ways they save energy in their everyday lives.

A • Read through the sets of statements as a class. Have students work in pairs to discuss the meanings of the phrases in blue. If necessary, inform them that the phrases in each set are synonyms—words that mean the same thing.
• Then have students discuss the difference between the phrases in each set. Ask them how the meaning of *reduce / cut back / cut down* is different than the meaning of *eliminate / give up*.

B • Read the cloze sentence aloud; then have students share their predictions with a partner.
• Play the introduction to the TV program one or more times. **Audio CD Track 5**
• Survey the class to find out how accurate their predictions were.

Sample Answer: take the (show's) "energy challenge"

C • Before listening to the interviews, have students read through the lists under each photo.
• Play the entire audio recording, pausing as necessary to allow students time to check off their answers. **Audio CD Track 6**

Answers: *The Novak family:* reduce air travel; *The Noguchi family:* change the temperature settings on the refrigerator; hang clothes to dry; *The Perez family:* carpool (to drive together with others); use solar energy for heating water or cooking

continued on page 29

Listening

A Look at these two groups of verbs in bold. What do they mean? Discuss your ideas.

1	I'm going to **reduce** my work week from forty hours to thirty. My doctor told me to **cut down** / **cut back** on desserts.
2	To be a vegetarian, you need to **eliminate** all red meat from your diet. I need to eat better, but I cannot **give up** chocolate completely. I love it too much!

B You're going to listen to the introduction to a TV program. What do you think it's about? Tell a partner. Then listen and complete the sentence in your own words.

The program *Our Green Planet* will be following everyday people as they ______________.

C Listen to each person. Check (✓) the energy-saving actions that they are taking.

The Novak family

☐ use a bicycle instead of a car for short trips
☐ reduce air travel
☐ grow their own food

The Noguchi family

☐ unplug all electronic appliances daily
☐ change the temperature settings on the refrigerator
☐ hang clothes to dry

The Perez family

☐ carpool (to drive together with others)
☐ buy only locally made products
☐ use solar energy for heating water or cooking

D Look at the items in Exercise **C** that you didn't check. Why doesn't the family do these things? Listen again and take notes using the pattern below. Then explain your answers to a partner.

The ____________ family doesn't ____________________ because . . .

Ask Answer Mr. Noguchi counted the electronic appliances in his home. How many are in your home? In the kitchen? In the living room? In your bedroom?

Extension

Have students convert the three lists in Exercise **C** into interview questions. Then, instruct them to role-play interviews, asking each other the questions. For any energy-saving actions that students (or their families) don't do, have them explain to each other why not.

Connections

A Read through the survey alone and underline any words you don't know. Then discuss the survey as a class. Can your classmates explain the unfamiliar words to you?

ARE YOU READY TO GO ON AN ENERGY DIET?

1. _____ Eliminate at least three chemical housecleaning products.
2. _____ Buy only locally made or grown products.
3. _____ Resist the urge to buy an item that you don't use often.
4. _____ Eat a vegetarian diet one day a week.
5. _____ Grow your own food.
6. _____ Give up at least one processed food that you normally eat.
7. _____ Use public transportation at least three times a week.
8. _____ Unplug phone chargers when they are not in use.
9. _____ Give up bottled water for tap water.
10. _____ Turn off the tap when you're brushing your teeth.
11. _____ Recycle all glass, aluminum, plastic, and paper.
12. _____ Eliminate the use of plastic and paper bags when shopping.

Chicago waterfront

B Working alone, take the survey above. Write the letter of a statement below (*a, b, c, d*) next to each item in the energy diet survey.

a. I do this already.
b. I'll try to do this in the next month.
c. I'm going to do this someday in the future.
d. I can't do this. It seems impossible.

C Compare your answers with a partner. How similar or different are you?

D Look at your **b** and **c** answers in the energy diet survey. Complete these sentences and talk about your personal energy diet plan.

Starting this weekend, one change I'll make is ____________________.

After I make my first change, I'll ____________________.

When I get discouraged about sticking to my energy diet, I'm going to ____________________.

By this time next year, I think I'll be ____________________.

Listening *continued*

D Play the audio recording again. Have students write their answers on a separate sheet of paper. Pause the recording after each family to give students time to write. **Audio CD Track 6**

Sample Answers: *The* Novak *family doesn't* grow their own food *because* Anica hates gardening and thinks it's too much work. She also hates to get dirty. *The* Novak *family doesn't* use bicycles instead of a car for short trips *because* children have to pass an exam before they are allowed to ride their bikes on public streets, and Anica's kids are too small to take the exam. *The* Noguchi *family doesn't* unplug electronic appliances *because* Akira can't remember to unplug all 37 of their appliances every morning before they go to work. *The* Perez *family doesn't* buy locally made products *because* it's hard for Dora to find things in their small town. Instead, she shops online.

Connections

5-10 min. A
10 min. B
10-15 min. C
15-20 min. D
Extension: 10-15 min.

A After the class identifies and explains any unknown words, read through the survey items as a class. Discuss how each one relates to energy consumption and give additional explanations as needed. For example, some students may not be aware that red meat production carries a significant environmental impact (item 4)—production of protein from grain-fed animals uses eight times the amount of fossil-fuel energy as the production of protein from plants.

B
- Encourage students to be realistic when selecting choices **b** and **c**.
- For any statement that students assigned a **d**, have them write a follow-up explanation of why they feel the action seems impossible.

D Direct students to the Grammar Chart of future forms on page 27 to help them complete the sentences. Then have students identify which future forms they used in each: *plan, promise, prediction, ongoing future action.*

Extension

Assign a point value to each response in Exercise **B**; have students calculate their scores. Pair up students that scored on opposite ends of the spectrum; have those in the energy-saving mindset try to convince others to adopt their practices and give them tips for doing so. Alternatively, if the majority of students answered **a** and **b**, have them work in pairs to create a pamphlet containing their best tips and practices for saving energy.

Reading

5-10 min. **A**
10 min. **B**
10-15 min. **C**
15-20 min. **D**
Extension: 20 min.

A Alternatively, take the quiz orally as a class; then have students find the supporting information in the reading.

Answers: 1. T; 2. F; 3. F; 4. T

B Have students share their ideas with the class; then have them read the passage.

C Have students compare their lists of advantages and disadvantages with a partner. Then, ask the whole class which method of gathering solar energy would be better suited to your community and why.

Answers: *Steam generation method:* Advantages: more efficient; converts more sunlight into electricity. Disadvantages: requires a lot of open space; long cables are needed and can be expensive. *PV panels:* Advantages: easy to place on rooftops; no extra cost to transmit energy. Disadvantages: when not sunny, people need to rely on battery backups; very expensive to buy.

Outcome: Upon completing this activity, students will have met the Outcome ***identify the pros and cons of an issue.***

D Allow students time to develop their persuasive arguments and questions about disadvantages. They may jot down notes, but encourage them to be spontaneous during the role-play.

Reading

A Take the quiz and compare ideas with a partner. Then scan the reading to check your answers.

SOLAR ENERGY Quiz

1. The sun generates more energy than humans can use.	T	F
2. Worldwide, most electricity is produced using solar energy.	T	F
3. Solar energy generates a lot of pollution.	T	F
4. Solar energy can only be used in places that get a lot of sunlight all year.	T	F

B Why aren't we using solar power more? List some of your ideas. Then read the passage to check your answers.

C Read the passage again. On a separate piece of paper, list at least two advantages and two disadvantages of each method of gathering solar energy (steam generation and PV panels).

Reading Strategy **Identifying key details** The article compares two ways of gathering solar energy. As you read, watch for keywords like *advantage, disadvantage, drawback, however, (al)though,* and *on the other hand* to help you identify key details.

D Use your answers from Exercise **C** to act out this role-play.

1. **Student A:** Imagine that you work for a solar energy company. You need to persuade the mayor of your city to invest more money in solar power. Give two or three reasons why this is a good idea.

   Student B: Listen to your partner's argument and ask at least two questions about the disadvantages. Did your partner convince you to invest more money?
2. Switch roles and practice again.

Our sun is the most powerful source of energy on Earth. Worldwide, humans use about 16 terawatts[1] of energy a year. The sun produces 120,000 terawatts annually—much more than we consume. Today, though, solar power is used very little; it generates less than one-tenth of 1 percent (0.1%) of the world's electricity each year.

Why don't we use solar power more? To answer this question, it's important to understand the two main ways we gather energy from the sun. The first way is to place flat, computer-guided mirrors in a field. The mirrors focus sunlight onto a receiver on a tower and this produces steam. The steam is then used to produce electricity. The second way of gathering energy from the sun is to use PV (photovoltaic) panels. The panels collect sunlight and convert[2] it into electricity. Most people have seen PV panels on buildings; small ones are also on some handheld calculators.

Both ways of gathering solar energy have their advantages. Unlike oil or coal, solar power

Extension

Ask students to use the Internet to research the advantages and disadvantages of another clean, sustainable energy source, such as wind or hydro. Then have students refer back to the lists they made in Exercise **C** and compare the benefits and drawbacks of solar power versus the other energy source. Ask them to write a comparison and give their opinion as to which is a more viable source of energy.

Plugging Into The SUN

Sunlight provides us with more energy than we need . . . so why aren't we using solar power more?

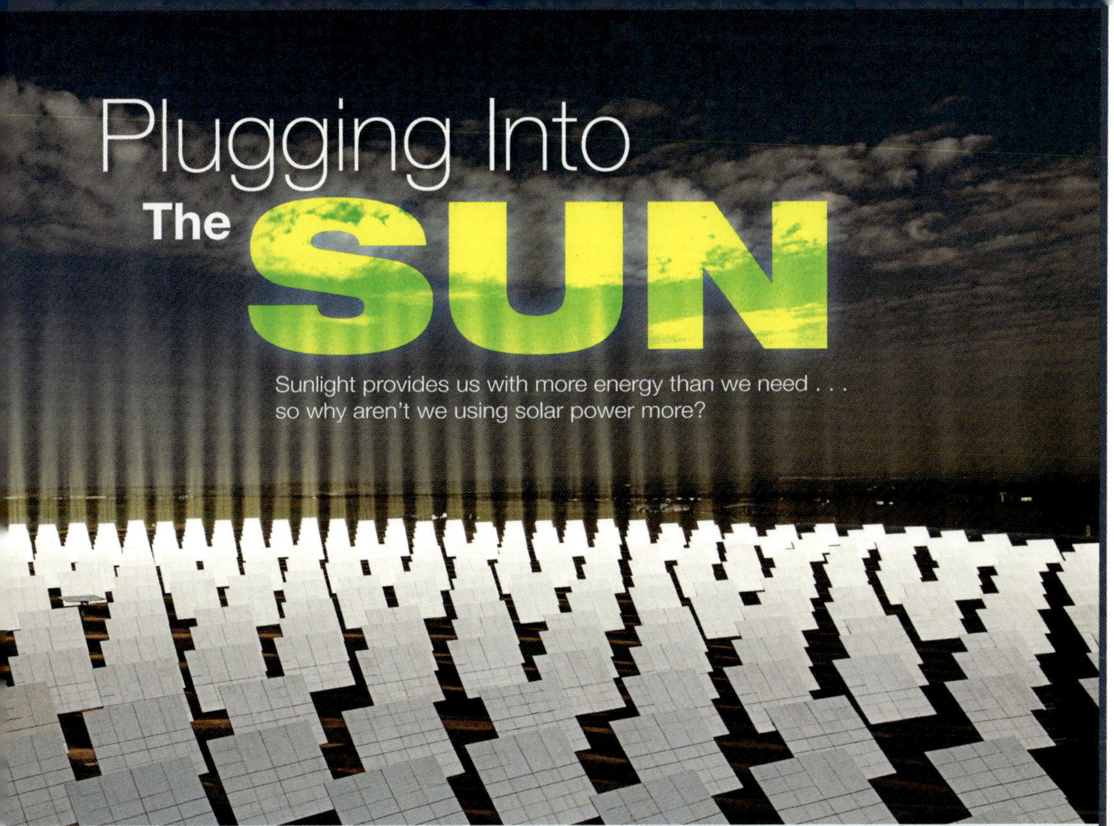

generates "clean" energy that produces very little pollution. However, the steam-generation method[3] is more efficient than the PV panel method because it converts more sunlight into electricity. The steam generation method requires a lot of open space, though (for example, a big field). Long cables are also needed to transmit[4] the power from an open space to the city, which can be expensive. PV panels, on the other hand, can easily be placed on rooftops where the power is needed. There is no extra cost to transmit the energy in this way.

Both methods have a similar disadvantage: they are unable to produce enough energy when it's cloudy or dark. Engineers are working on this problem. For now, though, people who use PV panels as their main source of energy must rely on batteries at night or when the weather is bad.

One of solar energy's biggest drawbacks is cost. PV panels are still very expensive to buy. In some places, though, people are earning their money back. Wolfgang Schnürer lives in Freiburg, Germany. He powers his home using solar energy. In the winter, the panels on the roof of Schnürer's apartment do not produce enough energy. But on a sunny day in May, the panels can generate *more* energy than he and his family consume. When this happens, Schnürer can sell the extra power back to the energy company in his city. In 2008, he made 2,500 euros ($3,700) from the extra power his solar panels generated.

Despite the challenges, solar energy use is increasing worldwide. In Germany, Japan, and the United States, governments are trying to make solar power more affordable for everyone. And as people find that they can save money—and even make money—using solar power, the number of countries using this energy source will surely grow.

[1] **terawatt** a measurement of electrical power
[2] **convert** change
[3] **method** a way of doing something
[4] **transmit** send from one place to another place

Background Information

- Commercial solar power stations were first developed in the 1980s; the biggest ones were built beginning in 2008. The world's largest solar power plant, which uses the steam generation method, is Solar Energy Generating Systems (SEGS) in California (US); it uses about one million mirrors that are spread over 6.5 square kilometers. The largest photovoltaic plant in the world is Golmud Solar Park in China.
- Italy, Spain, and Germany are also home to significant commercial solar power plants. Germany is by far the world leader in terms of electricity generated from solar energy.
- Photovoltaic installations on rooftops are used by companies, schools, and homeowners around the world, mostly in Asia, Europe, and North America.

Language Notes

As explained in the passage, a *watt* is the standard measurement of electrical power; it is defined as one joule per second. A *terawatt* is one trillion watts.

Photo Caption

This image is of the mirrors at the PS10 Solar Power Plant near the city of Seville in southern Spain. The plant, constructed in 2004, has 624 of these mirrors, called heliostats. Together, the mirrors reflect and concentrate the sun's rays to the top of a tower. A steam turbine is activated in the tower, producing electricity. The PS10 was Europe's first commercial solar power tower.

Beyond the Reading

Recommend that students watch one of the videos about solar power on the National Geographic Web site (nationalgeographic.com/video). Have them jot down notes as they watch. Then, in pairs, have students share what they learned and what facts were surprising to them.

Video

5 min. **A**
10 min. **B**
5-10 min. **C**
10-15 min. **D**
10-15 min. **E**
Extension: 20 min.

Background Information

- Greenpeace, founded in 1971, is a nongovernmental organization dedicated to environmentalism. The organization does not accept funding from any government, political party, or corporation. Greenpeace activists frequently engage in direct action, or activities that are undertaken outside of social or political channels.
- Bridgeport, Connecticut (pop. 144,000), is a coastal city in the northeastern part of the United States. The Greenpeace protest depicted in the video took place at the United Illuminating coal-fired power plant as part of the organization's "anti-coal" campaign.

Before You Watch

A • Ask students if they have heard of Greenpeace; have volunteers share what they know about the organization.
• Point out to students the compound word that gives the organization its name. Ask them what they think the name means.

B • After students watch the video without sound and make their guesses, ask what evidence from the video supports their guesses.
• Play the video a second time with sound. Have students raise their hands if they guessed correctly.

C • Have students read through the statements.
• Then play the video and have students complete the activity. Allow students to watch the video more than once if needed.

Answers: 1. dirty; 2. coal; 3. relying; 4. on; 5. clean; 6. air; 7. contributing; 8. pollution; 9. see; 10. shut; 11. down

continued on page 33

Video

VIDEO GLOSSARY

impact a strong effect
contribute to be one of the causes of something
injustice a lack of fairness in a situation
roadblock a situation or condition that prevents further progress; an obstacle

A In this video, you are going to meet Lauren, a Greenpeace activist. Read about Greenpeace below. Have you ever heard of it?

Greenpeace is the largest environmental organization in the world. It works to protect our oceans and forests and stop global warming. Greenpeace activists (people who work to achieve social or political change) sometimes take the initiative in effecting changes instead of working with political leaders, even to the extent of breaking the law.

B Watch the video once through with the *sound off*. What energy issue is the video about? Then watch the video with the *sound on* and check your ideas.

C Watch and answer these questions by completing each blank with the correct word.

What is the problem? (1) _______ (2) _______ energy is something the United States has been (3) _______ (4) _______ for way too long.

What does Lauren think is a basic human right? Having (5) _______ (6) _______

What has the plant been doing? (7) _______ a significant amount of (8) _______ to the community

What does the community want to do? They want to (9) _______ the coal plant (10) _______ (11) _______.

D Watch again and answer these questions. If an answer isn't given, write "NM" ("not mentioned").

1. What is Lauren deeply concerned about?
2. How does Lauren feel about the plant?
3. What does Lauren say the plant is a roadblock to?
4. According to Lauren, what can people do to stop the plant?

E Discuss these questions with a partner.

1. Do you think it's sometimes all right to get people to make changes without involving the proper authorities?
2. Lauren says, "Sometimes we need to be leaders ourselves." Do you agree with this statement?
3. Lauren is protesting at the plant in Bridgeport, Connecticut. What other things could people in that community do to shut down the plant?

32

Extension

Have students use the Internet to research other Greenpeace actions. Ask students to report what they learned to the class, who will ask follow-up questions. What were the activists' goals? Were they successful? How?

Writing

A Persuasive Paragraph

A Read the paragraph. Then answer the questions with a partner.

Change a Bulb, Save the Planet

Everyone wants to save energy and protect the environment. Now you can do both by using CFL bulbs instead of regular bulbs in your home, classroom, or office. How will this help? **For one thing**, according to National Geographic's *Lightbulb Buying Guide*, CFL bulbs use almost 75% less energy than regular bulbs. When we use less energy to light a room, we generate less CO_2. This helps the environment. **In addition**, because CFL bulbs use less energy, you'll save a lot of money on your electric bill over time. So remember: a regular bulb will light your home. However, a CFL bulb will help you save energy, spend less on electricity, and improve the environment. You can make a difference!

TIP The writer uses specific facts to support his point. He cites his source by using the words *according to.*

1. What is the main goal of this paragraph?
   a. to compare two similar things
   b. to explain why you should do something
   c. to describe the pros and cons of something
2. What two benefits are discussed in the paragraph? Which words introduce these ideas?

B Read the Writing Strategy. What do you notice about the words that follow *instead of, rather than*, and *by*?

Writing Strategy

Being persuasive To encourage people to do one thing instead of another, you can use structures like these:

1. **Instead of / Rather than** <u>using</u> regular light bulbs, use CFL bulbs. You'll save energy.
2. **By** <u>using</u> CFL bulbs **instead of / rather than** (<u>using</u>) regular bulbs, you'll save energy.

C You want to encourage people to change something they are doing now. Use the structures in the Writing Strategy and the information below. Write each sentence in two ways.

	You waste energy when you . . .	**You save energy when you . . .**
1.	drive everywhere.	ride a bike.
2.	throw away paper and plastic.	recycle paper and plastic.
3.	drink bottled water.	drink filtered water.
4.	always keep all electronics plugged in.	unplug electronics when you're not using them.
5.	Your idea: ___________	Your idea: ___________

Instead of driving, ride a bike sometimes. / By riding a bike sometimes instead of driving, you'll save energy.

Rubric	Very Good	Satisfactory	Needs Improvement
Content			
Use of persuasive phrases			
Use of grammar			
Organization			

Video *continued*

D After students have watched the video again and taken notes on these questions, have them write the answers in complete sentences.

Answers: 1. Lauren is deeply concerned about coal and its impacts on the climate and local communities. 2. Lauren feels the fact that the plant has been contributing a significant amount of pollution to Bridgeport for over 50 years is an injustice, and she wants to see it shut down. 3. Lauren says that the plant (specifically, reliance on coal for power) is the biggest roadblock to renewable energy coming in to the country and providing new jobs. 4. NM

Writing

5-10 min. **A**
5 min. **B**
10 min. **C**
15-20 min. **D**
5-10 min. **E**
Extension: 15-20 min.

Purpose of Writing

The purpose of this writing task is to persuade someone to change his or her current behavior.

A Inform students that *CFL* stands for "compact fluorescent lamp." They cost more than regular bulbs, but because they use less energy and have a longer life (8–15 times), CFL bulbs are considered financially and environmentally beneficial. However, they must be carefully disposed of, as they contain mercury.

Answers: 1. b; 2. (1) CFL bulbs use almost 75% less energy than regular bulbs; (2) you'll save a lot of money on your electric bill over time. *Words that introduce the benefits:* for one thing; in addition

B

Answer: The words are all in the gerund form (*-ing*).

C
- Encourage students to include an additional benefit for each item. For example, in item 1, riding a bike is also a good way to exercise.
- The information on wasting and saving energy is also used in the Speaking section on page 34.

continued on page 34

Writing *continued*

D Have students research statistics online to support their claims. Remind them to use the phrase *according to* when citing facts.

Outcome: Upon completing this activity, students will have met the Outcome *express an opinion and give examples to support it.*

Extension

Collect the papers and read them aloud. Have the class vote for the most convincing ones.

Speaking

20-30 min. **A**
10-15 min. **B**
10 min. **C**
Extension: 15 min.

A
- Refer students to the information on wasting and saving energy in the Writing section on page 33, Exercise **C**. Remind students to pick a different topic than the one they chose for their writing assignment.
- Review the Writing Strategy box on page 33; provide additional examples.

B **Outcome:** Upon completing this activity, students will have met the Outcome *persuade an audience to make a change.*

C After pairs have discussed their opinions, survey the class to find out which public service announcements were most effective and why.

Extension

Have students make videos of their public service announcements. Encourage them to be creative, using props and humor to make their announcements interesting and persuasive.

Internet Activity

Have students log on to www.storyofstuff.org and listen to *Take THAT, plastic bags!* Ask students to summarize what each interviewee has done to reduce plastic bag use. Also ask them to state who, in their opinion, has probably had a greater impact on persuading others to give up plastic bags.

D Choose a sentence from Exercise **C** (1–5). On a separate piece of paper, write a paragraph that explains the change and gives two reasons why people should do it.

Everyone wants to save energy and protect the environment. Now you can do both . . .

E Exchange papers with another student. Read your partner's writing and answer questions 1–3 in the Writing Checklist.

Writing Checklist

Does the paragraph . . .

1. clearly state what change people should make?
2. give two reasons to make the change, using *for one thing* and *in addition*?
3. convince readers to change their behavior?

Speaking

A Work with a partner. You are going to create a public service announcement* about saving energy. Choose an idea from Exercise **C** on page 33 or think of your own. Then do the following:

Design a public service announcement that is 45–60 seconds long. It should . . .

- explain what change people should make.
- give 2–3 reasons why people should make the change.
- be interesting and make your viewers want to make the change.

For ideas, reread the paragraph and information in the Writing Strategy box on page 33 again.

B Do your presentations.

Presenters: Present your public service announcement to the class.

Viewers: Take notes on each pair's public service announcement. Answer these questions briefly:

1. What change do they want you to make?
2. What reasons did they give for making the change?
3. Did they convince you to make a change? Why or why not?

C Compare your notes in Exercise **B** with a partner. In your opinion, which public service announcement was the best? Why?

*A public service announcement is an ad that tells people about an important issue.

Rubric	Very Good	Satisfactory	Needs Improvement
Persuasiveness of message			
Use of vocabulary			
Use of grammar			
Pronunciation and fluency			

Expanding Your Fluency

A We can add the suffixes *-ion* / *-tion* / *-sion* to some verbs to form nouns. Complete the chart with the noun or verb form of each word. Use your dictionary to help you. Then say the words with a partner.

Verb	Noun
1. consume	
2.	conversion
3. eliminate	
4. generate	
5.	pollution

Verb	Noun
6. prevent	
7.	production
8.	projection
9. reduce	
10.	transmission

B Use the correct words from the chart to complete the sentences. Check answers with a partner.

1. How is the air quality in your city? Is there a lot of ________________ or is the air clean?
2. Should we completely _____________ cars in cities and encourage people to walk and bike only?
3. What things can you do to cut down on energy _______________ and ______________ your electric bill each month so that you pay less?
4. Which sources ____________ the most energy today? Are there any energy sources we should stop using? Why?

C Think about your answers to the questions in Exercise **B**. Then do the following with a partner.

1. Take turns. Choose one of the questions.
2. Answer the question by talking for one minute without stopping, and you get a point.
3. Repeat steps 1 and 2 for a total of ten minutes. Continue until there are no more questions or the ten minutes are up.
4. The winner is the person with the most points at the end.

Check What You Know

Rank how well you can perform these outcomes on a scale of 1–5 (5 being the best).

________ refine your use of future tenses
________ identify the pros and cons of an issue
________ express an opinion and give examples to support it
________ persuade an audience to make a change

Expanding Your Fluency

15-20 min. A
10-15 min. B
15-20 min. C
Extension: 20 min.

A
- Do item 1 as a model with the class.
- Go over the answers as a class.

Answers: 1. consumption; 2. convert; 3. elimination; 4. generation; 5. pollute; 6. prevention; 7. produce; 8. project; 9. reduction; 10. transmit

B
- Have students first read through the questions and decide if each blank takes a verb or a noun. Then have them read the questions again and select the correct word.
- Go over the answers as a class.

Answers: 1. pollution; 2. eliminate; 3. consumption; reduce; 4. generate / produce

C
- Have students review the expressions from the Reading Strategy box on page 30 and the Writing Strategy box on page 33.
- Model answering a question. Encourage students to give examples in their answers.

Check What You Know

Refer students back to the exercises in the unit where each Outcome is addressed.

- *refine your use of future tenses:* Grammar, Exercise **B**, page 27
- *identify the pros and cons of an issue:* Reading, Exercise **C**, page 30
- *express an opinion and give examples to support it:* Writing, Exercise **D**, page 34
- *persuade an audience to make a change:* Speaking, Exercise **B**, page 34

Extension

Have students use the questions from Exercise **B**, plus one additional question, to interview a family member. Tell students that they should write a summary of their family member's responses, and state whether they agree or disagree with each one.

Unit 4 The World's a Stage

Unit Overview

- Unit 4 is about performers and their arts. Students will learn about how performers become successful in what they do, and how the meaning of success is often subjective. The unit mentions many kinds of performers, focusing mainly on singers who represent different types of music around the world: pop, salsa, hip-hop, and traditional Irish.
- Ask students what they think is meant by the unit title, "The World's a Stage." Explain that it comes from a play by William Shakespeare: *As You Like It,* Act 2, Scene 7: *All the world's a stage, And all the men and women merely players; They have their exits and their entrances, And one man in his time plays many parts, His acts being seven ages.* Further note that many common phrases in English come from the works of Shakespeare, including, "method in the madness" (*Hamlet*) and "one fell swoop" (*Macbeth*). Preview the unit by asking students the following questions:

1. How do you feel about performing in front of a crowd? Have you ever had to perform?
2. What artistic talent do you wish you had? Why?
3. What makes a performer successful?

Photo Caption

This image is of the members of a Mariachi band in Mexico. Mariachi music originated in the state of Jalisco, in western Mexico, in the 1700s. A Mariachi band usually includes guitars, violins, and trumpets, and the musicians often wear silver-studded costumes and wide-brimmed hats. They often play at weddings and other special occasions.

4 The World's a Stage

VOCABULARY	GRAMMAR	LISTENING	READING
The story of Esmee Denters, YouTube sensation	Infinitive complements (*persuade* verbs, *want* verbs, *believe* verbs, *plan verbs,* and *make* verbs)	Interview with a salsa band musician	*Hip-Hop Goes Home:* A Struggling Rapper in Africa

1 Where do you think this photo was taken? What type of music do you think is being played?

2 Do you think this performer is famous? What's more important, being famous no matter what or staying true to your roots?

3 Who are some of your favorite musicians and actors? Do you ever go to see live performances?

Unit Outcomes

In this unit, you will learn to:

- use infinitives to complement certain types of verbs
- state the pros and cons of making a decision
- use time expressions to order life events
- paraphrase information from other sources

37

5-10 min. **Warm-Up Questions**
Extension: 15-20 min.

Background Information

With the Internet and the availability of digital recordings of music, movies and books, the art scene has changed dramatically in the last decade. The total number of physical albums (CDs) released has dropped over the last few years as digital music has become more popular. In 2011, Apple's iTunes store sold its 10 billionth song.

Warm-Up Questions

- Read Question 1 as a class. Ask several volunteers to make a guess about the photo. Work as a class to describe the photo in detail.
- Ask students what they think *staying true to your roots* means.
- Have students write down their answers to Questions 2 and 3. Then survey the class on their responses. What is the class consensus on the importance of fame? What type of artists do the majority of students prefer?

Extension

Based on students' responses to Question 2, form small groups that have an equal number of students who believe that being famous is important and students who believe that staying true to your roots is important. Encourage students to discuss their different points of view within their groups. Then, bring the class back together and ask if anyone changed their views about performers and fame.

VIDEO	WRITING	SPEAKING	OUTCOMES
Songs Under a Big Sky (excerpt): Profile of Irish singer Iarla Ó Lionáird **Pronunciation:** Linking	Write a profile of a person that you admire **Strategy:** Paraphrasing	Analyzing a music contract **Strategy:** Talking about pros and cons	• use infinitives to complement certain types of verbs • state the pros and cons of making a decision • use time expressions to order life events • paraphrase information from other sources

Vocabulary

5-10 min. A
15-20 min. B
10-15 min. C
Extension: 15-20 min.

A • Ask if anyone in your class is a musician. Have these students think about what they might do if they wanted to become famous.
• Have students read the word bank definitions individually. Point out other collocations with *launch: ~ a business; ~ a Web site; ~ a career.*

Answers: Formed from verbs: *assistance (assist), disturbance (disturb), entrance (enter);* Formed from adjectives: *brilliance (brilliant), importance (important)*

B Have students read the profile individually, or read the profile aloud as students follow along silently.

Answers: 1. her friends; 2. when Justin Timberlake contacted her; 3. on the *Oprah Winfrey Show;* 4. She doesn't really have one.

C • Ask students what they know about the words *webcam, YouTube channel,* and *mainstream media.*
• Before pairing students, allow them to jot down some notes about the singer they like.

Extension

Have students write a profile of a singer they like (different than the one they discussed in Exercise **C**), using the profile in Exercise **B** as a model. In their profiles, have them consider these questions: *How did the singer get his or her start? What kind of music does he / she sing? How does the singer use mainstream and non-mainstream media to stay in touch with fans?* Then have them take turns reading their profiles aloud in small groups without mentioning the singers' names for their classmates to guess.

Vocabulary

A Your friend is a musician who wants to become famous. What would you tell him or her to do? Think of two or three ideas with a partner and then share them with the class.

audience a group of people watching a performance
commercial related to the buying and selling of goods and services
convince to persuade someone (to do something)
emerge to come out and be recognized or noticed
hard-core very committed (to something)
inspired (by) encouraged (by) or motivated (by)
launch to start
mainstream most typical or conventional
make an appearance to come out in public
performance singing, dancing, or acting for an audience

commercial ~ *success,* ~ *development,* ~ *use*

Which of the following ***-ance*** words are formed from verbs? From adjectives? *assistance, brilliance, disturbance, entrance, importance*

B Read this profile of Esmee Denters and answer the questions below with a partner.

This is the story of a 17-year-old Dutch teenager with a webcam and a dream. Esmee Denters loved to sing and her friends loved her voice. They convinced her to launch her own YouTube channel. Inspired by her friends' support, Esmee started recording videos. And they were soon a hit. Within nine months, her videos had 21 million views, and, just like any celebrity, she had hard-core fans. Esmee had definitely arrived on the scene.

Her big commercial break came when singer Justin Timberlake contacted her. They wrote several songs together. Esmee put out an album and even made an appearance on *The Oprah Winfrey Show*. The webcam singer was soon giving performances for audiences of 70,000 people. Unbelievably, with almost no attention from the mainstream media, the pancake waitress from the suburbs had emerged as a star!

1. Who convinced her to launch a YouTube channel?
2. When did her big commercial break happen?
3. Where did she make an appearance?
4. What is her relationship to the mainstream media?

C Think of a singer that you like, but don't tell your partner his or her name. Your partner will ask you questions about your choice to guess your singer.

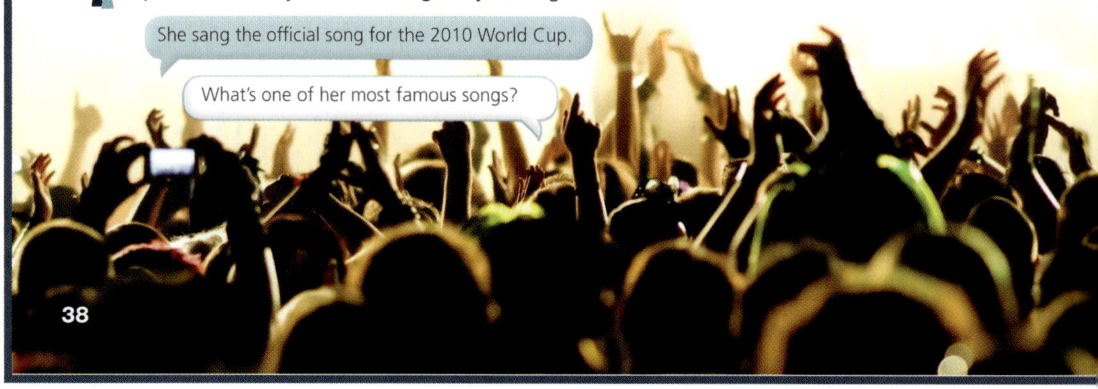

38

Internet Activity

Direct students to Esmee Denters's YouTube channel at http://www.youtube.com/user/esmeedenters and have partners choose two songs to listen to. Then have pairs play the roles of a friend of Esmee's and a talent agent. The friend should write an email to the agent telling Esmee's story, mentioning her songs, and explaining why the agent should work with her. The agent writes an email response expressing his or her opinion of Esmee's music and if she has the talent to make it as a singer. Students should use at least five vocabulary words in their emails.

Grammar

A Complete these sentences with *to*, *for*, or — (nothing).

1. They made me ________ practice every day.
2. We'll arrange ________ you ________ pick up the tickets.
3. They advised us ________ take the offer.

Infinitive Complements

Infinitive complements that follow the pattern **verb** + **object** + **infinitive** fall into some common verb groups including ❶ *persuade* verbs (*advise, cause, convince*), ❷ *want* verbs (*expect, need*), ❸ *believe* verbs (*consider, recognize*), and ❹ *plan* verbs (*arrange*). Group ❺ verbs are *have, let*, and *make*.

❶ Verb + object + infinitive	She **advised me to take** the job.
❷ Verb + (object) + infinitive	She **expects me to apply**. I **need to find** a job.
❸ Verb + object + infinitive of *be*	We **consider him to be** the best singer.
❹ Verb + *for* + object + infinitive	They **arranged for me to have** an interview.
❺ Verb + object + base form	His music **makes me feel** happy.

Group ❶: the object is required. Group ❷: the object is optional.
Group ❸: follows the pattern **verb** + **object** + **infinitive**, and the infinitive is usually *to be*.
Group ❹: follows the pattern **verb** + ***for*** + **object** + **infinitive**.
Group ❺: follows the same basic pattern, but requires the base form of the verb rather than the full infinitive.

B Read this story about Bree. The structure **verb** + **(object)** + **infinitive** appears nine times. Seven of them contain errors. Find and correct the errors. Compare your answers with a partner.

Just Acting or the Real Thing? This is the story of Bree, who became an Internet celebrity. To her hard-core fans, she was a young girl who posted videos from her bedroom about her life as a teenager. Her fans (1) wanted to hear from her frequently. They (2) expected her post videos four or five times a week. They posted notes to her and (3) advised to her to share more about her life.

The reality, however, was quite different: a man named Ramesh Flinders produced Bree's videos. He (4) arranged to an actress to play the part of 15-year-old Bree. Jessica Rose, a 19-year-old actress, had a paid job pretending to be Bree. The fans didn't know a thing. They simply (5) considered Bree to have a normal teenage girl.

After four months, a newspaper reporter discovered the secret. The producers (6) had Jessica to tell the truth in one of her videos. They (7) planned Bree's story to continue, but it was too late. The news of the fake story (8) caused viewers to stop watching.

Why did Mr. Flinders (9) let everyone to believe that Bree was a real person? And why did Jessica do it? What do you think?

C What do you think of Bree's story? Use the verbs in the chart to discuss her story with a partner.

I don't think anyone expected Bree to be an actress.

I don't think it was OK to let the audience believe her story. That's dishonest.

Extension

Have students write sentences to express their opinions about the media today, both mainstream and Internet. Their sentences should include at least two of the infinitive complements they learned in the chart. If students have trouble coming up with sentences, give the following as examples: *The Internet media needs to be as reliable as the mainstream media. People expect the media to tell the truth all the time. I consider the mainstream media to be less important than the Internet.* Ask for volunteers to read their sentences out loud, and have the class indicate whether they agree or disagree with them by a show of hands.

Grammar

10-15 min. A
10-15 min. B
10 min. C
Extension: 10-20 min.

A
- Go through the chart as a class. For each use, give additional examples and ask students to respond to these questions: *What is something your parents advised you to do? What is something your teacher expects you to do? What do you need to do today? Who do you consider to be the best singer? How does his / her music make you feel?*
- Point out to students that the rules mentioned here do not apply 100% of the time. Sometimes more than one structure is possible but does not sound natural. For example, in Group 3, *We consider him to be the best singer* is not technically incorrect, but we would be more likely to say *We think he's the best singer,* which is more natural.
- For the pattern in Group 2, when the object is dropped, it changes the meaning of the sentence. In the sentence, *She expects me to apply,* the speaker, *me*, is expected to apply. In the sentence *She expects to apply,* the subject, *she*, is the person who is expected to apply.

Answers: 1. –; 2. for, to; 3. to

B

Answers: 1. *correct*; 2. expected her to post; 3. advised her to share; 4. arranged for an actress to play; 5. considered Bree to be; 6. had Jessica tell; 7. planned for Bree's story to continue; 8. *correct;* 9. let everyone believe

Outcome: Upon completing this exercise, students will have met the Outcome ***use infinitives to complement certain types of verbs.***

C
- Review ways to express opinions (*I think…, I don't think…, In my opinion,…*)
- Encourage students to use at least three verbs from the grammar chart.
- Ask for volunteers to share their opinions with the rest of the class.

Listening

10 min. **A**
10-15 min. **B**
10-15 min. **C**
10-15 min. **D**
Extension: 10 min.

Background Information

Students will listen to an interview. In some ways an interview is easier to understand than other texts because someone asks a question, which focuses the information to follow. In this interview, Carlos discusses salsa. *Salsa* is a style of music and dance that began in New York in the 1960s by Cuban and Puerto Rican immigrants. It later spread to most Latin American countries. *Salsa* means "sauce" in Spanish and refers to its "spicy" nature. It has both African and Spanish influences.

A Read the quick facts together as a class. If students are not familiar with salsa, have them make predictions about what it might sound like. What kind of rhythm does it have? What instruments does it use?

B
- Make sure students know the meanings of these words from the audio: *skateboarding, energy, current, feature,* and *inspire.*
- Point out that in this interview Carlos says his band has "come of age." This expression means to have become successful. Students will also hear this phrase later in the video.
- Read through the Tip as a class. Call on students and ask what they are into.
- Point out that students may circle more than one correct answer for each question.
- Play the audio recording one or more times. **Audio CD Track 7**

Answers: 1. a, c; 2. b, c; 3. a, b, c; 4. b, c; 5. c

Language Notes

- Carlos uses adverbs to connect his ideas and add emphasis (*actually, really, anyway, finally, definitely*).
- In the Tip, students learned the expressions *be into* and *get into*. In the audio, they will also hear *be new to* and *be native to.*

C Play the audio recording again. Pause the recording after each event to help students keep track of the order. **Audio CD Track 7**

Answers: a. 4; b. 1; c. 3; d. 6; e. 5; f. 2

Listening

A What do you know about salsa? Do you like it? Discuss in pairs.

Salsa Music: Quick Facts
- a merging of musical styles from Cuba, Puerto Rico, Mexico, and South America
- the name "salsa" was created in New York City in the 1960s
- Colombian salsa, Cuban salsa, and other styles have emerged over the years

audition a short performance given by a person to demonstrate suitability for a show
promote to encourage the popularity or sale of something
realize to understand something, sometimes suddenly

TIP As you listen, notice how the word *into* is used to express interest in casual speech. *I **was into** skateboarding.* (I was interested in skateboarding and enjoyed doing it.) *I finally **got into** salsa music.* (I became interested in and started enjoying salsa music.)

B Listen and choose the correct answer(s).

1. What was Carlos interested in at first?
   a. rock music b. salsa music c. skateboarding
2. Who has Carlos played music with?
   a. Ben b. his brother c. his friends
3. Why does he like salsa?
   a. It's energetic. b. It's easy to dance to. c. It makes him happy.
4. How is his band different?
   a. They play covers. b. They write their own music. c. They play an older kind of salsa.
5. Who inspires Carlos?
   a. his brother b. his record company c. his fans

C Listen again and put these events in order.

_____ a. Carlos formed a band.
__1__ b. Ben quit the school band.
_____ c. Carlos studied music.
_____ d. Carlos made an album.
_____ e. Carlos played in small bars.
_____ f. Carlos sang in his friend's band.

D Use the information in Exercises **B** and **C** to summarize Carlos's story in pairs.

Ask Answer What kind of music are you into? What's popular now?

Extension

Play the recording again for the class. Have students write three true and three false statements based on the information in the recording. Then direct them to exchange their papers with a partner and identify which statements are true and false without listening to the recording again.

Connections

A Read this information about fundraising. Look up any words you don't know in your dictionary.

Fundraising is a way for schools and other organizations to raise money for a particular purpose, for example, a **charity**. A common way to fund-raise is to hold a **benefit** (a sporting event / a performance / a movie screening) and sell tickets for the event. The money earned from the ticket sales is given to the school or organization.

a benefit movie screening

B You are planning a benefit to raise money for your school. You need to organize an event. With a partner, answer the questions on a separate piece of paper.

Event type What type of benefit event will you have?

Entertainment You need a famous person or group to come to your event. Who will you invite? What do you want him / her / them to do at your event?

Venue Where will you have the event? Who will arrange for the space?

Schedule When will you hold the event?

Publicity How will you promote the event?

Event goals How many people do you expect to attend? How much money do you expect to earn from this event?

C Share your ideas with the class. Take notes on what your classmates say.

We are going to have ______ (Name) ______ make an appearance at our benefit because . . .

We are going to let people know about the event by ______________.

We will promote ticket sales by ______________.

We expect ______________ people to attend.

We hope to raise ______________ by the end of the event.

D Which fundraising plan is most likely to succeed? Vote to choose the best idea for a fundraiser.

a benefit dance performance

41

Internet Activity

Have students search online for information about benefits or other fundraising events in your city or nearby. Tell them to answer the questions in Exercise **B** as they take notes. Have students share their findings in pairs.

Connections

5-10 min. **A**
10-15 min. **B**
15-20 min. **C**
10 min. **D**
Extension: 10-15 min.

A
- Have students read the information individually or read it aloud as students follow along.
- Check comprehension by asking questions: *What is fundraising? What is an example of a charity? What are examples of benefits? Where does the money from a benefit go? Has anyone been to a benefit? What was it? What are other ways to raise funds?*

B Encourage students to come up with a specific "purpose" for the benefit. Have them think about one or more projects for which your school could use money. Explain that for many benefits, the organizers include the purpose of it in their promotional materials, and suggest that students do the same.

C Explain that students will use these sentences as models for presenting their ideas to the class. Remind students that, because the sentences are models, they don't have to use all of these sentences and can include extra sentences and information about their benefit if they choose to.

D You may choose to have students vote for plans privately or with a show of hands. After the vote, have students explain why they feel the chosen plan was the most likely to succeed.

Extension

For the winning plan, have students role-play a phone conversation in which the event organizers are trying to convince the celebrity to come to the event. In groups of three or four, have organizers explain the event and why the celebrity should make an appearance. One group member, in the role of the celebrity, should express doubts and ask questions. Ask for groups to volunteer to do their role-play in front of the class.

Reading

5 min. **A**
10 min. **B**
15-20 min. **C**
5-10 min. **D**
5-10 min. **E**
Extension: 15 min.

A • Focus attention on the map. Ask students to name which continent is shown and to guess what country is highlighted. (*Senegal*)

• Explain to students that they are only guessing the answers based on the photos, title, and quotation; wrong answers are acceptable.

Answers: A rapper (Assane); West Africa (Senegal); become famous / be heard

B Encourage students to scan the article once, then read the list of actions. Have them scan it a second time before checking off their answers.

Answers: *checked:* written songs about his life experiences; experienced difficulties in his life; lived in different places; shared his creativity with others; *not checked:* worked at the same job for all of his life; written about pop culture

C Remind students to look for capital letters in the reading in order to locate place names.

Answers: 1. Dakar. Assane was a popular DJ working in Dakar. 2. Toubab Dialaw. Assane returned to Toubab Dialaw, his village. It is located 40 kilometers from Dakar. 3. The Great Rock. Assane built his restaurant in the shadow of the Great Rock, which faces the Atlantic Ocean; at night, he and his brother and cousin sit by the Great Rock and write songs about their difficult lives as fishermen, being poor, and watching their town get crowded with rich Dakarians and French. 4. Chez Las. Assane's small restaurant.

D

Possible Answer: They are all about difficulties. He's trying to emphasize the difficult nature of their lives.

E

Answers: 1. Assane loves hip-hop music. 2. The life of a village fisherman is difficult and dangerous. 3. His town is getting crowded with rich Dakarians and even richer French. 4. Some of his relatives leave in the morning and never return. 5. Their dream is to make a record. 6. Rap music represents a bigger dream and a better life. 7. They want money to help their parents.

Reading

A Look at the photos and read the title of the article, the captions, and the quote. What do you think the reading is going to be about? Complete the sentence below with a partner.

This story is about ______________ who lives in ______________ and wants to ______________.

B Scan the article. Which of these things has Assane done? Mark your answers.

- ☐ written songs about his life experiences
- ☐ experienced difficulties in his life
- ☐ lived in different places
- ☐ worked at the same job for all of his life
- ☐ written about pop culture
- ☐ shared his creativity with others

C Read the article. As you read, look for these place names. Why does / did Assane go to each one? On a separate piece of paper, write about each place.

1. Dakar
2. Toubab Dialaw
3. the Great Rock
4. Chez Las

D With a partner, look at this sentence from the fourth paragraph. How are the underlined words similar? What is Assane trying to emphasize?

It has always existed here, because of our <u>pain</u> and our <u>hardships</u> and our <u>suffering</u>.

E How does Assane feel about these things? What does he say about them? Discuss your answers with a partner.

1. hip-hop music (first paragraph)
2. the life of a village fisherman
3. his town
4. his relatives
5. making a record
6. rap music (third paragraph)
7. money

Toubab Dialaw, Senegal

42

Extension

Review words and phrases that connect ideas and explain the sequence of events. Refer students to the sentence, <u>*Before*</u> *he left his Senegalese village to work as a DJ in Dakar, he was a fisherman...* Have students identify other connecting words and phrases in the reading. After they've read the article, have them create a timeline of events in Assane's life.

Hip-Hop GOES HOME

The voice of a generation demanding to be heard

Assane N'Diaye, 19, loves hip-hop music. Before he left his Senegalese village to work as a DJ in Dakar, he was a fisherman, just like his father, like his father's father before him. Tall, lean, with a muscular build and a handsome face, Assane became a popular DJ, but the equipment he used was borrowed, and when his friend took it back, he returned to his village of Toubab Dialaw. The village is located about 25 miles (40 kilometers) south of Dakar—marked by a huge boulder, perhaps 40 feet (12 meters) high—facing the Atlantic Ocean.

In the shadow of this Great Rock, Assane has built a small restaurant, Chez Las, decorated with hundreds of seashells. It is where he lives his hip-hop dream. At night, he and his brother and cousin sit by the Great Rock and face the sea. They write rap songs about their difficult lives as village fishermen, and about being poor, watching their town get crowded with rich Dakarians and even richer French. And they write about their relatives who leave in the morning and never return, losing their lives in the dangerous seas.

Their dream, of course, is to make a record. They have their own demo,[1] their own logo,[2] and their own rap group name, Salam T. D. (which stands for Toubab Dialaw). But rap music represents a bigger dream: a better life. "We want money to help our parents," Assane says over dinner. "We watch our mothers boil water to cook and have nothing to put in the pot."

He fingers[3] his food lightly. "Rap doesn't belong to American culture," he says. "It belongs here. It has always existed here, because of our pain and our hardships and our suffering."

After a dinner of chicken and rice, Assane says something in Wolof[4] to the others. Silently and carefully, they take every bit of the leftover dinner—the half-eaten bread, rice, pieces of chicken, the chicken bones—and dump them into a plastic bag to give to the children in the village. They silently rise from the table, walk outside, and head out to the darkened village, holding on to that bag as though it held money.

> Rap doesn't belong to American culture. It belongs here. It has always existed here.

[1] **demo** a brief recording illustrating the abilities of a musician
[2] **logo** a special design used by a company or group
[3] **fingers** touches
[4] **Wolof** one of many recognized regional languages of Senegal

Background Information

- Assane N'Diaye (pronounced UH-ZHAHN N-DJEYE-UH) is considered a modern griot—a West African storyteller. In Assane's native language of Wolof, he is known as a *Ngewal*—someone who records history through song.
- Toubab Dialaw is a small village in Senegal on the Atlantic Ocean with only a few thousand residents. According to legend, a local ruler led a group of people fleeing slave traders to this place. He was told by a white trader to go to Toubab Dialaw. When he arrived, the slavers followed, and there was fighting. The ruler fought bravely but was killed. The villagers buried him by the sea and marked his grave with a small stone, and over the years it is said to have sprouted like a tree. It became a huge, arching boulder that stares out to sea, protecting the village behind it. When the fishermen went deep out to sea, the boulder was like a lighthouse that marked the way home. The Great Rock of Toubab Dialaw is said to hold a magic spirit.

Purpose for Reading

Explain that this article is similar to the text on page 38 in that it is a profile. Profiles tell about a specific person or place, often to make a larger point about a topic. As students read the article on page 43, ask them to think about what this profile might tell them about hip-hop music.

Language Notes

- *build* (Line 4) = body type; Collocations include: *muscular build, athletic build, slight build, sturdy build, dancer's build*
- *fingers* (Line 28) = touches or works with one's fingers
- Point out that the article uses words that look like verbs but act like adjectives: *half-eaten* (Line 34), *darkened* (Line 38)
- *as though* (Line 39) = like; It is used to compare two things. In the last line, *Assane holds on to a bag of food as though it held money.* Ask students to explain in their own words what this sentence means.

Beyond the Reading

Recommend that students watch a video of another Senegalese hip-hop group called Daara J. Their song "Boomerang" can be found at http://video.nationalgeographic.com/video/music/genre-wm/african-pop/boomerang-wm/. Daara J fuses hip-hop, reggae, and tongue-twisting proverbs in their native Wolof language.

Video

5-10 min. **A**
15-20 min. **B**
20-25 min. **C**
Extension: 5-10 min.

Background Information

Ireland is an island in Europe west of Great Britain. The island is divided between the Republic of Ireland and Northern Ireland, which is part of the United Kingdom. The Celts originally colonized the island a couple thousand years ago. The last group of Celts were called the Gaels, which is where the name of the Irish language, Gaelic, comes from. English is the common language, but Gaelic is an official language and taught in schools. In 1800, Ireland became part of the United Kingdom. The part known as the Republic of Ireland became independent in 1921. Six counties in the north became Northern Ireland and stayed part of the UK.

Before You Watch

Iarla Ó Lionáird (pronounced EAR-lah oh LAY-nart) learned his style of singing in West Cork. He grew up in a small Irish-speaking area and comes from a family of singers. They sing traditional Irish music that is often unaccompanied. Ó Lionáird is perhaps the most famous performer of this ancient style of music.

A After students read the definitions, have them write a sentence that uses each word.

B Play the video. Pause it as necessary to give students a chance to record their answers.

Answers: a. 2; b. 6; c. 7; d. 3; e. 4; f. 1; g. 5

Language Notes

Ó Lionáird uses similes and metaphors to express his feelings. A simile is a direct comparison between two things using *like* or *as*. A metaphor also compares two things, but it is less direct. Ask students to identify which sentences in Exercise **C** contain similes. Students will learn more about using similes in writing on pages 130–131.

C Read through the statements as a class. Then play the video again.

Answers: 1. c; 2. a; 3. e; 4. b; 5. f; 6. d

Video

encounter to meet
enthusiasm a feeling of energetic interest in something

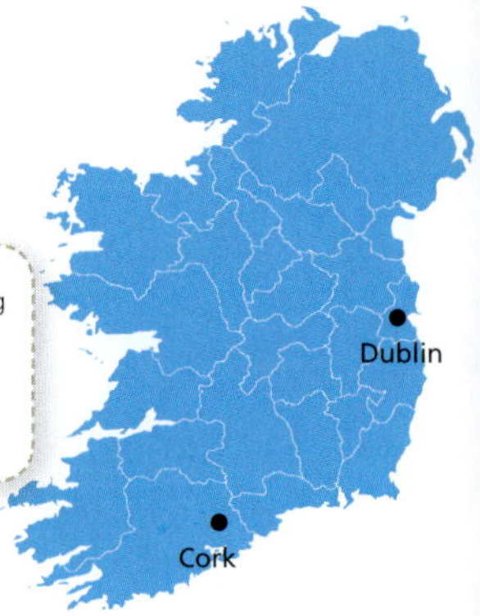

Sean-nós traditional "old style" Irish singing that combines oral history and song
Gaelic a language spoken in parts of Scotland and Ireland

A You are going to watch a video about Iarla Ó Lionáird, a singer from Ireland. First, read these definitions. What else do you know about Ireland? Discuss with a partner.

B Look at this list of events in Iarla's life. Then, watch the video. As you watch, put the events in the order in which they happened.

_____ a. started school
_____ b. joined the Afro-Celt Sound System
_____ c. started singing traditional music for audiences worldwide
_____ d. was encouraged to sing by his teacher
_____ e. became frustrated
__1__ f. learned to sing traditional Irish music with his family
_____ g. quit singing

C Read what Iarla and the narrator said. Pay attention to the underlined words. Watch the video again and match the sentence to its meaning.

__c__ 1. It was almost as if there was—there were kind of shoes (and) they were waiting for me to put my feet into it.
_____ 2. I felt a little bit like a museum piece, really.
_____ 3. That was like the coldest breakfast you ever had to eat.
_____ 4. Frustrated, despairing, Iarla found himself on a dead-end street.
_____ 5. He quit singing entirely until fortune revealed a path.
_____ 6. I suppose it just shook me to the foundations, you know.

a. It seemed that my music was old-fashioned and no one cared about it.
b. He was stuck and he didn't know what to do next.
c. Everyone was expecting me to carry on the singing tradition.
d. The experience had a strong impact on me.
e. It was something unpleasant that I experienced.
f. Luckily, he realized what to do next.

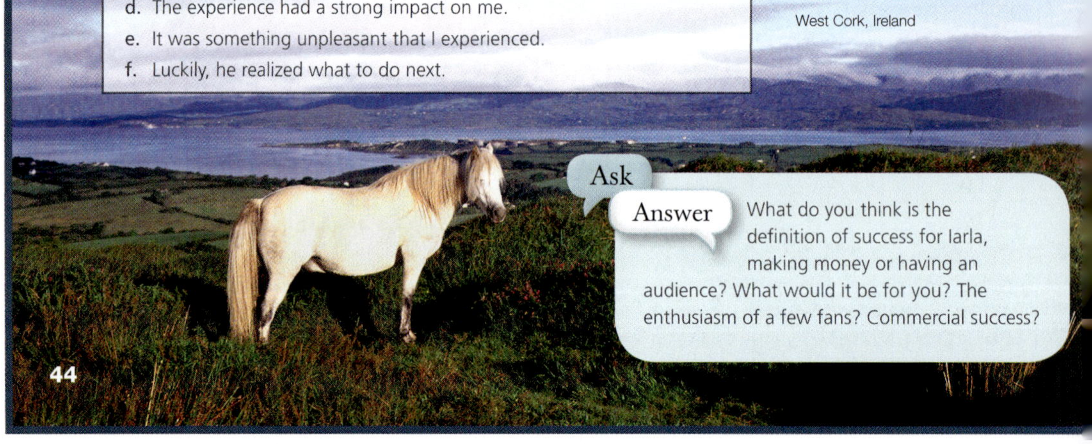

West Cork, Ireland

Ask Answer What do you think is the definition of success for Iarla, making money or having an audience? What would it be for you? The enthusiasm of a few fans? Commercial success?

44

Extension

In the video, Ó Lionáird tells how he almost gave up something he really enjoyed because others didn't understand or appreciate it. Have students write a paragraph about something they enjoy doing. Ask them, *What would you do if you had to give it up?* Encourage them to write about how important their particular activity is to them.

Writing

A Profile

A Use the time expressions in the box to complete the profile.

as an adult	from an early age	in those days	up to that point	today

Iarla was born into a family of singers in West Cork, Ireland. (1) In those days, his family were known Sean-nós performers. (2) ______, Iarla was encouraged to sing. (3)______, Iarla was living in the capital city of Dublin. The Sean-nós style was not so popular there. (4)______, Iarla had only performed traditional music. He felt lost. He wrote a letter to Real World Records, asking for an audition. His heartfelt letter and his music convinced them to give him a contract. At Real World Records, he met the Afro-Celt Sound System and joined their band. He learned a new style of music, but never forgot his roots. (5)______ Iarla tours the world and is loved by audiences. He inspires me because he's an excellent singer who stayed true to his roots, but he also was not afraid to try something new.

TIP Time expressions like these help your reader identify key events in a person's life.

B Follow the Writing Strategy and paraphrase each sentence below on a separate piece of paper.

Writing Strategy

Paraphrasing To paraphrase something means to express the same meaning by using different (your own) words. This is an important strategy when using information from a source (such as a book or Web site) in your own writing. Follow these steps to paraphrase:

1. Read the information and make sure you understand it.
2. Rewrite the main ideas using your own words.
3. Reread the original to make sure your version has not changed the basic meaning.
4. Put in quotation marks any phrases that you take directly from the original.

1. Singer Esmee Denters launched her own YouTube channel, and soon it became a big hit.
   Esmee Denters started to post her music online. Soon she had a big audience for her videos.
2. Her big break came when singer Justin Timberlake contacted her.
3. In time, with almost no attention from the mainstream media, she emerged as a star!
4. Today, she gives performances to audiences of 70,000 people or more worldwide.

C Write a profile of a musician or other person that you like, using Exercise **A** as a model.

1. Choose a person—what qualities make him or her special or interesting? Make notes.
2. What are some important events in the person's life? Make a timeline and list time expressions you can use.
3. How has the person inspired or impacted you? Make notes for your conclusion.
4. What are the best places to find information about this person? List three sources.
5. Use your notes and timeline to write a profile. Be sure to paraphrase the information you find from your sources.

D Exchange papers with another student. Read your partner's writing. Does it use time expressions well to describe major events in the person's life? Does it give you a clear idea of who the person is?

Rubric	Very Good	Satisfactory	Needs Improvement
Content			
Paraphrasing sources			
Use of grammar			
Organization			

Writing

5-10 min. **A**
10-15 min. **B**
15-20 min. **C**
10 min. **D**
Extension: 10-15 min.

Purpose of Writing

The purpose of a profile is to describe a person, their qualities, and life events. In both the Vocabulary and Reading sections, students read examples of profiles.

A

Answers: 1. In those days; 2. From an early age; 3. As an adult; 4. Up to that point; 5. Today

Outcome: Upon completing this exercise, students will have met the Outcome *use time expressions to order life events.*

B

- Read through the information in the strategy box. Go over the first paraphrase together.
- Have students discuss as a class the ways that they can paraphrase item 2 and write the options on the board.
- Have students work individually to paraphrase items 3 and 4, and then compare ideas with a partner.
- Have volunteers write their paraphrased sentences on the board.

Outcome: Upon completing this exercise, students will have met the Outcome *paraphrase information from other sources.*

C

If students don't want to write about a singer, suggest other people they could write about. For example, a famous artist, a person who inspires them, a person who they would like to meet someday.

Extension

Give students other sentences from the unit to paraphrase: *But rap music represents a bigger dream; a better life* (from the reading) and *I had spent like twenty years of my life perfecting as best I could this way of singing... to find out that nobody was interested, except the people I grew up with* (from the video). When students feel comfortable with paraphrasing, suggest they pick a paragraph from the reading to paraphrase.

Speaking

⏱	10 min. A 10-15 min. B 10-15 min. C 10-15 min. D Extension: 10 min.

A • Put students in pairs to answer the questions.
• Call on students to share their ideas with the class.

Possible Answers: 1. His life is hard. People in his village are poor. Fishing is dangerous. 2. The important people in his life are his family members (brother, cousin, mother), and the other people in the village. 3. His dream is to make a record, and to have a better life.

B • Check students' comprehension of the contract.
• Go over the information in the speaking strategy box. As a model, use the expressions to talk about the pros and cons of performing on YouTube: *On the one hand, many people will see you. On the other hand, they may not be people who can help you. One major benefit of performing on YouTube is that it is free. One big drawback is that...*

Outcome: Upon completing this exercise, students will have met the Outcome ***state the pros and cons of making a decision.***

C Go over the roles. Then put students in pairs to practice their role-plays.

D Put two pairs together to take turns performing their role-plays.

Extension

Have students identify a decision they might have to make in their own lives. Give them a few minutes to take notes on the pros and cons of making this decision. Call on students to tell the class about the pros and cons using the expressions in the speaking strategy box.

Speaking

A Answer these questions about Assane N'Diaye, the undiscovered musician who was featured in the reading on page 43.

1. What's his life like?
2. Who are the important people in his life?
3. What's his dream?

B Imagine that Assane has just been discovered by a talent scout who works for Global Rhythms Corporation (GRC), a recording company. They want Assane to sign a contract and leave his village in Africa. Follow these steps:

- Read the terms of the GRC contract below. Make sure you understand them.
- Discuss the terms of the contract with a partner. What do you think of it? What parts of the contract might be difficult for Assane to fulfill?
- Use the expressions in the Speaking Strategy to discuss the pros and cons of the contract.

> - Assane will sign a five-year contract. GRC will arrange for Assane to live alone in an apartment in London for six months. (Assane will need to leave his family behind.)
> - Assane will produce one or two albums per year. A producer will have final say in which songs get chosen for the album.
> - Assane will perform and promote his music 150 days a year in cities around the world.
> - Sixty percent of Assane's earnings will go to GRC. Assane will use the remaining 40% to cover his living expenses while performing on the road.
> - Assane will be given a new stage name ("MC Cube") and a new style of dress.

Speaking Strategy

Giving the pros (plus sides) and cons (downsides) of something

On the one hand . . . / On the other hand . . .
A(n) (dis)advantage of this contract is . . .
One major / minor benefit of signing is . . .
One big / small drawback to signing is . . .
The best / worst part is . . .

The best part is Assane gets to move to London!

Yeah, but a major drawback is he has to go by himself. It sounds so lonely.

C You are going to role-play a conversation between Assane and his possible future manager at GRC.

Student A: You are Assane. You want to sign the contract, but there are some parts of it you don't like. For the cons in the contract, suggest other ideas.

Student B: You work for GRC. You want Assane to sign the contract. Listen to Assane's questions and decide what to do.

I'm excited about living in London, but I don't want to leave my brother behind. Can he come with me for the first six months?

D Now do your role-play for another pair. When you are finished, listen to their role-play.

Rubric	Very Good	Satisfactory	Needs Improvement
Ability to negotiate terms of the contract			
Use of vocabulary			
Use of grammar			
Pronunciation and fluency			

Expanding Your Fluency

A Read these things you can do to start conversations with people you don't know very well. Which one of these things have you tried before? Which ones are new for you?

1. Talk about popular music, TV shows, movies, or other shared cultural experiences: *I saw the first movie, but not the sequel. How was it?*
2. Talk about recent events in the news: *The traffic was terrible today. Did you hear about the accident?*
3. Make a comment about something the person is wearing: *I love the design on your scarf. Where did you get it?*
4. Ask follow-up questions: *Are you studying music (or film) at Tokyo University? How do you like it there?*

B Imagine that you are at a party with many famous singers, dancers, actors, and other creative people. Follow the steps below.

1. Take the role of a famous creative person whom you know something about.
2. You are going to meet five different people at a party. Stand up and move around the classroom. Find a partner, introduce yourself, and make small talk for two minutes.
3. Try to use at least one of the strategies in Exercise **A** with each person you meet.

I'm not into comedy films, but this movie is special. I saw the first movie in the series, but not the sequel. How was it?

The sequel was much better. I'm a hard-core fan now!

I can't wait to see it. What exactly did you like about it?

TIP You can use these expressions to end your conversation. *(It's been) nice talking to you. Thanks. You too.*

Ask Answer Who was the most interesting person you met at the party? Was it always easy to start a conversation? Why or why not?

Check What You Know

Rank how well you can perform these outcomes on a scale of 1–5 (5 being the best).

_______ use infinitives to complement certain types of verbs

_______ state the pros and cons of making a decision

_______ use time expressions to order life events

_______ paraphrase information from other sources

47

Expanding Your Fluency

15-20 min. A
25-35 min. B
Extension: 10-15 min.

A Gauge students' familiarity with these strategies by asking for a show of hands. For any strategies that students aren't familiar with, ask for a volunteer to practice with you. Demonstrate ways to keep the conversation going.

B
- Go over the steps. Tell students it is acceptable to choose the person they wrote about in Writing.
- Have students stand and move around the room to introduce themselves as the famous person. Remember to keep track of time and to signal changing partners by using a cell phone alarm, clapping, or ringing a bell.

Check What You Know

Refer students back to the exercises in the unit where each Outcome is addressed:

- *use infinitives to complement certain types of verbs:* Grammar, Exercise **B**, page 39
- *state the pros and cons of making a decision:* Speaking, Exercise **B**, page 46
- *use time expressions to order life events:* Writing, Exercise **A**, page 45
- *paraphrase information from other sources:* Writing, Exercise **B**, page 45

Extension

Divide the class into two groups. One forms a circle facing outward. The other forms a circle facing inward (on the outside of the other circle) so that every student faces another student. Students will start talking to each other and try to keep a conversation going. Remind them of the topics they can talk about. When you say "Start," students begin talking. When you say "Switch," the inside circle moves one place to the right (clockwise). Keep the activity moving quickly; call "Switch" every 30 to 45 seconds. The goal is to increase fluency.

Unit 5
No Need to Panic

Unit Overview

- Unit 5 is about fear and the things that make us nervous. Students will learn how people react to stressful situations and how most people are equipped to get through them.
- The unit covers a variety of these situations, including a plane crash, becoming trapped, getting caught in bad weather, and being attacked by a wild animal. It also covers more everyday situations, like getting nervous for a test and going to a job interview.
- Ask students what they think is meant by the unit title, "No Need to Panic." Explain that panic is a sudden overwhelming fear that often causes people to act irrationally. The expression *no need to panic* is meant to assure people that they will get through a crisis.
- Preview the unit by asking students the following questions:

1. Is there a difference between feeling nervous and feeling scared? If so, explain the difference and give examples.
2. Is it good to be afraid of things? Why or why not?
3. How can people overcome their fears?

Photo Caption

This image is of a family on an amusement park ride at the Texas State Fair in Dallas, Texas, in 2008. In the United States, state and local fairs are open for a short amount of time, usually in the summer, and often feature fast-moving, high-flying rides like this one for thrill-seekers.

VOCABULARY	GRAMMAR	LISTENING	READING
People who have beaten the odds	Adverbial clauses	There's no need to panic	*Mount Everest's Deadliest Day:* Two teams compete to reach the summit first— with deadly results

1 Where are the people in the photo? Have you ever been on rides like this one? Do you like them? Why or why not?

2 Read the unit title. What kind of things make you feel nervous or scared?

3 Can you think of any recent news stories in which someone was in a dangerous situation? What happened?

Unit Outcomes

In this unit, you will learn to:

- use adverbial clauses to talk about challenging situations
- reach a compromise
- explain steps in a process
- follow steps to get through a difficult situation

49

5-10 min. **Warm-Up Questions**
Extension: 10-15 min.

Background Information

Some of the most common fears people have are of small critters (like spiders and mice), heights, water, storms, closed spaces, tunnels and bridges, crowds, and speaking in public. Many fears are natural and help people to survive. For example, a fear of fire keeps one from getting burned. When a fear is irrational, it is called a phobia. According to psychologists, phobias affect about 10% of adults.

Warm-Up Questions

- Read Question 1 as a class. Ask several volunteers to guess where the people are. Work as a class to describe the photo in detail. Ask students to describe their feelings about the experience.
- If necessary, explain what *panic* means. Ask students to describe moments when they have felt panic.
- Have students work with a partner to answer Questions 2 and 3. Then, ask volunteers to talk about the news stories they thought of. Ask students if they think they could get through similar situations.

Extension

Ask students to brainstorm out loud things that many people are afraid of. Write five ideas on the board. Have students work individually to rank the fears in order from 1 to 5, with 1 being the most frightening. Then have students share their ideas with a partner.

VIDEO	SPEAKING	WRITING	OUTCOMES
Surviving Deadly Everest	Discuss a difficult environmental issue Strategy: Reaching a compromise	Write a set of instructions describing how to do something Strategy: Explaining the steps in a process	• use adverbial clauses to talk about challenging situations • reach a compromise • explain steps in a process • follow steps to get through a difficult situation

Vocabulary

15 min. **A**
15-20 min. **B**
10-15 min. **C**
Extension: 10-15 min.

A • *Handle* can be a noun as well as a verb, but their meanings are not related.
- Other words with the same noun and verb forms on this spread include: *crash, pilot, lack, snowboard.*
- Remind students to make guesses based on the photos and headlines. Discourage them from reading the articles.

B • Check understanding of the words *engine*, *survivor*, *calm*, *recall*. Explain the difference between *trap* (*verb*—to keep someone confined) and *trapped* (*past participle*—unable to escape).
- Ask students in what situations they might say *Hang in there!* to someone. Mention that, as a phrase of encouragement, it can be used in situations where you're trying to cheer someone up.

Answers: 1. rescued; 2. injured; 3. ordeal; 4. handled; 5. collapsed; 6. trapped; 7. intense; 8. panic; 9. encouraged

C • As a follow-up, ask students to explain how they would react in the situation they chose.
- Before students respond to the Ask and Answer question, describe a stressful situation you have had and how you handled it.

Background Information

- Point out to students that the two news articles in Exercise **B** are true stories.
- On January 15, 2009, US Airways Flight 1549 took off from LaGuardia Airport in New York City and struck a flock of geese. The impact disabled the engines, and the pilot, Captain Chesley B. Sullenberger, successfully landed the plane in the Hudson River, saving all passengers on board.
- On August 5, 2010, near the city of Copiapó, Chile, a copper and gold mine collapsed, trapping 33 miners over 700 meters (2,300 feet) underground. The men were stuck in the mine for 69 days and eventually rescued. No one was killed or seriously injured.

Vocabulary

collapse to fall down suddenly
encourage to give someone confidence or hope
handle to deal with a problem or situation successfully
injure to damage a part of a person's body
intense very great or extreme
ordeal a very difficult, stressful situation
panic to feel very anxious or afraid all of a sudden
rescue to save someone from a dangerous situation
trapped unable to escape from a place or situation because something is stopping you

n. *handle **a job** / **a problem** / **a situation***
*handle **the pressure** / **the responsibility***
adj. ***difficult** / **easy** / **hard to** handle*

A Look at the photos and read only the titles of the two articles below. What do you think happened to these people? Use a sentence or two to describe each story to a partner.

B Read the two news articles and choose the correct option for each item.

Pilot lands plane; everyone safe

Shortly after Flight 1549 took off from New York, it lost power in both engines. The plane, flying over 3,000 feet (914 meters) in the air, was in danger of crashing. Luckily, the pilot landed safely in the Hudson River nearby. All 155 people were (1) trapped / rescued from the water and no one was seriously (2) injured / rescued. After the (3) ordeal / injury, survivors say that the pilot stayed calm and (4) encouraged / handled the situation perfectly.

Chilean miners reach the surface

After the mine they were working in (5) collapsed / rescued, thirty-three men were (6) encouraged / trapped for over ten weeks. During this time, they suffered (7) intense / trapped heat, a lack of food and water, and long periods of time in total darkness. One miner recalls times when he would get scared and start to (8) handle / panic. But whenever that happened, the others (9) injured / encouraged him. The men kept telling each other: "Hang in there! Help is coming!" And finally it did.

Hang in there! – Stay positive! Don't give up! (*said to encourage someone in a difficult situation*)

C Now cover up the articles with a piece of paper. Choose one and explain it to your partner. Use the questions to help you.

- What happened?
- How did the people involved handle it?

Ask Answer How do you handle scary or stressful situations—are you calm or do you start to panic? Explain with an example.

Extension

Point out that in the articles, the words *collapse*, *panic*, *rescue*, *trap*, *crash*, and *land* are all used as verbs. Tell students to write sentences using as many of these words as they can as nouns. Have students share their sentences with a partner.

Grammar

Adverbial Clauses	
Adverbial clauses explain when, why, where, or in what way something happened. Adverbial clauses begin with a *connecting word*. When the clause starts a sentence, it is followed by a comma.	
Time: *after, since, whenever, as soon as, until, while, before, when*	**After the mine collapsed**, the men were trapped. The men were trapped **after the mine collapsed**.
Reason: *because, since*	**Because the mine collapsed**, the men were trapped.
Contrast: *although, (even) though*	**Even though it was hard**, they survived for weeks.
Purpose: *so (that)*	They closed the mine **so (that) an accident doesn't happen again**.
Before, after, during, since, and *until* can also be followed by a noun phrase.	**Before** the collapse, the men heard a sound. **During** the collapse, one man was injured.

A Tom broke his leg in a snowboarding accident. He is explaining what happened. On a separate piece of paper, combine the two sentences into a single one using the correct connecting word.

1. I went snowboarding on a difficult run. I knew it was risky. (*so that, until, even though*)
   I went snowboarding on a difficult run even though I knew it was risky. / Even though I knew it was risky, I went snowboarding on a difficult run.
2. I crashed. I was coming down the mountain. (*while, whenever, since*)
3. I knew I was injured. I tried to stand up. (*so that, as soon as, until*)
4. I tried to walk. The pain was intense. (*after, though, because*)
5. My friend drove me to the hospital. I could see a doctor. (*although, so that, while*)
6. I can't snowboard. My leg is fully healed. (*so that, whenever, until*)
7. It's going to take time to get better. I was injured seriously. (*although, since, so that*)
8. I'm going to go snowboarding again. I feel better. (*as soon as, even though, while*)

risky dangerous
risk-taker an adventurous person, unafraid of taking chances

B Answer these questions with a partner. Use the information in Exercise **A**.

1. What mistake did Tom make?
2. When did he crash?
3. When did he know he was injured?
4. Why did his friend drive him to the hospital?
5. Why is it going to take time for him to get better?
6. When can he snowboard again?

C How much of a risk-taker are you? With a partner, answer each question and explain your reasons. Use at least one connecting word from the chart in each reply.

Would you ever . . .

1. parachute (jump) out of a plane even though it's dangerous?
2. sing or play music in a public place so that you could earn some extra money?
3. cut all of your hair off or dye it so that you could have a new look?

I'd never parachute out of a plane because I'd be too scared.

Extension

Write the following independent clause and connecting word on the board: *I'm nervous when I fly even though….* Ask students to complete the sentence. Then have them follow your model with their own ideas, using independent clauses and connecting words. Starting on one side of the class, call on a student to say his or her sentence starter. The next student finishes it then begins another sentence. Continue until everyone has participated.

Grammar

15-20 min. **A**
10-15 min. **B**
15 min. **C**
Extension: 10-20 min.

A
- Point out that students need to pay extra attention to two connecting words: *since* and *while*. *Since* can show time or reason. *While* can show time or contrast.
- Clauses with *so that* are usually after the independent clause.
- Have students review items 2–8 to see which ones can be written a different way.

Answers: 2. I crashed while I was coming down the mountain. While I was coming down the mountain, I crashed. 3. I knew I was injured as soon as I tried to stand up. As soon as I tried to stand up, I knew I was injured. 4. I tried to walk though the pain was intense. Though the pain was intense, I tried to walk. 5. My friend drove me to the hospital so that I could see a doctor. 6. I can't snowboard until my leg is fully healed. Until my leg is fully healed, I can't snowboard. 7. It's going to take time to get better since I was injured seriously. Since I was injured seriously, it's going to take time to get better. 8. I'm going to go snowboarding again as soon as I feel better. As soon as I feel better, I'm going to go snowboarding again.

B Before pairing students, ask the first question. Make sure students answer using an adverbial clause.

Answers: 1. He went snowboarding on a difficult run even though he knew it was risky. 2. (He crashed) while he was coming down the mountain. 3. (He knew he was injured) as soon as he tried to stand up. 4. (His friend drove him to the hospital) so that he could see a doctor. 5. (It is going to take time for him to get better) since he was injured seriously. 6. (He can snowboard again) as soon as he feels better. / He can't (snowboard again) until his leg is fully healed.

C After pairs have answered the questions, ask for volunteers to say out loud which person is more of a risk-taker, using a "reason" adverbial clause. For example, *Since Vicky would parachute out of a plane and I wouldn't, she's more of a risk-taker than I am.*

Outcome: Upon completing this exercise, students will have met the Outcome *use adverbial clauses to talk about challenging situations.*

Listening

5-10 min. A
15 min. B
10-15 min. C
10-15 min. D
Extension: 5 min.

Background Information

Students will hear an interview with a life coach. Life coaching, which developed from the field of athletic coaching, uses ideas from sports to help people reach their goals. For example, in sports, a coach might suggest that a runner create a mental picture of crossing the finish line. In other areas of life, a personal or life coach might suggest that someone make a mental picture of achieving a different goal.

A Call on students to tell the class about their partners.

B • Review the different parts of speech of the words below before having students listen to the audio. They will hear most of them in the interview. Give students a copy of this chart with some of the words missing and have them add the correct forms.

Feelings and Emotions		
noun	verb	adjective
anxiety	*none*	anxious
calm	calm (down)	calm
nerves	*none*	nervous
relaxation	relax	relaxed relaxing
stress	stress (out)	stressed stressful

• Play the audio recording one or more times. **Audio CD Track 8**

Answers: 1. Greg focuses on *everyday things that cause anxiety*. 2. One of Greg's clients recently *went on her first job interview*. 3. She got so nervous she *froze (and had a hard time answering questions)*. 4. In some situations, people panic because they're worried about *doing something poorly*.

C Ask students what they think Greg's going to say before you play the audio. Play the audio recording one or more times. **Audio CD Track 9**

Answers: 1. Breathe; 2. plan; imagine; before; 3. Follow

Listening

A How do the situations below make you feel? Rate each with a number: 1 (not nervous at all), 2 (somewhat nervous), or 3 (very nervous). Then explain your answers to a partner.

_____ taking an important test at school
_____ giving a presentation in front of a lot of people
_____ interviewing for a job
_____ speaking English

Giving a presentation in front of a lot of people makes me very nervous since I don't do it often.

client someone who pays a person or company for a service; a customer

freeze (*past*: **froze**) to suddenly stop and be unable to move or think

B Listen to an interview with life coach* Greg Ravetti. Then correct these false statements.

1. Greg focuses on dangerous situations that cause anxiety.
2. One of Greg's clients recently gave a presentation at work.
3. She got so nervous that she panicked and started laughing.
4. In some situations, people panic because they're worried about their appearance.

*A **life coach** helps people set goals and improve their lives (for example, by doing better at school or work, improving their appearance, etc.).

C Greg is now going to talk about three ways to calm down in a stressful situation. Read sentences 1–3. What do you think he's going to say? Tell a partner. Then listen and complete the sentences in the first column of the chart.

Ways to calm down in a stressful situation	How doing this helps you feel calmer
1. ______________ slowly for a minute.	
2. Make a simple __________. Also: Try to ________ the situation ________ you're in it.	
3. ____________ the plan you created.	

D How does doing each step in Exercise **C** help you feel calmer? Listen again and take notes in the second column of the chart.

Ask
Answer
Which of Greg's recommendations do you think is the most helpful? Why?

D Before playing the audio again, read each step from Exercise **C** and have students indicate with a show of hands if each one would make them feel calmer. Play the audio recording again. **Audio CD Track 9**

Answers: 1. It relaxes you so that you can think normally again. (When you get anxious, you start breathing faster. This makes you feel more nervous.) 2. It helps you feel more in control. 3. It helps you feel more in control and reduces your anxiety.

Extension

Play the audio again and have students take notes on what they hear. Then have them write two true statements and two false statements based on the recording. Put students in pairs to exchange their statements and mark them true or false. Call on students to read a statement to the class and ask if it is true or false.

Connections

A Listen to and read the dialog. Then answer the questions below with a partner.

Fatima: Hello?
Amina: Hey Fatima. It's Amina.
Fatima: Oh hi, Amina. What's up?
Amina: Not much. Hey, you sound upset. Are you okay?
Fatima: No, I'm freaking out. You know that project for our English class that's due tomorrow? Well I haven't started it.
Amina: What?! Why not?
Fatima: Because I thought it was due *next* week! What am I going to do? This project is 50% of our grade!
Amina: Fatima, don't panic, okay? Have you done *any* work?
Fatima: Yeah, I've got an outline.
Amina: So even though you haven't started the project, you have some ideas.
Fatima: Yeah.
Amina: Okay, just let me think for a minute . . .

1. What's Fatima's problem?
2. Is there anything positive about Fatima's situation?
3. What do you think the expression *I'm freaking out* means?

B With a partner, finish the dialog in Exercise **A** by thinking of a solution to Fatima's problem.

C Role-play your dialog for another pair. Did they like your solution?

D You are going to create a role-play that is similar to the dialog in Exercise **A**. Choose one of the situations below and do the following:

1. Student A: Explain to your partner what your problem is and ask for help.
   Student B: Try to calm your partner by coming up with solutions to his or her problem.
2. Practice your role-play. Be sure it includes at least three sentences with adverbial clauses.
3. Get together with another pair and role-play your entire dialog for them. Did they like your solution?

Situation 1	***The problem:*** You failed an important test because you didn't study enough. ***Why you're nervous:*** You have to tell your parents. You're not sure how they will handle the news. ***The good news:*** You're getting a good grade in the course so far.
Situation 2	***The problem:*** You borrowed your best friend's cell phone to make a call. While you were talking, you accidentally dropped it on the ground and broke it. ***Why you're nervous:*** The phone costs a lot of money. ***The good news:*** Your friend has been talking about getting a new phone for a while.

Before you tell your parents about the test, maybe you can . . .

Connections

10-15 min. **A**
10 min. **B**
5-10 min. **C**
15-20 min. **D**
Extension: 10 min.

A
- Point out places in the dialogue where words are italicized to show emphasis. Have students listen for the emphasized words in the recording.
- Have students listen for the differences in the way Fatima and Amina speak.
- Play the audio recording one or more times. **Audio CD Track 10**

Answers: 1. Fatima has a project due in her English class. She thought it was due next week, but it's actually due tomorrow. 2. She's got an outline of her ideas. 3. *I'm freaking out* is a phrase used to express panic. It means to act nervously and in an overly excited and emotional way.

Language Note

Amina tells Fatima *don't panic*. Other phrases that mean the same thing include: *Relax*; *Take it easy*; *Chill (out)*; *Calm down*; *Take a deep breath*; *Don't worry*; *Everything is going to be fine/okay/alright.*

B Tell students to imagine they are Amina giving suggestions.

C After pairs role-play their completed dialogues, have them note ways that their solutions were similar and different.

D Go over the steps and the situations. Then, put students in pairs to create role-plays.

Outcome: Upon completing this exercise, students will have met the Outcome ***follow steps to get through a difficult situation.***

Extension

Have students work in small groups to try out the advice they got from their partner. For example, students who worked on Situation 1 pair up with a new partner who will play the role of the mom or dad. They use the advice they were given to explain the situation. For Situation 2, students pair up with partners who will play the best friend.

Reading

5 min. **A**
10-15 min. **B**
15-20 min. **C**
10-15 min. **D**
Extension: 15 min.

A • As a preview to the reading on Mount Everest, show segment 1 of the video for Unit 5.

- Write these statements from the video on the board: *At over 29,000 feet Mount Everest* ***towers over*** *everything else on Earth*, and *Everest has* ***claimed the lives*** *of over 200 people.* Ask students if they can guess the meanings of the phrases *tower over* and *claim lives* from the context.
- Direct students' attention to the title of the reading. Based on the video preview, the phrases, and the title, ask students what they might conclude about Mount Everest.

Answers: 1. 8,850; 2.1953; 3. 200; 4. 60,000; The risks include dying from snow, intense cold and altitude sickness. The cost can be $60,000 per person. People climb Mount Everest because it is challenging, exciting, an adventure, etc.

B To focus their reading, have students read the questions before reading the title and paragraphs. Point out that the title and the first two paragraphs of a reading usually contain the main idea.

Answers: 1. Scott Fischer and Rob Hall owned adventure companies that allowed people to explore Mount Everest. 2. They often competed for clients. They also competed to be first to reach the summit with their teams. In the story, both decide to climb to the summit of Everest with their teams on the same day. 3. No, Rob and Scott thought that it was a perfect day to climb to the summit. But Ed Viesturs was worried about so many people climbing at the same time. 4. Answers will vary.

continued on page 55

Reading

A Complete the information about Mount Everest with numbers from the box. Then answer the questions with a partner.

200	60,000	8,850	1953

At 29,035 feet—(1) __________ meters—Mount Everest is the highest point on Earth. In (2) __________, New Zealander Edmund Hillary and Sherpa[1] Tenzing Norgay first reached the summit.[2] Although thousands of people from all over the world try to reach the summit each spring, it's not easy. Climbing Everest is risky: more than (3) ______ people have died on the mountain from snow, intense cold, and altitude[3] sickness. It's also expensive: guide services can cost up to (4) $__________ per person.

[1] **Sherpa** a local Nepalese climber who guides other climbers up Everest
[2] **summit** top [3] **altitude** height off the ground

A climber's map of Mount Everest

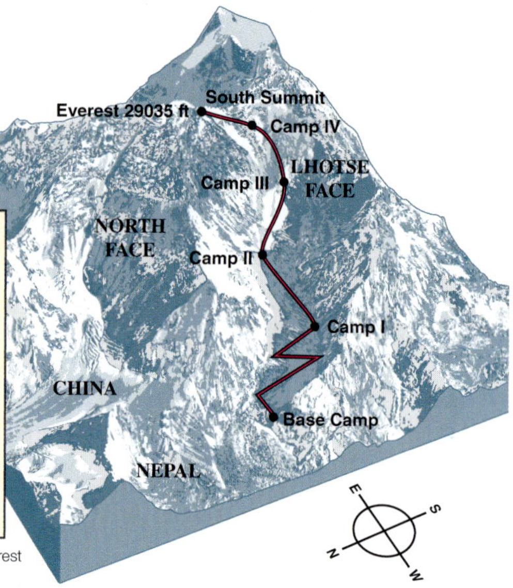

- What are the risks and cost of climbing Mount Everest?
- Even though climbing Everest is dangerous, many people do it every year. Why do you think they do it?

B Read the title and the first two paragraphs of the article. Then answer the questions in your own words with a partner.

1. Who are Scott Fischer and Rob Hall?
2. How did Scott and Rob compete?
3. Was there any reason to worry about people climbing to the summit on May 10?
4. What do you think is going to happen next in the story?

C Read the rest of the article. How are these dates and times important to the story? Write a sentence or two about each on a separate piece of paper.

May 10 2:00 p.m. 3:00 p.m. 10:00 p.m. May 11

D Summarize the story, using your answers in Exercises **B** and **C**.

Ask Answer Why do you think Rob and Scott didn't make their teams turn around at 2:00 p.m. on May 10? What lesson can we learn from this story?

Answers to **A**: (1) 8,850 (2) 1953 (3) 200 (4) 60,000

Extension

Have students close their books. Dictate the following sentences and have students write them down. Then, ask them to number the events in order, 1–7.

People were trapped between the summit and camp 4. (5)

A massive snowstorm started. (4)

Two groups began the climb. (1)

Ed checked on the climbers through a telescope. (2)

The groups ignored an important rule. (3)

Some people were rescued. (6)

Some collapsed and died on May 11. (7)

MOUNT EVEREST'S

Deadliest Day

Climbing Mount Everest is dangerous business, but even so, tourists pay enormous sums of money to take the risk. In 1996, there were more fatalities on Mount Everest than any other year . . . and half of those people died on just one day.

Scott Fischer and Rob Hall made a living guiding people up the mountain, but they didn't work together. They each owned adventure companies, Adventure Consultants and Mountain Madness, that allowed people to explore Mount Everest. Scott and Rob were good friends, but they were also rivals.[1] They each tried to get their groups to the summit first, and they often competed for clients. That May, both Scott and Rob decided that the 10th was the perfect day to set out for the summit. Scott's team had twenty three people in it, and Rob's had twenty five. There was also a twelve-person crew on Everest that day, making a movie about climbing the mountain. Consequently, there were more people trying to climb Mount Everest in May 1996 than at any other time before. One member of the movie crew, Ed Viesturs, was good friends with Rob and Scott and was worried about safety with so many people climbing at the same time.

Rob's and Scott's teams set off[2] early on May 10th. They left for the summit of Mount Everest from camp 4. It was a beautiful day, with perfect weather. Ed was at camp 2 and was monitoring[3] the progress of the climbers using a radio and telescope. Ed looked through the telescope at around 2:00 p.m. to check on the climbers. He noticed that the groups were moving very slowly. It is a rule on Mount Everest that at 2:00 p.m. you are to turn around and return to camp 4 in order to make it back before dark and avoid bad weather near the summit. Rob and Scott each wanted their groups to reach the top, so both groups ignored that critical rule and continued up the mountain instead of turning around.

Suddenly, at 3:00 p.m. a massive snowstorm started. By 10:00 p.m. that night, people from both Rob's and Scott's groups were trapped on the mountain in between the summit and camp 4 because of the storm. Some of the stranded climbers managed to survive the freezing cold and were rescued from the mountain the next day. However, on May 11th a few others collapsed and died in the snow, including Scott Fischer and Rob Hall. In total, eight people died on Mount Everest's deadliest day.

> "Rob and Scott each wanted their groups to reach the summit, so both groups ignored that critical rule and continued up the mountain instead of turning around."

[1] **rival** a person you compete with
[2] **set off** (for a place) to start a trip
[3] **monitor** to follow or check something regularly

55

Internet Activity

Direct students to this Web site containing facts and statistics about Mount Everest: http://www.mnteverest.net/history.html. In small groups, have them create a timeline that includes at least ten major events in the history of the mountain. Ask for volunteers to present their timelines to the class and explain why they believe the events they chose are significant.

Reading *continued*

C Remind students to scan the reading for numbers when locating dates and times.

Answers: *May 10*: This was the day that Rob's and Scott's teams decided to climb to the summit of Everest. It is also the day that a number of the climbers on both teams got trapped on the mountain. *2:00 p.m.*: This is the normal turnaround time on Everest. If you're at the summit, you have to return to camp 4 at this time. If you haven't reached the top yet, you must still turn around and return to camp at that time. *3:00 p.m.*: On May 10, it suddenly started snowing on Everest at this time. *10:00 p.m.*: By this time on May 10, a number of climbers from both teams are trapped on the mountain. *May 11*: Some of the climbers are rescued, but several others die, including Scott Fischer and Rob Hall.

D Remind students that summaries include only the most important information from a longer source.

Background Information

Mount Everest is located in the Himalaya Mountain range between Tibet and Nepal. Tibetans call it Chomolungma; the name "Everest" is in honor of George Everest who was the Surveyor General of India. Because of its status as the highest mountain in the world, Everest attracts many climbers. It has two main climbing routes: from the southeast through Nepal and the northeastern route from Tibet. Edmund Hillary and Tenzing Norgay used the southeastern route when they made the first successful climb to the summit in 1953.

Purpose for Reading

In recounting the circumstances of the deadliest day on Mount Everest, this reading mentions several causes and their effects. Review words and phrases that signal cause (*because*, *since*, *due to*) and ones that point to outcomes (*consequently*, *therefore*, *in order to*, *so*, *as a result*). To remind students about cause and effect as they read, ask these questions: *Why were there so many people on the mountain that day? Why do groups turn around at 2:00 p.m.? Why didn't the two groups turn around?*

Language Notes

The text includes several idioms and phrasal verbs. Point out the following: *make a living* = earn money; *set out*, *set off* = leave; *make it back* = return successfully; *turn around* = return, go back

Video

5-10 min. A
10-15 min. B
15 min. C
10-15 min. D
Extension: 5-10 min.

Background Information

Adventure Consultants is a mountain guiding company based in New Zealand that leads amateur climbers on expeditions throughout the world. Once owned by Rob Hall, the company is now operated by Guy Cotter, an experienced mountaineer who has climbed the world's tallest summits. Adventure Consultants leads only small groups on its expeditions in order to provide personalized service and limit the impact on the environment.

Before You Watch

- Go over the words in the word bank. Point out that the word *zombie* is something that exists only in fiction. In the video, it is mentioned in reference to climbers who were exhausted from climbing.
- Preteach other words and phrases from the video: *tower over*, *claim the lives*, *tragedy*, *blizzard*, *notorious*, *perish*, *minimize risk*

A Play segment 2 one or more times. Note that segment 1 gives the backstory of the 1996 tragedy that was highlighted in the reading.

Answer: Cotter and others have learned that safety must come first.

B
- Have students read the lists of numbered and lettered items before you play segment 3.
- Play the video one or more times. After students have listened, have them compare answers with a partner.

Answers: 1. c; 2. g; 3. f; 4. c; 5. a; 6. e or g; 7. b; 8. d

C Have students compare answers in Exercise **B** with a partner. Then play the video so they can check.

D

Answer: It took Team Canada almost two months to reach the summit from their start in April.

Video

caught off guard to be surprised by someone or something
disorientation confusion
oxygen a gas (O) in the air needed by humans to breathe
sea level on the ground, near the ocean
soak (something) in to look at or enjoy a place you are in as much as you can
zombie a dead person who has come back to life

A Read the information below. Then ask a partner: How do you think climbing Everest has changed since 1996 when Rob Hall ran Adventure Consultants? Watch **segment 2** of the video to check your answer.

Adventure Consultants, originally owned by New Zealander Rob Hall, continues to guide people to the top of Everest. Today it is run by climber Guy Cotter. In the video, he's going to lead a Canadian group (nicknamed Team Canada) to the summit.

B Look back at the map on p. 54. Then watch **segment 3** of the video. Match a sentence stem (1–8) with an answer (a–g). Sometimes an answer can be used more than once.

Team Canada's Everest Expedition

1. Team Canada sets out on foot to base camp . . .
2. Today, Adventure Consultants uses computers and satellite phones . . .
3. At base camp, the team does the Puja ceremony . . .
4. For weeks, Team Canada travels back and forth between camps 1 to 4 . . .
5. In mid-May, the guides prepare supplemental oxygen . . .
6. The team stops at the fourth and final camp before the summit . . .
7. The team sets off the next morning for the summit . . .
8. They take some photos and look at the view . . .

a. since they will need extra to survive on the mountain.
b. before daybreak.
c. because they need to adjust to the altitude.
d. after they reach the top.
e. so that they can rest.
f. before they are allowed to climb the mountain.
g. so that they can check the weather report.

During the Puja ceremony, climbers say prayers to Mother Goddess of the Earth (the Nepalese name for Everest).

C Watch the video again and check your answers in Exercise **B**.

D Use the map on p. 54 and your answers in Exercise **B** to explain Team Canada's Everest journey. How long was it from the start in April to the finish?

Ask Answer What do you think of people who climb Everest? Would you do it? Why or why not?

Extension

Divide the class into two teams. Have a member from each team approach the board. Ask a question about the video (for example, *What is located on Everest at 17,000 feet?*). The first student to write the correct answer gains a point for his or her team. Continue asking questions until all students have had a chance to answer. Tally points and declare one team the winner.

Speaking

A Read the information below. What problem are people meeting to discuss?

Local business people, mountain climbers, and interested parties from around the world are debating closing Mount Everest. Some want to stop all climbing and camping for environmental and, above all, safety reasons. Others say that this will cause many people to lose their jobs. Should Everest be closed?

Speaking Strategy — Reaching a compromise

Making a suggestion
One option / idea would be to . . .
Another (option / idea) would be to . . .

Disagreeing with a suggestion
The problem with that is . . .
Sorry, but that doesn't work for me because . . .

Agreeing with a suggestion
I could do that / agree to that.
That works for me.

Offering a compromise
If you'll agree to . . . , I'll agree to . . .

B Work in groups of four. Follow these steps and use the expressions in the Speaking Strategy to help you.

1. **Assign** each role from the box below to one person.
2. **Read** the information about your part only.
3. **Introduce** yourself and explain your opinion.
4. **On your own**, think of one or two possible solutions (close Everest completely; keep it open year round to everyone; something in-between). Try to think of a solution everyone can accept.
5. **Start the discussion**. One person suggests a possible solution and explains the reasoning. The others should then respond. Continue negotiating until you all agree on one solution.

Everest guide: You lead groups of international climbers up Mount Everest each spring. You employ nine people. Even though some of your clients are not fully trained to make the climb, none have ever been injured. However, you have recently almost had a couple of accidents, and you are not enjoying your work like you used to. If Everest closes, your business will collapse.

Mountain climber: You've been training to climb Everest for a year. It's your dream to reach the top, and you don't want the mountain to close. You've heard stories about inexperienced climbers being injured—or worse. You think these people should not be allowed on Everest.

Environmentalist: Everest gets thousands of visitors every year. The result: water and air pollution have increased. Climbers leave garbage on the mountain. There are also over a hundred dead bodies still on Everest. You believe the mountain must close so that it can be cleaned up and preserved for the future.

Local Sherpa guide: You've been a mountain guide for several years. Even though you make good money doing it, you're very concerned about safety. Your brother was also a trained guide. Last spring, though, he died in an avalanche* near the summit. In your opinion, something has to change.

C Explain your group's solution to the class.

One option would be to close Everest for a year so that we can clean it . . .

***avalanche** a large amount of snow that falls down a mountain

Speaking

5-10 min. **A**
20-25 min. **B**
15-20 min. **C**
Extension: 20 min.

A

Answer: Closing Mount Everest.

B
- Go over the steps and the expressions in the box. Check comprehension.
- Put students in groups of four and assign each person one of the roles: Everest guide, mountain climber, environmentalist, local Sherpa guide.
- Allow students time to jot down notes on their position before they begin the discussion.

Outcome: Upon completing this exercise, students will have met the Outcome ***reach a compromise.***

C
- Call on groups to share their solutions.
- Ask students if they know any places in your country, such as a national park or beach, that gets a lot of tourists each year. Have them compare it to the problems on Everest.

Extension

With the class, create a list of problems about one of the local places mentioned above. Write the issues on the board and which people are most interested in the outcomes of them (the stakeholders). Assign roles and have students try to reach a compromise on at least one of the problems.

Rubric	Very Good	Satisfactory	Needs Improvement
Use of expressions to reach a compromise			
Use of vocabulary			
Use of grammar			
Pronunciation and fluency			

Writing

5 min. **A**
10 min. **B**
5 min. **C**
15-20 min. **D**
5-10 min. **E**
Extension: 10-15 min.

Purpose of Writing

In this writing assignment, students describe the steps in a process. When writing about a process, students need to use expressions that tell the order of events. Remind students to use expressions like the boldfaced ones in Exercise **B** and adverbial clauses as in the Grammar section.

A Have students indicate their guesses by a show of hands.

B Ask for volunteers to read sections of the box about surviving a shark attack out loud.

C
- Brainstorm other ideas with students that would require following steps. For example: *asking your teacher for a better grade, getting along better with your parents or sibling, stopping someone from choking or other first-aid, stopping a bully, making a certain type of dish from your country.*
- To prepare students for writing the steps in a process, review a routine that everyone typically does, such as getting ready for school, doing laundry, and so on. Ask questions using signal phrases: *What do you do first? What do you do after that? When do you . . . ?*

D **Outcome:** Upon completing this exercise, students will have met the Outcome *explain steps in a process.*

Extension

Have students rewrite the process they described in Exercise **D**. This time they will write each step on a separate card or strip of paper and they will not use signal phrases. Have students exchange their sentence strips with a partner to reorder and add their own phrases to organize the process.

Writing

A Set of Instructions

A If you are swimming and you see a shark, what is the first thing you should do?

a. Pretend you are dead. b. Splash and attract attention. c. Remain still.

B Read the information. Then answer the questions below with a partner.

Surviving a Shark Attack

Last summer, I was a lifeguard at a beach near my house. Before I started, I had to take a class. In it, I learned different water safety skills, including how to handle the situation if a shark attacked.

Although shark attacks are rare, they are very dangerous. If you see a shark while you're in the water, you should follow these steps. **The first is** to stay very still. Do not panic and start moving a lot because this will attract the shark. Also, do not pretend you are dead and assume the shark will just go away. Dead animals attract sharks! **The next thing you should do is** to get out of the water quickly and calmly. Don't splash around or attract attention. **While** you are moving toward the shore, keep watching for the shark so that it doesn't come back and surprise you. If the shark *does* come and attack, then **the only thing you can do is** to fight back. Hit the shark in the nose and eyes very hard. Because these are sensitive areas on the shark's body, it might scare the animal so that you can get away safely. **As soon as** you're out of the water, report the shark sighting right away. Following these steps can help you stay safe.

1. Was your guess in Exercise **A** correct?
2. What do the boldfaced words show the reader?
3. Close your book. Can you recall the instructions the lifeguard gave?

C Read the Writing Strategy. Then choose one of the topics below to write about.

Explain how to . . .

- tell someone bad news (pick something specific).
- improve your English conversation skills.
- prepare for an important exam.
- stay safe if there is a fire.
- your idea: ____________________

D Make a list of steps in the process. How is each step helpful? Then write a paragraph or two on a separate piece of paper.

E Exchange papers with another student. Read your partner's writing. Does it follow the Writing Strategy?

Writing Strategy — **Explaining steps in a process**
When you describe how to do something, (1) identify specific steps in the process; (2) use signal words and phrases such as *first, next, then, last, when, while,* and *as soon as* to mark the steps. (See the boldfaced words in Exercise **B**.); and (3) briefly explain why each step in the process is helpful: *The first (thing you should do) is stay very still.* <u>Do not panic and start moving a lot because this will attract the shark.</u>

Rubric	Very Good	Satisfactory	Needs Improvement
Content			
Clear explanation of steps in a process			
Use of grammar			
Organization			

Expanding Your Fluency

A On your own, read the situation below. Then make an escape plan. Be prepared to explain the steps in your plan and why you think each step is a good idea.

You and a friend were on a sailing tour. During the trip, there was a storm and your boat sank. Luckily, you and your friend survived and were able to swim to a small island, but you are now trapped on it. What are you going to do?

The island

You're on a beach and the weather is hot. There's no fresh water, but there are lots of coconut trees. (Coconuts usually have drinkable water in them.)

You can see a tall mountain in the center of the island. There are no buildings or people on your side of the mountain. You don't know what's on the other side. You thought you saw smoke coming from there, but you aren't sure.

Your supplies

Before the boat sank, you saved your waterproof backpack. Inside you find matches, a small first-aid kit, a fork, a sharp knife, a spoon, and a cell phone with a GPS system. The cell phone works but it isn't getting any reception right now.

Your situation

During the storm, your boat was blown off course. Even though a rescue team will search for you, they might not know where to look.

One of you injured your leg in the ordeal. You can walk, but it's painful.

B Imagine that you and your partner are trapped on the island. Explain your plans to each other. Use the expressions on p. 57 to help you negotiate and create <u>one</u> escape plan together.

> One option is to hike to the other side of the island and see what's there.

> The problem is that I injured my leg and can't walk very well. Also, before we hike to the other side, we need to . . .

C Share your escape plan with the class. When all pairs have presented their plans, vote for the best one.

Check What You Know

Rank how well you can perform these outcomes on a scale of 1–5 (5 being the best).

________ use adverbial clauses to talk about challenging situations
________ reach a compromise
________ explain steps in a process
________ follow steps to get through a difficult situation

Expanding Your Fluency

10-15 min. A
15-20 min. B
15-20 min. C
Extension: 10-15 min.

A
- Explain the meaning of the term *blown off course.*
- Note for students that *GPS* is an acronym that stands for *global positioning system*. If necessary, explain that a device with a GPS can track a person's location on the earth through satellites in space.

B
- Encourage students to be creative but realistic in their solutions for escaping the island.
- Remind students that when reaching a compromise with their partner, they will have to reorder the steps in their own processes to come up with a master escape plan. This will include abandoning parts of the plan they came up with on their own in Exercise **A**.

C Tally votes for the best plan by a show of hands. Ask those who voted for the winner to explain why they believe it's a good plan.

Check What You Know

Refer students back to the exercises in the unit where each Outcome is addressed.

- *use adverbial clauses to talk about challenging situations:* Grammar, Exercise **C**, page 51
- *reach a compromise:* Speaking, Exercise **B**, page 57
- *explain steps in a process:* Writing, Exercise **D**, page 58
- *follow steps to get through a difficult situation:* Connections, Exercise **D**, page 53

Extension

On pieces of paper or cards, write questions about scary situations (e.g., *What can you do when a shark attacks? What can you do when you are stuck in a bad snowstorm? What can you do when your car breaks down in the middle of nowhere?*). Prepare enough so each student gets one. Have students stand and walk around the room to ask and answer questions. After ten minutes, stop the activity and ask students to tell the class how people answered.

Unit 6
In Style

Unit Overview

- Unit 6 is about shopping and fashion. Students will learn how the choices we make in fashion and shopping reveal something about who we are.
- Different factors motivate shopping: a desire for a bargain, prices, brand names, responsible planning, and how new and exciting a product is.
- Online shopping is another trend popular around the world. South Korea does the most online shopping of any nation, followed by the United Kingdom, Germany, Japan, and the United States.
- Preview the unit by asking students the following questions:

1. Do you enjoy shopping? Why or why not?
2. Do you consider yourself stylish in the way you dress? Explain.
3. How often do you buy things online? In stores?

Photo Caption

This image is of a market street in Tokyo, Japan, called Ameyoko. The street attracts shoppers interested in buying a variety of products, from clothing to food to electronics. "Ameyoko" is an abbreviated form of its full name, "Ameya Yokocho," or "candy store alley," as it was traditionally a place that sold candies.

6 In Style

1 What is happening in this photo? Have you ever been to a place like this?

2 A trend is something that is popular or in style. Do you follow fashion trends? Why or why not?

3 What is more important to you when it comes to fashion: quality or price?

Unit Outcomes

In this unit, you will learn to:

- describe shopping habits and fashion preferences
- use adjective clauses to explain and define people and things
- react to other points of view
- present and defend an argument

VOCABULARY	GRAMMAR	LISTENING	READING
The Dubai Shopping Festival	Adjective clauses with subject relative pronouns **Pronunciation:** Intonation patterns in relative clauses	Conversations at a shopping mall	*Every Shoe Tells a Story:* They say a lot about us, even when we're not wearing them

5-10 min. **Warm-Up Questions**
Extension: 10-15 min.

Background Information

Fashion has long been valued in many cultures. Stores and designers have held fashion shows or fashion parades since the nineteenth century. The modern fashion show with runway models became more popular after 1940. People involved in American fashion organized a week of fashion shows to highlight American designers. The idea caught on, and now fashion shows with a runway, or catwalk, are popular all around the world. The most influential fashion shows are held in the cities of Paris, New York, Milan, London, Hong Kong, Singapore, and Sao Paulo.

Warm-Up Questions

- Read through Question 1 as a class. Ask several volunteers to guess where the place is. Work as a class to describe the photo in detail. Ask students if they have ever been to a place like this.
- Make sure students understand what a trend is by asking students to name a trend they know about.
- Have students work with a partner to answer Questions 2 and 3.

Extension

Put students in pairs or small groups to describe their favorite places to shop for clothes, electronics, food, and so on. Call on students to describe the places and why they like to shop there.

VIDEO	SPEAKING	WRITING	OUTCOMES
How to Spot A Fake Louis Vuitton Bag	Give your opinions in a shopping and fashion survey Strategy: Reacting to someone else's point of view	Present and defend an argument Strategy: Making a successful argument	• describe shopping habits and fashion preferences • use adjective clauses to explain and define people and things • react to other points of view • present and defend an argument

Vocabulary

15-20 min. A
25-35 min. B
Extension: 10-15 min.

A • Point out to students that while *bargain* and *deal* have the same meanings as nouns, they do not quite have the same meanings as verbs. *To bargain* means to come to an agreement about the cost of something; *to deal* can mean to distribute or trade.

- Word partnerships with *sale*: *be on ~, be for ~, go on ~, salesperson, sales tax*
- Word partnerships with *bargain*: *strike a ~, recognize a ~*

Outcome: Upon completing this exercise, students will have met the Outcome ***describe shopping habits and fashion preferences.***

B Before putting students in pairs to discuss the Ask and Answer question, tell the class about a shopping event or sale that you're familiar with.

Answers: 1. recommend; 2. goods; 3. bargain; 4. purchase

Language Note

Note the uses of the word *brand* on this page: alone as a noun, as a noun with the word partner *designer*, and as an adjective with the word partner *name*.

Photo Caption

This image is of the Gold Souk in the city of Dubai, United Arab Emirates. *Souk* is an Arabic word that means "open-air market." Dubai's Gold Souk includes over 300 vendors that sell mostly jewelry. The gold for sale at the souk is relatively cheap and of high-quality. Bargaining is part of the culture at the Gold Souk, and shoppers can talk down the price of certain goods by as much as half the asking price.

Vocabulary

affordable reasonably priced, inexpensive
bargain to talk with someone to try to get a lower price on something
brand a type of product made by a particular company
browse to look around a shop casually
deal something good you buy, usually for a low price
discount a reduction in the usual price of something
goods products you buy
purchase to buy something
quality how good or bad something is
recommend to suggest to someone that a thing or person would be good or useful

Usage: *bargain* and *deal* *Bargain* can also be a noun and means the same thing as *deal. The shoes cost only $25. What a bargain/deal!*

deal *bad ~, fair ~, good ~ great~, real ~*

A Choose the expressions in 1–3 that best describe your shopping habits. Then explain your responses to a partner.

1. When I shop, I like to **take my time and browse / hurry up and buy what I need.**
2. I **occasionally / never** try to bargain to get a discount on something.
3. The most important thing to me is that my purchases are **high quality / affordable.**

I love shopping at the Dubai Shopping Festival. Every year, over forty shopping malls and stores join together in January and February to offer big discounts on everything from brand name clothing to high-quality electronics and cars.

B Read what Nadia says about the Dubai Shopping Festival.

1. Complete the profile with a word from the vocabulary list.
2. Then ask a partner: Would you like to shop there? Why or why not? How is it similar to or different from shopping where you live?

Best time to shop: *I* (1) ____________ *going in the early morning or late evening so you can avoid the crowds. You can find the best deals late in the day. Also, many people speak English so you don't have to worry about communicating with the locals.*

Best place to browse: *A traditional marketplace, called a souk. You can buy a variety of* (2) ____________ *there, including furniture, jewelry, food, and spices. Merchants typically start with a high price and then* (3) ____________ *with you for a more affordable one.*

What makes it special: *Over three million people attend. Also, people who* (4) ____________ *items during the festival are entered into a daily lottery. Winners receive cars, money, and even gold!*

Ask / Answer In your city, is there a time of year when stores offer big discounts on goods? Do you ever shop at these sales?

62

Extension

Put students in pairs to write a description of a shopping place they know. Suggest they use Exercise **B** as a model and as many words from the word bank as possible. Have each pair join another pair to exchange and read the descriptions.

Grammar

A Complete 1–3 with the correct word(s). Explain your answers to a partner.

1. People **who / which / that** enter the lottery can win prizes.
2. Did you buy the jacket **who / which / that** was on sale?
3. Dubai's traditional souks, **who / which / that** sell many goods, are very interesting.

Adjective Clauses with Subject Relative Pronouns	
who = for people	❶ People **who visit Dubai during the shopping festival** can get some great deals.
which = for things	❷ The festival, **which gets over three million visitors**, lasts several weeks.
that = for people and things	❸ Nadia is someone **that spends a lot on clothes**. ❹ It's a festival **that takes place every year**.
subject-verb agreement	❺ It's a shop **that sells discount electronics**. ❻ They're shops **that sell designer handbags**.

Adjective clauses give more information about a noun and begin with a relative pronoun (*who, which, that*).
In ❶, the adjective clause gives necessary information about the subject. It completes the meaning of the sentence.
In ❷, the adjective clause gives extra information about the subject. You don't need it to complete the meaning of the sentence. It is separated from the main clause by commas.

TIP When an adjective clause gives extra information, *that* cannot be used: *The festival, ~~that~~ which gets over three million visitors . . .*

TIP Don't repeat the subject after the relative pronoun: *He's a person who ~~he~~ spends a lot on clothes.*

B Correct the mistake in each sentence. Then check your answers with a partner. In which sentences do the adjective clauses give necessary information? Which give extra information?

1. Men which live in Europe spend more money on clothes than men in North America.
2. Clothing and books are the most popular products that they are sold online.
3. Most people who lives in South Korea have purchased something online at least once.
4. The Bugatti Veyron, who is the most expensive car in the world, costs almost $2,500,000.
5. The Dubai Mall, that is one of the largest in the world, has over 1,200 stores.

C Combine the sentences using an adjective clause to form a single question. Then take turns asking and answering the questions with a partner.

Which shops have good bargains? I want something near here.
Which shops that are near here have good bargains?

1. Have you ever bought something? It was really expensive.
2. Can you name any clothing designers? They are known around the world.
3. Do you have any friends? They are very stylish.
4. Can you recommend a good place for vacation? It's fun and affordable.

PRONUNCIATION Notice the different meaning and intonation patterns in these two examples.

The shopkeeper who sells such beautiful goods will make a lot of money.
The shopkeeper, who sells such beautiful goods, will make a lot of money.
For more information on intonation patterns in relative clauses, see p. 149.

Extension

Bring in photos from department store flyers or magazines. Give a photo to each student to write a description using at least one adjective clause (e.g., *The red dress that has five buttons down the front is on sale today*). Collect the photos and post them around the room. Collect the descriptions and redistribute. Have students walk around the room to match the description to the photo.

Grammar

10-15 min. A
15-20 min. B
15-20 min. C
Extension: 10-20 min.

A
- Explain to students that in everyday spoken English, *that* tends to be used more frequently to describe things than *which*. In number 2, for example, people would be more likely to say *Did you buy the jacket that was on sale?* than *...which was on sale?* But grammatically, both are correct.
- Write sentences 1 and 2 from the grammar chart on the board. To highlight the difference between necessary information and extra information, erase the adjective clause in each sentence. Then have students read the remaining sentences. Ask them why the adjective clause in sentence 1 is necessary. (Because it describes a specific place where people can get deals.)
- To help students understand the Pronunciation box, read the two example sentences aloud with the correct intonation.

Answers: 1. who / that; 2. that / which; 3. which

B

Answers: 1. Change *which* to *who.* or *that.* 2. Cut the word *they.* 3. Change *lives* to *live.* 4. Change *who* to *which.* 5. Change *that* to *which.* The adjective clauses in sentences 1, 2, and 3 give necessary information. The adjective clauses in sentences 4 and 5 give extra information.

C Go over the correct forms of the questions before pairing students.

Answers: 1. Have you ever bought something that/which was really expensive? 2. Can you name any clothing designers who/that are known around the world? 3. Do you have any friends who/that are very stylish? 4. Can you recommend a good place for vacation that/which is fun and affordable?

Outcome: Upon completing this exercise, students will have met the Outcome *use adjective clauses to explain and define people and things.*

Listening

5 min. **A**
10-15 min. **B**
10-15 min. **C**
20 min. **D**
Extension: 10 min.

Background information

Robson Street in Vancouver is named after John Robson who was the premier of British Columbia from 1889–1892. After train tracks were laid down next to the street in 1895, shops and other businesses began to gather there. Many Europeans opened businesses on Robson Street after World War II, and it became known as Robsonstrasse. Now it is home to many diverse stores and restaurants. Vancouver is one of the most expensive places to have a business, and Robson Street is the most expensive retail space in Vancouver.

A Point out that *goods* are products.

B
- Focus students' attention on the image of the tablet to make sure students are familiar with the term before you play the audio.
- Go over these words and expressions from the audio: *affordable* (within someone's price range), *there's no way* (not possible), *hang on* (to wait), *loan* (to give temporarily), *max* (short for *maximum*).
- Play the audio recording one or more times. Pause the recording after each conversation to give students the time to write their answers. **Audio CD Track 11**

Answers: 1. a; 2. No. She decides to shop for it online instead. 3. b; 4. Yes; Price: $75; 5. b; 6. Yes; Price: $560

Language Notes

- Conversation 1: *See anything…* is an abbreviated construction of *You see anything…?* which is an abbreviated construction of *Do you see anything…?*; *discount* is a noun in the word bank on page 62 but is used as an adjective in the conversation: *discount electronics*
- Conversation 2: *You shopping…* is an abbreviated construction of *Are you shopping…?* An even more abbreviated construction would be *Shopping for shoes?*

Listening

a tablet

A Where can you get good deals on electronics, clothes, and other goods? Have you ever purchased anything in one of these places? What did you buy? Discuss with a partner.

B You're going to hear three different conversations happening in Robson Street, a popular shopping district in Vancouver, Canada. Read the information below. Then listen and choose the correct answers.

Conversation 1

1. The man and woman are looking at a tablet. The man _____.
   a. tells the woman not to buy it   b. bargains with the woman for it
   c. recommends another product
2. Does the woman purchase the tablet? **Yes** Price: ________ **No** Why not: ____________________

Conversation 2

3. The woman who is shopping for shoes wants _____.
   a. evening shoes   b. reasonably priced shoes
   c. shoes like her friend's
4. Does the woman purchase any shoes? **Yes** Price: ________ **No** Why not: ____________________

Conversation 3

5. The man _____.
   a. can't decide which bike to buy   b. bargains with the saleswoman
   c. is confused about the prices
6. Does the man purchase a bike? **Yes** Price: ________ **No** Why not: ____________________

C Read the sentences below. Then listen again. Choose the correct answer for each one.

1. When the man says, "What a *rip off*!," he means "What a **cheap / high** price!"
2. When the woman says, "*Check out* this pair," she means, "**Look at / Forget about** these shoes."
3. When the woman says, "*It's worth it*," she means, "The bike is **cheap / expensive** because its quality is **good / bad**."

D Imagine that you are at the mall with your partner. Create a short dialog in which you use at least two of the new expressions from Exercise **C**. Then perform your dialog for another pair.

Vancouver, Canada

C Play the recording one or more times. Note that this track contains excerpts of each conversation from the previous track. Pause the recording after each excerpt to give students time to write their answers. **Audio CD Track 12**

Answers: 1. high; 2. Look at; 3. expensive, good

Extension

Photocopy the script of the conversations in Exercise **B**, found on pages T–172 to T–173. Make enough copies for pairs of students. Cut the lines of dialogue into strips and shuffle them. Then, give a set of strips to each pair of students for them to place the dialogues in order. Finally, play **Audio CD Track 11** again so students can check their work.

Connections

A Two people are bargaining at a flea market. Listen to and read the dialog. What's special about the pen the man is selling? Would you buy this product?

Buyer: This is an interesting looking pen. How much do you want for it?
Seller: $20.
Buyer: For this old pen?!
Seller: Ah, but it's not just *any* old pen. It's a pen that never runs out of ink.
Buyer: A pen that never runs out of ink? Really?
Seller: Yes. It's perfect for the person who never wants to buy another pen again! But I've only got three left. They're selling fast.
Buyer: Hmmm . . . Well, it *is* pretty . . . and you say it'll never run out of ink? I'll give you $5 for it.
Seller: Ten. Come on; think of all the money you'll save. Ten is a great deal.
Buyer: Six. That's all I can afford.
Seller: Six it is!

The Estremoz flea market in Portugal.

At a flea market, people sell old or used goods. You can often find odd objects, fantastic deals, and . . . a lot of junk!

B You're going to sell an item at a flea market. Do the following:

1. Think of an everyday item (cell phone, watch, umbrella, article of clothing). Then give it a "special power." Answer the questions to describe your special item:
   - What does it do? It's a ______ that ________________.
   - Who is it perfect for? It's perfect for people who ________________.
2. Take four small pieces of paper. On each, write the item you listed in step 1. This paper now represents your merchandise. You are going to sell four of the same items at the flea market.
3. Decide on a cost for the item. It cannot be more than $100.

C Your instructor will divide the class into sellers and buyers. Read your information below.

Sellers	Buyers
Your goal: To sell all four of your items for as much money as you can before time is up	**Your goal:** To buy as many products as you can before time is up. You start with $100 to spend.
Talk to different customers at the market. Explain what your item is and why it's useful. When you sell an item, give the paper to the buyer and add the amount you earned below.	Talk to different sellers. If you want to buy a product, bargain for a lower price. When you buy an item, deduct the amount you paid below. Also write the price on the paper the seller gives you.
Starting amount: 0	Starting amount: 100
+ ______ + ______ + ______ + ______	– ______ – ______ – ______ – ______ – ______ – ______ – ______ – ______
Total earned: ______	**Total left:** ______

D Start the bargaining! You will have fifteen minutes to buy or sell as many items as you can. When time is up, share your results with the class. Who were the most successful bargainers?

E Switch roles (those who were sellers are now buyers) and repeat Exercises **C** and **D**.

Internet Activity

Have students research different countries and the shopping customs there. Do people typically bargain at markets? What rules do people follow when they bargain? Suggest that students do a search for "bargaining in (*name of the country*)." Students should note what they find and share the information in pairs or small groups.

Connections

5 min. **A**
5-10 min. **B**
5 min. **C**
15 min. **D**
10-15 min. **E**
Extension: 10 min.

Photo Caption

This image is of the Saturday market in the town of Estremoz, Portugal. Located in southeastern Portugal near the border of Spain, Estremoz is known for its old marble architecture. The Saturday market takes place in the main square of its lower town and is one of the biggest in Portugal. Vendors sell, among other things, earthenware pottery and cheese.

A Before students do Exercise **A**, have them look at the photo and read the caption. Ask them if there are flea markets near their community and if they have ever been to one.

Answer: The pen is special because it never runs out of ink.

B
- Brainstorm ideas for items and powers: *backpack that's bottomless, sweater that makes you invisible, cup that refills itself, painting that you can step into.*
- If necessary, help students figure out the monetary equivalent of $100 in their own currency.

C
- Before students begin, write a few bargaining expressions on the board: *What a bargain! / It's a great deal. / Can you give me a discount? / I can't go any lower than that. / That's all I can afford. / I can spend __. / How much if I buy two? / That's my final offer.*
- Students in the role of "buyers" may have to add more lines as they buy more items and subtract money from the original total.

D Point out to students that successful bargaining for sellers is selling all of their items for the most money possible, while for buyers it's getting the most items possible and still having money left over.

Extension

After the bargaining activity, conduct a survey to see what items were sold and for how much. Have students create a chart that lists the items and their sale prices. Take a vote to see which item they felt was the most creative and sold the most cheaply.

Reading

5 min. **A**
10-15 min. **B**
15-20 min. **C**
10-15 min. **D**
Extension: 15 min.

A Draw students' attention to some of the common adjective endings: *-ous*, *-ing*, *-ed*, *-able*, *-al*.

B Remind students to refer to the adjectives in Exercise **A** when describing what kind of people might wear each type of shoe.

Possible Answers: 1. *high-heeled boots:* a professional woman, one who is fashion-conscious and sophisticated; 2. *casual boots, comfortable shoes and sneakers:* students, people who are practical and don't need to dress up. 3. *UK flag sneakers:* someone young, who doesn't need to spend a lot of money on clothes, wants to be comfortable, wants to make a statement, has a strong personality, is daring

C Have students read the text individually, or call on students to read sentences from the text as the class follows along silently.

Answers: *high-heeled shoe or boot for women:* is a daring and self-confident person; also possible: powerful; *low-heeled or flat shoes for women:* is a serious, practical, dependable person; *heavy men's boots:* may work outside as a construction worker or fire fighter; *men's designer shoes:* may need to dress formally at work, might have money to afford expensive shoes; *bright, multi-colored shoes:* is an outgoing and adventurous person; *neutral or darker colored shoes:* is a sophisticated person, has a lot of self-control; *worn sneakers:* is a bit of a rebel—a person who doesn't care what others think; *designer sneakers:* is a fashion-conscious person who is interested in the latest trends, whatever the cost

D Alternatively, have students match the shoes their partners are wearing to the descriptions in Exercise **C**. Then have them say whether they think the description is true for the partner, even if they don't know each other well.

Reading

A The adjectives below are used to describe people. Mark the ones you know. Look up the ones you don't know in your dictionary. Then circle the ones that describe you.

adventurous	fashion-conscious	self-confident
daring	outgoing	serious
dependable	practical	sophisticated

B Read the title and the first paragraph of the article on the next page. Then look at the photos and ask a partner: Who might wear each pair of shoes? What can you tell about each person by looking at only his or her shoes?

C What does each type of shoe tell us about a person? Read the article and then complete the chart with information from the reading.

high-heeled shoes or boots for women	**low-heeled or flat shoes for women**
heavy boots for men	**designer shoes for men**
bright, multi-colored shoes	**neutral or darker colored shoes**
worn sneakers	**designer sneakers**

D How much can you tell about your partner by looking at his or her shoes? Describe him or her using the information in Exercise **C** to help you. Then share your description with your partner. Was it correct?

Extension

Write the words from Exercise **A** on the board. With their books closed, have students write a summary of the reading using all of the words. Put students in pairs to compare summaries. Allow them to look at the reading to check if their summaries are accurate and make changes as needed.

Every Shoe Tells a Story

A Christian Louboutin stiletto

Humans have been wearing shoes for thousands of years. They protect our feet from the heat and cold; they allow us to walk comfortably or to run faster. Our shoes do more than this, though. They can also tell others a lot about us. If your shoes could talk, what would they say about you?

Boy or girl?

One of the first things your shoes tell others about you is your gender. A high-heeled shoe, for example, probably belongs to a woman. This kind of shoe wasn't always associated with[1] women, though. For hundreds of years, wealthy men and women in Europe and Asia wore high-heeled sandals or boots to protect their feet and clothes from mud and water on the ground.

Though today's streets are cleaner, 4- to 5-inch stilettos are still very popular among women. Beautiful? Perhaps. Practical? Not really. So why do so many women continue to wear them? Natacha Marro, who has designed shoes for pop stars like Christina Aguilera, explains. "You put on heels, and suddenly you are 6 inches [15 centimeters] higher. It's a power thing." Wearing stilettos (or any high-heeled shoe or boot) tells others that you're daring and self-confident. Some people find that very attractive. Low-heeled or flat shoes, on the other hand, project a more serious image. They tell others that you're practical and dependable.

What do you do?

For hundreds of years, shoes also told others about a person's occupation or social position. In early Japan, for example, merchants, actors, and soldiers wore shoes specific to their line of work. Although we usually can't tell what a person does by looking at his or her shoes anymore, we can still make some guesses. A man who wears heavy boots on the job, for example, may work outside; perhaps he's a construction worker or firefighter. A man with a closet full of designer shoes, however, may need to dress more formally at work. Perhaps he's an attorney or business executive. Or maybe he just has the money to buy a lot of expensive shoes.

What are you like?

In ancient Rome, the wealthy could be identified by the red or orange shoes they wore. Though shoe color no longer indicates[2] one's social status, it does still tell us something about the shoe owner's personality. Bright, multi-colored shoes or those with lots of details suggest an outgoing, adventurous character. Neutral or darker colors, on the other hand, signal sophistication and self-control. Even the sneakers we wear can tell others a lot about us. A worn[3] pair, for example, suggests that you're a bit of a rebel—a person who doesn't care what others think. A pair of $400 designer sneakers, however, tells others you're a fashion-conscious person who is interested in the latest trends, whatever the cost.

Our shoes say a lot about us, even when we aren't wearing them. Look at the shoes you've got on right now. What do they tell others about you?

[1] **associated with** to be connected or related to another thing
[2] **indicate** to show
[3] **worn** old, damaged, used a lot

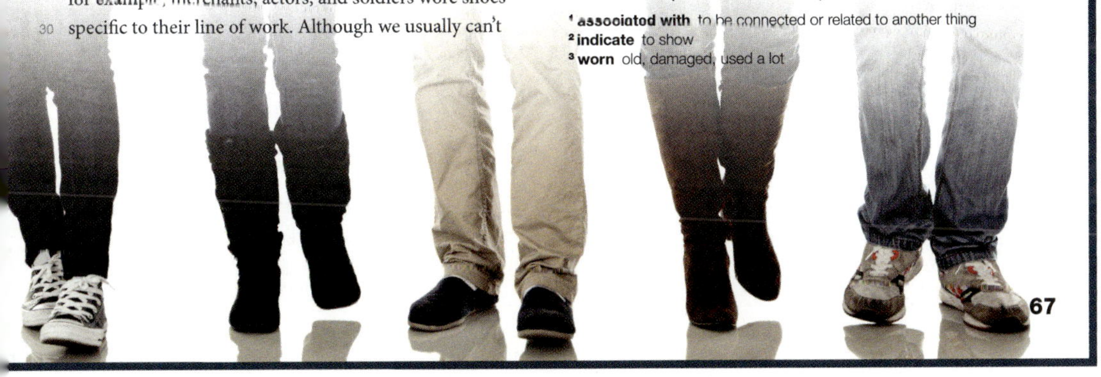

67

Background Information

- Sturdy footwear probably originated between 40,000 and 26,000 years ago, according to Erik Trinkaus, an anthropologist at Washington University in St. Louis. Trinkaus studied the foot bones of people living thousands of years ago and says that shoe wearers developed weaker toes because of the reduced stress and increased support that shoes allow.
- Jenna Tedrick Kuttruff, a textile expert at Louisiana State University, points out that of the group of fiber sandals (some as old as 8,000 years) found in a Missouri cave she has examined, no two are alike. Although they didn't need to make them different, people liked having an individual look or style even then.
- Natacha Marro is a boot and shoe designer in London. She has also designed shoes and boots for movies like *Star Wars*.

Purpose for Reading

This article focuses on fashion and personality. The headings of each section can help readers locate information quickly. Suggest to students that they number the sections. Then call out details from the article and ask students which section the information is in (e.g., *attorney, power for women, a rebel, men and women hundreds of years ago, construction worker, Japanese merchants, outgoing character*).

Language Notes

- Point out that in Line 46, the word *signal* means "indicate."
- In the English-speaking world, different words are used to describe the same thing. These variations are called regionalisms. For example, *sneakers* are also called *tennis shoes* in some places, *Keds* in other places, and *running shoes* in others. Also, *high heels* are called *pumps* in some regions.
- There are several hyphenated adjectives in this article: *fashion-conscious, self-confident, high-heeled, 5-inch, low-heeled, multi-colored.* In most cases, these words are hyphenated because they are two adjectives used together to modify one noun. For example, a "high, heeled shoe" might refer to a tall boot with a heel, but a "high-heeled shoe" means a shoe with a high heel.

Beyond the Reading

Have students do research on a certain kind of shoe (e.g., *running shoes, ballet toe shoes, clogs, flip-flops, pumps, slippers, construction boots*). Suggest they search for "history of the (*name of shoe*)." They should look for information on the earliest record of this type of shoe, its purpose, what it is usually made of, and how it has changed over time.

Video

10 min. **A**
10-15 min. **B**
10-15 min. **C**
10-15 min. **D**
Extension: 15-20 min.

Background Information

Louis Vuitton is a famous French fashion house that began in 1854. It is known for the "LV" monogram. They design canvas bags of all sizes, leather goods, and other accessories. When the company started, they made trunks. Louis Vuitton displayed their goods at the Chicago World's Fair in 1893. In 1913, the company opened a store on the famous Champs-Elysees in Paris. At the time, it was the largest travel goods store in the world.

A
- Tell students that they're going to watch a video that will tell them how to spot a fake bag. Direct their attention to the photos. Ask them to predict some of the ways that someone might be able to tell a fake bag from a real bag.
- Preteach the meanings of these words: *crease* (fold), *genuine* (real), *oxidize* (get darker), *monogram* (initials), *piping* (lines along a stitch), *plethora* (many)

Answer: The top right bag is a fake.

B
- Students can write their guesses on a separate sheet of paper before they watch the video, then fill in their actual answers in the book while they watch.
- Play the video one or more times.

Language Notes

Point out these phrases from the video: *go with your gut* = trust your instincts or feelings; *spring for* = buy.

C

Answers: *Step 1:* wrong, 1,000, fake; *Step 2:* crooked, stitch; *Step 3:* tan, red, yellow, brown; *Step 4:* dealer, online, return; *Step 5:* instinct, how much

Video

authentic real, genuine
canvas a type of strong, heavy cloth, used for making clothes and bags
crooked not straight; bent or curved
dealer someone who sells something
fake not real
imitator someone who copies what someone else does
instinct your feeling about something
spot to identify

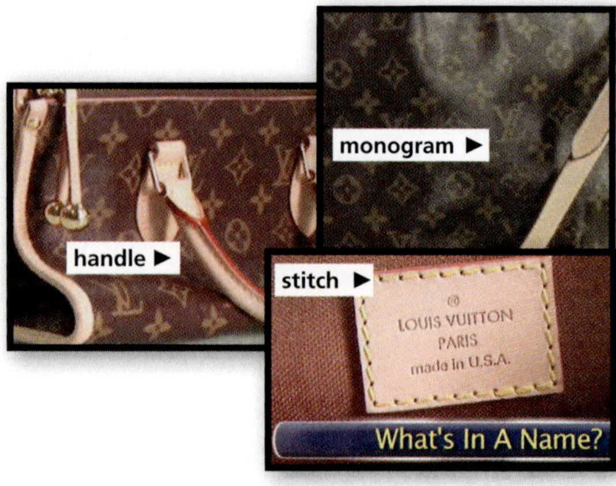

A Discuss the questions with a partner.

1. Do you ever see people selling fake designer goods? What kinds? Why do you think fake goods are so popular?
2. Look at the photos of the handbags. Can you guess which one is real and which is fake? How?

B Read the title of the video. In pairs, try to guess the answers in steps 1–5. Then watch the video once through—without writing anything—to check your ideas.

How to Spot a Fake Louis Vuitton Bag

Step 1: The price is (a.) ____________.
- Most bags sell for over (b.) $ ____________. If you pay less than $300 for a new bag, you're not getting a deal, you're getting a (c.) ____________.

Step 2: Usually the "LVs" on a fake bag are (d.) ____________.
- If you have any LVs that are in a crease or in a (e.) ____________, it is not the real thing.

Step 3: The color of the leather handles should be a light (f.) ____________, with the edge dyed (g.) ____________ and the stitching in (h.) ____________.
- After a few weeks, the handles should change to a darker (i.) ____________. If they don't, the bag is a fake.

Step 4: If you buy a Louis Vuitton bag from a street (j.) ____________, it's not genuine.
- You should also be careful about buying bags (k.) ____________.
- Pay attention to seller feedback and ask about buyer protection and the (l.) ____________ policy.

Step 5: Trust your (m.) ____________.
- If you feel funny about (n.) ____________ you're paying, walk away.

C Watch the video again and complete the first sentence in steps 1–5 in Exercise **B**. Then watch it again and complete the rest of the blanks.

D In addition to designer clothing and accessories, other fake goods sold worldwide include music, movies, car parts, computer software, electronics, and even food and medicine. Would you ever buy any of these goods? Why or why not? Discuss with a partner.

Extension

This video is an example of a how-to video. Have students work in pairs to create the script for a how-to video related to fashion. Brainstorm some ideas with them before they start: *how to tie a tie, how to wear a scarf, how to polish shoes, how to French-braid hair, how to dress for a job interview*. Remind students of the phrases speakers use to indicate the order of events (from Unit 4). Have students present their "videos" to the class.

Speaking

A On your own and on a separate piece of paper, complete statements 1–4 with your opinion.

Shopping and Fashion: What Do You Think?

1. I think people who buy designer goods …
2. I think people who always dress casually …
3. I think men who wear …
4. I think women that wear …

B Get into a group of three people and do the following:

1. Take four small pieces of paper and write a number (1, 2, 3, 4) on each one. Then shuffle them and place them face down on the desk.
2. One person starts by picking up a number. Read your corresponding sentence from Exercise **A** aloud and explain your reasons to the group.
3. The other people in the group should then use the expressions in the Speaking Strategy below to agree or disagree with the statement and each other. When you state an opinion, remember to explain your reasons.
4. Return the number to the pile and then it is another person's turn. Repeat steps 1–3 until everyone has shared all of their sentences from Exercise **A**.

I think people who buy designer goods are probably rich. You need a lot of money to afford those things.

I'm not so sure about that. I know someone who owns several pairs of designer shoes and she isn't rich; she just likes high-quality goods.

Speaking Strategy

Expressing strong agreement
I couldn't agree (with you) more.
Yeah, no question / doubt about it.

Questioning another's point of view
I don't know / I'm not so sure about that.
I guess so, but at the same time . . .
I see / know / understand what you're saying . . . but don't you think . . .

Expressing strong disagreement
I completely disagree.
Are you kidding? (Informal)
No way! (Informal)

Informal phrases can sound rude. Only use these when you strongly disagree and with someone you know well.

69

Rubric	Very Good	Satisfactory	Needs Improvement
Expressing and reacting to opinions coherently			
Use of vocabulary			
Use of grammar			
Pronunciation and fluency			

Speaking

5-10 min. A
35-45 min. B
Extension: 20 min.

A
- Direct students to the "A" speaker in the example dialogue in Exercise **B** to show one way that sentence 1 could be completed. Brainstorm with students some other possible opinions that could be used to complete sentence 1. For example, *I think people who buy designer goods… are probably rich / are wasting their money / are fashion conscious and enjoy dressing well / care about quality*
- Then have students work on sentences 2–4 to create opinion statements of their own.

B
- Go over the steps, the Speaking Strategy, and the Tip. Get students started by stating your own opinion about a fashion topic (e.g., *I think high heels are unhealthy. They damage women's feet and backs.*). Then, call on students and ask what they think. Encourage them to use an expression in the strategy box to respond.
- Put students in groups of three. Monitor groups' conversations to complete the rubric.
- Call on groups to share their ideas with the class.

Outcome: Upon completing this exercise, students will have met the Outcome ***react to other points of view.***

Extension

Write the sentence stems from Exercise **A** on the board. Call a group of students (different from the groups in Exercise **B**) to the front of the room. Have one of the students complete a sentence stem. Call on 2–3 others to express agreement or disagreement using the expressions from the strategy box. Continue with other sentence stems and other students. When everyone has expressed an opinion, call another group to the front.

Writing

10-15 min. **A**
10-15 min. **B**
10-15 min. **C**
10 min. **D**
Extension: 10-15 min.

Purpose of Writing

When presenting and defending an argument in writing, students will usually need to use expressions of contrast and concession. A strong argument acknowledges the strengths of the opposite point of view, but the writer follows by demonstrating how his or her argument is stronger or better. Review these expressions that signal contrast or concession: *While that may be true… / However, … / Although … / Even though … / While …*

A Have students read the paragraphs individually, or read them aloud as they follow along silently.

Answers: 1. Selling fake goods is wrong. 2. People who sell knockoffs sometimes trick buyers into purchasing something. 3. (1) *opposite opinion:* Most people can't afford to pay full price for designer items. (2) *opposite opinion:* A lot of people think it's easy to spot fake goods because the quality is poor or the brand name is different.

B After students have created their charts, have them show the charts to a partner in order to ensure that everything makes sense.

C Write ways to introduce opposite opinions on the board. (*Many people think … / A lot of people think … / Some people believe / feel … / For some people, ….*

Outcome: Upon completing this exercise, students will have met the Outcome *present and defend an argument.*

Extension

Have students think of two arguments they could make about fashion. Then have the students stand in two lines facing each other. Students in line A give an opinion and a reason to support it. Their counterparts in line B must respond with the opposing opinion and a reason. Remind them that their responses do not necessarily reflect their own opinion. Then A and B switch roles. When they have had a turn in both roles, have line A move one position to the right and repeat.

Writing

Present and Defend an Argument

A Read the paragraphs. Then complete the steps below with a partner.

I think selling fake goods is wrong. Some people might disagree with this opinion, but I believe there are two important reasons why I'm right. First, people who sell fake goods, or "knockoffs," are stealing money from the original product manufacturer.* This is not fair. Of course, <u>many people who buy fakes say</u> they can't afford to pay full price for name brands. **While that may be true**, buying or selling fake goods is still a form of stealing and it is wrong.

Second, people who sell knockoffs sometimes trick buyers into purchasing something. These days, there are lots of Web sites that sell fake products as "the real thing." Shoppers think they are buying a designer handbag or MP3 player at a discounted price. In reality, they are buying a knockoff, but they don't know it. <u>A lot of people think</u> it's easy to spot fake goods because the quality is poor or the brand name is different. **However**, it's often hard to tell the difference between fake and real items that are sold online. For these reasons, I think selling fake goods is wrong.

***manufacturer** maker

TIP Stating an opposite opinion and explaining why you think it is weak can help support your argument.

1. List the writer's main argument (paragraph 1) in the chart below.
2. The writer gives two reasons to support the argument. Write the second one under "reasons."
3. He also states two opposite opinions from other people. What are they?

The main argument: ______	
Reasons	**Opposite opinions**
1. *People who sell fake goods are stealing money from the original manufacturer.*	1. *Most people can't afford to pay full price for designer items.*
2.	2.

B Read the sentence and follow the steps below:

I **think / don't think** buying designer brands is a good way to spend your money.

1. Circle the word(s) in the sentence that express your opinion.
2. On a separate piece of paper, create a chart like the one in Exercise **A**. List two reasons to support your argument. Also think of an opposite opinion for each of your reasons.

Writing Strategy

Making a successful argument When you argue a point, you should . . .

- clearly state what your opinion is. Are you for or against something?
- give reasons that support your opinion.
- include opposite opinions using expressions like the ones underlined in the sample. You should also show why you disagree with those opinions using expressions like the ones in bold in Exercise **A**.

C Write two or three short paragraphs that argue your point, using the information in your chart.

D Exchange papers with another student. Read your partner's writing. Does your partner successfully follow the Writing Strategy?

Rubric	Very Good	Satisfactory	Needs Improvement
Content			
Defending an argument against opposite opinions			
Use of grammar			
Organization			

Expanding Your Fluency

A Read the short passage. Then answer the questions with a partner.

You've been to sales at department stores. You've purchased things online at discount prices. Perhaps you've even visited a flea market and found a few bargains. But have you ever shopped at a store where everything was *free*? Stores like this have existed for years all over the world, and today they are growing in popularity.

How does a free store work? People bring in goods that they don't use anymore: clothing, electronics, bikes, furniture, art, jewelry, books, music. The items must be good quality; they can't be old, worn, dirty, or broken. People who come into the store can also take anything they want—without paying for it. A free store isn't only for those who can't afford to buy new things, though. The goal of these stores is to encourage *all* people to reuse items, not to throw them away or to keep buying new stuff all the time.

1. What is a free store and how does it work?
2. Who shops at a free store?

B Complete the sentences with your opinions. Think of two reasons to support each opinion.

1. I think a free store **would / wouldn't** be a good addition to my neighborhood because. . . .
2. I think everyone **should / shouldn't** be allowed to shop in a free store because. . . .

C Discuss your opinions in pairs. Use the expressions in the Speaking Strategy on p. 69 to agree or disagree with each other.

Check What You Know

Rank how well you can perform these outcomes on a scale of 1–5 (5 being the best).

_________ describe shopping habits and fashion preferences
_________ use adjective clauses to explain and define people and things
_________ react to other points of view
_________ present and defend an argument

Expanding Your Fluency

10-15 min. A
10-15 min. B
20-25 min. C
Extension: 10-15 min.

A Read the paragraphs aloud to the class, or have students read them silently to themselves. Alternatively, students can form pairs first, with each reading a different paragraph out loud to the other.

Answers: 1. A free store is a store where everything is free. People bring in the things they don't use anymore, and other people can take them home. 2. Anyone can shop at a free store. The goal is to encourage everyone to reuse things.

B Provide alternative sentences for students to complete with their own opinions:

- I would / wouldn't shop at a free store because ___.
- I think shopping at free stores is / isn't better than shopping at regular stores because ___.
- I think free stores are / aren't good for the economy because ___.
- Free stores are / aren't a good way to reuse items because ___.

Check What You Know

Refer students back to the exercises in the unit where each Outcome is addressed.

- *describe shopping habits and fashion preferences:* Vocabulary, Exercise **A**, page 62
- *use adjective clauses to explain and define people and things:* Grammar, Exercise **C**, page 63
- *react to other points of view:* Speaking, Exercise **B**, page 69
- *present and defend an argument:* Writing, Exercise **C**, page 71

Extension

Have students write down three things they have at home that they no longer use and could give to a free store. Put students in small groups to describe the items. Have their classmates make suggestions about different ways the thing could be reused. Encourage them to be creative. For example, if someone has an old armchair, they could cut off the legs and make a doggie bed or they could use it as a coat rack by the front door.

Unit 7
On the Move

Unit Overview

- Unit 7 is about transportation and how we get around. Students will learn about different modes of transportation. They will discuss the advantages and disadvantages of each in a variety of contexts and think about the impact of their choices.
- Many factors influence the decisions we make about how to get around: distance, location, transportation options, timing, cost, effect on the environment.
- Ask students what they think is meant by the unit title, "On the Move." Explain that the expression "on the move" refers both to the physical act of transportation and to a general sense of action, busyness, or progress.
- Preview the unit by asking students the following questions:

1. How many different forms of transportation have you used in your life? Name as many as you can.
2. What is your favorite way to travel to a friend's house? To school? To another part of your country?
3. How do you think transportation will change in the next fifty years?

Photo Caption

This image is of the Royal Scotsman Train on a bridge over Loch Awe in Scotland, United Kingdom. The Royal Scotsman, or Royal Scot, was an express passenger train that first ran in 1862. It traveled between London Euston and Glasgow Central stations. Originally powered by steam engines, the train converted to diesel and electric engines in the twentieth century. The Royal Scotsman stopped running in 2003.

7 On the Move

VOCABULARY	GRAMMAR	LISTENING	VIDEO
Advice on how to get around your city	Comparative forms	A commuter's diary **Strategy:** Listening for connections between ideas	*Capital Bikeshare*

1 What do you think of when you hear the expression "on the move" (traveling to school or work, taking a trip, moving to a new place, or something else)?

2 Look at the photo and imagine the people that are traveling. Who are these people and where are they going? Why do you think they're on the move?

3 What's the most routine trip you take? What's the biggest trip you've ever taken?

Unit Outcomes

In this unit, you will learn to:

- make comparisons
- recognize cause-and-effect relationships
- make a complaint and propose a solution
- use facts and evidence to defend a position

73

5-10 min. **Warm-Up Questions**
Extension: 10-15 min.

Background Information

The United States has a reputation as a car culture. Over 254 million personal vehicles are registered in a country whose population is just over 300 million. The United States also has the world's most extensive railway network, with nearly 140,000 miles of track. Russia, China, and India occupy the second, third, and fourth places in this ranking. However, much of this track is used to transport freight, not passengers. Japan, India, and Germany transport the most people by train each year, and Belgium is the country where the highest percentage of people travel by train in relation to other modes of transportation.

Warm-Up Questions

- Read Question 1 aloud. Have students share their ideas about movement. For each type of movement mentioned, ask them what mode of transportation they use.
- Divide the class into small groups to discuss Question 2 and then report back to the class. Ask students if they have ever traveled by train. Have volunteers describe their experiences.
- Ask students what is meant by a *routine trip*. If necessary, explain that a routine trip is a trip someone takes regularly, perhaps every day or every week, such as the trip to school or work.

Extension

Divide the class into four groups. Assign each group a different mode of transportation: train, car, bicycle, and subway. Have the groups discuss their assigned modes of transportation and prepare a list of pros and cons to present to the class.

WRITING	READING	SPEAKING	OUTCOMES
Write a letter of complaint	*One Foot on the Gas:* Children of Immigrants Discover American Car Culture	Consider the facts in an immigration case Strategy: Presenting facts and announcing a decision	• make comparisons • recognize cause-and-effect relationships • make a complaint and propose a solution • use facts and evidence to defend a position

Vocabulary

15-20 min. A
10-15 min. B
15-20 min. C
Extension: 10-20 min.

A • Ask students, *Which mode of transportation is the most comfortable? The safest? The most environmentally friendly?*
- Explain to students that the noun form of *commute* is presented here, but it can also be used as a verb: *Ryan commutes by bus.*
- Ask students to explain the literal meaning of *fit (in)* and explain how it is related to the figurative meaning of belonging.
- Explain that the verb form of *transfer* is presented here, but it can also be used as a noun: *You need to make a transfer at the bus station.*

B Ask students if Vanessa's advice would be good advice for their town or city.

Answers: 1. overwhelming; 2. options; 3. delays; 4. punctual; 5. keep in mind; 6. rush hour

C Ask volunteers to present to the class the best ways to get around your town or city. For extra practice, give students these additional sentences to complete: 6. Rush hour here is between . . . and . . . ; 7. . . . is (not very) punctual and (or) reliable. 8. People here tend to . . .

Photo Caption

This image is of a mass of commuters making their way through Grand Central Terminal in New York City. Commonly known as Grand Central Station, it is one of the biggest train stations in the world with 44 platforms and 67 train tracks. Over 21 million people pass through Grand Central each year.

Vocabulary

A **How do people get around where you live—by bike, car, train? Make a list of all the modes of transportation (including walking). Then answer these questions with a partner.**

Which mode of transportation is best when you . . .

1. are going to work or school?
2. want to take a long trip?
3. don't have a lot of money?

commute the daily journey you make between your home and work or school
cramped not big enough for the number of people or things in it
delay when you have to wait longer than expected for something to happen
fit in to feel that you belong to a particular group and are accepted by them
keep in mind to remember something important (often a warning / advice)
option something you can choose from a group of alternatives
overwhelming difficult to fight against
punctual on time; not late
reliable trusted to work or behave well
rush hour the times of day when most people are traveling to and from work
tend likely to behave in a particular way
transfer to go or move something from one place to another

Other expressions with *keep: ~ your promise/ word, ~ an appointment, ~ a secret, ~ up*

B **Read Vanessa's tips about getting around her city. Use words from the list above to complete her advice.**

Getting around a big city can be (1) __________. There are so many transportation (2) __________ that it's hard to know which one to choose. Here's my advice. When you have to travel a long distance, think twice before getting into a taxi. They can be expensive, and heavy traffic can result in frequent (3) __________. Take the subway instead. It may not always be (4) __________, but it's reasonably priced, clean, and reliable. You should (5) __________, though, that most locals use the subway to commute to and from work or school. Allow extra time if you have several transfers to make. If you don't like cramped spaces, it's best to avoid the subway during (6) __________. For short trips, you can simply walk to your destination. If you do all these things, you'll fit in just like a local!

74

C **How does your city or town compare to Vanessa's? Work with a partner to complete these sentences.**

1. When you have to go a long distance, you should . . .
2. For short trips, it's best to . . .
3. When it comes to commuting, most locals . . .
4. The best way to avoid delays is to . . .
5. The most important thing to keep in mind is . . .

Extension

Have students consider their suggestions from Exercise **C** and discuss with a partner how transportation could be improved in their city or town. Ask them to choose one suggestion and write a paragraph describing their proposed improvement and why it is necessary.

Grammar

A Compared to five years ago, which of these sentences describes rush hour in your city or town today? Complete the sentences with the correct comparative form of *convenient*. Then choose an answer.

a. It's ________________ to get around than it was before. (It's better.)
b. It's ________________ than it was before. (It's worse.)
c. It's about the same.

TIP We don't usually use *less* with one-syllable adjectives. We use *not as . . . as* instead. *~~The bus is less fast than the train~~. The bus is not as fast as the train.*

Comparative Forms			
	more than . . .	**less than . . .**	**equal to . . .**
Adjectives	Taking a taxi is **faster** and **more reliable than** taking the subway.	The subways are **less reliable than** they used to be. They are **not as nice as** they once were.	During rush hour, walking is **as fast as** taking the bus.
Adverbs	The trains run **faster** and **more frequently** than the bus.	The trains run **less frequently** on weekends than they do on weekdays.	The old trains run **as smoothly as** the new ones.
Noncount nouns	After I quit, I had **more time than** I used to.	As a new parent, I have **less time than** I used to.	I spend **as much** time working **as** (I did) before.
Count nouns	The local train makes **more stops than** the express (does).	The express train makes **fewer stops than** the local (does).	The Blue Line has **as many riders** as it did last year.
Irregular forms: good → better, bad → worse, far → further			

B Make sentences comparing these two subway lines. Which would you prefer to ride?

	Blue Line	**Green Line**
number of riders	140,000 per month	100,000 per month
train tracks	2 years old	15 years old
daily schedule	weekdays: every 5 minutes weekend: every 16 minutes	weekdays: every 5 minutes weekends: every 12 minutes
on time schedule	arrives late 8% of the time	arrives late 2% of the time
cleanliness	moderately clean	very clean
hear the announcements	clear 97% of the time	clear 82% of the time

C You are going to talk about the best way to travel between two points. Work with a group.

1. Choose a starting point and an ending point in a place you know well. The points should be far enough apart to require a combination of public transportation, driving, or walking to get there.
2. Think of two different routes you could take to get to your final destination.
3. Compare the pros and cons of the two routes using comparative language.

Extension

Share the following information with students about commuting patterns in the United States. According to a 2009 survey, 76% of people drive alone to work, 10% carpool, 5% take public transportation, 3% walk, and 4% work at home. Explain that *carpooling* means driving to work with a group of people. Have pairs of students write six sentences comparing the different modes of transportation and comparing these trends to transportation patterns where they live.

Grammar

15-20 min. A
10-15 min. B
15-20 min. C
Extension: 10 min.

A
- Go through the chart as a class. For each comparative form, give additional examples relating to your city or town. Have students compare where they live to another place they have seen or learned about.
- Tell students that *far* has two different comparative forms: *further* and *farther*. Explain that *farther* is used to compare physical distances (*I have to travel farther than you do to get to school.*), while *further* is used in figurative comparisons (*Check our Web site for further information.*).
- Read through the Tip as a class. Have students repeat Exercise **A** with the comparative forms of *easy*, *hard*, and *difficult* in order to practice the forms of single- and multiple-syllable adjectives.

Answers: a. more convenient; b. less convenient

B To reinforce comparative forms, ask students to compare which characteristics of the two lines are more important, less important, and not as important in their opinions.

Sample Answers: The Blue Line has more riders per month than the Green Line. The Green Line has fewer riders per month than the Blue Line. The train tracks on the Blue Line are newer than / not as old as the train tracks on the Green Line. The train tracks on the Green Line are older than / not as new as the train tracks on the Blue Line. The Blue Line runs as frequently as the Green Line on weekdays. On weekends, the Green Line runs more frequently than the Blue Line. The Blue Line doesn't run as frequently as the Green Line. The trains on the Blue Line arrive late more often than the trains on the Green Line. The Green Line is more punctual than the Blue Line. The Green Line is cleaner than the Blue Line. The Blue Line is not as clean as the Green Line. You can hear the announcements on the Blue Line more clearly than the announcements on the Green Line.

C **Outcome:** Upon completing this exercise, students will have met the Outcome *make comparisons.*

Listening

5-10 min. A
15-20 min. B
20-25 min. C
Extension: 15-20 min.

Background Information

Students will hear a radio news broadcast about commuting in a big city. After an introduction from the radio host, a reporter describes his morning commute to work as an audio diary.

A
- Review the phrasal verbs *pull in, pull out,* and *get in.* Explain that the subject of *pull in* or *pull out* is either the vehicle itself or a person who is driving or riding in the vehicle: *The train pulled in on time. We pulled out of the station late.*
- Survey the class to find who has the longest commute. The shortest? The most transfers?
- Review comparatives by having pairs of students compare their commutes.

B
- Read through all the items with the class before playing the recording. Have students guess what Jeremy's commute is like and what topics he will address.
- Point out the expression *break down*, which is stated twice in the audio. Explain that *break down* means to stop working.
- Play the audio recording of the news broadcast one or more times. **Audio CD Track 14**

Answers: 1. increasing; 2. the suburbs; 3. common; 4. near; 5. standing; 6. more than one train

C
- Give the class time to read the items before you play the recording.
- Play the audio recording, and pause after each break in the story for students to mark their answers. **Audio CD Track 15**
- Have students discuss the Ask and Answer questions in pairs. Explain that a *hub* is a central place where you can transfer between two or more types of transportation. Ask students to write four sentences comparing their city's transportation hub to Central Station.

Answers: 1. older, more, less, less; 2. cleaner, more; 3. worse, slower

Outcome: Upon completing this exercise, students will have met the Outcome *recognize cause-and-effect relationships.*

Listening

get in arrive
pull in / pull out arrive / depart (especially used for vehicles such as trains, trucks, and cars)

A Look at the photo below. How long is your typical commute to school or work?

B Listen to a news broadcast in which the reporter, Jeremy Wexler, talks about his commute. As you listen, mark the correct answer for each item.

1. The average commuting time is **increasing / decreasing**.
2. Jeremy probably lives in **the suburbs / the city**.
3. It is **common / not common** for the 8:12 train to be late.
4. His office is **near / far from** the train station.
5. He's probably **sitting / standing** on the train.
6. Jeremy takes **one train / more than one train** to work.

Listening Strategy **Connecting ideas** Listen for expressions like these that connect ideas. They show a cause-and-effect relationship between one idea and another: *As a result . . . / Because of that . . . / That means that . . . / When that happens . . .*

C Read the Listening Strategy. Then listen again. Mark your answers to show the cause-and-effect relationships that Jeremy describes.

1. The trains are **older / newer**. → They break down **more / less** often. → They run **more / less** frequently. → People are **more / less** likely to find a seat.
2. The stations are **cleaner / not as clean**. → The commute is **more / less** pleasant.
3. Traffic is **better / worse** these days. → Commuting by car is **slower / faster**.

Ask Answer Central Station seems to be the busiest commuting hub in Jeremy's city. What about your city or town? What is the busiest center for transportation? How does it compare to Central Station?

76

Extension

Have students write down some observations about their commute to school in a commuter diary. Encourage them to be creative and challenge them to describe at least two cause-and-effect relationships using the expressions in the Listening Strategy. Have the class vote on the most entertaining story.

Video

availability the fact that something can be used or reached
bottom line the total amount of money a company has made or lost over a particular amount of time
perfect match two things that go or work together successfully

A Read about bikeshare programs. Is there anything like this where you live?

Bikeshare programs provide bicycles for public use as an alternative to driving or taking public transportation. For a small fee, individuals can join the program and use the bicycles for short trips around the city. There are currently about two hundred bikeshare programs worldwide.

Word Partnership

Look at the verbs in blue. What do they mean? Use your dictionary to help you.

I use bikeshare to **get around** town.

I **get on** the bike near the station and **drop** it **off** ten minutes later.

I use bikeshare when I have to **pick up** my son at school.

B Washington, DC is the capital of the United States. The city has a bikeshare program. Follow these steps.

a. Read through items 1–6 below. Can you guess any of the answers?
b. Watch the video once. Don't write anything.
c. Watch again and complete the sentences.

1. **Chris Holbern:** Bikesharing works well in ________ areas. There are 114 ________ and 1,100 bikes. You can join for a year, a ________, or a day. Bikesharing is not only open to residents but ________ too.
2. **Matt Pearson:** The program is great for ________ and it brings more people to the ________ area.
3. **Chris:** The bike has ________ speeds, a basket, a bell, and a ________ for use at night.
4. **Matt:** The bikes are not only safe but ________ too.
5. **Chris:** We have to keep the system ________ and fix the bikes. When a station gets too full, we have a ________ that picks up bikes and transfers them to another ________.
6. **Matt:** Businesses think that bikeshare has improved their ________ ________.

C Read the sentences. Then listen to each speaker in the video and choose the correct answer.

1. 
2. 
3. 
4. 

5. 

____ a. Bikesharing helped me to lose weight.
____ b. I don't worry about anyone stealing my bike.
____ c. I use bikeshare day or night when I'm visiting Washington.
____ d. You can check ahead to see if any bikes are available.
____ e. A lot of professional people like me use bikeshare.

Ask Answer Would you use bikeshare? What are some of the disadvantages of a bikesharing program?

Internet Activity

Have students go to the Capital Bikeshare Web site (http://www.capitalbikeshare.com) to learn more about the program. Then have them write a paragraph promoting the program to tourists planning on traveling to Washington, DC.

Video

10-15 min. A
20-25 min. B
10-15 min. C
Extension: 10-15 min.

Background Information

Students will watch a documentary video about the Capital Bikeshare program in Washington, DC. The city started its bikeshare program in 2008 with only 120 bicycles. In only a few years, the program grew to over 1,200 bikes.

Before You Watch

A
- Point out to students that *bikeshare* is a made-up compound word: *bike + share*. Ask them why they think the program is called "bikeshare."
- Write the words "Pros" and "Cons" side-by-side on the board. Based on the information in the paragraph, have students guess the pros and cons of a bikeshare program.
- Ask volunteers to explain the meanings of *get around* and *get on* in their own words. Have students brainstorm other transportation-related expressions with the word *get*. For example: *get in*, *get off*, *get home*, *get lost*.

B Play the video twice for students.

Answers: 1. urban, stations, month, tourists; 2. business, downtown; 3. three, (built-in) light; 4. solid; 5. clean/operating, van, station; 6. bottom line

Language Notes

Get into the swing of something is to become accustomed to something. *In a big way* means that something will be an important change. *We couldn't be more happy* is another way to say *We couldn't be happier*. *Alleviate* is to reduce or make something easier. *Mobility* is being able to move around easily. *Constructive* is helpful, or improving something. *Zooming* is moving quickly.

C

Answers: a. 5; b. 3; c. 2; d. 4; e. 1

Extension

Have pairs of students discuss the Ask and Answer questions. Each partner should choose one side of the issue and prepare a list of arguments for or against a bikeshare program in their community. Then bring the class together and have the two sides debate the issue.

On the Move 77

Connections

10-15 min. A
15-20 min. B
15-20 min. C
Extension: 10-15 min.

A Ask students to share their experiences with bicycles in the city. Have them consider these questions: *Should bicycles be allowed on sidewalks? Should there be special lanes for bicycles in streets? Should cyclists follow the same traffic rules as automobile drivers? Is it dangerous to encourage tourists to ride bicycles in a city they don't know well?*

B Point out the phrase *sustainable transportation* in Henry's list. Ask for volunteers to explain what they think this phrase means. Explain if necessary. Have the class brainstorm additional modes of transportation that can be considered sustainable.

C
- Encourage students to use the speaking skills they learned in the Unit 6 Speaking Strategy: Reacting to someone else's point of view.
- Have students switch roles and repeat the activity.
- Ask students who they agree with more, Henry or Giovanni, and why.

Extension

Have students imagine they're in the local government and want to address Giovanni's concerns. Have pairs discuss changes they could make to the program that would solve the problems Giovanni mentions. Have them list proposed changes to the program and present them to the class.

Connections

A Read the description of a bikesharing program in Exercise **A** on page 77. Would it work in your city or town? Why or why not?

B Read the facts about the bikesharing program. Then read about Henry's and Giovanni's opinions on bikesharing. Add one more item to each person's list.

Bikesharing program, FACTS
- Membership costs $90 a year.
- Helmets are not provided.
- Five hundred single-speed bikes are available.

Henry

I support bikesharing. I think we should introduce a bikesharing system in my city.

The bikesharing system . . .

— gives you an easy and reliable way to get around town.
— promotes sustainable transportation.
— is a good option when the subways are delayed.
— is easy to navigate—anyone can use it.
— saves you time between transfers.
— means you can avoid cramped subway cars.
— ______________.

Giovanni

I'm against bikesharing. I think we should lower the fares and encourage people to use the subway.

The bikesharing system . . .

— will take taxpayer money to maintain and take money away from other transportation projects.
— will overwhelm the streets with too many bikes.
— doesn't provide helmets for riders and therefore puts people's lives at risk.
— is not suitable for long-distance trips.
— is not affordable for some people.
— ______________________.

C Do a role-play.

Student A: You agree with Henry. Explain why you support bikesharing. Compare it to riding the subway.

Student B: You agree with Giovanni. Explain why you are against bikesharing. Compare it to riding the subway.

Bikesharing is a good idea. For shorter distances, it's faster than waiting for a bus or the subway.

It may be faster in some cases, but it's not as safe. Keep in mind that bikesharing will put more bicyclists on the road. As a result . . .

Internet Activity

Tell students to research bikesharing programs in another city or country. How do the details of the program compare to the proposed bikesharing program in Henry and Giovanni's city? If there are no comparable programs, ask students to describe a bikesharing program that would work in their community. Remind them to use the comparative forms they learned on page 75.

Writing

A Letter of Complaint

A What would you do if bus and subway fares increased two times in one year?

- ☐ 1. Call or e-mail my complaint to the city.
- ☐ 2. Complain to my family and friends about how unfair it is.
- ☐ 3. Just accept it and do nothing.

B Read Joanna's letter of complaint. Then answer the questions with a partner.

Dear Representative Meyer,

Recently you voted against a bikesharing plan for our city. I'm writing to ask that you support it.

As a commuter on the Blue Line, I used to transfer from the subway to the B41 bus to get to my office. As you know, because of the weak economy, there have been transportation cuts. As a result, the B41 bus line has been eliminated, and I have no reliable way to get to work easily.

The distance between the subway station and my office is too far to walk. A cab is one option, but taking a taxi is expensive. I'm feeling very frustrated by this situation.

A bikesharing system would not only be good for the city (fewer people riding in cars means less pollution), but it's also convenient for someone like me: I need to travel between the subway and my office quickly and safely, and riding a bike would be the perfect solution for me!

Thank you for your attention to this matter,

Joanna O'Shea

TIP State your request up front. Present the problem. Show cause and effect where possible.

TIP Offer a solution and explain how it helps.

1. Who is the letter written to?
2. What's Joanna's problem?
3. What caused it?
4. What's her solution?

C Think of a problem you'd like to see changed. Choose from the problems below or use your own idea. On a separate piece of paper, write notes about the problem, its causes, and a solution.

If you live in a city, write about . . .

- the increasing cost of public transportation
- traffic congestion
- cuts in transportation services

If you live in a town, write about . . .

- the lack of a subway or bus system
- poor transportation options to nearby towns
- the lack of easy access to a major airport

D Write a letter of complaint using your notes. Be sure to use the writing tips. Then exchange papers with another student. Read your partner's letter. Does it do the three things on the Writing Checklist? Do you think the request will be granted? Why or why not?

Writing Checklist

Does the letter . . .

1. state the writer's request clearly?
2. explain what the problem is and what caused it?
3. offer a possible solution?

Rubric	Very Good	Satisfactory	Needs Improvement
Content			
Expressing problems and solutions			
Use of grammar			
Organization			

Writing

5 min. **A**
15-20 min. **B**
10-15 min. **C**
10-15 min. **D**
Extension: 15-20 min.

Purpose of Writing

The purpose of a letter of complaint is to identify a problem and its cause(s) and propose a solution to the problem.

A Survey the class to find which approach is most popular. Ask students what issues would drive them to write a letter of complaint.

B
- Remind students of the phrases they learned on page 76 to express cause and effect. Ask them to identify any of these expressions they see in Joanna's letter (*because of*, *as a result*, *means*).
- Brainstorm with students some phrases they can use to state their requests (e.g., *I'm writing to ask / to request / to propose / to suggest* . . .).

Answers: 1. It's written to Representative Meyer, a politician. 2. Her bus line was cut and she has no easy way to get to work. 3. There were cuts in transportation because the economy is poor. 4. She wants the city to start a bikesharing system.

C Have students consider these questions as they plan their letters: *What is the problem and what caused it? Who is responsible for the problem? Who can solve it? In other words, who should they write to? How can the problem be solved? Are there any negative consequences to this solution?*

D Have students present their problems and solutions by reading their letters aloud. Then have the class vote on the most achievable solution.

Outcome: Upon completing this exercise, students will have met the Outcome ***make a complaint and propose a solution.***

Extension

Have students write responses to their partners' letters. Remind them to thank the writer and then address each suggestion. As someone in government, explain which suggestions might be possible to implement and which might be more challenging or impossible.

Reading

5-10 min. **A**
15-20 min. **B**
10-15 min. **C**
10 min. **D**
Extension: 15-20 min.

A Have partners read and discuss the statistics in the chart. Ask them to consider additional questions: *What are the major immigrant groups in your country? What attitudes and traditions from your country are difficult for immigrants to understand? Do you have friends or family who have moved to another country? Where? What attitudes surprised them about their new country?* Refer students to the explanation of *attitude* on page 81.

B Have students read the article, read the options for main point, and reread the article before answering.

Answers: c. The student body is diverse, but they all share an interest in cars.

C
- Give students time to read the questions and review the article before grouping them with their partners.
- After students have identified the answers to these questions in the reading, have partners answer them again from the perspective of students in their culture.

Answers: 1. 16 years old; 2. A car means freedom and you can go anywhere. You can get away when life is overwhelming. 3. They want to go to the beach or to New York. 4. They want a cool, attractive car that makes a statement. 5. Their parents want their car to be economical, affordable, and safe. 6. No talking or texting on your cell phone while driving. Wear your seatbelt. Don't drive too fast. Driving in rush hour is not allowed. Bring the car home on time.

D
- Explain that *get away* means to go somewhere different, not just a long distance from where one is.
- Point out the expression *make a statement* and ask students what they think it means. If necessary, explain that *to make a statement* is to do something that shows what you like and what you think is important. Ask students for examples of other ways that people make statements (for example, with clothing, music, food, etc.) and have them explain their answers to a partner.

Reading

A Read the statistics below and then ask your partner: How does your country compare to the ones in the chart? Do many people from other nations come to live in your country permanently or temporarily? If so, where do they come from?

People all over the globe are on the move, with many moving permanently or temporarily to a country other than their own.

Country	% of the population that is foreign-born
Canada	18.7%
India	0.5%
Singapore	42.6%
Germany	12.3%

B Read the article. What is the main point of this article?

a. The parents and students disagree over cars and driving rules.
b. All students dream about getting away and going somewhere fun.
c. The student body is diverse, but they all share an interest in cars.
d. The students' diverse backgrounds help them to get a driver's license.

C Quickly find and underline the answers to questions 1–6 in the reading. Then take turns asking and answering them with a partner.

1. How old do the students need to be to get a license?
2. Why do they want a car?
3. Where do they want to go?
4. What kind of car do they want?
5. What kind of car do their parents want them to drive?
6. What are some of the rules they have to follow?

D Look at these ideas from the reading about driving. What do you think they mean? Which ones do you agree with?

1. "Your car is your life."
2. "Doesn't everyone want to get away?"
3. "The teens want a new car that makes a statement."

Ask Answer In the United States, a driver's first car symbolizes independence and adulthood. Does driving have the same meaning for you? What symbolizes independence in your culture?

Extension

Have pairs of students imagine that one of them is a teenager who wants a car and the other is a parent who does not want him or her to have a car. Have them role-play the conversation, using the strategies for proposing a solution they learned on page 79.

ONE FOOT on the GAS

Everyone has a backpack. Boys tend to wear jeans and T-shirts; girls wear skirts or pants. Boys and girls wear earrings and talk about the same music. To an outsider, it looks like just another typical day at J.E.B. Stuart High School.

But running beneath the common fashion and attitude[1] are their cultural differences at home: many of the students have parents who came to the United States from other countries. Walking through the halls of Stuart, one meets students from a variety of different backgrounds: an African American, an Afghan Italian, a Cambodian, and a Palestinian. The students take pride in their diversity even as they try to fit in as everyday American teenagers.

Conversations, especially among the boys, quickly turn to cars. "A car means freedom," one says. "You can go anywhere—your car is your life." One boy, who is saving his part-time job earnings[2] for a car, says, "With a car I could go with my friends to the beach or to New York. Life in general can get overwhelming sometimes. Doesn't everyone want to get away?"

And get away they do. Teenagers in many states in the United States can get a license at the age of 16 and most are eager to start driving right away. Teen drivers have a higher rate of road accidents, however. Because of that, the student drivers at Stuart will have to follow their parents' rules: No talking or texting on your cell phone while driving. Remember to wear your seat belt. Don't drive too fast. Commuting to school is all right, but driving in the city's rush hour is not allowed. When taking the car out, remember to bring it home on time. Being safe, reliable, and punctual is important, say parents.

For most new drivers, it's important for a car to be attractive and cool: They want a new car that can "make a statement." Their parents, on the other hand, are looking for a car for their child that is economical, affordable, and most of all, safe. As a result, most teens start driving with the family car that's available—which is usually the oldest, least attractive one of the bunch.

Back at Stuart High, at 2:05 p.m., the school day ends, and a rush to buses and cars begins. Some students get rides with parents or friends. Others get to drive themselves. Music blares[3] from car radios and the kids who are left behind sit on the grass talking, laughing, and just hanging out with friends.

These are normal American teenagers whose parents happen to come from all over the world. They may have one foot in their parents' culture, but they share one thing with their US-born classmates: They all have one foot on the gas pedal . . . and they are ready to go!

[1] **attitude** the way you think and feel about something
[2] **earnings** the money you make while working
[3] **blare** to make a loud, unpleasant sound

81

Purpose for Reading

Throughout this unit, students have been discussing different modes of transportation, but primarily public transportation options in cities. In this article, students will read about American teenagers' feelings about cars and driving. Ask students: *Do you have a car? Would you like to have a car? What are the advantages and disadvantages? Is it dangerous for a 16-year-old to drive a car? Is it common for teenagers in your country to have their own cars?*

Photo Caption

The students in this image are in a convertible, a car whose roof can be removed. For some drivers, a convertible is a symbol of freedom and leisure. Ask students: *Do you know anyone who drives a convertible? Are convertibles cooler than hardtop cars? Are they more practical? Where do you think the students are in this photo? What are they looking at?*

Language Notes

- Explain that *running beneath* (line 6) describes something that exists without being seen.
- *Take pride in* (line 12) means *are proud of*.
- When a conversation *turns to cars* (line 16), the topic changes to be about cars.
- *Bunch* (line 40) refers to a group of things; in this case, the cars that a family has.
- When the author says that students have *one foot in their parents' culture* (lines 49–50), it means that part of the students' identity is their parents' culture, but part of it (the other foot) is not.

Beyond the Reading

Point out the sentence *Get away they do (line 22)*. Ask students to rephrase this sentence in a more familiar word order: *They (do) get away*. Have them guess why the author expresses the idea this way. Point out that the phrase *get away* appears at the end of the paragraph immediately before this sentence, and show them how the repetition of this phrase at the beginning of the next sentence draws attention to it and makes a clear transition between the paragraphs. Have students write their own paragraphs using this structure and share them with the class.

Speaking

10-15 min. **A**
30-40 min. **B**
Extension: 10-15 min.

A
- Have students use the Internet to learn more about Mali (http://travel.nationalgeographic.com/travel/countries/mali-guide). Ask volunteers to share what they know about the country.
- Before students begin reading, review the meanings of words and expressions related to immigration: *papers* refers to visas or permits that allow someone to be in a country legally; if someone is *undocumented*, they do not have the proper papers.
- Quickly survey the class to see if there is consensus about whether Amadou should be allowed to stay. What about his parents?

B
- Give students time to work independently, or with their groups, on their arguments for the case. Alternatively, divide the class into three groups, and have all of the judges and the lawyers for each side discuss additional arguments.
- Review the Speaking Strategy with the class, and ask volunteers to use each of the expressions in a complete sentence.
- Model some possible opening statements for the lawyers. Refer students to the writing tips on page 79 for ways to make a request, present a problem, and show cause-and-effect relationships. Model: *I am here today to ask that Amadou be allowed to stay in this country for several important reasons . . .*
- If there is time, have each group role-play their court case for the class.
- Survey the class again to see if their opinions about the case have changed.

Outcome: Upon completing this exercise, students will have met the Outcome *use facts and evidence to defend a position.*

Extension

Have students switch roles and repeat the role-play, this time discussing the case for Amadou's parents. Does the judge come to a different conclusion?

Speaking

A **Read this information about Amadou and his parents. Then discuss the questions with a partner.**

- Amadou is a first-year college student studying urban planning and transportation. He's an excellent student.
- His parents are from the Republic of Mali. They came to your country with Amadou when he was 2 years old.

- His parents have been working in your country for years without the proper work visas.
- Three months ago, Amadou was stopped for speeding in his car and the police realized he didn't have the proper papers.
- The government wants to send Amadou and his parents back to Mali because they are in the country illegally.
- Amadou wants to stay in your country, finish his education, and get a job.
- Amadou hasn't lived in Mali since he was a baby and he doesn't speak the language.

In your opinion, what should happen? Should Amadou be allowed to stay?

B **Get into a group of three people. Two students will be attorneys (one supporting Amadou's position, the other against it). The other student will be a judge. Follow the steps below:**

1. **Attorneys for and against Amadou:** Read the arguments below. Together, add one or two more reasons to your list. Also think about how you will address the arguments the other attorney presents.

   Judges: Read the arguments below. Together, add one or two more reasons. Also think about how you will address the arguments the attorneys will present.

Why Amadou should stay	Why Amadou should go
1. Amadou only knows this country. If he has to leave now, he may miss the chance to finish his education and have a better life.	1. The law is clear. Amadou's family broke the law when they entered your country on tourist visas and stayed on. They must all leave.
2. Amadou and his parents have worked hard and have never been in trouble with the law.	2. If you allow Amadou to stay in your country, many other foreigners will try to do the same thing.
3. Amadou did nothing wrong. He was brought to your country as a baby.	3. The economy is doing poorly, and many people are unemployed. Amadou and his parents will take jobs away from legal residents.
4. Last year, the government gave special work permits to 200 undocumented foreigners.	4. ______ 5. ______
5. ______ 6. ______	

2. **Begin the role-play.** The attorneys will argue their case for or against Amadou. The judges will listen to each point and can ask questions at any time. Use the Speaking Strategy to help you.

3. **Make a decision.** At the end, the judges should review their notes, consider the attorneys' arguments, and make a decision about Amadou's future. They should then explain their ruling.

Speaking Strategy

Presenting facts When making an argument, it is important to support your position with facts and evidence.

Considering that/Given that Amadou's parents broke the law . . .
Keeping in mind (that) Amadou doesn't want to be separated . . .
If you think about it, Amadou only knows life in this country . . .

Announcing your decision To show that you are making a fair, informed decision, acknowledge that you have heard and understood all the facts presented.

When I look at all the options, it's clear that . . .
After weighing all the options / factors, I have decided . . .
After much consideration, . . .

Rubric	Very Good	Satisfactory	Needs Improvement
Presenting a reasoned argument			
Use of vocabulary			
Use of grammar			
Pronunciation and fluency			

Expanding Your Fluency

Read these statements. Then join a partner and follow the steps below.

Talk about . . .

- the worst commute you ever had
- the first time you drove a car / flew in a plane / took a train
- the longest distance you've ever traveled
- your favorite car and why you like it
- why you would or wouldn't like to join a bikeshare program
- the best way to get around your city or town
- the worst thing about owning a car

1. Flip a coin to decide who goes first (Student **A**). **A** picks a statement and talks about it for a minute without stopping.
2. **B** goes next and can choose any statement except for the one that **A** already talked about.
3. Take turns talking for a minute until all the statements have been chosen once.
4. Award one point when a person can talk successfully for one minute without stopping. The winner is the person with the most points at the end.

Check What You Know

Rank how well you can perform these outcomes on a scale of 1–5 (5 being the best).

_______ make comparisons
_______ recognize cause-and-effect relationships
_______ make a complaint and propose a solution
_______ use facts and evidence to defend a position

83

Extension

Have each student choose an additional topic of conversation related to the unit theme and write it on a piece of paper. Collect the papers and write the topics on the board. Repeat Exercise **A** with these new topics of conversation. Challenge the class to talk for one and a half minutes about each topic.

Expanding Your Fluency

40-55 min.
Extension: 10-15 min.

- Have students read through the topics for conversation. Give them time to work on their own and write notes about each topic on the list.
- Divide the class into pairs and answer any questions they have about the instructions. Give personal examples of your own if necessary. Tell students that you will alert them at the beginning and end of each minute, using your own watch or a clock in the classroom.
- Once students have completed the activity, have them switch partners and repeat. Encourage students to choose topics they did not talk about in the previous round.
- Then, as a class, have volunteers share the most interesting or unusual story they heard from a classmate about each topic.

Photo Caption

This image is of a businessman from Kuwait driving an experimental sports car, a 1960 Plymouth XNR. The XNR was a concept car, meaning a car that was an idea but never mass-produced. It was designed by Virgil Exner, who named it after himself. This model was the only one ever made and was once owned by the Shah of Iran. Survey the class with a show of hands: *Would you like to drive a car like this?*

Check What You Know

Refer students back to the exercises in the unit where each Outcome is addressed.

- ***make comparisons:*** Grammar, Exercise **C**, page 75
- ***recognize cause-and-effect relationships:*** Listening, Exercise **C**, page 76
- ***make a complaint and propose a solution:*** Writing, Exercise **D**, page 79
- ***use facts and evidence to defend a position:*** Speaking, Exercise **B**, page 82

Unit 8
Think Twice

Unit Overview

- Unit 8 is about how closely one's activities are monitored and the consequences for breaking rules. Students will learn about how their actions can have both short-term and long-term implications, and how it's not always easy to foresee the impact that their choices will have.
- Personal information is becoming available to a wider audience online, not only to family, friends, and acquaintances, but to companies and governments. The sharing of this information—sometimes without our knowledge—raises questions about privacy and blurs the line between public and personal.
- Ask students what they think is meant by the unit title, "Think Twice." Explain, if necessary, that it's an expression that means one should consider things carefully before acting.
- Preview the unit by asking students the following questions:

1. How closely do you feel that people are watching what you do every day? Who's watching your activities?
2. What are some things that people might do because they know they won't get into trouble? Do you ever bend the rules?
3. Do you think there should be more rules about what people do online, or more freedom? Explain.

Photo Caption

This image is of a traffic guard watching pedestrians cross the street in the neighborhood of SoHo in New York City. SoHo is known for its appeal to artists, and many live and have studios in the neighborhood. It is also distinguished by its architecture, with many buildings made of cast-iron. Located in Lower Manhattan, SoHo gets its name from its location on "SOuth HOuston" Street.

VOCABULARY	GRAMMAR	LISTENING	WRITING
Text messaging during class	Past modals	Problems with posting online **Strategy:** Determining a speaker's attitude **Pronunciation:** Reduction with past modals	Give an opinion on an event **Strategy:** Writing an effective online post

1 Look at the photo. Where do you think these people are? What do you think is happening?

2 Who is the man in orange? What would he say to the people walking? To the people in the car? Come up with a brief conversation.

3 Is it ever OK to break the rules? If so, when? If not, why not?

Unit Outcomes

In this unit, you will learn to:

- use past modals to consider possibilities, express disbelief and regret, and make logical conclusions
- compare actions to their consequences
- recognize hardship and express sympathy
- respond to a news story with your own opinion

5-10 min. **Warm-Up Questions**
Extension: 10-15 min.

Background Information

Advances in technology in recent years have made individuals more visible and more watched than ever before. The Internet is probably the most obvious example of technology's ability to expose people publically. Much of that exposure is voluntary when people contribute to social networks like Facebook, Twitter, and YouTube. But some exposure is also involuntary, as people's actions can be recorded nearly anywhere and at any time with video surveillance equipment and smartphone cameras. Whether we're aware of it or not, the potential exists for people to see what we're up to nearly every minute of the day.

Warm-Up Questions

- Read through Question 1 as a class. Ask several volunteers to guess where the people are. Work as a class to describe the photo. Ask students if they can guess what is happening.
- Point out the blurry, out-of-focus look of the image. Ask students why they think it appears this way. Is it a mistake, or is the photographer trying to tell us something?
- Have students work with a partner to answer Questions 2 and 3.

Extension

Put students in pairs or small groups to discuss recent stories in the news in which people broke the rules. Have them note whether the circumstances involved people who were caught breaking rules secretly, or people breaking rules publically to make a statement. Encourage them to explain the stories objectively (just facts, no opinions). Then, ask for their points of view on what they reported.

VIDEO	READING	SPEAKING	OUTCOMES
Protecting Reputations Online	*Nowhere to Hide:* What happens when our private lives become public	Evaluate different surveillance practices	• use past modals to consider possibilities, express disbelief and regret, and make logical conclusions • compare actions to their consequences • recognize hardship and express sympathy • respond to a news story with your own opinion

Vocabulary

5-10 min. A
10-15 min. B
10-15 min. C
15 min. D
Extension: 10 min.

A • Conduct a brief survey of the class, asking students if they text message, how often, and when.
• Have students create word families for as many of the vocabulary words as they can. For example, *criticize* → *critic, criticism, critical*.

Language Notes

- Word partnerships with *consequences*: *negative ~, unintended ~, serious ~, long-term ~, suffer / face / consider / accept / understand the ~*
- Word partnerships with *trouble*: *get in / into ~, get out of ~, stay out of ~, cause / make / start ~, run into ~*

B • Ask students what clues in each statement led them to answer as they did.
• Lead a brief discussion with students about the regulations on texting in your class.

C As a class, have students come up with three additional behaviors in class that are disruptive. Then have them answer the questions again for those behaviors.

D • Encourage pairs to work a compromise into the role-play that includes a consequence that is not as severe as the teacher demands at first.
• Ask volunteers to perform their conversations for the class.

Vocabulary

A Students often send text messages during class. Why do you think they do it? Discuss your answers with a partner.

consequences results or effects (of an action)
criticize to express disapproval by saying what's wrong with something
discipline self-control; an action taken to correct inappropriate behavior
disruptive causing trouble and stopping something from continuing as usual
get away with to do something wrong or risky and not suffer any consequences
get into trouble to be in a position where you will be punished for something
punish to take action against someone for inappropriate behavior
regulation an official rule (e.g., made by a government or school)
respectful to be polite and well-behaved towards someone (in authority)
restriction a limit on something

B Read these statements about texting in class. Who do you think said each one? Mark your answers and discuss with a partner. Which statements do you agree with? Why?

	Student	Teacher	Parent
1. I don't know of any restrictions on texting in class. It's not against the regulations, is it?			
2. I think there should be consequences for texting in class: for example, you should be punished in some way.			
3. It's a problem with discipline. Students who text in class are being disrespectful to their teachers and their classmates.			
4. All students would text during class if they weren't afraid of getting into trouble and being criticized by their classmates.			
5. Texting in class may be disruptive, but as long as they can get away with it some students will continue to do it.			

C Read the statements below. Answer the questions with a partner to discuss your opinions of these behaviors. Be prepared to share your thoughts with the class.

- talking in class without raising your hand
- looking at another student's work during a test
- coming to class without completing your homework

1. How are these behaviors disruptive? Which ones are serious discipline issues?
2. What are the consequences of these behaviors?
3. Which of these behaviors do people usually get away with?
4. What kinds of restrictions or regulations should be made to prevent these behaviors?

D In pairs, prepare a conversation where a student is caught texting in class by a very strict teacher. the teacher wants to punish him / her; the student asks for pardon. Use vocabulary from Exercise A.

Extension

Have students write a paragraph about a time that someone broke a rule at school, work, in a game, or some other situation. Encourage them not to use the person's real name. Remind them to use as many vocabulary words (or words in the same word family) as they can. Put students in pairs to share their stories.

Grammar

A Stella got in trouble for texting in class. Read the sentences in the chart to see what other students had to say about it. Then answer the questions.

Past Modals	
Use past modals with past participles to assess real or imaginary past actions.	
Disbelief / impossibility	Jen: Stella **couldn't have**[1] **been** texting. She lost her cell phone recently.
Possibility	Tom: She **might have**[2] **borrowed** a friend's phone to do it.
Logical conclusion	Amy: I heard she was texting her mother. It **must have been** something important.
Regret over an action that <u>wasn't</u> taken	Ed: Even so, she **should have waited** until after class to send a text.
Regret over an action that <u>was</u> taken	Min: I agree. She **shouldn't have disrupted** the class.
[1]or *can't have*	[2]or *could have* or *may have*

1. Who is certain that Stella needed to send a text in class?
2. Who is certain that Stella was *not* texting in class?
3. Who thinks that Stella made a mistake?
4. Who thinks it is possible that Stella was texting in class?

B Choose the correct answer to complete each item.

1. She loves scary rides. She **could have / must have** been excited to go on the roller coaster.
2. He **shouldn't have / can't have** been in the meeting. He was sick at home that day.
3. I'm not sure where Mike is. He **might have / should have** gone to the store.
4. We just needed one more goal and we **could have / couldn't have** won.
5. Our team is better. We **may have / should have** won the game.

C What happened? Read about these five situations. On a separate piece of paper, write 2–3 sentences for each one. Use past modals. Then take turns reading your sentences aloud with a partner.

1. You arrived at your friend's soccer game. You see your friend on the ground being helped by another player. Everyone looks worried.
2. Your coworker gets a phone call and looks surprised. She picks up her car keys and runs out of the office. She leaves her purse behind.
3. You've arrived at school and it's time to submit your homework. When you look in your backpack, it isn't there.
4. Earlier this afternoon, you saw your friend's parents talking to your homeroom teacher. Later you find out your friend has been punished for a month.
5. This morning, you saw your neighbor sitting on the back of an ambulance with a bandage on his head. His car is damaged on one side.

Extension

Bring in photos from magazines or newspapers that show actions in progress or their aftermath (such as a car accident, a natural disaster, people expressing emotions). Distribute the photos and ask students to come up with at least two statements with past modals about the photo. If you have time, students can write sentences and share them in pairs.

Grammar

10-15 min. **A**
5-10 min. **B**
25-30 min. **C**
Extension: 10-15 min.

A Review the chart as a class. Have students practice each type of past modal by coming up with humorous statements. Get them started with one of your own. For example, *John couldn't have talked during class. He was asleep for the whole thing!*

Answers: 1. Amy; 2. Jen; 3. Ed and Min; 4. Tom

Language Notes

- Contrast the use of *mustn't* meaning prohibition (*You mustn't be late.*) with *mustn't have*, meaning logical conclusion (*He mustn't have known what time to come.*).
- There are two more subtle meanings of *could have*: (1) *She could have borrowed it.* —a possibility, but the speaker isn't sure if it happened or not; (2) *She could have had a scholarship.* —a possibility that she didn't take, a missed opportunity.

B As a follow-up, have students make a note of which type of past modal is reflected in each statement (i.e., disbelief, possibility, logical conclusion, regret over action taken, regret over action not taken).

Answers: 1. must have; 2. can't have; 3. might have; 4. could have; 5. should have

C Encourage students to use many different types of past modals.

Possible Answers: 1. It must have just happened. The player should've been punished. 2. She may have received some bad news. She should've taken her purse. She must have been upset because she forgot her purse. 3. I must have left my homework at home. I should've put my homework in my backpack after I finished it. 4. My friend must have done something really bad. They shouldn't have punished my friend for a whole month. 5. He might have had a car accident. He should have been more careful.

Outcome: Upon completing this exercise, students will have met the Outcome ***use past modals to consider possibilities, express disbelief and regret, and make logical conclusions.***

Connections

5-10 min. **A**
10-15 min. **B**
10-15 min. **C**
15 min. **D**
Extension: 10 min.

A
- As a preview, conduct a survey of the class to see how many students have entered their names into a contest for something free. Then ask how many people have ever won anything.
- *enter a contest* = participate in a contest; *entry* = a submission to the contest

Answers: Rules: You have to register online. You have to be 18 or older. You can only enter once.

B Ask for a volunteer to read Mary's situation out loud.

Answers: 1. She entered a contest for herself and her friend Paola. 2. Paola decided to sell the ticket. 3. Mary criticized Paola and now they're not speaking.

C
- Remind students that there are no right or wrong answers in this exercise and that they should respond based on their own opinions about Mary's situation.
- Point out the phrase *after all* in item 5. If necessary, explain to students that it means the same thing as *in the first place* or *to begin with*.

D As an alternative to students' pairing with the same partners they had in Exercise **C**, match students based on which person, Mary or Paola, they are more sympathetic toward. First, ask the class to indicate by a show of hands whom they side with more. Then, match Mary supporters with Paola supporters to make the conversations more interesting.

Connections

A Read the information about a contest. What are the rules of the contest? Would you ever enter a contest like this? Why or why not? Discuss with a partner.

THE CONCERT OF A LIFETIME!
Register at www.freeticket.cengage and win a free ticket to the upcoming rock concert by the Regulation Nation.
Restrictions: Must be 18+. Limit one entry per person.

B Now read about Mary's situation. Then discuss the questions with a partner.

Recently I entered a contest to win a free ticket to a concert featuring my favorite band, Regulation Nation. The contest regulations were clear: only one entry per name. To increase my chances of winning, I also entered the name of my best friend, Paola, without telling her.

My friend's name was chosen and she won the ticket to the concert. I expected her to give me the ticket because I was the one who signed up for the contest and she knows the band is my favorite. I was shocked when my friend said she was going to sell the ticket at full price.

When I refused to buy the ticket, she sold it to someone else. I missed the concert and I criticized Paola for what she did. Now we're not speaking.

1. What did Mary do? 2. How did Paola respond? 3. What happened in the end?

C Read these statements. Indicate if you agree with each one. Then explain your answers to a partner.

	Agree	Disagree
1. Paola must have needed the money.	☐	☐
2. Mary shouldn't have broken the rules in the first place.	☐	☐
3. Mary couldn't have known that Paola would sell the ticket.	☐	☐
4. Mary shouldn't have criticized Paola.	☐	☐
5. Paola and Mary must not have been very good friends after all.	☐	☐
6. Mary should have just accepted the consequences.	☐	☐

D What should Mary and Paola do now? Come up with a solution with your partner and act out a conversation where they repair their friendship.

Extension

In Exercise **B**, students read Mary's side of the story. Have students work on their own to write about the same situation from Paola's perspective. Encourage them to change details slightly to make it sound like Mary has some of the facts wrong. Then ask for volunteers to read their situations aloud as if they were Paola.

Listening

big deal something important
get suspended temporarily not allowed to go to school or class because you've done something wrong
private only for one person or group; not for everyone
sympathetic showing that you understand and care about someone's suffering

A You are going to hear a conversation about student Micah Green. Read this excerpt from the conversation. What do you think Micah did? Discuss in pairs.

Carly: Did you hear what happened? Micah got suspended from school. For five days!
Mark: You're kidding!
Carly: No, I'm not. He got in trouble for posting something online.
Mark: What exactly did he do?

B What happened to Micah? Listen and complete the story.

Micah Green went online to (1) _______ a teacher. He deleted the post a (2) _______ later, but it was too (3) _______. The school (4) _______ Micah by suspending him. The principal said that Micah's posting was disruptive to (5) _______ life. Micah is going to write a letter of (6) _______ to the teacher he criticized.

Listening Strategy **Determining a Speaker's Attitude**
Some set expressions can give clues to a speaker's attitude or feelings. **Sympathy:** *I'm so sorry to hear that. / That's too bad. / I can't imagine what she's / he's going through.* **Surprise:** *No way! / You're kidding!* **Agreement:** *I know! / Tell me about it!*

C Listen again. In your notebook, write key words to answer each question. Write "NM" if the answer isn't mentioned.

1. What does Micah think of Mr. Salazar?
2. What is Mark's opinion of Mr. Salazar?
3. How did Mr. Salazar react?
4. How did Ms. Stevens describe the incident?
5. How do Mark and Carly feel about Micah's situation?
6. What do Mark and Carly think about posting opinions online?

PRONUNCIATION Notice how Mark pronounces *should have* as *should've* in the sentence. *He should've kept it private.* For more information on reduction with past modals, see page 150.

89

Extension

Have students work in pairs to create a conversation between Mr. Salazar and Micah after Micah's suspension. Imagine what each person might say to the other about the incident. Encourages students to use past modals in the dialogue. Then, ask for volunteers to role-play the conversation for the class.

Listening

10-15 min. A
15-20 min. B
15-20 min. C
Extension: 15 min.

Background Information

The practice of "blogging," or writing one's thoughts online for others to read, is a popular way to communicate. The term *blog* is a combination of the words *web log* (*log* is another name for a journal). People blog on various topics. While the mainstream media—newspapers and magazines and their online equivalents—must report the truth, bloggers do not follow the same kinds of rules. They can generally write whatever they want without getting into legal trouble. But sometimes their postings cause enough criticism that they are forced to remove what they've blogged.

A
- Point out that students have learned three idioms with *get*: *get suspended*, *get in trouble*, *get away with something.* Other similar expressions include: *get expelled* (permanently not allowed to go to school or class), *get to someone* (bother someone).
- Write students' guesses on the board about what Micah did. Circle the correct guess after students have listened to the audio.

B
- Play the audio once, and have students complete the activity. **Audio CD Track 16**
- Play the audio a second time, and have students listen for phrases in the Listening Strategy.

Answers: 1. criticize; 2. day; 3. late; 4. punished; 5. school; 6. apology

C
- Play the audio again and have students listen for the words and intonation that show the speakers' attitudes. **Audio CD Track 16**
- Go over the Pronunciation note. Point out to students that Carly also uses a reduction when she says "must've." Mention that in natural speech, these reductions are often pronounced *shoulda* and *musta*.

Answers: 1. worst math teacher; 2. strict; likes his class; 3. NM; 4. disruptive (to school life); 5. angry, sympathetic; 6. actions online have consequences

Outcome: Upon completing this exercise, students will have met the Outcome ***recognize hardship and express sympathy.***

Writing

5-10 min. A 10-15 min. B 15 min. C 10-15 min. D Extension: 10-15 min.

Purpose of Writing

Students will react to an event by writing an opinion as if it would be posted online. Point out to students that online postings should be written clearly, concisely, and respectfully. Remind them that they learned some of the language for expressing opinions in the Speaking Strategy in Unit 6 on page 69.

A

Answers: He criticized one of his teachers online. He was suspended from school for a week.

B
- Ask for a show of hands for who agrees with each of the posts.
- Point out the usernames of the people who posted their opinions. Remind students that people often have unique online names that say something about who they are.

C Before students begin writing, go through the post by "celticsfan" in Exercise **B.** Help them identify how the student's response follows each step in the Writing Strategy. For example, 1. "I go to Micah's school." 2. "As a student…" 3. "Does the punishment fit the behavior, though?" 4. "I think the school could have punished him a different way." 5. "I can certainly sympathize…"

Outcome: Upon completing this exercise, students will have met the Outcome *respond to a news story with your own opinion*.

D Have students write the numbers of the steps from the Writing Strategy on their partners' papers to keep track of which tips were covered.

Extension

For more writing practice, present another scenario: At a public event, someone took a video of a classmate breaking the law and posted it online. Your classmate was arrested and got kicked out of school. Was it okay to take the video without permission? Should the person have been expelled? Have students write their opinions.

Writing

Give Your Opinion on an Event

invasion of privacy when your private life is disturbed in an unpleasant way
responsibility something that is your job or duty to deal with

A Read the short article about student Micah Green. What did he do and how was he punished for it? Discuss with a partner.

> Student Micah Green was suspended from school for a week for criticizing one of his teachers online. Micah is the first student at the school to get into trouble for posting something on a social media site. Micah's parents will be meeting with the school's principal later this week.

B Read these online responses to Micah's situation. Which posting(s) do you agree with? Discuss with a partner.

soccermom As the parent of a child who goes to school with Micah, I'm upset. This is an invasion of privacy. Micah was at home and using his own computer. He was not at school nor was he using school property. I don't know of any school regulations that say you can't express your opinions about a teacher on your own time. Are there any?

celticsfan I go to Micah's school. As a student who spends a lot of time online myself, I can certainly sympathize with his situation. Does the punishment fit the behavior, though? Micah didn't use strong language and he took his post down after a short time. I think the school could have punished him in a different way—maybe by asking him to apologize to the teacher.

teacherman78 Being a teacher is hard work. We don't have very many behavior problems in my school, but there are some students who are disrespectful—just like Micah was. When an incident like this happens, you have to stop it right away. I think you need to make an example of the student. Was suspending Micah the right thing to do? I think so. Students need to take responsibility for their actions. What they do in and out of school has consequences.

C What do you think? Should Micah have been suspended? Write your own opinion to be posted online. Use the tips in the Writing Strategy.

D Exchange papers with another student. Read your partner's writing. Did your partner follow the tips in the Writing Strategy? Is your opinion similar to your partner's? How are your opinions different?

Writing Strategy — **Effective Online Posts**

When posting online . . .

1. Identify your role. *As the parent of a child . . . / I go to Micah's school.*
2. Explain how the issue relates to you. *As an Internet user myself . . . This is an invasion of privacy.*
3. Ask questions for further discussion. *Is that true? / Does the punishment fit the behavior?*
4. Try to summarize your ideas clearly or your audience may lose interest.
5. Remember to be respectful in your posting.

Rubric	Very Good	Satisfactory	Needs Improvement
Content			
Clear, concise, and respectful			
Use of grammar			
Organization			

Video

goofy silly or ridiculous
illegal not allowed by law
reputation the opinion that people have about someone or something; how much they respect or admire it

reputation good / bad / solid ~; impact / harm / hurt / ruin one's ~; put one's ~ at risk

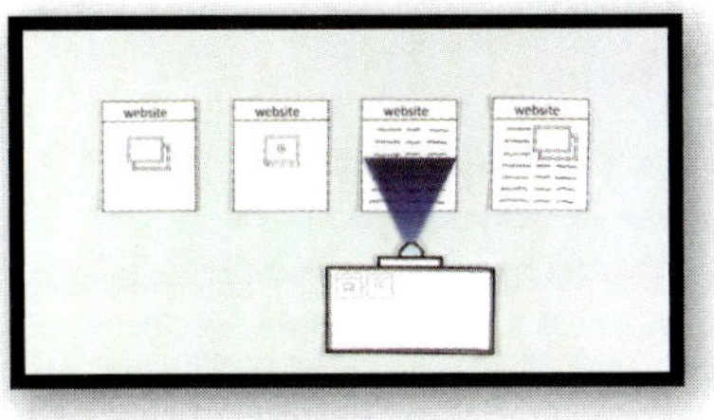

A You're going to watch a video about how to protect your reputation online. Discuss the questions with a partner.

1. What kind of information is available about you on the Web?
2. How could someone harm your reputation online?

B Watch the video. Mark each statement true or false.

	True	False
1. Search engines take pictures of everything posted on the Internet.	☐	☐
2. You don't have to worry about a problematic photo if the image is deleted.	☐	☐
3. It's easy to control who sees the photos you put online.	☐	☐
4. It's possible to hide your postings from search engines.	☐	☐

C Read this list of do's and dont's for posting online. Try to guess the missing words. Then watch the video and check your answers.

Do . . .	**Don't . . .**
think of the ________ who will see the posting (grandfather, boss, etc.)	share everything ________
take ________ for images, videos, and stories you share	use people's ________
ask your ________ to think about what they ________ on the Web	
________ before you click	
________ the person who posted a bad photo of you and ask them to ______ it	

Ask Answer Look back at your answers in Exercise **C**. Do you follow any of these suggestions already? In general, are you careful about protecting your reputation online?

Internet Activity

Refer students to Question 1 in Exercise **A**. In order to answer the question more accurately, have them enter their names into a search engine to find out what kind of information is available about them online. Then conduct a class discussion about what students found. Ask them if their searches revealed anything surprising about them on the Internet.

Video

5-10 min. **A**
15-20 min. **B**
20-25 min. **C**
Extension: 15-20 min.

Background Information

Students will watch an instructional video. Instructional videos are designed to provide helpful information in simple language for people who may not have a lot of previous knowledge about a topic. This video explains the steps that people can take to protect their online reputations.

A Direct students' attention to the word *illegal*. They should know the word *legal*, meaning "related to laws." Point out that the prefix *il-* means "not," so *illegal* means "not legal."

B
- Alternatively, before watching the video, have students guess the answers to items 1–4. Then have them check their guesses as they watch.
- Play the video at least once.

Answers: 1. True; 2. False; 3. False; 4. True

C
- If students prefer, have them write their guesses on a separate sheet of paper and their final answers in the book.
- Play the video again.

Answers: *Do. . .*: think of the people who will see the posting (grandfather, boss, etc.) / take responsibility for images, videos, and stories you share / ask your friends to think about what they share on the Web / think before you click / contact the person who posted a bad photo of you and ask them to delete it; *Don't. . .*: share everything publicly / use people's names

Extension

Have students work in pairs to brainstorm two other things not mentioned in the video that people should *not* do when posting things online. Then have pairs share their ideas with the class as you write them on the board. Once everyone has shared, ask students which idea they think is best by a show of hands. Tally the votes, and have students write the top three ideas in the blank spaces under the "Don't. . ." column of Exercise **C**.

Reading

5 min. **A**
5-10 min. **B**
10 min. **C**
10-15 min. **D**
10-15 min. **E**
Extension: 15 min.

A Point out that the noun form of *anonymous* is *anonymity*.

Answer: a

B Have students read individually, or call on students to read aloud paragraph by paragraph.

C If students have trouble finding the correct words or expressions, you can help them by directing them to the line number where each is found: 1. Line 4; 2. Line 5; 3. Line 6; 4. Line 37; 5. Line 43.

Answers: 1. anonymous; 2. interfere; 3. private; 4. damaged; 5. removed (a video)

D

Answers: 1. the professional and the student; 2. the professional; 3. the student; 4. the professional; 5. the professional; 6. the student

E Remind students that summarizing means using your own words to describe the highlights of a longer story or situation.

Answers: *Consequences for the professional:* everyone still criticizes her for her behavior; *consequences for the student:* he and his friends apologized to the car owner, almost suspended from school, punished by parents.

Outcome: Upon completing this exercise, students will have met the Outcome ***compare actions to their consequences***.

Reading

anonymous made or done by a person whose name is not known

A Look at the photos and the title of the reading. What do you think is the main point of the article? Choose your answer and discuss your choice with a partner.

a. What we do in our private lives can show up online so there's a loss of privacy.
b. There are new ways to uncover a person's identity online so it's impossible to hide.
c. Anyone can post online so it's possible to get away with writing mean comments.
d. Two videos online show that there are negative consequences to behaving disrespectfully in public.

B Read the article and check your answer in Exercise **A**. Were you correct?

C Find the words and expressions in the article that are the opposite of the ones listed below.

Paragraph 1

1. Opposite of *identified* or *known:* ____________
2. Opposite of *leave alone:* ____________
3. Opposite of *public:* ____________

Paragraph 4

4. Opposite of *repaired:* ____________
5. Opposite of *posted (a video):* ____________

D Mark the statements that apply to the professional, the student, or both.

	The professional	**The student**
1. The person's behavior was caught on video.		
2. The video is online even now.		
3. The person damaged someone else's property.		
4. The person acted alone.		
5. The person knows that no laws were broken.		
6. The person said, "I'm sorry."		

E Summarize the professional's and student's stories using the chart in Exercise **D**. Then answer the questions with a partner.

- What were the consequences of their actions?
- Do you think video of them should have been posted online? Why or why not?

Ask
Answer
Imagine that everything you said and did today was posted online. How would you feel? How might you change your behavior?

Extension

Write the words "the professional" and "the student" on several strips of paper. Place them in a container, mix them up, and have each student pick one strip. Then instruct them to write an online post responding to the incident involving the person on their paper. Remind them to use the Writing Strategy on page 90 as they write. Ask for volunteers to read their responses aloud to the class.

Nowhere TO Hide

We used to view the Internet as a place of freedom—a world all its own. When you went on the Web, you could be yourself, take on a new identity and pretend to be someone else, or simply remain anonymous. Whatever you said or did stayed online and did not interfere with your life offline. Likewise, your private life was your own, completely separate from your online identity. You didn't have to worry about things you said or did at work or school showing up[1] on your computer. You could act goofy and it was no big deal.

Nowadays, new technology has changed everything, so that the separation between our two lives is no longer well-defined. What we do offline (in our "real" lives) can now be posted on the Web with a few easy clicks. With cheap cell phone cameras and free video hosting sites like YouTube readily available to anyone, photos and videos taken in public can be put online within minutes, sometimes with damaging results.

A professional in New York City discovered this the hard way. She was filmed on a commuter train on her way home, arguing with the train's conductor. "I lost control," the woman said. "I was very tired from a long day at work and I said some things I wish I hadn't." That short argument had negative consequences because the scene was filmed by another passenger on the train and posted online that evening. Thousands of people are still watching the video every month. "I was disrespectful, it's true," said the woman. "I didn't do anything illegal, but it feels like I did . . . because everyone is still criticizing me. It's been terrible."

A similar story happened in England when a young college student and his friends were filmed roughhousing[2] after a big football match. The young men damaged a car parked on the side of the road, and a video of the incident[3] was posted online and viewed by hundreds of thousands of people. "My friends and I apologized to the owner of the car and offered to pay him for the damages," said the student. "We felt so bad. But the video didn't show that. It only showed us damaging the car." The video was removed after a couple days, but the damage had been done. "I almost got suspended from school over this. My parents punished me. This experience has practically ruined my reputation."

We know that we're losing our anonymity online. And now, it seems we are losing privacy and anonymity offline as well. There are no restrictions around recording video of what happens in public and putting it on the Web. For now, you can get away with doing it.

It used to be a choice to go online and share yourself with the world. Now we are entering a time when someone else may be making that choice for us. In short, we may end up having a public face online—whether we like it or not.

[1] **showing up** appearing
[2] **roughhousing** fighting in a playful way
[3] **incident** an event

Background Information

- YouTube is a video-sharing Web site that currently has 800 million users per month and gets sixty hours of new videos every minute. It was founded in 2005 by Chad Hurley, Steve Chen, and Jawad Karim, three colleagues who had worked together at PayPal, an online payment service. Of all the video content on YouTube, three-quarters is posted from outside the United States.
- The first cell phone with a built-in video camera was released in 2002 by Sprint and Sanyo.

Purpose for Reading

The first two paragraphs of the reading use a common technique in introducing a topic, sometimes called a "turnabout." The first paragraph sets up one situation or set of expectations as it applied to the past. The second paragraph turns it around to express opposite ideas in the present day. You can have students create a T-chart with "Past" and "Present" as the headings where they can note the differences between the two.

Language Notes

This article uses a number of phrasal verbs with non-phrasal synonyms:

take on = assume
show up = appear
get away with = escape
end up = become

Beyond the Reading

Direct students to the second-to-last paragraph (Lines 47–51). In groups of three, have them discuss if they think there should be restrictions against recording some videos in public. They should talk about when it is acceptable and when it isn't. Then have them write two or three regulations that they would like placed on recording public videos. Encourage them to consider the consequences for breaking the regulations they come up with.

Internet Activity

Have students read the blog at http://learning.blogs.nytimes.com/2011/06/22/do-you-worry-about-the-lack-of-anonymity-in-the-digital-age/#more-70851. Specifically direct them to the questions posed to students at the end of the blog. Have students discuss these questions in groups of three or four. Ask for volunteers to share what their groups discussed.

Speaking

5-10 min. **A**
25-30 min. **B**
10-15 min. **C**
Extension: 10 min.

A Direct students' attention to the three images. Ask them to jot down what they think each image depicts without reading the captions. Then have them read the captions for each image and ask if their predictions were correct.

B
- Alternatively, you can assign one of the three surveillance practices to each pair of students in order to focus their discussion more. Encourage everyone to contribute their points of view for each question before moving on to the next one.
- Encourage students to take notes on their partners' observations so that they can report back to the class in Exercise **C**.

C
- If you chose to take the alternative approach mentioned above, ask for one pair of volunteers for each practice to share their conclusions. Other pairs that discussed the same situation should feel free to contribute to the presentation.
- After all topics have been covered, ask by a show of hands which practice students feel is the most important to have in place, and which they feel is the biggest invasion of privacy.

Extension

After your class has determined which of the surveillance practices is the biggest invasion of privacy, have students draft short statements to lawmakers in which they try to persuade them to pass laws against the practice. Refer students to the Writing Strategy on page 33 about using persuasive language in writing. Then ask for volunteers to read their statements to the class as if presenting them to a group of lawmakers.

Speaking

surveillance the careful watching of someone, especially by the police

A We are under surveillance in different ways in our lives. Read about these situations in the boxes near each photo. What do you think about them?

B Discuss the three practices shown on this page and the questions below with a partner. Be prepared to share your opinions with the class.

- How do these different methods help us? How might they be an invasion of privacy?
- Which one do you think is most disruptive to our everyday life?
- What restrictions should be put on these different surveillance methods?
- Are you sympathetic to people who get into trouble in any of these situations? Why or why not?
- What should the punishment be if you get caught doing something illegal in each of these situations?

In the UK, there are more CCTVs (closed circuit televisions) per person than anywhere else in the world. They are used to track and photograph your every move.

Large numbers of people pass through airports every day. To keep everyone safe, new technology is being used to scan passengers who may be carrying dangerous items.

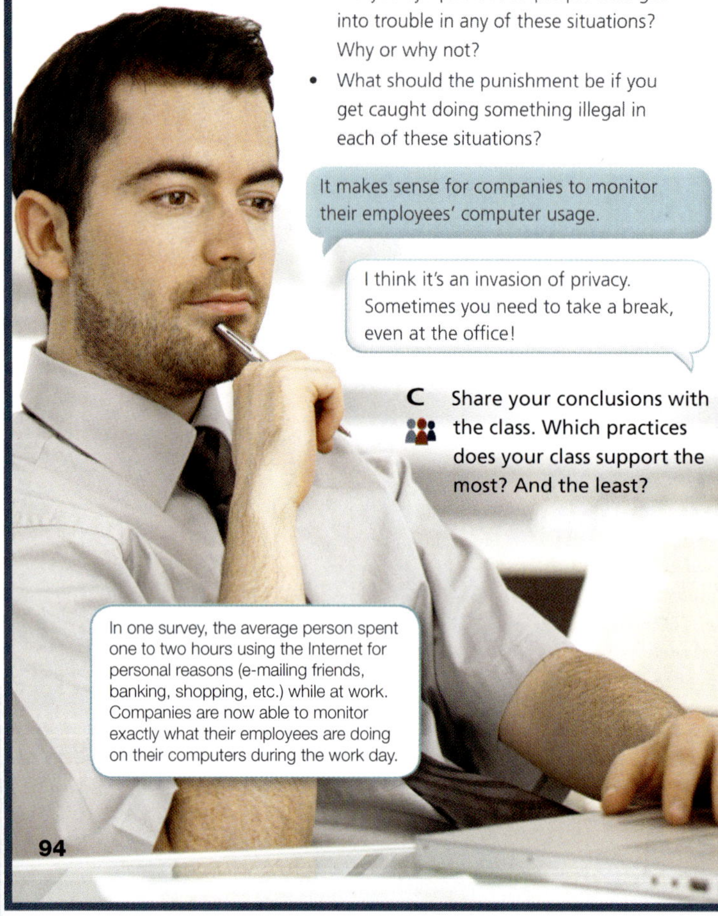

It makes sense for companies to monitor their employees' computer usage.

I think it's an invasion of privacy. Sometimes you need to take a break, even at the office!

C Share your conclusions with the class. Which practices does your class support the most? And the least?

In one survey, the average person spent one to two hours using the Internet for personal reasons (e-mailing friends, banking, shopping, etc.) while at work. Companies are now able to monitor exactly what their employees are doing on their computers during the work day.

94

Rubric	Very Good	Satisfactory	Needs Improvement
Ability to reach conclusions after a discussion			
Use of vocabulary			
Use of grammar			
Pronunciation and fluency			

Expanding Your Fluency

A Look at these two pictures. Where are these people? What do you think might happen in each case? Discuss with a partner.

B Now read about the laws shown in the photos in Exercise **A**.

1. Where I live, your ticket is not checked when you get on the metro. Sometimes, however, police officers make spot checks to see if all passengers have a ticket. Last month, my friend got caught on the train without a ticket. She was so embarrassed. She has to pay a fine of 40 euros.
2. If you smoke, you have to put your cigarette butt in the trash. It's illegal to litter. Last week, my coworker was in a hurry. There was no trash can nearby, so he threw his cigarette on the ground. Then he heard a police officer calling after him. This is the second time he's been caught for littering in a year. He may have to pay a large fine. He's very upset.

C Create a role-play about one of the situations in which you or your partner pretends to know the person involved.

Student A: Tell Student B about your friend or coworker. Explain what happened and how you feel about the situation.

Student B: Listen to the story. Ask questions to get more details. Tell how you feel about it.

My friend Hannah got in trouble on the metro.

What did she do?

She got on the train without a ticket.

Really? She shouldn't have done that!

I know, but she was in a hurry and . . .

Check What You Know

Rank how well you can perform these outcomes on a scale of 1–5 (5 being the best).

________ use past modals to consider possibilities, express disbelief and regret, and make logical conclusions

________ compare actions to their consequences

________ recognize hardship and express sympathy

________ respond to a news story with your own opinion

Expanding Your Fluency

10-15 min. **A**
5-10 min. **B**
25-30 min. **C**
Extension: 10-15 min.

A Point out to students that the man in the left image is a police officer in Berlin, Germany, and that *Polizei* is the German word for "police."

B Ask for volunteers to read each of the laws aloud for the class.

Language Notes

make a spot check = check random people

litter = throw trash on the ground

C Remind students that in real conversations, asking questions is a good strategy for keeping the conversation going. Encourage students playing the "**B**" role to continue asking questions if they feel the conversation slowing down.

Check What You Know

Refer students back to the exercises in the unit where each Outcome is addressed:

- *use past modals to consider possibilities, express disbelief and regret, and make logical conclusions:* Grammar, Exercise **C**, page 87
- *compare actions to their consequences:* Reading, Exercise **E**, page 92
- *recognize hardship and express sympathy:* Listening, Exercise **C**, page 89
- *respond to a news story with your own opinion:* Writing, Exercise **C**, page 90

Extension

Have students review the vocabulary and grammar from the unit. Students will tell a story about a time they made a mistake for which there was a consequence. The situations can be real or imaginary. Give them a few minutes to take notes. They need to use past modals and at least five vocabulary words. Put students in pairs to tell their stories. Call on students to tell the class about their partner.

Unit 9
In the Wild

Unit Overview

- Unit 9 is about animals. Students will learn about the different ways that humans interact with the animal kingdom and the numerous reasons why animals deserve our attention.
- There are more than 40,000 endangered plant and animal species in the world, and over 16,000 of them are at risk of extinction. Among the most critically endangered animals are the tiger, the polar bear, the Pacific walrus, the leatherback turtle, the mountain gorilla, the rhinoceros, and the giant panda.
- Ask students what they think is meant by the unit title, "In the Wild." In this phrase, "the Wild" means natural environments, so it refers to something found in nature or in its natural state.
- Preview the unit by asking students the following questions:

1. Do you have any pets at home? If so, what kind? If not, what pets do other people you know have?
2. Why is it important to help endangered animals?
3. Are the needs of animals ever more important than the needs of humans? Explain.

Photo Caption

This image is of a family of Japanese macaques, or snow monkeys, bathing in the warm waters of an onsen (hot spring) in Nagano, Japan. Macaques are native to Japan and live in the snowy regions of the country. They are the only species of primate—except for humans—known to live in cold climates. Macaques can climb and leap and are known to be excellent swimmers.

9 In the Wild

1 The animal in the photo is a macaque, or snow monkey, and is native to Japan. Is there an animal that is native to or often associated with your country?

2 In your opinion, can animals be intelligent? Which ones?

3 What story about animals was in the news recently? What happened?

Unit Outcomes

In this unit, you will learn to:

- use different forms of the passive voice
- use an outline to summarize ideas
- raise people's awareness about an issue
- write strong sentences to capture your readers' attention

VOCABULARY	GRAMMAR	LISTENING	READING
Three of our favorite pets	Review of the passive voice	Bonobos: Humans' closest relative **Strategy:** Listening for probability	*Orphan Elephants:* A center in Kenya rescues, rehabilitates, and researches baby elephants

5-10 min. **Warm-Up Questions**
Extension: 10-15 min.

Background Information

People have kept wild animals in places where they could be seen by the public for centuries. Long ago, these places were called menageries and were the private collections of kings and emperors. They evolved into zoological gardens or parks, and then eventually public zoos. The oldest existing zoo is in Vienna, Austria. It was the private collection of the Hapsburg monarchy before it opened to the public in 1765.

Warm-Up Questions

- Read through Question 1 as a class. Inform students that snow monkeys are only found in Japan. If students have trouble thinking of an animal that is unique to their country, encourage them to consider species that are common.
- Have students discuss Question 2 with a partner. As a follow-up, ask them if all animals are intelligent in the same way or different ways.
- Have students work with a partner to answer Question 3. If necessary, have them search for stories online.

Extension

Write on the board: *What animal are you most like?* Have students write down their responses and think of reasons why they are similar to the animal they chose. Ask for volunteers to share their answers and explanations with the class.

VIDEO	SPEAKING	WRITING	OUTCOMES
Great Migrations (excerpt), *Saving Elephants from Harm*	Debate what to do about three animals at risk	Write an informational brochure **Strategy:** Getting the reader's attention	• use different forms of the passive voice • use an outline to summarize ideas • raise people's awareness about an issue • write strong sentences to capture your readers' attention

Vocabulary

15-20 min. **A**
25-35 min. **B**
Extension: 15 min.

Language Notes

- Point out other vocabulary word partnerships: *endangered* + ~ species, ~ animal, ~ habitat; *wild* + ~ guess, ~ idea
- Explain that the noun *pet* is also used as a verb, meaning to stroke an animal's fur.
- Point out some words that describe animal behaviors: *scratch, bite, sting, lick, sniff*
- Point out some words for the noises animals make: *bark, meow, chirp, growl, purr, squawk*

A
- Before students match the sentences to the three pets, have them underline the vocabulary words found in the sentences. Clarify their meanings in context, if necessary.
- After students have completed the exercise, you may choose to share these animal facts with them: *Dogs:* Humans have had domesticated dogs for about 10,000 years (#2). Domestic dogs are all members of the species *Canis familiaris*, which is related to wolves, foxes, and jackals (#6). *Parrots:* The African gray parrot is the best mimic of human language in the entire animal kingdom (#3). Some parrot species are highly endangered, but others that had been domesticated have been released into the wild and thrive (#5). Many parrots that are kept as pets live in cages and have clipped wings to prevent them from flying far (#7). *Cats:* The estimated global population of cats is 202 million, more than any other domestic animal (#1). Ancient Egyptians worshipped a cat goddess and even mummified pet cats (#4). While dogs tend to wag their tails to show excitement, cats often swing their tails back and forth while stalking or hunting something (#8).

Answers: 1. Cat; 2. Dog; 3. Parrot; 4. Cat; 5. Parrot; 6. Dog; 7. Parrot; 8. Cat

B
- If necessary, explain the meanings of these phrases: *for sport* = for fun, pleasure, or competition; *at risk* = in danger
- Encourage students to use as many vocabulary words as they can as they discuss the questions.

Vocabulary

attack to try to hurt someone with physical violence
capture to catch a person or animal and confine it
cruel very mean or unkind
domesticated raised by people for agricultural purposes or living with people as household pets
endangered in danger of dying out completely
evolve to slowly change and develop over time into a different form
hunt to chase and kill an animal, usually for food
species a class of plants or animals that have the same characteristics
train to teach a person or animal how to do something
treat to behave in a certain way toward someone
wild free, untamed, not taken care of by people

Notice!
in the wild in nature

adv. *treat (someone)* ***cruelly / fairly / poorly / well***
prep. + n. *treat (someone)* ***with kindness / respect***
neg. ***mistreat*** to treat someone poorly

A Work with a partner to match an animal with a sentence. Then check your answers with the class.

Humans have been keeping animals as pets for thousands of years. How much do you know about three of the most common ones?

	Dog	Parrot	Cat
1. This is the most common household pet in the world.	☐	☐	☐
2. This was the first wild animal that humans domesticated.	☐	☐	☐
3. Not only can this animal sing, it can also be trained to talk!	☐	☐	☐
4. Ancient Egyptians treated this animal like a god.	☐	☐	☐
5. Many wild species of this animal are endangered.	☐	☐	☐
6. This animal evolved from the wolf and was originally used for hunting.	☐	☐	☐
7. Some people believe capturing this animal and keeping it in a cage is cruel.	☐	☐	☐
8. If this animal wags (moves) its tail from side to side, watch out. It's warning you that it might attack!	☐	☐	☐

A parrot

B Discuss the questions with a partner.

1. Do you, or does someone you know, have a pet? Is it trained to do anything?
2. What do you think of people who treat dogs like people (e.g., dressing them in clothes, feeding them at the table)?
3. Do you think it's cruel to hunt wild animals for sport? What about capturing and keeping them in zoos?
4. Name an endangered animal. Why is this animal at risk?

Extension

Explain to students that animal names are sometimes used metaphorically to describe people or their actions. Write the following mismatched list on the board:

chicken	a liar; someone you can't trust
snake	a person who is scared to do something
pig	a follower; someone who isn't able to think on his or her own
sheep	a tattletale; someone who tells on you
rat	a very sloppy, dirty person who eats too much

Have volunteers come forward and draw lines to match the animal to its description (answers in order of the descriptions: snake, chicken, sheep, rat, pig). Point out that all of these names have negative connotations.

Grammar

A Complete the sentences in the chart with the passive form of sentences 2–6. Item 1 has been done as a model. Then check your answers with a partner.

1. People keep the animals in tiny cages.
2. Humans domesticated dogs 15,000 years ago.
3. Humans have trained them to do police and rescue work.
4. A volunteer is caring for the lost cat at the animal shelter.
5. The animal shelter will return the cat to its owner tomorrow.
6. Owners should keep their dogs on a leash.

Review of Passive Voice	
simple present	The animals **are** *kept* in tiny cages. It's cruel.
simple past	Dogs ______ __________ 15,000 years ago.
present perfect	They ______ __________ **trained** to do police and rescue work.
present continuous past continuous	The lost cat **is / was** __________ **cared for** by a volunteer at the animal shelter.
simple future	The cat ______ **be** __________ to its owner tomorrow.
with modals	Parrots **can** *be taught* to communicate with humans. Dogs **should** ______ __________ on a leash.

❶ Forming the passive: Use a form of *be* + the past participle. With modals: modal + *be* + past participle
❷ To show who does the action, use *by* + noun: *The lost cat* **was found** *by a neighbor*.
If it's clear who does the action, or if it's not important, don't use *by* + noun: *Parrots* **can be taught** *to speak*.
❸ You might use the passive if:
- It's obvious who did something or the doer of the action is a general group of people: *Parrots can be taught to speak*. (We know humans are the ones teaching.)
- The action is more important than who does it: *The boy was bitten by a spider*.

B Complete the sentences using the passive form of the verb provided in parentheses.

1. Every year, thousands of cats and dogs (simple present: *abandon*) are abandoned by their owners.
2. Recently a celebrity wearing a fur coat (simple past: *attack*) __________ by a group of animal activists. They say wearing fur is cruel. The celebrity says she (*should / allow*) __________ to wear whatever she wants.
3. In the last forty years, almost 20% of the Amazon rain forest (present perfect: *cut down*) __________ so that cattle (*can / raise*) __________ there. Scientists fear that another 20% of the forest (simple future: *destroy*) __________ by 2030.
4. A millionaire recently died, leaving all her money to her pet dog and nothing to her children. Now her wishes (present continuous: *challenge*) __________ by the family. They say it is unfair that a dog (simple present: *treat*) __________ better than a person.

C What should be done about the issues in Exercise **B**? Work with a partner to find at least one solution for each issue. Then share your ideas with another pair.

Every year, thousands of cats and dogs are abandoned by their owners.

I think the owners should be found and fined!

Grammar

15-20 min. **A**
10-15 min. **B**
15-20 min. **C**
Extension: 10-15 min.

A
- Write the first sentence on the board. Point out the subject (*people*), verb (*keep*), and object (*the animals*). Walk through the formation of the passive, changing the object (*the animals*) to the subject and changing the verb (*keep*) to *are* + past participle (*kept*).
- Point out that *in tiny cages* is a prepositional phrase that does not change when changing from the active to the passive.

Answers in chart: *simple past:* were domesticated; *present perfect:* have been; *present / past continuous:* being; *simple future:* will be returned; *with modals:* be kept

B If necessary, explain the meanings of *abandon* (to leave something behind) and *millionaire* (a person who has over $1 million in assets). Remind students that they learned about *activists* in Unit 3 on page 32.

Outcome: Upon completing this exercise, students will have met the Outcome *use different forms of the passive voice.*

Answers: 2. was attacked; should be allowed; 3. has been cut down; can be raised; will be destroyed; 4. are being challenged; be treated

C Remind students to practice using the passive voice in their discussions of each issue. Circulate around the room to monitor students' practice.

Extension

Have students write six sentences about something they did in the past, something they do in the present, and something they will do in the future. Remind them that these sentences should be in the active voice. Then, have students exchange their sentences with a partner. Direct them to rewrite their partners' sentences in the passive voice.

Listening

5-10 min. A
15 min. B
10-15 min. C
10-15 min. D
Extension: 15 min.

A • Explain that what sets *primates* apart from other animals is that they have larger brains, binocular vision (both eyes facing forward), and the ability to grasp things with their hands.
• Encourage students to write their guesses on a separate sheet of paper. They will fill out the fact sheet in Exercise **B**.
• After students have finished discussing with partners, direct their attention to the map of Africa. Point out that the shaded region is the Democratic Republic of the Congo.
• Explain that there are two countries in Africa with the name Congo; the other is immediately to the west of the shaded one and is called Republic of the Congo. Bonobos are found only in the Democratic Republic of the Congo.

B • Refer students to the Listening Strategy. Have them brainstorm other expressions of probability (e.g., *maybe, it could be*).
• Play the audio of the first part of the interview one or more times. Remind students to write down only key words and numbers.
Audio CD Track 17

Fact Sheet Answers: 1. The Democratic Republic of the Congo; 2. 98%; 3. Peaceful, don't attack each other as much as other primates; 4. Probably endangered; Reasons: humans expanding, bonobos hunted for meat. **Item 2 Answer:** Numbers 1 and 2 are facts; 3 and 4 are possible. Dr. Stern says, "the theory that bonobos are a peaceful species has never really been proven." When asked if they are endangered, he says, "It's hard to say for sure, but we think they probably are."

C Play the second part of the interview once. Pause it after each item is addressed to give students time to write their answers. Then play the recording again straight through to allow students to check their work.
Audio CD Track 18

Answers: 1. communicate with humans; 2. trained; 3. children; 4. his mother; 5. communicate / speak; 6. thousands; 7. special keyboard; 8. piano

Listening

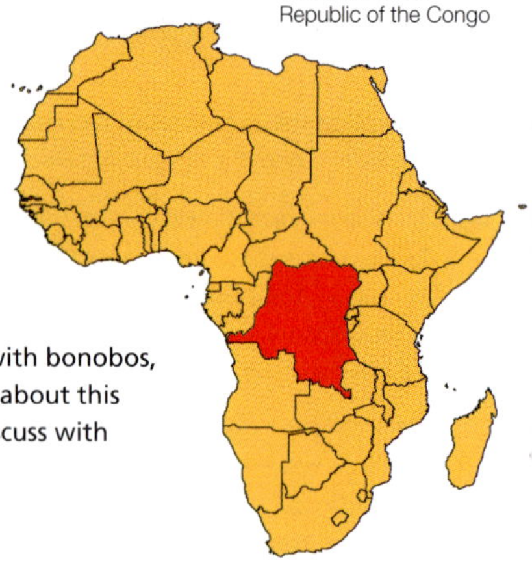
The Democratic Republic of the Congo

habitat the natural environment in which an animal or plant normally lives or grows
primate a type of mammal that includes humans, monkeys, and apes

A You are going to hear an interview with a man who works with bonobos, a type of ape. Look at the photo below. What do you know about this animal? Can you guess any of the answers to 1–4 below? Discuss with a partner.

Bonobo Fact Sheet
1. Country of origin in Africa: ____________________
2. How similar to humans: ____% of the same DNA
3. Behavior: ____________________
4. Endangered status: ____________________
Reason: ____________________

Listening Strategy **Listening for probability** Listen for words and expressions like *possibly, probably, it's hard to say for sure, I think so, it hasn't been proven.* They are used to signal that a person is not 100% certain about something.

B Read the Listening Strategy. Then listen to the first part of the interview and do the following:
1. Complete items 1–4 above. Write only key words and numbers.
2. Then ask a partner: Which items are facts? Which are possible but haven't been proven? How do you know?

C Dr. Stern is going to describe a bonobo named Kanzi. Read the summary below. Then listen. Complete each blank with no more than three words.

Scientists are studying Kanzi because he's the first bonobo to learn to (1) __________. The most surprising thing is that he wasn't (2) __________ to use language. He learned it in the same way (3) __________ do: he heard scientists talking to (4) __________. Later, he tried to use words to (5) __________ with people. Today, Kanzi can understand (6) __________ of spoken words and communicates with people using a (7) __________. He also plays (8) __________!

D Discuss the questions with a partner.
1. How is Kanzi special? If you could ask him a question, what would it be?
2. Do you think capturing and studying animals like Kanzi is useful or cruel? Explain.

Name: Kanzi
Species: Bonobo
Home: Great Ape Trust (in the United States)

Photo Caption

Kanzi the bonobo was born in captivity in 1980 in Atlanta. He now lives at the Great Ape Trust of Iowa. He learned language the way human children do: by being exposed to it from an early age. He is able to respond appropriately to unique sentences because he has learned some of the rules of English syntax. The word *kanzi* means "treasure" in Swahili.

Extension

Ask students to think of a story about themselves that they could tell a partner. When they tell their stories, have them leave off the endings. Encourage everyone to take notes on the stories they hear. Then ask for volunteers to retell their partner's story to the class and include a possible ending using phrases of possibility from the Listening Strategy. Students whose stories are told should then say whether the ending was true or not.

Connections

Mammoths were a relative of the elephant that became extinct about four thousand years ago.

clone a genetic copy of an animal that has been made in a lab using the DNA of another animal

A **On your own, read the three situations. Come up with as many reasons *for* and *against* each situation as you can. List your ideas.**

1. Ana is moving to another city and can't bring her dog with her. The pet needs a new home or it will be taken to an animal shelter. George has been thinking about getting a dog for some company and to encourage him to exercise more. However, he lives alone in a small apartment and tends to work long days, so the animal might be alone a lot. Should he take the dog?
2. Liz recently saw a movie that showed how animals are raised for food and she was shocked by how the animals were treated. Because of this, she's thinking about becoming a vegetarian. Should she?
3. Using cloning technology, scientists say that it is possible to bring back extinct animals, including those that died out recently (like some species of tiger) as well as those that became extinct thousands or millions of years ago (like mammoths or dinosaurs). Some of these animals would be kept in zoos; others would be released into the wild. Should scientists do it?

B **Get into a group of four people. Follow the steps to discuss the situations in Exercise A.**

1. Take ten small pieces of paper. Write "Yes" on five pieces and "No" on the other five. Shuffle the papers and place them face down.
2. Take nine small pieces of paper. Write the number 1 on three pieces. Do the same with the numbers 2 and 3. Shuffle the papers and place them face down next to the other pile.
3. One person starts. Turn over a paper from each pile.
   - 1, 2, or 3 is the situation you will speak about. *Yes* or *No* is the answer you will give to the question.
   - State your answer and give a reason to support it, using one of your *for* or *against* ideas from Exercise **A**. You cannot repeat a reason already given.
   - If your group members think you have given a good reason, you get a point. If you don't give a good reason or can't think of an answer, it's the next person's turn.
   - When you finish, return the papers to the bottom of each deck.
4. Play until everyone has answered as many questions as possible. Who has the most points?

No, he shouldn't take the dog. It's cruel for a pet to be left alone all day in a small apartment. No animal should be treated like that.

Extension

Ask for a volunteer who gave reasons in favor of Situation 1 and another volunteer who gave reasons against Situation 1 to stand in front of the class and have a debate. Allow each student to speak three to five minutes. Then, ask the class to vote on which person was the most convincing. If there is time, move on to Situation 2 and do the same.

Connections

15-20 min. **A**
25-35 min. **B**
Extension: 10 min.

A
- Ask for three volunteers to read the situations aloud while the class follows along silently.
- If students need help understanding the questions posed in each situation, give them short summaries of each: 1. Question: *Should George take Ana's dog or not?* 2. Question: *Should Liz become a vegetarian because of what she saw in a movie?* 3. Question: *Should scientists bring back extinct animals?*
- Challenge students to list at least three reasons for and three reasons against each situation.

B Alternatively, for smaller classes, you may choose to have students do this exercise in pairs. Students may use fewer pieces of paper (six "yes," six "no," and two each of "1," "2," and "3"). Instead of gaining points, partners can take notes on the reasons given for each situation and argue the other side. Students continue until they have debated each situation.

Possible Answers: 1. *Reasons for (yes):* George wants company and can walk the dog before and after work. He can also hire a dog walker to exercise the dog during the day. *Reasons against (no):* The dog will not get enough exercise because the apartment is too small and George is away most of the day. It's not fair to the dog. 2. *Reasons for (yes):* Liz can eat a well-balanced diet without meat. *Reasons against (no):* You can't get enough protein from a vegetarian diet. 3. *Reasons for (yes):* Diversity is good for all species. *Reasons against (no):* The world has changed and some of those animals can't survive in today's world.

Reading

5 min. A
10-15 min. B
10-15 min. C
15-20 min. D
Extension: 15 min.

A • If necessary, point out to students that "stats" is short for *statistics*. Remind them that they learned this word in Unit 1, page 2.
• Remind students that they are only guessing the answers with a partner at first. Encourage them to keep the Quick Stats covered while they work together to come up with their guesses.

B • Point out the use of the word *trust* in the photo caption of Kanzi on page 100 and here in the reading. Explain that a *trust* is something set up for the purpose of caring for a particular thing. The Great Ape Trust takes care of endangered great apes like bonobos. The David Sheldrick Wildlife Trust takes care of endangered elephants and rhinoceroses in Kenya.
• Encourage students to scan the reading for proper nouns like *Wildlife Trust* and *Nairobi* to help them locate some of the information for the outline.

Answers (outline): *What it does:* strong enough to return; 100. *History:* 1987; Daphne Sheldrick. *How it works:* nursery; keepers, 24 hours; two, moved to a rehabilitation center; wild, several years; a new family. *The benefits:* the well-being of existing elephants.

C

Possible Answers: Humans and elephants live in groups and are social animals. Family is very important to them. Elephants have emotions, self-awareness, and memory like humans. The loss of a stable adult role model negatively influences the young. (Note that this is not stated explicitly in the reading, but students should be able to infer it.)

continued on page 103

Reading

A Cover the Quick Stats to the right and try to answer the questions with a partner. Then check your answers.

1. How many years do elephants usually live?
2. How long do male elephants stay with their mothers? How about female elephants?
3. Are elephants endangered?

Quick Stats: Elephants

1. Average life span in the wild: seventy years
2. Female elephants live in family groups called *herds*. Males stay with the herd until they are about 14; female relatives stay together for life.
3. Many are killed by poachers* for their ivory tusks and by farmers protecting their land. Some species are endangered.

***poacher** a person who illegally catches and kills an animal

B Read the title of the article, look at the photos, and read the outline below.

1. What do you think the Wildlife Trust in Kenya does?
2. Read the article to check your answer. Then complete the outline with information from the reading.

The David Sheldrick Wildlife Trust in Kenya

WHAT IT DOES
The Wildlife Trust raises orphan baby elephants until they are ____________________ to the wild.
To date, it has returned over ________ elephants to the wild.

HISTORY
The Wildlife Trust was started in 19___ by ________________.

HOW IT WORKS
Orphan babies arrive at the __________ in Nairobi.
Babies are cared for by ____________ who stay with them ________ a day.
When elephants are ______ years old, they are ____________________________.
Keepers reintroduce elephants to the ________ over ________________________.
Final goal: Elephants join ____.

THE BENEFITS
The work keeps elephant numbers from decreasing.
It maintains ____.

C What are some ways that humans and elephants are similar? Underline ideas that you find in the article. Did any of this information surprise you? Tell a partner.

D Using the outline, summarize for a partner what the David Sheldrick Wildlife Trust is doing in Kenya and why this work is important. In your opinion, what else can be done to help?

Extension

Have students practice reading the article out loud to each other. Suggest that they take turns by alternating readers at every paragraph. Encourage partners to correct any errors in pronunciation. Circulate around the room and monitors students' reading fluency.

Orphan Elephants

Elephants, among the most intelligent creatures on Earth, may have no future without our help.

It's feeding time for the baby elephants at the David Sheldrick Wildlife Trust in Kenya. Here, orphan[1] elephants from all over the country are raised until they are strong enough to return to the wild. Most of them have lost their mothers and other family members to poachers or farmers protecting their land.

Moved[2] by the suffering of these animals, a woman named Daphne Sheldrick started a nursery[3] in Nairobi for orphan baby elephants in 1987. She named the project after her husband. Prior to this, she had cared for many of Kenya's native animals, but none interested—or challenged—her as much as the elephants. "Elephants are very human animals," says Sheldrick. "Their emotions are exactly the same as ours." In fact, studies now show that structures related to memory, self-awareness, and emotion in the elephant brain are very similar to those in humans. When young elephants arrive at the nursery, explains Sheldrick, "they've lost their families, and they come here filled with sadness and fear."

Enter the caregivers at the Nairobi nursery. With humans acting as their mothers, orphans are cared for by people called "keepers" who stay with them twenty-four hours a day. The other young elephants at the nursery help, too. Like humans, explains Sheldrick, "they are extremely social animals. Whenever we get a new baby here, the others will come around and lovingly put their trunks on its back to comfort it. They have such big hearts." When they are about 2, elephants are moved to a rehabilitation center in Tsavo National Park. Here, keepers slowly reintroduce the animals to the wild over several years, encouraging them to join one of the park's elephant families.

To date, Sheldrick's team has returned more than a hundred orphan elephants to the wild. The work being done not only helps to keep elephant numbers from decreasing; it has also helped to maintain the well-being of existing elephant populations. "The loss of older elephants," says one scientist, "and the extreme stress of seeing their family members killed, negatively influences a young elephant's normal development." When orphan females become adults, for example, they are less likely to care for the young properly. Male elephants become much more aggressive, which can also make them more of a danger to humans. When the young elephants are raised by stable[4] adults, however, these behaviors disappear.

Even after adult elephants have joined a new family in Tsavo National Park, some still come back to visit their human caretakers. In December 2008, Emily, a female that came to the Nairobi nursery in 1993, arrived at one of the rehabilitation centers one afternoon. "She'd given birth the day before, about a mile away," recalls one keeper. "She brought the baby here to show us her newborn." Even with a new life and family of her own, Emily—like other elephants—still remembered those at the Wildlife Trust who had loved and cared for her.

[1] **orphan** a child or animal whose parents are dead
[2] **moved** influenced emotionally
[3] **nursery** a place where the young are cared for
[4] **stable** calm, responsible

Reading *continued*

D
- Remind students that they should not read the outline to their partners, but instead should use the information in the outline to summarize what the Wildlife Trust is doing.
- Since students will be referring to the same outline, encourage partners to divide the outline in half and summarize the information under two of the headings.
- Encourage students to discuss additional information from the reading that is not accounted for in the outline.

Outcome: Upon completing this exercise, students will have met the Outcome ***use an outline to summarize ideas.***

Background Information

Elephants generally live between 50 and 70 years. Young elephants live in a herd with their mothers, who protect them from attack. Elephants have many behaviors in common with humans. They bury and mourn their dead. The young adolescent males have been known to form gangs. Elephants also can paint and play music.

Purpose for Reading

This article makes a case for the benefits of human intervention in the lives of young elephants. It particularly asserts the human-like qualities of elephants and the bonds that take place between "keepers" and the animals. As students read, direct their attention to quotations from people who are involved in the care of elephants. Point out that while articles are usually written without bias, opinions can often be found in quoted speech. Challenge students to find the opinions mentioned in the article.

Language Notes

The phrase *Enter the caregivers* (Line 20) is used to mean that caregivers start to get involved in elephants' lives. The expression *enter the…* comes from stage directions for plays. It is used to signal the appearance of an important player in a story.

Beyond the Reading

Direct students to the elephant orphan profiles on the David Sheldrick Wildlife Trust Web site at http://www.sheldrickwildlifetrust.org/asp/orphans_history.asp. Have students look through a few of the profiles and choose one elephant to read about. After taking notes on the orphan elephant, have them share the story with a partner.

Video

10-15 min. **A**
10-15 min. **B**
10-15 min. **C**
10 min. **D**
Extension: 5-10 min.

Background Information

Because elephants in East Africa sometimes wander into areas where humans live, causing damage, and, in some cases, killing people, they are often at risk of being killed themselves. This video follows a team that tags an elephant with an electronic device so that its movements can be monitored.

A
- Students should draw from the information they learned in the reading to answer Question 1.
- Turn the volume of your video player down so that students can make guesses based on what they see. Play both segments of the video.
- Students will see an elephant collapse after being shot. Remind them that the title of the video is *Saving Elephants from Harm*. Ask students if they think the video is showing people helping or harming the elephant and why.

Answers: 2a. Iain Douglas-Hamilton is a biologist and expert on elephants. David Daballen is a researcher for the Kenya Wildlife Service. 2b. Elephants are tranquilized and tagged with a GPS device so that researchers can keep track of where they are at all times and intervene if they get too close to human settlements; the process is called geo-fencing.

B Play the first segment of the video with the sound on. Have students complete the paragraph individually and answer the questions posed in Exercise **A** in pairs.

Answers: 1. airplane; 2. ground; 3. collared; 4. 20; 5. collar; 6. communicate; 7. alert

C
- Before playing segment 2, have students guess what the collar on the elephant will do and why it will be helpful.
- Play the second segment.

Answers: 1. c; 2. d; 3. b; 4. a

D

Possible answer: Geo-fencing lets researchers know if an elephant is getting too close to a human settlement so that they can keep people safe from the elephants and elephants safe from the people.

Video

VIDEO GLOSSARY

alert a warning, an alarm
anesthetic a drug that stops pain or causes you to fall asleep
collar (*noun*) an item that an animal wears around its neck; (*verb*) to capture an animal
GPS (global positioning system) a tool that allows you to locate or follow people or things on Earth
intercept to interrupt and stop something from happening
tag (*noun*) a device attached to someone or something that sounds an alarm; (*verb*) to put a tag on someone or something

A Work with a partner and do the following:

1. Explain what you already know about elephants. Why are so many of them being killed?
2. The title of the video is *Saving Elephants from Harm*. Watch the entire segment once through with the sound off. Then try to answer the questions.
   a. The people in the video are in Kenya. Who do you think they are?
   b. What exactly is being done to "help save elephants from harm"?

Did you know?

Elephants live in a group called a *herd*. The female lead in an elephant herd is called a *matriarch*. Everyone in the herd follows her.

B Read the paragraph below and try to predict some of the answers based on what you've seen. Then watch segment 1 of the video with the sound on and complete the summary. Finally, use it to answer questions 2a and 2b in Exercise **A** again with your partner.

Iain Douglas-Hamilton and David Daballen locate and then follow a herd. Iain is in an (1) __________ and David is on the (2) __________. When they identify the female to be (3) __________, they shoot her. The anesthetic drug causes her to fall down. Once she's unconscious, the team has only (4) __________ minutes to attach the (5) __________. It will allow the elephant to (6) __________ with Douglas-Hamilton by sending an (7) __________ to a cell phone via text message.

C Watch segment 2 of the video. Then match an item (1–4) with an action (a–d).

How geo-fencing works

1. An elephant	a. gets it and stops a herd before it reaches a human settlement.
2. The GPS in the collar	b. sends an alert to a list of recipients.
3. The server	c. crosses a virtual fence line.
4. A person	d. sends a text message (SMS) to a server in Nairobi.

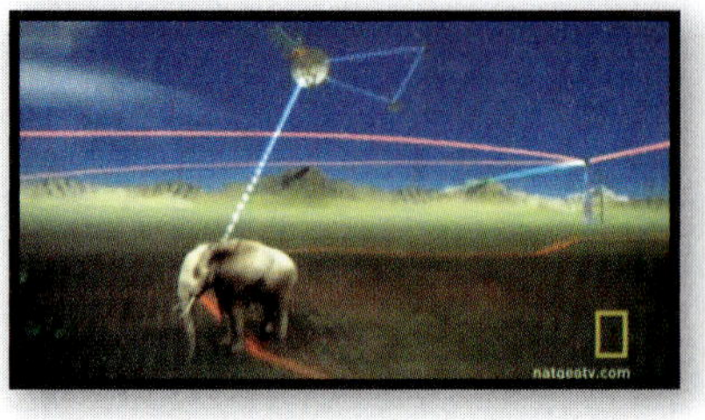

D Using the photo and your answers in Exercise **C**, explain to a partner how geo-fencing works. How does geo-fencing benefit the local people and help save elephants from harm?

Extension

Play both segments of the video again for students. Tell them to take notes on the process of putting collars on the elephants and then how geo-fencing works. Have them write a brief summary of the process that uses at least five passive sentences (e.g., *The female elephant is identified. Then she is shot with anesthesia. A collar is put on her neck. A signal is transmitted to satellites.*).

Internet Activity

Direct students' attention to Quick Stat #3 about elephants on page 102. Point out that the video they watched explains how elephants can be in danger from people protecting their land. Have students investigate the other reason for danger: *many are killed by poachers for their ivory tusks*. Students should search online for what "ivory tusks" are and why poachers would kill for them. Have students discuss what they learned about poaching and ivory.

Speaking

pesticides chemicals put on plants to kill insects

A Get into a group of three. Each person should choose one of the animals featured on this page. Then follow the steps.

1. **On your own**, read about your animal.
2. **Explain to your partners** in your own words the animal's current status and why people are concerned about this. Discuss what you think can be done about the problem.

Name: Siberian Tiger

Status: For years, tigers have been hunted for their fur and body parts (which are used in some cultures' traditional medicines). Their numbers have also been seriously reduced by the destruction of their forest habitat. Today, only 400–500 Siberian tigers—the world's largest cat—can be found in the wild.

Why the concern: Animal activists worry that the Siberian tiger may become extinct. In addition, because the tigers' habitat is being destroyed, it is harder for them to hunt. Though these tigers tend to avoid humans, they will attack and eat people if they can't find food.

Name: American Bumblebee

Status: According to a recent study, bumblebee numbers in the United States have dropped dramatically in the last twenty years. Some species have decreased by almost 96%. What's causing this? Climate change, pesticides, or something else—scientists aren't sure.

Why the concern: Domesticated bees are used to pollinate plants that give us many foods. Without the bees, less food will be produced, resulting in higher costs for consumers. Jobs are also at risk.

Name: Bottlenose Dolphin

Status: Though not listed as endangered, these animals are hunted worldwide for meat. Others are captured and sold for large amounts of money to aquariums around the world and used in animal shows.

Why the concern: Studies have shown that dolphins are not only playful, social animals, but that they are quite intelligent. Protesters argue that it is cruel to kill or cage an animal as smart as a dolphin.

B Imagine that you and your partners work for an international organization that will donate money to help one of the causes above. Which one would you give the money to? Why? Explain your reason to another group.

Speaking

25-35 min. A
15-20 min. B
Extension: 10-15 min.

A • Alternatively, you can assign animals to students and have those with the same animal discuss it in a group first. Then place students with different animals in groups of three.
• Circulate around the room to monitor students' discussions. Make sure that students are explaining the situations of their animals in their own words.

B Refer students to the Speaking Strategy in Unit 6 on page 69 about expressing opinions. Encourage students to use those expressions in their discussions about which organization to give money to.

Outcome: Upon completing this exercise, students will have met the Outcome ***raise people's awareness about an issue.***

Extension

Take a survey of the class to see if there is a majority opinion on which cause is most deserving of money. If so, have students discuss in their groups of three what would be the best way to spend the money to help the animal. Have them reread the animal's status and why there's a concern. If groups need help, offer some ideas: *education, habitat preservation, activism*, etc.

Rubric	Very Good	Satisfactory	Needs Improvement
Expressing information and ideas in own words			
Use of vocabulary			
Use of grammar			
Pronunciation and fluency			

Writing

15-20 min. A
15-20 min. B
10-15 min. C
Extension: 10-15 min.

Purpose of Writing

A brochure provides basic information about a topic and tries to persuade the reader to feel a certain way or take action. In the example brochure, the writer wants the reader to support the koala. Students will write a similar brochure to raise awareness about another animal.

A
- If necessary, explain that *raise awareness* means to help people learn more about something.
- Point out that the writer of the brochure sometimes refers to the animal in the plural, *koalas*, and sometimes the singular, *the koala*. Explain that the singular form refers to a species in general. Provide other examples: *the black bear*, *the Canadian goose*, *the African elephant*.

B
- Students may choose to write about animals that have been profiled in this unit, including: *bonobos*, *elephants*, *the Siberian tiger*, *American bees*, *the bottlenose dolphin*, *parrots*. Or students may choose to focus on other animals, such as *pandas*, *polar bears*, *baby seals*, *whales*, etc.
- Point out the question in the headline. Tell students that many headlines ask a question to try to grab people's attention and bring readers into a situation.
- Explain to students that a call to action often involves using commands or the imperative form of verbs, such as *Support… Join… Donate… Call…*

Outcome: Upon completing this exercise, students will have met the Outcome ***write strong sentences to capture your readers' attention.***

Extension

With their partners from **B**, have students use their brochures to create public service announcements. Explain that a public service announcement, or PSA, is like a brochure that is recorded. Encourage students to use props to make their PSAs more interesting and persuasive. Ask for volunteers to play their PSAs for the class.

continued on page 107

Writing

Create an Informational Brochure

World Animal Day
When: October 4
Why: to appreciate and learn about animals; to raise awareness of endangered animals

A A student created the brochure below to raise awareness about koalas for World Animal Day. Read the brochure. Then discuss the questions with a partner.

1. What kind of headline did the writer use? (See the Writing Strategy on the next page.)
2. Describe the image. Why do you think it was chosen? Do you like it?
3. Does the background information explain clearly why this animal is in trouble?
4. Which fact makes the strongest argument for helping the koala?
5. Is the call to action written clearly? What is one more thing you could do to help?
6. Overall, do you like the brochure? How would you improve it?

Use **an attention-grabbing sentence** that uses one of the writing strategies.

Use **images** that grab your readers' attention.

Include **a call to action** that tells people what to do.

This little guy might lose his home. Won't you help?

WHAT CAN YOU DO? Support or become a member of an organization like the World Wildlife Fund (WWF). Visit the site to learn more about how you can help.

BACKGROUND Though they can be seen in zoos all over the world, in the wild koalas can be found in only one place on Earth: the forests of Australia. For years, these unique animals were killed for sport and for their fur and almost became extinct. Fortunately, hunting koalas is now illegal. Protection programs have also introduced them into the wild again, which has helped their numbers to increase. Unfortunately, the koalas' natural habitat is still threatened as human populations expand into their forested land. Many koalas also die each year when they are hit by cars or are attacked by domesticated dogs that people keep as pets.

KOALA FACTS
- Although it looks like a cute little bear, the koala is actually a kind of animal called a marsupial. Female marsupials carry their babies in a pouch on their stomach.
- For the koala, the tree is life. They live and sleep in trees, they eat tree leaves, and they get most of their water from the leaves they eat. If the Australian forests disappear, so will the koalas.

B Work with a partner. You're going to create a brochure that raises people's awareness about an animal issue of your choice. Choose one of the animals in this unit or think of your own. Then design your brochure. Remember that it should have:

- an attention-grabbing headline.
- one or two compelling images.
- background information explaining what the issue is and two to four brief facts that will get people to care. You can use information you learned in this unit.
- a clear call to action that tells people what to do.

Rubric	Very Good	Satisfactory	Needs Improvement
Content			
Use of attention-grabbing words, sentences, and images			
Use of grammar			
Organization			

Writing Strategy

Getting a Reader's Attention When we write something—a brochure, a story, a news article—we want to get our readers interested in the subject matter immediately. One way to do this is to use an attention-grabbing headline or opening sentence. This might be . . .

- a question that makes you think: *Does having a pet make you healthier?*
- an interesting, surprising, or shocking fact: *In the last twenty years, 96% of these bees have vanished.*
- an emotional appeal: *Adopt a dog . . . save a life.*

C Exchange your brochure with another pair. Read their brochure and then answer questions 1–6 in Exercise **A** about it.

Expanding Your Fluency

Monkey freed from zoo by keeper, still hunted by police	Drowning surfer rescued by dolphins happy to be alive	Critics and supporters battle as bullfighting banned in Barcelona

A You are going to create a minute-long TV interview with a partner. Choose a news headline and, using it to help get you started, do the following:

Student A: You are the person from the news story (the zookeeper, the surfer, the critic or supporter of bullfighting). You're going to be interviewed by a TV news reporter about your experience. Work with your partner to invent a story. Think of answers to his / her questions that tell your story in a memorable way.

Student B: You're a TV news reporter. Think of five or six questions that you can ask your partner about his / her experience. If your interview is interesting enough, it will be shown around the world.

B Get together with another pair. Do your role-plays for each other. After you listen to the other pair's interview, answer the questions.

You say that while you were surfing, you were rescued by dolphins. What happened exactly?

- Who was being interviewed? What happened?
- Did the person tell an interesting story? Do you think the story will be shown around the world?

C Change roles and repeat Exercises **A** and **B**.

Check What You Know

Rank how well you can perform these outcomes on a scale of 1–5 (5 being the best).

_______ use different forms of the passive voice
_______ use an outline to summarize ideas
_______ raise people's awareness about an issue
_______ write strong sentences to capture your readers' attention

Extension

Have students get into groups of three to act out the bullfighting news story. One student should be the interviewer, one should be a supporter of the ban on bullfighting, and the third should be an opponent of the ban. Direct the students in the role of the interviewer to act as a moderator between the two opposing sides. Explain that a moderator ensures that each side has an equal opportunity to explain their points of view.

Writing *continued*

C
- Explain to students that if an attention-grabbing phrase, sentence, or headline is effective, it will make the reader want to keep reading. Encourage them to think of things they have read to make them want to keep reading.
- When students are finished writing and revising, have them post their brochures in a place where people will read them. Try to monitor how often people stop to read them.

Expanding Your Fluency

10-15 min. **A**
10-15 min. **B**
20-25 min. **C**
Extension: 10-15 min.

A
- Point out that the passive voice is often used in a reduced form in headlines (e.g., *Monkey freed from zoo by keeper, still hunted by police = A monkey that was freed from the zoo by its keeper is still being hunted by the police.*) Have students write full sentences of the other two headlines.
- You may choose to have students find their own partners and decide which headline to use. Alternatively, you can assign A / B roles to students and then assign a different headline to each pair so that all three stories are covered.

B When pairs of students team up with other pairs, make sure that each pair has discussed a different news story.

C Direct the students who were the reporters in the first round (Student B) to play the role of the person from a different news story in the second round.

Check What You Know

Refer students to the exercises in the unit where each Outcome is addressed.

- *use different forms of the passive voice:* Grammar, Exercise **B**, page 99
- *use an outline to summarize ideas:* Reading, Exercise **D**, page 102
- *raise people's awareness about an issue:* Speaking, Exercise **B**, page 105
- *write strong sentences to capture your readers' attention:* Writing, Exercise **B**, page 106

Unit 10 Decisions, Decisions

Unit Overview

- Unit 10 is about making decisions. Students will learn about the factors that influence the decisions they make including biology, peer pressure, and societal expectations.
- Ask students what they think is meant by the unit title, "Decisions, Decisions." Explain that it is often used when someone is contemplating a difficult or important decision; the person says this phrase as they consider the options.
- Preview the unit by asking students the following questions:

1. How did you decide what clothes to wear today?
2. How did you decide to study English?
3. When you have to make a decision, how do you know if it's the right one?

Photo Caption

This image is of a hedge maze on the property of Traquair Castle in Scotland. The castle, located about 30 miles south of Edinburgh, dates back to the 12th century and was once the residence of the kings of Scotland.

The hedge maze was constructed in 1981 and is a big attraction, especially for children at Easter, when the castle hosts an egg hunt in the maze each year. Such mazes are commonly found on the grounds of large estates to entertain guests. The Traquair maze has no dead ends, so visitors must remember the turns they take to avoid going in circles.

10 Decisions, Decisions

VOCABULARY	GRAMMAR	LISTENING	READING
Brain teaser: What do you know about the brain and decision-making?	Review of the conditional	Three everyday decisions	*The Teenage Brain:* Why teenagers act the way they do **Strategy:** Recognizing cause and effect

1 What does this image represent to you?

2 What was the last important decision you made? Did you make the right choice?

3 When you have to make a big decision, do you typically ask for help? If so, who do you ask and why? If not, why not?

Unit Outcomes

In this unit, you will learn to:

- use the conditional to make predictions and talk about hypothetical situations
- identify cause and effect relationships
- identify factors that influence decisions
- give reasons to justify a decision

109

5-10 min. **Warm-Up Questions**
Extension: 10-15 min.

Background Information

Cognitive psychology, which is the study of how our brains work, applies the scientific method to studying the way people think. Researchers have found that making decisions uses up "mental energy"; the more decisions we have to make, the harder it is for us to carefully consider new decisions. As a result, people who have already made several decisions in one day are more likely to make impulsive, rather than well-reasoned decisions, or to avoid making decisions at all, due to a condition referred to as "decision fatigue."

Warm-Up Questions

- Have students consider Question 1 before you tell them the information in the photo caption. Ask them to identify the game represented in the photo, and what they think the person pictured has to do. Ask them why they think this image is appropriate for a unit about decisions.
- Have students discuss Question 2 with a partner. As a follow-up, ask students to guess what would have happened if they had decided differently.
- As a follow-up to Question 3, ask students to discuss whether they ask different people for advice for different types of decisions.

Extension

Have students create a diagram showing the factors that influenced an important decision that they've made (for example, the decision to study English). Tell them to list at least four factors that influenced their decision.

SPEAKING	VIDEO	WRITING	OUTCOMES
Analyze how you handle peer pressure	*Moral Dilemma* (excerpt)	Use cause and effect to explain a decision you'd make **Strategy:** Showing cause and effect	• use the conditional to make predictions and talk about hypothetical situations • identify cause and effect relationships • identify factors that influence decisions • give reasons to justify a decision

Vocabulary

15-20 min. A
15-20 min. B
10-15 min. C
Extension: 10-15 min.

Language Notes

- Point out the words *affect* and *effect.* Explain that *affect* is usually a verb (*The weather affects my mood.*), while *effect* is usually a noun (*The effect is that I get grumpy.*). Ask students to create their own sentence pairs to practice using these two words correctly.
- Explain to students that the verb form of *process* is presented here, but it can also be used as a noun: *The process of making a decision can be very complex.*
- Point out the difference between *rational* and *rationale*, both in meaning and pronunciation. *Rational* has the spoken stress on the first syllable, and is an adjective meaning *logical. Rationale* has the spoken stress on the final syllable, and is a noun meaning *the reason someone makes a decision*.

A
- Have students review the Word Partnership feature, and ask them if they know any other expressions with *mind*.
- Challenge students to use at least two vocabulary words in their description of each photo.

B
- Have students work independently to read the information and complete the exercise.
- After partners discuss their answers and their impressions, survey the class to find out what each pair found most surprising.

Answers: 1. process; 2. figure out; 3. rational; 4. react; 5. effect

C Have partners discuss these additional questions: *What kinds of decisions are easy for you to make? What kinds of decisions do you most often regret? What other effects does lack of sleep have on you?*

Vocabulary

affect to influence or cause something to happen
change your mind to change your decision or opinion about something
concentrate to pay close attention to something
effect the result or change that one thing causes in a second thing
figure out to discover an answer or a solution to a problem
hesitate to not speak or act for a short time, usually because you are uncertain about something
process to review and consider information in order to understand it
rational logical, reasonable
react to respond or act in a certain way because of something that has happened
regret to feel very sorry about the outcome of something

A Look at the photos below. What are the people trying to do? Tell a partner.

B How much do you know about the brain and decision making? Complete each blank with a word from the word bank. Did any information surprise you? Tell a partner.

Word Partnership

Match each phrase with its definition:

keep (something) in mind	tell others honestly how you feel
make up your mind	remember
speak your mind	decide to do something

Did you know?

Your brain is able to (1) ___________ large amounts of information at speeds of 200 miles (322 km) per hour! That's faster than a supercomputer.

When we have too many choices, it can be difficult to (2) ___________ which *one* is best. In a situation like this, we often hesitate, change our mind many times, and then regret the choice we made!

A lack of sleep not only affects our ability to make (3) ___________ decisions; it also makes it hard to concentrate and (4)___________ quickly. People who don't get enough sleep have a big (5) ___________ on road safety, for example. Sleepy drivers cause over 100,000 car crashes a year!

C Complete the sentences with the words that describe you. Then explain your answers to a partner. Do you have anything in common?

1. When I have to make an important decision, I usually **react quickly and make a choice / take my time so I can make a rational decision / change my mind several times before I decide**.
2. I **often / sometimes / rarely** regret the decisions I make.
3. A lack of sleep **often / sometimes / rarely** affects my ability to concentrate in class.

Extension

Divide the class into small groups, and have students reread the last paragraph of Exercise **B**. Then have groups create public service announcements warning people about the effects of sleep-deprivation and present them to the class. Encourage students to research additional information on the Internet and draw from their own experiences.

Grammar

A Max is a college student who needs money for school. Read the advice he gets and then answer the questions with a partner.

Sam: You could get a part-time job in the evenings.

Max: Great idea. **If I <u>do</u> that, I'<u>ll have</u> enough money.**

Jess: **If you <u>had</u> a scholarship, you <u>would have</u> enough money.**

Max: I know. I don't have a scholarship yet, but I'm planning on applying for one.

1. Look at the two **bolded** sentences. What does each describe: a possible future event or an imaginary situation? Write the sentences in the chart below.
2. What do you notice about the underlined verb forms?

The Conditional

❶ With possible (real) future events		❷ With imaginary (unreal) present situations	
if clause	*result clause*	*if clause*	*result clause*

❶ This form of the conditional is used to make predictions and talk about possible future events. The verb in the *if* clause is in the <u>simple present</u>. In the result clause, the verb is in the <u>simple future</u>.

❷ This form of the conditional is used to talk about imaginary present events. The information in the *if* clause is not true right now. The result clause describes an imagined result. The verb in the *if* clause is in the <u>simple past</u>. In the result clause, <u>*would(n't)* + *verb*</u> is used. Note: *be* → *were* for all subjects in the *if* clause: If I / you / he <u>were</u> the teacher . . .

B Complete the sentences with the correct word(s). Then explain your answers to a partner.

1. If the teacher is sick tomorrow, we **won't / wouldn't** have class.
2. We'll go to the beach this weekend if the weather **is / will be** nice.
3. I'm broke, but if I **have / had** a lot of money, I **will / would** start my own business.
4. I **will / would** travel to the year 2100 if I **have / had** a time machine.

C Complete each item with your own ideas and discuss your answers with a partner.

1. If you ______________________, you'll probably get a good job.
2. You'll score high on the TOEFL if you ______________________.
3. If you drink too much coffee before bed, you ______________________.
4. If you miss more than a week of this class, ______________________.
5. If I were ______________, I would(n't) ______________.
6. I ______________________ more often if I had the time.
7. I'd be happier if ______________________.

Extension

Have each student write two *if* clauses on separate pieces of paper: one for a possible future situation, and one for a hypothetical situation. They should only write the *if* clauses. Collect the papers and have students take turns choosing one paper from the pile and completing the sentences aloud with a logical ending.

Grammar

15-20 min. **A**
10-15 min. **B**
15-20 min. **C**
Extension: 10-15 min.

A
- Ask for three volunteers to read the conversation aloud.
- Point out that students should use *will + verb* when they are talking about a possible future event and *would + verb* when they are talking about an event that did not happen.
- Remind students to use the simple present tense, not the future, in the *if* clause of a sentence about possible future events, even though the clause expresses a future idea.
- Show students that the clauses in these sentences can be rearranged. When the *if* clause comes second, they don't need to use a comma between the two clauses: *I'll have enough money if I do that.*

Answers: 1. Max's first sentence describes a possible future event; Jess's sentence describes an imaginary situation. 2. In the first sentence, the verb in the *if* clause is in the simple present and the verb in the result clause is in the simple future. In the second sentence, the verb in the *if* clause is in the simple past and the verb in the result clause is in the conditional.

B
- Have students read through each item first and note if the sentence is a real possibility or an imaginary situation. Remind them that identifying the difference between the two will help them complete the exercise.
- As a follow-up, ask students what they would do if they had a time machine.

Answers: 1. won't; 2. is; 3. had, would; 4. would, had

C After they have completed the sentences and discussed their answers, have students rewrite each sentence reversing the order of the clauses.

Answers: Answers will vary. Items 1–4 should use the simple present / simple future. Items 5–7 should use the simple past / (*would + verb*).

Outcome: Upon completing this exercise, students will have met the Outcome *use the conditional to make predictions and talk about hypothetical situations.*

Listening

20-30 min. **A**
20-25 min. **B**
Extension: 10-15 min.

Background Information

Students will hear three conversations in which people make decisions in different situations.

A • Before playing the recording, have students work with partners to read the items and possible answers. Ask them to predict what they think each conversation will be about based on the answers.
• Play the recording, pausing after each conversation so that students can mark their answers. **Audio CD Track 19**

Answers: 1. a; 2. c; 3. b; 4. c; 5. b; 6. c; 7. a

B • Point out to students that the conversations all include ironic statements in which a speaker says something that is the opposite of what he or she really thinks or feels. Review the concept of intonation with students and show them how the same words can have very different meanings depending on the intonation of the speaker.
• Play the recording. **Audio CD Track 20**
• Explain to students that many English speakers use sarcasm when they speak. Ask students what clues can help them understand the true meaning of what someone says (e.g., intonation, facial expressions, the context of the conversation, etc.).
• Have pairs of students discuss the Ask and Answer question together. As a follow-up to the discussion, ask them this question: *If someone asked you to do something that you didn't want to do, but you wanted to avoid hurting his / her feelings, what would you say?*

Answers: 1. isn't; 2. annoyed; 3. I'm not sure. 4. unhappy

Listening

refund money you get back when you return something you've bought

return policy store rules about returning items that have been bought

A Listen to the conversations. After each, choose the best answer to the questions.

Conversation 1

1. The woman ____ a cooking class.
   a. regrets enrolling in
   b. wants to take
   c. has dropped

2. The man ____ the class.
   a. really enjoyed taking
   b. isn't familiar with
   c. has heard good things about

Conversation 2

3. Why does the man want to return the cell phone?
   a. There's something wrong with it.
   b. He's decided he doesn't want it.
   c. He's found a cheaper one somewhere else.

4. To get a full refund immediately, you must return the phone within ____ with ____.
   a. three weeks; the original packaging
   b. a month; a receipt
   c. two weeks; a receipt

5. Will the man be able to get a full refund in the store?
   a. Yes
   b. No
   c. It's not clear from the conversation.

Conversation 3

6. The man and woman ____.
   a. can't figure out when to meet
   b. are studying together from 4:30 to 6:30
   c. may or may not meet later today

7. When the woman suggests meeting at 4:30, the man hesitates because ____.
   a. he's made other plans
   b. he has class
   c. he wants to invite someone else

B Read the sentences below. Then listen again, paying attention to each speaker's intonation. Choose the best answer for each one.

1. **Conversation 1** The woman says *I can't wait* because she **is / isn't** looking forward to her class.
2. **Conversation 2** The man says *Oh, that's great* at the end, because he's **pleased / annoyed**.
3. **Conversation 3** When the man says *Uh, yeah . . . maybe* he means ***I'm not sure / Yes, I think so***.
4. **Conversation 3** The woman says *Oh, well . . . have fun* because she's **unhappy / happy** with the man's choice.

Ask Answer If you invited someone to do something (study together, see a movie) and the person said "maybe," would you expect the person to go with you?

Extension

Have students write at least two sentences using each of the italicized expressions from Exercise **B**. The expressions should have different meanings in each sentence (sarcastic, sincere, excited, etc.). Then have students exchange their sentences with a partner and practice reading the sentences out loud. They should use intonation to give each expression its intended meaning.

Connections

hang out with the wrong crowd to spend time with bad people

A If a friend of yours started doing poorly in school, what would you do? Explain your choice to a partner.

a. I'd ask what was going on and give some advice—even if he/she didn't want it. I always speak my mind.
b. I'd talk to my friend, but I'd only give advice if I were asked for it.
c. I'd probably wait for my friend to talk to me. His / Her problems are none of my business.

Other: ______________________________

B Read the situation below with a partner. Then choose roles and create a role-play. Perform your role-plays for another pair.

STUDENT A You and your twin sibling (brother or sister) attend a very well-known and expensive private school. You each receive a scholarship to go there, but must maintain good grades to keep it. Your twin used to be a really good student, but recently started hanging out with the wrong crowd and studying less. His / Her grades are beginning to suffer. You can't figure out what to do, but you're worried that if your sibling doesn't concentrate on school, he / she will lose the scholarship. You're also worried your parents will be angry with *you* for not helping your sibling.

You want to find out what's wrong and persuade your twin to start doing better in school. Use the conditional to . . .

- make some predictions about what will happen if he/she doesn't make some changes.
- brainstorm some possible solutions to his/her problem.

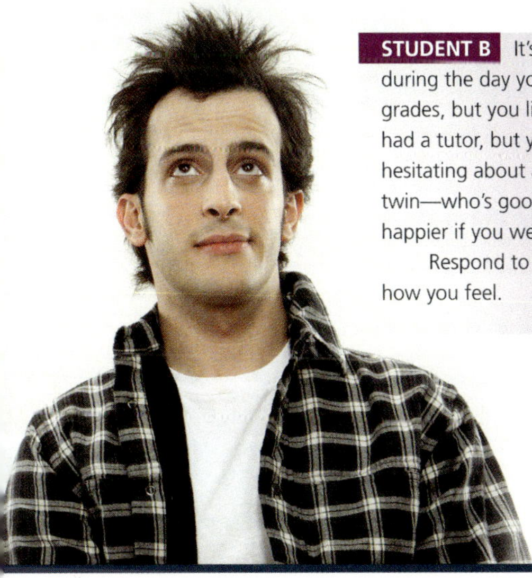

STUDENT B It's true: you're staying out late with your friends, and during the day you're having a hard time concentrating. It's affecting your grades, but you like hanging out with these people. It would help if you had a tutor, but you're not sure if your parents can afford one. You're also hesitating about asking for help because everyone compares you to your twin—who's good at everything. Sometimes you think maybe you'd be happier if you went to a different school.

Respond to your sibling's predictions and suggestions and explain how you feel.

If you stopped hanging out with those people, maybe you'd do better in school.

Yeah, but I'd also never have any fun. I'm tired of studying all the time.

Internet Activity

Encourage students to read more about the similarities and differences between identical twins. Direct them to the following feature article: http://ngm.nationalgeographic.com/2012/01/twins/miller-text. After students read the article, survey the class to see if students think heredity (nature) or our environment (nurture) is more influential in determining who we are and the decisions we make. Then ask them which factor seems to be contributing to the differences between the siblings in the situation on this page.

Connections

15-20 min. **A**
25-35 min. **B**
Extension: 15-20 min.

A
- Ask students who might use the expression *hang out with the wrong crowd*. Survey the class to see if there is a consensus about who is in the "wrong crowd."
- Explain that the expression *none of my business* means *not my concern*. Encourage students to give examples of situations where they might use the expression (e.g., when somebody does not want to be involved in a situation).
- Ask students follow-up questions: *Have you ever been in a situation where you noticed that a friend was having a problem? Which of the three options did you choose? Why?*

B
- Assign roles to the students, and give them a few minutes to read their descriptions.
- Have each student write two predictions and two hypothetical statements about their character's situation in preparation for their role-plays. Encourage them to refer to the model dialogue.
- After pairs have performed their role-plays for each other, have them switch partners and play the other role.
- Ask students which sibling they most resemble. What would they do in each situation?

Extension

Have students imagine that they are a parent to the twins in Exercise **B**. Have them compose an e-mail to either Student A or Student B in which they explain their concerns. They should also suggest what they think each sibling should and should not have done, and what they think the siblings should and should not do now. Encourage them to make the parent's advice different from the sibling's. Ask for volunteers to share their e-mails with the class.

Reading

5-10 min. **A**
15 min. **B**
5-10 min. **C**
10 min. **D**
5-10 min. **E**
Extension: 15-20 min.

Purpose for Reading

Students will read a cause-and-effect essay about teenagers' brains. The article discusses how people's decision-making patterns change as they get older. Draw students' attention to the question in the subtitle. Point out that when an article's subtitle poses the question *Why?*, they should expect to learn the answer—the cause—in the body of the essay.

A Give students 60 seconds to write down all of the adjectives they can think of that describe teenagers. Ask volunteers to share some of the words they came up with and write them on the board. Lead a discussion about whether or not all of the adjectives are accurate or fair.

B
- Ask students why they think the author put the word *irrational* in quotation marks in Line 10. Have them contrast it with the way quotation marks are used with *yes* in the previous sentence (Line 9).
- Have students answer Question 3 from their own perspective and give reasons for their answers.

Answers: 1. Our decision-making ability is developing and we're learning to make good choices. At the same time, we're more likely than ever to take risks. 2. We have a love of thrills; we have an intense need for peer approval. 3. The author thinks these things are mostly good; they can help us develop into successful, independent adults.

C Have students write four personalized sentences using each of the words in italics. Circulate around the room and check their sentences to make sure they comprehend the meaning of the words.

Answers: 1. developing; 2. want; 3. your own age; 4. admire

continued on page 115

Reading

A **Read the title and subtitle and look at the photo. What do you think this reading is going to be about? Tell a partner.**

B **Read the article. Then answer the questions with a partner.**

1. According to paragraph 1, what happens to us during our teenage years?
2. In paragraphs 2 and 3, the author describes two factors that increase our tendency to take risks during our teen years. What are they?
3. Does the author think these two behaviors are mostly good or bad? Why?

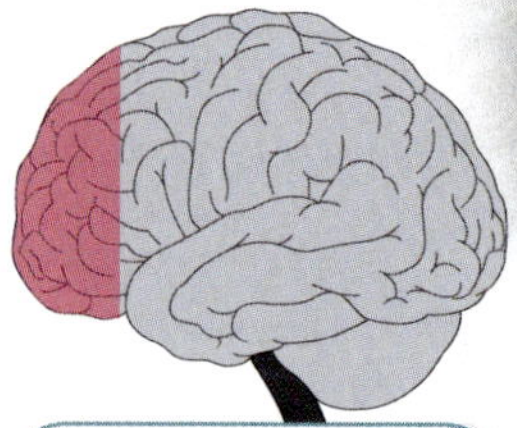

The prefrontal cortex—the part of the brain involved in making decisions, controlling our emotions, and planning for the future—isn't fully developed until we're 25.

C **Choose the correct option for each item.**

1. If something or someone is *maturing* (line 5), it is **developing / reducing**.
2. If you're *eager* (line 16) to do something, you really **hate / want** to do it.
3. Your *peer* (line 28) is someone who is **your own age / older than you**.
4. If you *impress* (line 43) someone, you cause the person to **dislike / admire** you.

ir- = not
What does *irrational* mean?

D **Study the Reading Strategy. Then complete the cause / effect charts with information from the passage. Use no more than three words per blank.**

Reading Strategy **Cause and Effect** In the article, the writer examines the cause / effect relationship between the brain and behavior. A cause / effect essay answers these questions: Why does something happen? What is the result of that event? As you read, think about these questions to help you identify key details.

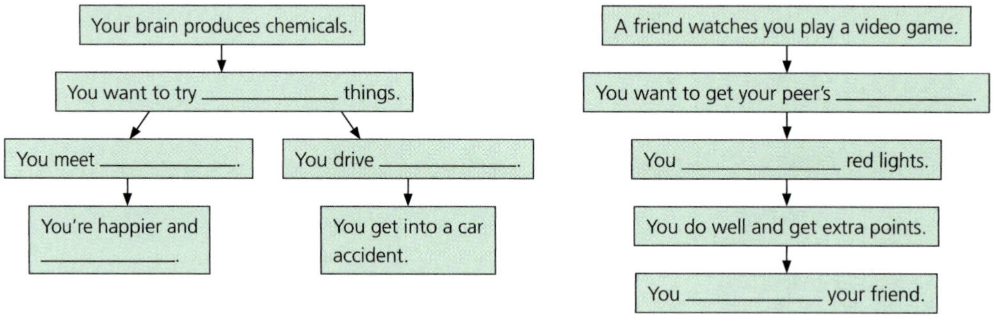

E **Use the charts in Exercise D to answer the questions with a partner.**

1. During our teen years, why are we so eager to experience new and exciting things? How can this benefit us? How can it be dangerous?
2. Peer approval is very important to us when we're teenagers. Why? How does the author use the video game to explain this?

Ask **Answer** How important is peer approval to you? Do you care a lot about what others think?

Internet Activity

Have students do research on the Internet to learn more about the human brain. Refer them to the following Web site to start: http://kids.nationalgeographic.com/kids/stories/spacescience/brain/. Ask them to write a brief paragraph explaining the information they found most interesting or surprising in their research.

The Teenage Brain

Why do teenagers act the way they do? Science may have the answers.

For years, scientists believed that human brain development was completed by the time we were 10 or 11. Recent studies, however, show that during our teenage years, our brain—especially the prefrontal cortex—is still maturing in important ways. When we're teenagers, our decision-making ability is developing and we're learning to make good choices. At the same time, we're more likely than ever to take risks. Is this normal? Scientists who study the brain say "yes." In fact, they believe that risk-taking and other "irrational" behaviors may actually help teens to become successful adults.

Take, for example, the teenager's love of thrills. We all like new and exciting things, but never as much as we do during our teenage years. During this time of our lives, say scientists, our brains produce chemicals that make us very eager to experience new things—the more exciting, the better. Although the need for excitement can lead to dangerous behaviors (like driving a car too fast and getting into a car accident), it can also generate positive ones. The desire to meet new people, for instance, can help us make friends, which usually makes us happier and more successful in life. Taking risks and trying new things can be challenging or even dangerous, but this behavior can also lead to useful experiences that will benefit us as adults.

Psychologist Lawrence Steinberg created a video game to explore an important factor that affects typical teenage behavior: the intense need for peer approval.[1] In the game, players try to drive across a town as quickly as possible. Along the way there are several traffic lights. Some lights turn from green to yellow as you approach them. You must make a decision: should you slow down and prepare to stop when you see the yellow light or speed up and try to go through the light before it turns red? If you get through the light before it turns red, you get extra points. If you fail, you lose time and points. When teens played the game alone, they took as many chances as adults. When a friend came into the room to watch, though, the teen almost always tried to go through more red lights. Their goal: to get more points and impress their friend. Adults who took part in the experiment, however, drove no differently with a friend watching.

Why did the teens react this way and try to impress their friends? We enter a world made by our parents, say scientists. But we will live most of our lives and succeed (or not) in a world run by our peers. Therefore, it is important that we are accepted—and respected—by that group, even if it means taking some risks to fit in.

Anthropologists[2] have found that almost all of the world's cultures recognize the teenage years as a time during which people seek excitement, take more risks, and struggle for peer approval. Doing these things can help us become successful, independent adults. But, say scientists, we must also learn that our actions can have serious consequences and find a balance between the two.

[1] **approval** support or praise; respect
[2] **anthropologists** scientists who study people, societies, and culture

Practice the Reading Strategy

Have students create their own cause-and-effect chart like those in Exercise **D** about decisions they have made, such as why to study English, attend a certain school, buy a certain product, etc. Their charts should include at least five levels. Remind them that since they're relating the cause-and-effect relationship of a past event, their sentences will be in the past tense, not the present.

Reading *continued*

D After students have completed the charts and checked their answers, show them that they can connect the different levels of the chart using the word *because*. Examples: You impress your friend *because* you do well and get extra points. You do well and get extra points *because* you go through more red lights.

Answers: *Left chart:* new and exciting / new people / too fast / more successful; *Right chart:* approval / go through more / impress

Outcome: Upon completing this exercise, students will have met the Outcome ***identify cause and effect relationships.***

E
- Have students rank how much they like to take risks on a scale of 1–10, with 1 being the least risky, and 10 being the riskiest. Then ask a student with a low number to describe the dangers of risk-taking and someone with a high number to describe the benefits.
- Have students reread the last two paragraphs of the essay and identify what two things the author is referring to with the line *find a balance between the two* (Line 55).

Extension

Write these sentences on the board. (1) *Teenagers take too many risks and are a danger to themselves and others.* (2) *Teenagers can only learn to be responsible adults by making mistakes and learning from them.* Assign each student one of the sentences and have them form pairs to debate and defend their positions.

Language Notes

- Line 12: *The teenager* here refers to teenagers in general.
- Line 12: *Thrills* are feelings of excitement.
- Line 34: *Go through the light* means to drive through an intersection that has a traffic light.
- Line 50: *Recognize* in this case means *acknowledge* or *understand*.
- Line 55: *Find a balance* means to avoid extreme actions or behavior.

Speaking

5-10 min. **A**
10-15 min. **B**
15 min. **C**
10-15 min. **D**
Extension: 10-15 min.

A
- Explain that *pressure* is both a noun (*I am under a lot of pressure at school.*) and a verb (*Ed's brother pressured him into buying the more expensive computer.*).
- Have students consider these additional questions: *What types of decisions are affected by peer pressure? What situations make you more vulnerable to peer pressure?*

B
- Explain that a *compulsive shopper* is a person who buys things that he or she does not need and spends money without thinking about the consequences.
- Have students write their answers to these questions anonymously. Collect their answers and write the tally on the board.

C
- Ask students what they think the expression *have a mind of your own* means. Encourage them to look for clues in the rest of the description (e.g., "[you] don't always give in to peer pressure").
- Explain that the expression *the in crowd* refers to a popular group. Based on this description, ask students to explain what is meant by "the in-and-out crowd."
- Remind students that these situations are hypothetical, or imaginary present, situations. Encourage them to refer to page 111 for a reminder of which verb forms to use.

Outcome: Upon completing this exercise, students will have met the Outcome ***identify factors that influence decisions.***

Extension

Have students choose a celebrity (a politician, an actor, an athlete, etc.) and describe to a partner what peer pressure rating they would give that person. Encourage them to cite examples from that person's life to explain why they would give him or her that rating.

Speaking

A Read the definition of **peer pressure**. Have you ever felt pressured to go along with the group even when you didn't want to? Tell a partner.

If you do something because of ***peer pressure****, you do it because other people in your social group are doing it.*

B Read each situation and think about your answers to the questions.

1. You have a close friend that your other friends don't like. You're having a party at your house this weekend. If you invite your good friend, your other friends will be angry with you. If you don't and your close friend finds out, he/she will be hurt. What would you do if . . .
   a. you were in this situation?
   b. you knew your close friend wouldn't find out about the party?
2. You're assigned to work on a group project with three other people in your English class. You have to agree on a topic. One person suggests an idea and everyone else seems to like it. What would you do if . . .
   a. you had a better idea?
   b. you were new in the school and the most popular person in your class suggested the original idea?
3. Your cousin is a compulsive shopper: the minute he gets money, he spends it. Recently, he lost his job and he's asked you for a loan. You have the money but don't want to loan it to him. What would you do if . . .
   a. your other relatives started pressuring you to change your mind?
   b. you found out that your cousin just bought himself a new cell phone and laptop?

C Take turns asking and answering the questions in Exercise **B** with a partner. Explain your reasons for your answers. What factors most influenced your decisions? At the end, rate yourself and your partner on how affected by peer pressure you each are. Do your ratings match?

Peer Pressure Ratings

- **Approval addict** Peer pressure affects you a lot; your decisions tend to be strongly influenced by the group. You need their approval!
- **The in-and-out crowd** Sometimes you're influenced by others' opinions, but you also have a mind of your own and don't always give in to peer pressure.
- **Independent forever** You're not affected at all by peer pressure. You think for yourself and speak your mind, whatever the consequences might be.

D With your partner, come up with your own question about peer pressure (like the ones in Exercise **B**). It can be about friends, family, school, or work. Then exchange your question with another pair. Answer the question you get.

Rubric	Very Good	Satisfactory	Needs Improvement
Content			
Use of details to explain reasoning			
Use of grammar			
Organization			

Video

appropriate the correct thing to do
cognition a mental process used to think about things
inclination a feeling that makes you want to act in a certain way
intuition (*adj.* **intuitive**) a feeling that something is true even when you have no proof of it
plea an emotional request
rudimentary simple, basic

A Read the information below and then ask a partner: Who is Tyler and what kind of research project is he participating in?

At Princeton University in the United States, neuroscientists (people who study the brain) are doing research. They want to find answers to these questions: When we are faced with a dilemma (a difficult choice), how do we decide what to do? Which part(s) of the brain do we use to make our decision?

Tyler, the research subject, is put into a machine called a *scanner*. Tyler will look at some pictures and he will be asked some questions. The scanner will record his brain activity.

B Watch segment 1 and answer the questions. Check your answers with a partner.

1. What decision does Tyler have to make? Summarize it in two or three sentences.
2. What do you think Tyler is going to do?
3. If you were in this situation, what would you do? Why?

C Watch segment 2. Then mark the correct answers.

1. **The majority / very few** of the people who participated in this study **would / would not** help the woman.
2. When we're faced with a dilemma, there's increased activity in which part(s) of the brain? Mark your answer(s) on the image.
3. The findings from this study suggest that we're more likely to help _____.
   a. an attractive person than an unattractive one
   b. a woman in danger than a man in danger
   c. someone nearby than someone far away

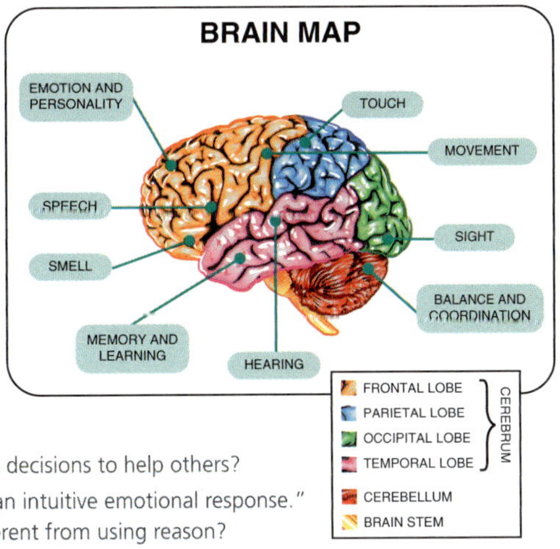

D Discuss the questions with a partner.

1. What does this study teach us about how we make decisions to help others?
2. Tyler's decision to help the woman was based on "an intuitive emotional response." How is using your intuition to make a decision different from using reason?
3. In what situations might you rely on your intuition to make a choice?
4. Do you think our intuition can help us make good decisions? Why or why not? Do you tend to rely more on your intuition, reason, or both when you make important choices? Why?

Extension

Lead a class discussion with students about the following situations. *Imagine there is a trolley speeding down the tracks with no brakes and there are four men working on the tracks. If you pull a lever, you can switch the trolley to a track where only one man is working. Would you pull the lever? Now, imagine that you are on a bridge over the trolley tracks, and you can stop the trolley by pushing a man onto the track in front of the trolley. Would you do that? Why or why not? What is the difference between these situations?* This dilemma is known as the "Trolley Problem" and was first posed by philosopher Philippa Foot.

Video

10-15 min. **A**
10-15 min. **B**
10 min. **C**
10-15 min. **D**
Extension: 10-15 min.

Background Information

Students will watch a documentary video about how scientists study decision-making. Neuroscientists study the brain and use a machine called an fMRI to see which parts of the brain we use when we make different types of decisions. In this video, a man must decide whether to help another person in a hypothetical situation.

Before You Watch

A Have students give an example of a time when they made a decision based on intuition instead of logic. Ask them if their intuition turned out to be correct.

B Play only segment 1 for the class. Give students time to take notes on their own answers before they get together with their partners.

Answers: 1. Tyler has to decide whether or not to help the injured woman. If he doesn't, she'll probably die. If he does help her, he'll ruin his suit. (He doesn't think about ruining his suit, even though it might be the "rational" thing to do. Instead, he is immediately concerned about the woman.)

C Have students discuss the answer to Question 3. Ask them why they think we are more likely to help someone nearby than someone far away.

Answers: 1. The majority / would; 2. the part of the brain that deals with emotion; the frontal lobe; 3. c

D

Possible Answers: 1. It teaches us that there are many factors that influence our decisions, including how close we are to a person in need. 2. When we use reason, we gather and analyze information and then make a choice about what to do. When we use intuition, we use feelings rather than facts. 3. We might use intuition over reason in an emergency; when forming a first impression of someone; when we have all the facts, but still can't decide what to do; or when we have too many options.

Writing

10-15 min. A
5-10 min. B
15-20 min. C
10 min. D
Extension: 10-15 min.

Purpose of Writing

The purpose of a cause and effect essay is to explain the reasons for a certain decision or situation. Cause and effect essays clearly show how certain factors lead to specific results.

A
- Give students time to read the scenario on their own, then ask a volunteer to read the sample response out loud to the class.
- Ask what the student means when he writes "we're all really close." Explain that he is referring to an emotional connection, not physical closeness.
- Refer students to the points in the chart about each school. Have them brainstorm possible effects of each point. e.g., Point: *You'll live at home in your own room.* Possible result: *You'll be more comfortable.* Point: *You'll live in the dorm with two roommates.* Possible results: *You'll be less comfortable. / You'll make new friends.*

B
- As students prepare for their writing, have them rank the points in the chart in order of importance to them.
- Ask students to consider what their intuitive choice would be and whether that choice is the same as their logical, reasoned decision.

C
- Have students review the Writing Strategy before they start writing their paragraphs.
- Point out that *so* is used to introduce a clause (I go to school in my town, so I live at home.). *As a result, because of this,* and *consequently* are transitions between sentences and should be used at the beginning of a sentence.
- Explain that an action can be both a cause and a result: e.g., "I'd probably eat out a lot." *If I lived in the dorm, I'd probably eat out a lot. As a result (of eating out a lot), I'd spend a lot of money.* I live in the dorm. > I eat out a lot. > I spend a lot of money.

continued on page 119

Writing

Showing Cause and Effect

A Read the scenario below and then one student's response to the question. What does he decide to do? What reasons does he give? Tell a partner.

You've been accepted to two universities. One is based in a small city near your hometown, where you're now living. Another is over 400 km away in a big city. Below is some information about the schools.

School near your hometown	School in the big city
• You'll live at home in your own room. • You'll be living in your hometown where everything is familiar. • All of your friends are going to this school, so you'll still see them all the time. • Classes will be small and you'll get lots of attention. • Your school will be a local college where you'll get a good education. • Tuition is affordable and you'll save money because you'll be living at home. • Your parents prefer this college.	• You'll live in a dorm with two roommates. • You'll be living in a big city that you've never been to before. • You won't know anyone, so you'll make new friends. • Classes will be very large. • Your school will be a prestigious school where you'll get a good education. • Tuition is affordable, but doesn't cover other school-related expenses. • Your teachers prefer this college.

Question: If you were in this situation, which school would you attend? Which factors would affect your decision the most?

Response: If I were in this situation, I'd probably go to the local school for two main reasons. First, it would be cheaper. When you go away to school, you typically eat in the dorm cafeteria, which costs extra. You also have a lot of living expenses that you don't have when you live at home. It can get expensive. If I went to a local school, I wouldn't have to pay to live in a dorm. I also wouldn't need to decorate my room. I'd save money on food, too, because I'd be eating my meals at home. **Consequently**, I'd be able to use my money for other things. Another reason I wouldn't move is that I would miss my friends and especially my family. I'm one of three children and we're all really close. If I moved, I'd only see my family during breaks. **As a result**, I'd probably be kind of lonely. If I went to the local school, though, I'd still see my friends and family all the time. **Because of this**, I'd probably be happier and do better in school. For these two reasons, I'd choose to go to the local school.

B Think about how you would answer the question in Exercise **A**. Then do the following:

1. On a separate piece of paper, list . . .
   - the school you'd go to.
   - two or three reasons for your choice.
   - what effects your choice would have.
2. Get together with a partner and explain your choice. Answer any questions your partner has and edit your notes.

118

Rubric	Very Good	Satisfactory	Needs Improvement
Content			
Use of conditional statements to show cause and effect			
Use of grammar			
Organization			

C Using your notes, write a paragraph answering the question in Exercise **A**. As you write, remember to give two reasons for your choice. Also, explain what effects your choice would have. Use the information in the Writing Strategy to help you write about causes and effects.

D Exchange papers with a new partner. Does it follow the instructions in Exercise **C**?

> **Writing Strategy**
>
> **Showing Cause and Effect** Conditional statements show a cause / effect relationship. Words and phrases like *as a result, because of this, consequently*, and *so* also describe results.
>
> If I lived in the dorm, I'd probably eat out a lot. (Living in the dorm would cause me to eat out.) **As a result / Because of this / Consequently**, I'd spend a lot of money.

Expanding Your Fluency

A Get into a group of four. Come up with two "What if" questions together.

What would do you if you could change one thing about yourself?

B On your own: Take two small pieces of paper. On each, write a question and your reply **using the conditional (*if* clause in the past + *would*)**. Don't explain your answer, and don't write your name.

C Put your two slips of paper in the middle of the desk and mix them up with everyone else's answers. Then follow the steps.

1. One person should choose a paper from the pile. (If you get your own, choose another.) Read the question and the reply aloud. Try to guess who said it.
   - If your guess is *correct*, you get a point. You must ask the author one more question about his or her answer. Then remove the paper from the pile.
   - If your guess is *incorrect*, put the paper back in the pile.
2. Now it's another person's turn. Repeat step 1 until all of the questions have been answered. The winner is the person with the most points.

Check What You Know

Rank how well you can perform these outcomes on a scale of 1–5 (5 being the best).

_______ use the conditional to make predictions and talk about hypothetical situations

_______ identify cause and effect relationships

_______ identify factors that influence decisions

_______ give reasons to justify a decision

Extension

Have students create a flow chart describing what they would do if they didn't have to come to class today. Tell them to include at least five items in the chart. Then have students get together with a partner and describe what they would do, making sure to include conditional statements and expressions to show cause and effect (e.g., *If I didn't have to come to class today, I would go to the beach. If I were going to the beach, I would have to bring my lunch, so I would stop by the sandwich shop.*)

Writing *continued*

C • Have students develop their own flow charts to organize their ideas before they begin writing.

Outcome: Upon completing this exercise, students will have met the Outcome *give reasons to justify a decision.*

Extension

Have students imagine that they are teachers at the student's high school. Ask them to write a letter to the student explaining why they think he should go to the school in the big city.

Expanding Your Fluency

5-10 min. **A**
5-10 min. **B**
30-35 min. **C**
Extension: 10–15 min.

C • Alternatively, do not have students read the reply aloud as written. Instead, have them rephrase the answer as a third-person statement (e.g., *If I could change one thing about myself, I would be a better soccer player. > If this person could change one thing about himself / herself, he / she would be a better soccer player.*).

- Have students repeat the game with different groups and a new set of questions. For the second round of questions, tell students to answer using a negative statement (e.g., *If I could change one thing about myself, I would not change my height.*).

Check What You Know

Refer students to the exercises in the unit where each Outcome is addressed.

- *use the conditional to make predictions and talk about hypothetical situations:* Grammar, Exercise **C**, page 111
- *identify cause and effect relationships:* Reading, Exercise **D**, page 114
- *identify factors that influence decisions:* Speaking, Exercise **C**, page 116
- *give reasons to justify a decision:* Writing, Exercise **C**, page 119

Unit 11
Rain or Shine

Unit Overview

- Unit 11 is about the weather. Students will learn about different types of weather, from everyday patterns to extreme weather events. They will discuss how the weather affects peoples' moods and impacts their lives.
- Ask students what they think is meant by the unit title, "Rain or Shine." Explain that "shine" in this expression refers to sunshine. "Rain or shine" is an expression that is often used to explain that an event will take place regardless of what the weather is like.
- Preview the unit by asking students the following questions:

1. How does the weather change where you live? What type of weather do you like most?
2. What is the worst storm you have ever been in? Describe the experience.
3. If you could move anywhere on Earth because of the weather, where would you go?

Photo Caption

This image shows lightning generated by electrically charged particles in volcanic ash from the eruption of a volcano at the Eyjafjallajökull ice cap in Iceland in 2010. A very active volcano that erupts frequently, the Eyjafjallajökull eruption pictured here spewed so much ash into the atmosphere that it disrupted air traffic across Europe for weeks.

Lightning occurs when particles in the atmosphere become charged and act against each other. A lightning bolt can travel at 220,000 kilometers per hour (140,000 miles per hour). About 16 million lightning storms occur on Earth every year.

11 Rain or Shine

1 Look at the picture. What do you think the weather will be like in an hour?

2 Describe your perfect day. What's the weather like? What kind of weather is your least favorite?

3 Have there been any major storms in the news lately? Where? What happened exactly?

Unit Outcomes

In this unit, you will learn to:

- explain how weather affects your life
- make inferences based on information you have learned
- understand and use similes
- use phrasal verbs

VOCABULARY	GRAMMAR	LISTENING	VIDEO
Bad weather traps a doctor on the South Pole	Separable and inseparable phrasal verbs	Reactions to the weather	*Sinking England*

5-10 min. **Warm-Up Questions**
Extension: 10-15 min.

Background Information

What makes weather? A combination of wind, humidity, temperature, and air pressure determines if the weather is rainy, sunny, cloudy, or snowy in a given place on Earth. These conditions are influenced by both the time of year and geographical location. In the summer months, temperatures are higher because the Earth tilts towards the sun and receives more hours of sunlight. Some regions have dry summers; others have heavy rains, strong storms, and dramatic changes in wind patterns. A region's latitude (distance from the equator) and elevation (height above sea level) also play a role in its weather.

Warm-Up Questions

- Read Question 1 aloud. Have students divide into groups that (1) like thunderstorms (2) are indifferent about thunderstorms and (3) can't stand thunderstorms. Have each group discuss their opinions.
- Have students discuss Question 2 in pairs. Then survey the class to find out if they agree about their favorite and least favorite weather.
- After students answer Question 3, ask them to describe major storms that have happened in their region.

Extension

Divide the class into four groups and give them this information. Group 1: Kampala, Uganda; Temperature: 29° (Celsius); thunderstorms in the afternoon. Group 2: Helsinki, Finland; Temperature: 2°; windy and snowy. Group 3: Tokyo, Japan; Temperature: 11°; sunny. Group 4: Santiago, Chile; Temperature: 31°; sunny and dry. Have each group prepare a weather report for the class and suggest what to wear and what activities to do.

SPEAKING	READING	WRITING	OUTCOMES
Which weather story is false?	*Storm Chasers:* Scientists risk their lives to gather data about tornadoes Strategy: Making inferences	Describe a time weather impacted your life Strategy: Using similes	• explain how weather affects your life • make inferences based on information you have learned • understand and use similes • use phrasal verbs

Vocabulary

10-15 min. **A**
10-15 min. **B**
10 min. **C**
10-15 min. **D**
Extension: 10-20 min.

Language Notes

- Ask students to give examples of temperatures they would consider *freezing* or *frigid*. Point out that *freezing* is often used to describe the feeling of being cold and does not always mean that the air temperature is below the freezing point.
- Explain that the word *after* in the phrasal verb *look after* does not relate to time.
- Explain that *mild* can also mean *moderate* when describing food (not a strong flavor) or personality (gentle).

A Ask students a follow-up question: *Has weather affected any of your major life decisions?*

Outcome: Upon completing this exercise, students will have met the Outcome ***explain how weather affects your life.***

B • Ask volunteers to read the photo captions aloud. Explain that *–60°C* is read "sixty degrees below zero (Celsius)" or "minus sixty degrees (Celsius)."
• Tell students that in the United States, temperature is usually measured in degrees Fahrenheit. For reference, tell students that –60°C is –76°F; 0°C is 32°F; 25°C is 77°F; 38°C is 100°F.

C

Answers: 1. refuse; 2. assessed; 3. postponed; 4. mild; 5. considered; 6. intervened; 7. freezing; 8. looked after; 9. recovered

Photo Caption

The original Amundsen-Scott South Pole Station was built by the US government in 1956, and there have been people living on the South Pole ever since then. It is named after Roald Amundsen and Robert F. Scott, two explorers who reached the South Pole in 1911.

Vocabulary

assess to judge or decide the quality or amount of something
consider to think about something carefully
cut off to disconnect
freezing very cold
frigid extremely cold
give up to part with; to let go of
intervene to become involved in a situation and try to change it
look after to keep someone healthy or safe
mild moderately warm
postpone to delay (an event)
recover to become well again
refuse to decline something
take off to depart
tolerate to accept something that you may not like

A Weather can impact our lives in many ways. What is one way it affects your daily life? Discuss with a partner.

B Look at the photos and captions. What do you think happened to Jerri Nielsen? What risks are involved in taking this type of job?

Jerri Nielsen
Jerri Nielsen is a physician who gave up her job to work in Antarctica as the medical doctor for the Amundsen-Scott staff.

C Read Jerri Nielsen's story. Choose the correct verb to complete the sentences.

When Jerri was given an opportunity to work on the South Pole, she was so excited that she couldn't (1) **recover / refuse** the offer. She arrived in Antarctica ready for an adventure and she loved her new job. Halfway through her time on the South Pole, Jerri was shocked to discover she had cancer. At that point, Jerri (2) **assessed / postponed** her situation. It was too cold for a plane to come and rescue her. Any attempt would have to be (3) **assessed / postponed** until the weather became more (4) **mild / frigid**. Jerri's employers (5) **considered / looked after** sending a plane to rescue Jerri, but they canceled the plan because it was too dangerous. That was when the military (6) **cut off / intervened** in the situation because they had a plane that could fly in the (7) **freezing / cut off** air for a short period of time. A plane flew overhead without landing and dropped equipment and medicine for Jerri. She took the medicine to treat herself for several months. At the same time, she (8) **looked after / gave up** her colleagues as the doctor. And she waited. . . . Months later, she was rescued. Upon her return, Jerri received treatment and (9) **assessed / recovered** from her cancer. She wrote a book about her experience called *Ice Bound*.

D With a partner, retell Jerri's story in your own words.

Ask Answer Would you ever give up everything to move far away for a job? Would you be able to tolerate living in a place like the South Pole, cut off from everyone else?

Amundsen-Scott South Pole Station, Antarctica
From February through October, the temperature stays around –60°C. It's too cold for flights to take off or land. During this time, the workers there are cut off from the outside world.

122

Extension

Have students imagine they are planning a trip to the South Pole. Have them write a paragraph describing what they will bring on their trip and what preparations they need to make before leaving. Encourage students to research the South Pole online at http://education.nationalgeographic.com/education/encyclopedia/south-pole/.

Grammar

Phrasal Verbs

A phrasal verb is a verb + preposition/particle. Some phrasal verbs are "separable;" the verb can be "separated" from the preposition/particle by an object (noun or a pronoun). Notice the placement of the pronoun in the separable verbs. Phrasal verbs have different meanings than the base verb on its own, as you will see in Activity **A**.

	With an object	Without an object
separable	She **gave up** her job. / She **gave** her job **up**. ~~She gave up it~~. / She **gave** it **up**. Other examples: *put off, size up, think over*	She **bounced back** (recovered) from her illness. The plane **took off** on a dangerous mission.
inseparable	She **looked after** her colleagues. The doctor **looked after** them. Other examples: *find out, put up with*	Other examples: *die down, pick up, step in*

Some phrasal verbs have three words. They are always inseparable: *How much longer do we have to* ***put up with*** *this rain?*
Every winter I ***come down with*** *a cold.*

Bangkok floods of 2011

A Tam lives in Bangkok. Read his e-mails to his friend Pierre in Canada. Match each phrasal verb in the reading with a verb in this list that has the same meaning.

_____ assess	_____ discovered; learned	_____ postpone
_____ became less	_____ increasing	_____ recover
_____ consider	_____ intervene	_____ tolerate

October 6 It took me forever to get to the airport, where I (1) **found out** my flight was canceled. The winds are (2) **picking up** and it looks like it's going to start raining again.

October 7 It rained all night. The winds (3) **died down** this morning, so I went out to (4) **size up** the situation. This is the worst flooding I have ever seen. I'll have to (5) **put off** my trip for a couple of days.

October 9 I haven't been able to write since Internet service has been cut off because of the storm. They're saying the military is planning to (6) **step in** to help people with the flooding. I can't (7) **put up with** drinking soda and eating noodles much longer. I wonder when Bangkok will be able to (8) **bounce back** from this storm.

October 10 I'm going to have to cancel my plans to visit you. Why don't you come and visit me in December? (9) **Think** it **over** and let me know your answer.

B Work with a partner. What do these weather expressions mean? Look up any you don't know. Then give an opinion or make predictions about these types of weather. Use phrasal verbs where you can.

torrential rain	a cold spell	scattered showers	pouring rain
boiling hot	a heat wave	snow flurries	heat stroke

I can't put up with boiling hot temperatures. I prefer pouring rain!

Extension

Have students imagine they are Tam's friend Pierre in Canada. Have them write brief e-mails in response to each of Tam's messages, using at least one phrasal verb in each e-mail.

Grammar

20-30 min. **A**
20-25 min. **B**
Extension: 10-15 min.

Language Notes

- Ask students to point out the phrasal verbs in the vocabulary they learned on page 122 (*cut off, give up, look after, take off*).
- To show how phrasal verbs have different meanings from their base verbs alone, ask students to find the two phrasal verbs using *put* in the chart (*put off, put up with*).
- Explain that a phrasal verb can have more than one meaning. Additionally, some phrasal verbs can be used both with an object and without an object. Point out *pick up* and indicate the difference in its meaning with and without an object: *The wind picked up as the rain started. / Gwen picked up her toys.*

A
- Encourage students to refer to the Word Bank on page 122 when completing Exercise **A**.
- After reviewing the answers, check overall comprehension by asking students: What is Tam trying to do? Why can't he do it?
- Have students work with a partner to identify the phrasal verbs used in Tam's e-mails. Ask them to list these verbs in two categories: phrasal verbs that do not have an object and phrasal verbs that do take an object. For those verbs that do take an object, ask students which verbs are separable and have them rewrite the sentences (*size the situation up, put my trip off*).

Answers: 1. discovered; 2. increasing; 3. became less; 4. assess; 5. postpone; 6. intervene; 7. tolerate; 8. recover; 9. consider

B Challenge students to use four separable phrasal verbs and four inseparable phrasal verbs in their predictions.

Sample answers: I found out there will be a cold spell tomorrow—we might have snow flurries. The scattered showers are picking up—soon it will be pouring everywhere. I can't put up with boiling hot weather. Let's hope we don't have another heat wave. It's hard to bounce back from heat stroke.

Outcome: Upon completing this exercise, students will have met the Outcome ***use phrasal verbs.***

Listening

10-15 min. A
15-20 min. B
15-20 min. C
Extension: 15-20 min.

A • Explain to students that English has many idiomatic expressions related to the weather that are used to describe people and their moods. Share these weather-related expressions and their meanings: *under the weather* (ill) and *a sunny disposition* (cheerful). Ask students if they can think of any others.
• Ask students to explain how the weather words in the expressions to describe people are related to the action or state that each describes.

B • Before you play each conversation, give students time to read the questions and guess what the conversation will be about.
• Play the audio recording of the conversations one or more times. **Audio CD Track 21**
• Read through the Tip with the class and ask students to identify the meaning of *pick up* used in Conversation 3 (to lift). Replay that conversation if necessary.

Answers: 1. b; 2. a; 3. c; 4. a; 5. c; 6. a; 7. b; 8. b

C • Play the audio recording again. Pause after each conversation for students to write down their definitions. **Audio CD Track 21**
• Have students work with the same partners they had in Exercise **A** and compare their original guesses to their final answers. Ask students whether they guessed right.
• Have students discuss the Ask and Answer questions in pairs.
• Explain that the expression *chill out* can have different meanings depending on the context. It can mean *spend time relaxing*. When used as a command, as in Conversation 3, *chill out* means *don't worry*.
• Point out that the verb *break through* is an open compound, while the noun *breakthrough*, meaning *a sudden improvement*, is a closed compound.

Possible answers: *storm out* = to leave a place angrily; *hold off* = to delay, not happen immediately; *break through* = to emerge; *come down* = to descend; *chill out* = to relax; *freeze up* = to become stuck; unable to move

Listening

A Look at the expressions below. What do you think they mean? Working with a partner, take a guess.

To describe weather	To describe people
break through	chill out
come down	freeze up
hold off	storm out

TIP You might notice that many phrasal verbs have more than one meaning. *Pick up*, for example, can mean (1) *to increase* (without an object), (2) or *to lift* (with an object, as in *pick up a bag*), (3) *to physically obtain* (as in *pick up a newspaper from the store*), or (4) *to learn* (as in *picking up a new language*). Which meaning is used in Conversation 3?

B Listen to the four conversations. Choose the answer that completes each sentence.

Conversation 1

1. Jill went to a(n) ___ party.
   a. anniversary
   b. birthday
   c. retirement
2. There was a(n) ___.
   a. argument
   b. performance
   c. announcement

Conversation 2

3. Bill is worried that ___.
   a. people won't come
   b. he isn't prepared
   c. it will rain
4. Dan is ___.
   a. confident
   b. unsure
   c. unhelpful

Conversation 3

5. Carrie wants to meet her friend at ___.
   a. school
   b. Deena's house
   c. the theater
6. In the end, Carrie is ___.
   a. staying home
   b. going out
   c. going to Deena's house

Conversation 4

7. Andy wants to ___.
   a. be on the baseball team
   b. appear in the school play
   c. graduate early
8. Andy feels ___ about his chances.
   a. unclear
   b. negative
   c. positive

C Listen again. What do these words mean?

1. storm out (Conversation 1)
2. hold off (Conversation 2)
3. break through (Conversation 2)
4. come down (Conversation 3)
5. chill out (Conversation 3)
6. freeze up (Conversation 4)

Ask Answer Have you ever stormed out of a room? If so, what made you so upset? What do you and your friends do to chill out? Think of a time when you froze up and didn't know what to do. What was the situation? How did it end?

Extension

After students have discussed the meanings of the expressions in Exercise **C**, have them get with a partner and play charades to act out each one. Explain to them that charades is a game in which one person performs actions without speaking while another guesses the word or phrase. Then ask for six volunteers to perform a charade for each expression in front of the class to see if everyone can guess the expressions they're demonstrating.

Connections

break down to stop working properly
call off to cancel

A Look at the photos and answer the questions. Work with a partner. Where do you think these images are from? What do you know about the weather surrounding events like the ones you see here?

dust storm

blizzard

hurricane

B Work with a different partner. You are going to role-play a telephone call, sitting back to back so that you can't see each other's faces. Follow the steps. Use phrasal verbs in the box in your conversation when you can.

break down	*call off*	*chill out*	*come down*	*cut off*	*die down*
hold off	*put off*	*put up with*	*size up*	*be snowed in*	*take off*

Student A

Choose one of the photos above. You are on vacation in that place. Something has happened and now you have to cancel or change your plans. Imagine you are calling home to your friend, Student B. You should tell your partner:

What's happened

What you plan to do next

Student B

Your friend, Student A, is away on vacation (but you're not sure where). Suddenly the phone rings. It's your friend, calling you while still on vacation! You should ask your partner:

Where he/she is

How the vacation is going

C Switch roles and repeat Exercise **B** using a different photo.

Student A: There's been a huge snowstorm.

Student B: Is your flight going to take off as scheduled?

Student A: I don't think so. The snow is really coming down.

Student B: What are you going to do?

Internet Activity

Have students do research to learn more about hurricanes at the following Web site: http://environment.nationalgeographic.com/environment/natural-disasters/hurricane-profile/. Then ask students to imagine they are in an area where a hurricane is predicted. Have them write a paragraph describing what they will do to prepare, using at least four phrasal verbs.

Connections

10-15 min. **A**
15-20 min. **B**
15-20 min. **C**
Extension: 10-15 min.

A
- Inform students that *call off* is a separable phrasal verb. Have them use these phrasal verbs in sentences about the photos. e.g., *My car broke down in the blizzard. My brother called off his wedding* (or: *called his wedding off*) *because of the hurricane*.
- After students have discussed the photos with their partners, write the words *dust storm*, *blizzard*, and *hurricane* side-by-side on the board. Invite students to come forward and write any weather words and expressions they can think that relate to each of these events.

Photo Captions

- Left image is the Sydney Harbour Bridge in Sydney, Australia, during a dust storm on September 23, 2009.
- Middle image is of vehicles stranded on a highway in Chicago, Illinois, USA, after a blizzard in February 2011.
- Right image is Hurricane Wilma in downtown Miami, Florida, USA, in October 2005. Before it reached land, Wilma was the most intense tropical storm ever recorded in the Atlantic Ocean.

B
- Review the meanings of the phrasal verbs in the box before students begin the activity.
- Encourage pairs of students to decide who will play which role.
- Remind Student A not to tell Student B which photo he or she has chosen before they begin their role-play.
- Give students time to write notes to prepare their conversations.
- Encourage students to look at the speech models in Exercise **C** for ideas.
- When students finish the role-play, ask them these questions: *Was it harder to communicate? If so, what made it harder?*

Extension

As a follow-up to Exercises **B** and **C**, have students find another partner and role-play phone conversations in which they explain their first partner's ordeal. If necessary, preview for them reported speech, which will be covered in the Grammar section of Unit 12 on page 135.

Video

15-20 min. A
10-15 min. B
15-20 min. C
Extension: 10-15 min.

Background Information

Students will watch a documentary video about how changes in the climate are affecting the coastline of Great Britain. Inform students that Great Britain is an island made up of the countries England, Scotland, and Wales.

Before You Watch

A
- Review the word bank with the class. Point out to students that *batter* and *defend* are words related to fighting. Ask students to guess what fighting has to do with the photo of a coastline.
- Point out the relationship between the words *coast* (land near the sea) and *coastline* (the boundary between the land and sea).

B
- Tell students that another way to say *in a sorry state* is *in a bad way*.
- Ask students to explain why *paper over the cracks* describes a temporary solution. If necessary, explain with this example: *When a wall has a crack in it, putting paper over the crack only makes it look nicer, but does not fix the problem. The wall still might break.*

Answers: 1. develop naturally; 2. poor; 3. temporarily

C
- Before showing the video, direct students' attention to the four prompts in the chart. Ask students to rephrase each prompt as a question that will be answered in the video. e.g., *What is the problem? Why is it happening? What is the government doing? What are they doing in Essex?*
- Play the video, and have students practice taking notes with the purpose of addressing each of the four prompts in the chart. Have them divide a piece of paper into four parts, and write one prompt in each corner. As they watch the video, have them take notes when they hear information related to each topic.

Answers: 1a. North; 1b. shrinking; 2a. rises, falls; 2b. warming; 3a. defend; 3b. building, repairing; 4a. protect; 4b. sea walls

Video

batter to hit something with strong force
coastline the boundary between land and sea
defend to protect something against attack
erosion the gradual removal of rock and dirt by the weather (wind, the sea, etc.)
shrink to become smaller

A Look at the word bank and the photo. Answer the questions with a partner.

1. What is the video going to be about?
2. What do you think is causing it to happen?

B Read these sentences from the video. What do the underlined expressions mean?

1. If we didn't defend, nature would take its course and we'll lose more land. *to take its course* = **develop naturally / change direction** and come to an end
2. The sea walls themselves are in a sorry state. *in a sorry state* = in **good / poor** condition
3. We simply can't continue to paper over the cracks. *to paper over the cracks* = to fix something that is damaged so that it works **temporarily / permanently**

C Watch the video. Complete the chart with key words.

1. The problem a. The _______ Sea is eroding the coastline. b. Great Britain is _______.	3. What the government is doing a. The government is spending a lot of money to _______ the coastline. b. Most of the money is used for _______ new sea walls and _______ older ones.
2. Why it's happening a. The country is gradually tilting: Scotland _______ and England _______. b. Sea levels are rising due to global _______.	4. What they're doing in Essex a. They are flooding the salt marshes to _______ the coast. b. They are not building more _______.

Ask Answer Do you know of other places in the world that are slowly disappearing? Why is it happening?

salt marsh

126

Extension

Have students make notes about another weather problem—either in their region or another part of the world. Tell them to use the chart in Exercise **C** as a model for the questions they need to answer. Then have them write out a descriptive paragraph, including a description of the problem, why it is happening, and what different groups are doing to fix the problem.

Speaking

A Get into groups of four. Each student should read one story and then follow the steps.

1. Take turns explaining your story to the group.
2. What did you find surprising about each story? Discuss with your group.

❶ OTTO THE OCTOPUS

The staff of the Berlin Zoo look after many exotic animals, but none as popular as Otto the Octopus. He has a special skill. His handlers believe that Otto can predict when the sea is going to rise. When he floats at the top of the tank, it means that the seawater will soon be going up and the waves will be rough. If he sits at the bottom, the opposite effect will occur—winds will die down and the seas will be calm. The zoo staff recently postponed a boat trip to a nearby island due to Otto's prediction of "bad weather."

❷ THE DISAPPEARING CITY

The capital city of Mauritania (a country in West Africa) is known for its mild weather and central location within the country. It's also slowly disappearing . . . sections are being buried under sand from the nearby desert. After assessing the situation, residents tried building fences and pouring gasoline on the dunes, but nothing has seemed to work. At this point, they are used to putting up with the sand, but worried that they are losing their city.

❸ THE DAY IT RAINED FISH

On February 8, 2008, a strange rain started to come down in Kerala, India. As the winds picked up, local villagers reported that small, moving objects were falling out of the sky during the storm. It didn't take long to discover that they were fish! Scientists have some theories but are not sure how this could happen. The people who experienced it will never forget "the day it rained fish."

❹ MAKING IT RAIN

Have you ever considered what it would be like to change the weather? In the summer of 2010, scientists in Abu Dhabi did just that. They used a special machine to create more than fifty rainstorms—some with strong winds, hail, and lightning—on days when there were clear skies and no forecast of rain. They plan to keep on using this technology in areas where there is little to no rainfall. Needless to say, local residents were completely confused.

B These stories might all seem unbelievable, but only one of them is false. Which one do you think it is? Discuss with your group. Give reasons for your answer.

C Present your choice to the class and explain your reasoning. Your instructor will give you the correct answer. How many groups guessed correctly?

Rubric	Very Good	Satisfactory	Needs Improvement
Ability to relate a story elaborately			
Use of vocabulary			
Use of grammar			
Pronunciation and fluency			

Speaking

20-25 min. A
10-15 min. B
10-15 min. C
Extension: 10-20 min.

A
- Divide students into their groups, and assign the stories to the different group members. Give students 5–10 minutes to read through their assigned stories independently. Address any questions they have.
- Then have students work with partners and practice reading their stories aloud. Remind students to use intonation and hand gestures to draw attention to the most interesting parts of their stories.
- Next, have students gather in their groups of four to share their stories. Encourage students to retell the stories in their own words dramatically and enthusiastically.
- As the groups are discussing the stories, walk around the classroom and make sure each student is participating in the conversation.

B
- For each story, make a chart on the board with two columns, labeled "true" and "false."
- After groups have discussed the stories, have a representative come forward and mark if the group thought that each was true or false. Ask the representative to explain the group's reasons.

C
- If no one has noticed the contradiction, point out that Berlin is not near the ocean. Encourage students to locate Berlin on a map.
- Tell students that Story 1 is based on an actual German octopus named Paul, who lived in the aquarium in Oberhausen. During the 2010 soccer World Cup, some people believed that Paul was able to predict the winners of the soccer matches. Paul died later in 2010.

Answer: Story 1, "Otto the Octopus," is false.

Extension

Based on this game, have students play "two truths and a lie." Tell them to think of three interesting facts about themselves but make one of them not true. Divide them into groups of three and have them share their facts. Encourage other group members to ask questions and decide which story is false.

Reading

10-15 min. **A**	
10-15 min. **B**	
10 min. **C**	
10-15 min. **D**	
Extension: 15-20 min.	

A Have students read the title of the article and ask them these additional questions: *What do you think storm chasers do? Why do they do it? Do you enjoy storms or do you think they are scary? What would you do if there were a tornado warning in your neighborhood?*

B

Answers: time of day; a whole day; crowded areas; winds from the north

C
- Review the word *percent*. Remind students that when they see the percent symbol (%), they should read out "percent."
- Review the pronunciation of *kph*. Tell students that *kph* stands for *kilometers per hour* and that they should read out the phrase "kilometers per hour" when they see this abbreviation.

Answers: *about 1,000*: how many tornadoes happen in the United States each year; *40%*: the percentage of tornadoes that happen in the central plains; *48 kilometers (wide)*: how large supercells (massive thunderstorms) can become; *one in a thousand*: how many thunderstorms become a supercell; *one in five or six*: how many supercells become a tornado; *F0 (winds of 64–116 kph)*: a storm that does light damage; *F5 (winds starting at 419 kph)*: a storm that does horrible damage

D
- Read through the Reading Strategy with the class, and make sure that students understand what is meant by *inference*.
- Give students some simple examples of inferences they can make: *Gary is sweating and he turned on the fan*. Inference: He's probably hot. *Monica put on her coat and picked up her keys*. Inference: She's probably leaving.

continued on page 129

Reading

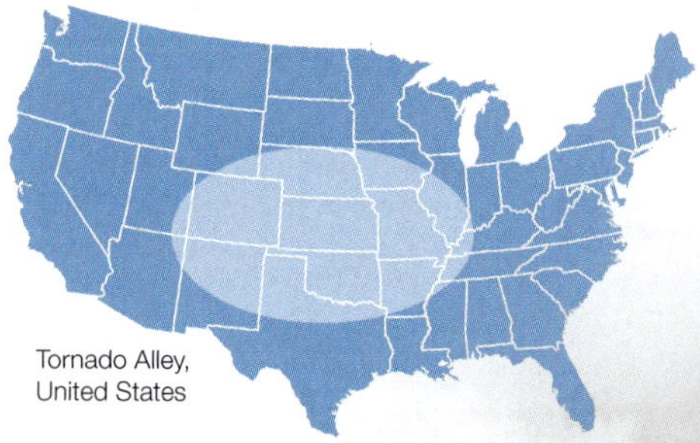

A Look at the photo of a tornado and answer the questions. Discuss with a partner. Then read the article to check your answers.

1. What do you know about tornadoes?
2. Where and when do they occur most often?

B Read the article again. Cross out the one item from each list that doesn't belong. Then check your answers with a partner.

What the storm chasers measure	How long tornadoes can last	Where many tornadoes occur	Conditions necessary for tornadoes to occur
wind speed humidity temperature time of day	a whole day an hour or more a few seconds	flat ground crowded areas good places for farming central plains states	warm wet air cool dry air winds from the north

C What do these numbers refer to in the reading? Write your answers on a separate piece of paper.

about 1,000	40%	48 kilometers (wide)	one in a thousand
one in five or six	F0 (winds of 64–116 kph)	F5 (winds starting at 419 kph)	

D Read these inferences that are based on information in the article. Then explain why you think the inference is true, based on what you read.

> **Reading Strategy**
> **Making Inferences** An inference is a conclusion that you draw about something you read. You can guess something is true based on the information you have—even when it isn't stated directly in the article.
> Statement: *The tornado caused more than light damage.*
> Inference: *On the Fujita scale, the tornado was greater than an F0.*
> (This is probably true because an F0 tornado only causes light damage.)

1. Inference: The storm chasers are driving in a rural area. (paragraphs 1 and 3)
   This is probably true because . . .
2. Inference: No one has ever filmed the inside of a tornado. (paragraph 2)
3. Inference: Tornadoes are not easily formed. (paragraph 5)
4. Inference: The path of a tornado is unpredictable. (paragraph 9)

Ask Answer Tim Samaras has a dangerous job. What can you infer from the article about his personality? How similar are you to Tim? Would you ever do what he does? Why or why not?

Extension

Have each student write five true statements about the weather in your region (e.g., *It rains a lot.*). Then have them switch papers with a partner and write five new sentences based on their partners' statements. Each new sentence should imply the information in the original sentence without directly stating it (e.g., *People carry umbrellas with them every day.*).

STORM CHASERS

Two cars rush down a nearby dirt road straight at an approaching tornado. Storm chaser Tim Samaras, a 45-year-old electronics engineer from Denver, and his partner, Pat Porter, are in a van carrying equipment used to measure the tornado's wind speed and direction, air pressure, humidity (the amount of water in the air), and temperature.

Photographer Carsten Peter hangs halfway out the window of the other speeding car, which is driven by expert storm chaser Gene Rhoden. Carsten is excited. He wants to be the first person to film a tornado from the inside of the tornado itself.

The chasers can hear the tornado's jet engine roar and see it snapping power poles as they travel east past the local farms and directly into the path of the storm. It is not too far away, and the winds are picking up.

Tornadoes are among Earth's most violent natural acts. About a thousand of them happen in the United States each year, more than in any other country in the world. Some are weak and last only seconds, while others can cause damage for an hour or more.

Forty percent of all US tornadoes occur in the central plains states, agricultural[1] areas that are mostly flat. The "tornado season" occurs from March through July, when cool, dry air from the Rocky Mountains meets warm, wet air coming up from the Gulf of Mexico. In such open country you can see entire supercells (a rare kind of thunderstorm with especially strong winds), some as large as 48 kilometers wide. Only one in a thousand thunderstorms becomes a supercell, and only one in five or six supercells gives birth to a tornado.

Scientists measure tornadoes by the damage they cause. On the Fujita scale, named after Ted Fujita of the University of Chicago, an F0 storm does light damage with winds between 64 and 116 kph. The worst tornado, at level F5, does horrible damage with winds starting at 419 kph.

> "Storm chasers" are people who get close to violent storms in order to study and photograph them.

The clouds in the sky are spinning swiftly, and a confused bird flies in front of Gene Rhoden's car. And then a part of one cloud lowers and gathers into the shape of a funnel.[2] It spins like an angry ghost, no more than 3 kilometers from the storm chasers, looking like an alien[3] has come to Earth. The storm chasers are moving closer to the storm.

The tornado moves quickly through the fields, where it's destroying bushes and trees. Tim considers the situation carefully. He wants to find out all he can about the storm, but at the same time he must look after his team.

Before he can finish his assessment, the tornado does something strange. It seems to stand almost still, and then suddenly . . . it takes off, lifting up overhead. It's as if the sky were pulling a finger back into its fist. The winds have died down completely. The storm chasers pull their cars over to the side of the road to take a break. They've given up the chase for today.

[1] **agricultural** the science or practice of raising crops and animals (farming)
[2] **funnel** an object, which has a wide round opening at the top and a narrow tube at the bottom, used for pouring liquids
[3] **alien** a creature from another planet

129

Reading *continued*

D

Answers: 1. This is probably true because they are driving on dirt roads and seeing farms. 2. This is probably true because Carsten Peter wants to be the first person to do this. 3. This is probably true because only one in a thousand thunderstorms becomes a supercell and only one in five or six supercells becomes a tornado. 4. This is probably true because the storm snakes across the ground and then suddenly takes off.

Outcome: Upon completing this exercise, students will have met the Outcome ***make inferences based on information you have learned.***

Background Information

Tornadoes occur most commonly in the central plains region of the United States. This area is sometimes called "Tornado Alley" and includes parts of South Dakota, Colorado, Nebraska, Kansas, Oklahoma, and Texas. Any area that is prone to tornadoes usually has "tornado sirens" that alert the community when a tornado has been spotted. Students can learn more about tornadoes, including safety tips, at http://environment.nationalgeographic.com/environment/natural-disasters/tornado-profile/.

Language Notes

- Line 12: Point out that the word *chasers* is a shortened term for *storm chasers*.
- Line 12: Explain that the expression *jet engine roar* is a metaphor that means that the tornado sounds similar to a jet engine.
- Line 15: Explain that *too* means *very* in this context.
- Line 23: Explain that the writer uses quotation marks around "tornado season" to explain that it is an invented time frame when tornadoes are most common.
- Line 30: Point out that *gives birth to* means *results in* in this context.
- Lines 46–47: Point out the similes *like an angry ghost* and *like an alien has come to Earth*. Explain that similes are examples of figurative language that make the article more interesting for the reader, and that students will learn more about them in the Writing section on page 130.
- Line 56: Point out the phrase *as if the sky were pulling a finger back into its fist* is also a simile. Explain that with this image, the writer imagines that the tornado looks like a finger and the cloud looks like a person's fist.

Beyond the Reading

Have students imagine a different ending to the article. Ask them to rewrite the final paragraph imagining that the tornado does not disappear. They should begin their paragraphs with the phrase "Before he can finish his final assessment . . ." Encourage them to use at least three phrasal verbs and to use as much figurative language as possible. Ask for volunteers to read their endings in front of the class.

Writing

5 min. **A**
10-15 min. **B**
5-10 min. **C**
10-15 min. **D**
10 min. **E**
Extension: 10 min.

Purpose of Writing

The purpose of a vivid description is to describe something in such a way that the readers will understand how the writer feels. Vivid descriptions often use figurative language.

A Ask students how often they pay attention to weather in the news. Survey the class to find out how many students read or heard a weather report today. Ask who knows what the weather will be like tomorrow.

B
- Before they read Aleksei's description, direct students' attention to the photo. Ask them what type of weather they think Aleksei is going to describe.
- Explain that when Aleksei writes that his sister "can be as annoying as a puppy," he uses *can* to mean that she *sometimes is*, not that she *is capable of being*, annoying.

Answers: 1. some snow; not too cold; sunny; changeable; 2. a cold spell; got cold and stayed cold; temperature got down to –20°C; 3. bus was often late; sometimes had to walk to school; 4. had to turn off the water; had to get up earlier; had to stay home every day after school; 5. couldn't get warm and that put him in a bad mood; frustrated; a little bored

C Explain that when students use the expression *as if* + [*to be*], they should always use the past subjunctive form *were*: *It was as if the wind were calling my name.*

Possible Answers: 1. The weather was crazy, like we were on another planet. 2. I felt as if I were going to be sucked up into the sky. 3. The wind was as strong as a tsunami.

Extension

Use Aleksei's description to review phrasal verbs. Have students underline the phrasal verbs in the description and find the separable phrasal verb that is used. (turn off)

continued on page 131

Writing

A Vivid Description

A Discuss the questions with a partner.

1. How much does weather affect your daily life?
2. Why is there so much information (in newspapers, on TV, on the Internet) about the weather?

B Read Aleksei's essay about how a change in weather affected his daily life. What did you learn? Complete the first column about Aleksei's life in the chart below.

Where I live, we can have cold temperatures in the winter and gray skies with some snow. It doesn't typically get too cold, though, and it's usually sunny. That's why I was so surprised one week last February. We had a cold spell like no other. At one point, the temperature dropped down to –20°C. No matter how many layers of clothing I wore, I couldn't get warm. It was so frigid that we had to turn off the water because otherwise the pipes would freeze and burst.

To get to school on time, I had to get up early because I couldn't depend on the bus. Usually I take a short bus ride to get to school, but during the cold weather the bus was often late, so I had to walk to school. When I arrived, I felt so cold, like an ice cube. That put me in a bad mood. It was too cold to be outside for very long, so I stayed home every day after school. I got a little frustrated and bored. My little sister is cute, but she was always bothering me. She can be as annoying as a puppy—always running around and making noise.

When the weather finally became more mild, I didn't have to wear as many layers of clothing so it felt as if I had lost 10 kilos. I hope we don't have another cold spell like that again!

	Aleksei	You
1. typical weather		
2. change in the weather		
3. impact on getting around		
4. impact on home life		
5. impact on mood		

C Read the Writing Strategy. Then look back at the reading on page 129; use the strategy to complete the sentences below.

Imagine you were with Tim Samaras, chasing a tornado.

1. The weather was crazy, like ______________.
2. I felt as if ______________.
3. The wind was as strong as ______________.

Writing Strategy **Using Similes** A simile is an expression that compares two things that the reader is familiar with in an unexpected way. We use similes (phrases with *like, as if,* and *as . . . as*) to make our writing more interesting and colorful for our readers.

When I arrived at school, I felt so cold, **like an ice cube**.

She can be **as annoying as a puppy**.

I didn't have to wear as many layers of clothing so it felt **as if I had lost 10 kilos**.

Rubric	Very Good	Satisfactory	Needs Improvement
Content			
Use of descriptive language			
Use of grammar			
Organization			

D Now write about a time when the weather affected your life. First, complete the second column in the chart in Exercise **B** with your information. Then, write your paragraphs. Use Aleksei's essay as an example. Include two or three comparisons using "like," "as if," and "as . . . as."

E Exchange papers with another student. Read your partner's writing. Does it clearly explain how weather affected daily life? Does it use similes to create a vivid image?

Expanding Your Fluency

A Some phrasal verbs have more than one meaning. Read about these three situations. What does "break down" mean in each case? Match each usage to its definition below.

1. You are driving in the country with your friend when your car **breaks down**. There is a thunderstorm approaching and you realize you've left your cell phone at home and your friend's phone isn't getting any reception.	2. You're studying in London and it's been a long and cold winter. You have a friend who is originally from the Caribbean who isn't used to cold weather. You see your friend at school and ask, "How are you?" Your friend **breaks down** and starts crying.	3. You borrowed money from a friend to repair your car windows after a storm. You recently got paid at work and were supposed to pay your friend back but you **broke down** and bought a new surfboard instead. What will you say to your friend?

a. to give in to something; lose control

b. to stop working properly

c. to get upset; become emotional

B Work with a partner. Choose one of the situations and create a minute-long role-play about it. In your dialog, you must also use three or four phrasal verbs that you learned in this unit.

C Get together with another pair and do your role-plays for each other. At the end of the other pair's role-play answer this question: How did they resolve the problem?

Check What You Know

Rank how well you can perform these outcomes on a scale of 1–5 (5 being the best).

________ explain how weather affects your life

________ make inferences based on information you have learned

________ understand and use similes

________ use phrasal verbs

Writing *continued*

D Review the Writing Strategy and have students generate similes of their own. Have them brainstorm possible descriptions by first choosing an adjective and then listing several nouns that could be described by that adjective. Then have them work with a partner to discuss a context in which the similes might be used.

Outcome: Upon completing this exercise, students will have met the Outcome ***understand and use similes***.

Expanding Your Fluency

15-20 min. **A**
15-20 min. **B**
10-15 min. **C**
Extension: 10-15 min.

A
- Give students these additional sets of sentences. Have them use a dictionary to find the different meanings of the phrasal verbs.
- *add up*: 1. His story doesn't add up. 2. The final bill adds up to $40.
- *back up*: 1. My computer crashed. I should've backed it up. 2. If you don't believe me, talk to Jon. He can back me up. 3. Let's back up right away and get out of here!
- *blow up*: 1. The grenade blew up. 2. Can you blow up this balloon? 3. We need to blow up the image in order to see the details.
- *take off*: 1. The plane eventually took off. 2. His career is really taking off. 3. He won't take his hat off. 4. I took three weeks off last summer.

Answers: 1. b; 2. c; 3. a

B
- So that not all pairs are preparing the same situation, assign one situation to each.
- Challenge students to incorporate similes into their role-plays. Give them a few examples if necessary. e.g., *I feel so trapped here, like a prisoner. I felt as if you didn't think about what I need. I was as scared as a puppy in a thunderstorm.*

C As students are discussing their classmates' role-plays, refer them to the chart on page 126. Have them name the problem, explain why it is happening, and what each person is doing to fix the problem.

Extension

Play a game using similes. Have each student call out one noun and one adjective, and write all of their suggestions on the board. Then give students five minutes to write as many similes as they can using the words on the board. Take a class vote on which simile makes the best comparison between two things.

Check What You Know

Refer students back to the exercises in the unit where each Outcome is addressed.

- ***explain how weather affects your life***: Vocabulary, Exercise **A**, page 122
- ***make inferences based on information you have learned***: Reading, Exercise **D**, page 128
- ***understand and use similes***: Writing, Exercise **D**, page 131
- ***use phrasal verbs***: Grammar, Exercise **B**, page 123

Unit 12
What's Your Game?

Unit Overview

- Unit 12 is about playing sports, games, and activities. Students will learn about how the games they play and activities they participate in can reveal something about their personalities.
- Ask students what they think is meant by the unit title, "What's Your Game?" Explain that *game* is sometimes used to refer to a person's profession, interests, or passions. Asking, "What's your game?" is an informal way to ask what someone does or what someone likes to do.
- Preview the unit by asking students the following questions:
  1. What's your favorite sport to watch? To play?
  2. If you had a choice between playing a board game and a video game, which would you choose? Why?
  3. Are you competitive? How do you feel when you lose a game?

Background Information

Sports play an important part in cultures all over the world. In the United States, the most popular team sports that people watch are (American) football, baseball, basketball, and ice hockey. In the rest of the world, soccer (football) is the most popular. Participation in sports is high among children due to organized programs at schools and in local youth leagues. In the United States, over 26 million children play basketball. Baseball follows a distant second with 15 million, then soccer at 14 million young players.

Photo Caption

This image is of the women's National Cycling Championship race at Seward Park in Seattle, Washington, United States, in 1994. Bicycling, a popular pastime throughout the world, is also a competitive sport that requires athletes to be in peak physical condition. The most famous cycling competition in the world, the Tour de France, takes place each July, lasting three weeks and covering more than 3,600 kilometers (2,200 miles).

12 What's Your Game?

VOCABULARY	GRAMMAR	LISTENING	READING
Team and individual sports	Reported speech	A professional basketball player in China	*The Battle for the Soul of Kung Fu:* A Shaolin master faces changes in the world of kung fu

1 What is this a picture of? Have you ever done this sport?

2 What do you prefer: watching sports or playing them?

3 List as many sports, games, and activities as you can. Circle the ones that are competitive. Underline the ones you do with a team. Which do you prefer and why?

Unit Outcomes

In this unit, you will learn to:

- use reported speech to explain what someone else said
- evaluate the relationship between activities and personal qualities
- pace yourself as you write a timed essay
- use an outline to support a presentation or essay

5-10 min. **Warm-Up Questions**
Extension: 10-15 min.

Warm-Up Questions

- Read Question 1 aloud and ask students to provide any information they know about competitive cycling. Ask them if they know any famous cyclists or well-known races.
- Take a survey of the class to see what students prefer when it comes to sports: watching, participating, or neither?
- Have students work with a partner to answer Question 3.
- **Examples of sports, games, and activities:** auto racing, baseball, basketball, biking, billiards, bowling, boxing, card games, cheerleading, chess, cricket, dancing, debate team, fencing, football (soccer), golf, gymnastics, hiking, hockey, horse / camel riding or racing, kayaking, kickboxing, lacrosse, martial arts (e.g., karate, judo, kung fu), pilates, ping pong (table tennis), rock climbing, rowing, rugby, running, sailing, skateboarding, skating, skiing, snowboarding, surfing, swimming, tennis, video games, volleyball, water skiing, weight lifting, wrestling, and yoga.

Extension

Survey the class to find the most popular answers to Question 3. Invite students to come forward one at a time and write their responses on the board. If a sport or activity has already been written, have students place a check mark next to it. Then ask the class these questions: *What is the most popular team sport in the class? Which sports are not as popular? What is the most unusual sport mentioned?*

VIDEO	WRITING	SPEAKING	OUTCOMES
Alain Robert: The French Spiderman	Write about important qualities **Strategy:** Pacing yourself as you write a timed essay	Present how to be good at an activity **Strategy:** Speaking from an outline	• use reported speech to explain what someone else said • evaluate the relationship between activities and personal qualities • pace yourself as you write a timed essay • use an outline to support a presentation or essay

Vocabulary

15-20 min. A
10-15 min. B
15-20 min. C
Extension: 10-15 min.

A • Explain that the verb *beat* is used with the name of the losing person or team, while *win* is used with the event (e.g., *we beat our rivals*; *we won the game*).

- Point out that *coach* can also be a verb, meaning "to train or guide players in a sport."
- Teach students the opposite of *in shape: out of shape*.
- Students will learn in Exercise **B** that the photos show people playing rugby, a team sport, and doing kickboxing, an individual sport.

Language Notes

- The construction *to get* + adjective often means *to become*. Contrast it with *to be* + adjective. Note the difference in usage between *to be used to* / *to be in shape* and *to get used to* / *to get in shape*.
- Ask students to explain the difference between these sentences: *You'll* ***get used to*** *the exercises.* / *Bob* ***is in*** *great* ***shape***.

B Have students read the Word Partnership feature before they complete Exercise **B**. After they have read the paragraphs, ask them to write definitions of *self-discipline* and *self-confidence*.

Answers: 1. coach; 2. beat; 3. commitment; 4. defend; 5. in better shape; 6. achieve

C Point out the phrase *on and off the playing field*. If necessary, explain that it refers to success while participating in a sport (on the field) and in other areas of life (off the field). Explain that a variation of the phrase is *on and off the court*.

Answers: 1. Derek grew up watching rugby with his father; Ana's friend convinced her to join a kickboxing class with her. Benefits: Winning games (national champs), getting in shape. Possible answers: great way to meet people, make friends, great way to relieve stress when you play or practice, etc. 2. Trying to achieve something even when it's difficult; motivation; self-discipline; teamwork / learning to work well with others; 3. Answers will vary.

Vocabulary

achieve to succeed in doing something after a lot of effort
beat to win against someone and defeat them in a competition
championship a competition to find the best player or team in a particular sport
coach a person who trains others to play a sport
commitment dedication to doing something
defend to protect from harm or injury
get used to to become accustomed to something
in shape fit, healthy
motivation a strong desire or willingness to do something
obsessed constantly thinking about something
opponent a rival, especially in a game

Word Partnership

self- (combined with words in descriptions that relate to a person's own self). For example: *self-centered, self-conscious, self-defense, self-employed*. Find two more examples in Exercise **B**.

A Look at the photos below and tell a partner anything you know about these sports.

B Read what Derek and Ana have to say about rugby and kickboxing, respectively. Complete each profile with a word from the list.

I'm a huge rugby fan. I grew up watching it with my dad and have been obsessed with the sport ever since. I played in university and now I'm the (1) ____________ of a high school rugby team that has won several national championships. People ask me how we've managed to (2) ____________ so many of our opponents. Part of it is talent and a team that works well together. But a big part is also each player's (3) ____________ to training hard and giving his best *every* day. It takes a lot of motivation and self-discipline, but that's what wins a game.

A friend told me that she was taking a kickboxing class and convinced me to join her. At first, every session was an intense workout, and I'd be exhausted by the end. After several classes, I got used to the exercises and started doing really well. Not only have I learned to (4) ____________ myself, now I'm (5) ____________ too, which has really increased my self-confidence. Studying kickboxing has taught me that you can (6) ____________ anything if you work hard enough.

C Discuss the questions with a partner.

1. How did Derek and Ana get interested in their sports? What are the benefits of each one?
2. Which personal qualities do these sports help people develop? Add ideas to make a list.
   - Commitment to hard work
   - ____________________
   - ____________________
   - ____________________
3. How can these qualities help you succeed both on and off the playing field?

Extension

Have students choose a sport, game, or activity they enjoy and write their own paragraph modeled on the paragraphs in Exercise **B**. Tell them to use at least five words from the vocabulary list. In their paragraphs, students should address these questions: *How long have you played this game / sport? Why did you start? What are the benefits of this game / sport?*

Grammar

Notice! Some verbs (*convince, remind, tell*) can follow more than one pattern.

Reported Speech

Use reported speech to explain what someone else has said. The verb tense, certain time words (such as *now, last week*), and pronouns can shift in reported speech.

Patterns in reported speech:

❶ verb + (*that*) clause: Ana **said (that) she was taking a kickboxing class.**
use with verbs: *explain, insist, mention, say*

❷ verb + pronoun/noun + (*that*) clause: Derek **told me (that) he played rugby.**
use with verbs: *convince, promise, remind, tell*

❸ verb + pronoun/noun + infinitive: Derek **encouraged his team to practice** more.
use with verbs: *beg, convince, encourage, invite, remind, tell*

Notice! Pattern 3 verbs are often used to ask for something or to give advice or instructions.

A Study the information in the chart. Then read sentences **a** and **b** below and do the following:

1. In sentence **b**, underline the pronouns and verbs that shift.
2. Which reported speech pattern (1, 2, or 3) does sentence **b** follow?
3. Use the verb *tell* and reported speech pattern 2 to report the sentences in **a**.

a. Direct speech: "I can't come tonight because I'm sick," said Al. "I think I ate some bad fish."
b. Reported speech: Al said he couldn't come tonight because he was sick. He thought he'd eaten some bad fish.

B Read the profile. With a partner, take turns reporting each statement about Marta's life.

When Marta was 14, a famous coach saw her playing soccer.

1. Coach → Marta's mother (*encourage*): "You should enroll Marta in a professional soccer camp."
   The coach encouraged Marta's mother to enroll Marta in a professional soccer camp.
2. Marta's mother (*explain*): "I don't have the money to do that."
3. Coach → Marta's mother (*promise*): "I'll take Marta to Rio and train her there."
4. Marta → her mother (*beg*): "Please let me go."

Marta's mother agreed. At 17, Marta was offered a spot on the Swedish women's soccer team Umea IK.

5. Coach → Marta (*convince*): "Take the job in Sweden."
6. Her opponents (*say*): "We've never seen anyone run that fast."

C Work with your class. One person says something about sports or games. The next person must repeat what that person said using reported speech and add something new. How long can you keep going?

I play chess.

Naomi said that she played chess. I've never played chess.

Naomi said that she played chess. Al said he'd never played chess. I like video games . . .

Marta Vieira da Silva
*Born in Brazil in 1986
*Soccer's greatest female player
*The female equivalent of soccer legends Pele and Ronaldo
*Is a Goodwill Ambassador for the UN

135

Extension

Divide the class into pairs. Have each pair interview each other about their favorite sport or game and why they like it. Each interviewer should take notes. Then, give students ten minutes to write a paragraph explaining what their partner told them using reported speech. Tell them to write at least five sentences and to use at least two of the verb patterns they learned.

Grammar

15-20 min. A
15-20 min. B
10-15 min. C
Extension: 10-15 min.

A • Ask students for examples of when they might use reported speech. Possible examples: *when telling a story, when relating news stories,* etc.
• Demonstrate how the verb tenses shift in reported speech by giving examples: *"I'm starting a chess club." > Marina said she was starting a chess club. / "My brother helped me." > Charlie told me that his brother had helped him.* In the second example, point out the shift from *my* to *his*.

Answers: 1. he, couldn't, he, was, he, thought, he, had eaten; 2. pattern 1; 3. Al told me (that) he couldn't come tonight because he was sick. He thought he'd eaten some bad fish.

B • Have a volunteer relate the information in the photo caption aloud in complete sentences. For example, *Marta Vieira da Silva was born in Brazil in 1986.*
• After each statement, have students report what their classmate said about Marta Vieira da Silva. For example, *Sally told us that Marta was born in Brazil in 1986.*

Answers: 1. *The coach encouraged Marta's mother to enroll Marta / her in a professional soccer camp.* 2. Marta's mother explained (that) she didn't have the money to do that. 3. The coach promised Marta's mother (that) he / she would take Marta to Rio and train her there. 4. Marta begged her mother to let her go. 5. The coach convinced Marta to take the job in Sweden. 6. Her opponents said (that) they had never seen anyone run that fast.

C **Outcome:** Upon completing this exercise, students will have met the Outcome *use reported speech to explain what someone else said.*

Listening

5-10 min. **A**
10-15 min. **B**
10 min. **C**
10 min. **D**
5-10 min. **E**
Extension: 15-20 min.

A Have students look back at the profile of Marta in Exercise **B** on page 135. Ask them what challenges she may have faced when moving to Sweden.

B
- Students will hear a TV interview with an American basketball player. Play the recording of the TV anchor and reporter's introductory comments about Jason Jennings once or twice. **Audio CD Track 22**
- Remind students to write only key words and numbers as they listen.

Answers: 1. He's famous because he is one of a handful American basketball players to leave the NBA to play in China. 2. He's in the news because he decided to retire from the team after one season.

C Play the recording of the interview with Jason Jennings once and have students answer the questions. Play it again and have students check their answers. **Audio CD Track 23**

Answers: 2. Missing familiar foods; 4. Making friends and socializing; 6. A lack of privacy

D
- Play the recording several times so that students have a chance to take notes on Jason's comments and turn them into reported speech. **Audio CD Track 23**
- Point out the expression *Don't get me wrong*. Ask students to guess what it means. Explain that it softens opinions that may seem strong.

Answers: *Missing familiar foods*: He said that the food in China was great, but that there were times when he would start missing certain foods back home. *Making friends and socializing*: He said that he didn't speak Chinese so he had to rely on interpreters for most things. He said it had been hard getting used to that. He also said not speaking the language had made it difficult to socialize with people outside the game. *A lack of privacy*: He said that the constant media attention had made it difficult to go out in public a lot, too. He said reporters were always following him and that he had no privacy.

E Ask students what they think would be the hardest part about living and working in another country.

Listening

adjustment a change
handful a small amount of something
interpreter a person who translates what someone is saying into another language
NBA the professional basketball organization in North America
recruit to choose and try to persuade someone to work for your organization

A Professional athletes often play for teams in other countries. What challenges do you think they face when they move? Look at the profile of the basketball player below. What challenges do you think he might face? Discuss in pairs.

Name:	Jason Jennings (USA)
Age:	22
Years played a professional:	2
Country currently playing in:	China

B You're going to hear an interview with a professional basketball player. Listen and answer the questions below with key words and phrases. Then compare answers with a partner. Use reported speech to explain what the news announcers said.

1. Why is he famous?
2. Why is he in the news now?

The news announcer said that Jennings was . . .

C What challenges has Jason struggled with? Listen and mark your answers.

_____ 1. Difficult teammates and coaches
_____ 2. Missing familiar foods
_____ 3. Getting used to the weather
_____ 4. Making friends and socializing
_____ 5. Being the youngest on the team
_____ 6. A lack of privacy

D What did Jason say that made you choose your answers in Exercise **C**? Listen again and note the key phrases you hear on a piece of paper. Use reported speech to explain your answers to a partner.

He said that it was hard . . .

Olympic Stadium, Beijing

E Discuss the questions with a partner.

1. In general, how do you think Jason feels about his first overseas experience playing basketball? What did Jason say during the interview that makes you think this?
2. What is Jason planning to do next? Do you think his experience with his next team will be different?

Extension

Have pairs role-play a conversation between Jason's parents about his decision to leave China. Encourage students to be creative and imagine what he would have told his parents that he might not have told a TV reporter. Remind them to use reported speech for the things Jason said. Ask for volunteers to perform their role-plays for the class.

Connections

physical education (PE) a school subject in which students exercise or play sports

role model someone you admire and try to imitate

violence an act that hurts, injures, or kills people

A Answer the questions in the chart. Then interview three people and take notes on their answers.

What's the best way to get in shape? Why?			
Me	Partner 1	Partner 2	Partner 3

B Get together with a new partner. Report your findings in Exercise **A** using four of the following verbs: *say, tell, suggest, insist, explain*. Which response do you agree with?

Carla explained that the best way to get in shape was to . . .

Notice! *Suggest* can be followed by a gerund or a *that clause*:
Carla suggested doing yoga to get in shape.
Carla suggested that the best way to get in shape was to do yoga.

C With your partner, do the following:

1. Choose one of the interview questions about sports below or come up with your own.
   - Do athletes make good role models?
   - Is there too much violence in professional sports?
   - Do professional athletes make too much money?
   - Should kids be required to take PE in school?
   - Should a person leave school before graduating to pursue a professional sports career?
   - Is the popularity of video gaming a problem?
   - Your idea: ______________________________
2. Using the question you chose, interview three people each. You and your partner should not interview the same people. On a separate piece of paper, take notes on what each person tells you. Remember to ask people to explain their answers.
3. Share your answers with your partner using three of these verbs: *say, tell, suggest, insist, explain*. Then evaluate all six responses. Which answer was the most common? Which was the most convincing?

D Summarize your findings. Then share them with another pair.

We asked, "Do athletes make good role models? Most people said . . ., but one person had a different opinion. He suggested . . .

Connections

10-15 min. A
5-10 min. B
15-20 min. C
10-15 min. D
Extension: 15-20 min.

A
- Direct students' attention to the word bank. Survey the class to see how many students have had to take classes in physical education.
- Have students tell a partner about one of their role models. They should explain what they admire about these people and what they do in order to try to imitate them.
- Remind students to write down their classmates' responses in note form instead of complete sentences.

B Circulate around the room and listen to pairs of students report their findings. Ensure that students are using a variety of verbs to report what others said.

C
- Explain that *video gaming*, or simply *gaming*, means *playing video games*. Regular video game players are sometimes called *gamers*.
- Clarify that students and their partners will be using the same question but interviewing different people.
- Before students interview their classmates, have them create a chart like the one in Exercise **A** for their notes. Have students write down their own answer to the question before they interview their classmates. After they have discussed their classmates' opinions, ask students whether their own opinions have changed at all.

D When pairs present their findings, have them report them as a ratio (e.g., *Four out of six people said that* … or *Half of the people we talked to believe* …).

Extension

Have pairs choose a different question from the list and repeat Exercise **C**. This time, instead of explaining their answers to another pair, have students work on their own to write a paragraph summarizing what they learned from their classmates. Explain that in written analyses of statistics, it is common to end with a conclusion about the information they learned (e.g., *In summary, most of the people I talked to feel* …).

Reading

5-10 min. **A**
10 min. **B**
10-15 min. **C**
5 min. **D**
10-15 min. **E**
Extension: 15-20 min.

A
- Explain to students that *martial arts* are any of several techniques of combat and self-defense that are practiced as a sport. Examples include karate, judo, taekwondo, and jiu-jitsu. Ask students to name other martial arts they know.
- Point out that the term *martial* is related to war and fighting. The word *martial* comes from the name Mars, the god of war in classical Roman mythology.

B
- Review with students the technique of scanning. Remind them that scanning is reading a text quickly to look for specific information. Direct students to read each item in Exercise **B**, look for a key word in the article, and then read the context to learn about the connection to kung fu.
- For further practice scanning, have students scan for *Yang Guiwu* and *celebration of violence*.

Answers: 1. *the birthplace of kung fu*; 2. the century that an Indian teacher introduced kung fu to monks at the Shaolin Temple; 3. what the monks originally used kung fu for; 4. China's modern-day kung fu capital; 5. jobs people hope to get by studying kung fu

C

Answers: 1. Hu is the owner of a kung fu academy and a teacher there. As a boy, he was obsessed with kung fu films. He also wanted to learn kung fu to get revenge on bullies in his village. As he studied kung fu, he discovered that it also helped one build character and taught discipline and respect for others. 2. The battle is between traditional Shaolin kung fu and the more modern form of kung fu taught in many kung fu academies. In addition to self-defense, traditional Shaolin kung fu focuses on self-discipline, character, responsibility, and respect. While many modern academies work on developing self-discipline, the focus is on acrobatics, and entertaining audiences or attacking opponents. Though it's not stated explicitly, we can infer that Hu feels the more modern form of kung fu is winning.

continued on page 139

Reading

A You are going to read an article about a Chinese martial art called *kung fu*. Look at the photos and then tell a partner anything you know about it.

B What is the connection of the items below to kung fu? Scan paragraphs 1 and 2 and write your answers on a separate piece of paper. Then check your answers with a partner.

1. the Shaolin Temple in China *the birthplace of kung fu*
2. the fifth century
3. self-defense and battle
4. the city of Dengfeng
5. movie star, famous kickboxer, police or military officer

C Read paragraphs 3 and 4. As you read, think about the questions below. When you are done, answer the questions with a partner using your own words.

1. Who is Hu Zhengsheng? As a boy, why did he become interested in kung fu? How have his beliefs about it changed?
2. Think about the title of the article. According to Hu, what two sides are "battling for the soul of kung fu"? In his opinion, which one is winning?

D Choose the correct word(s) to complete each sentence.

1. *Adversity* (line 31) is a very **easy / difficult** situation.
2. A person with *character* (line 33) **is / isn't** able to deal effectively with difficult situations.
3. If you *get revenge* (line 37), you try to **understand / hurt** someone who has hurt you.
4. If a person *shows off* (line 51), he does things to **get attention / hide** from others.

E Read the statements. Circle T (for *true*) if you think Hu would agree and F (for *false*) if he would not agree. Underline the information in the article that helped you choose your answers. Then explain your answers to a partner.

1. A kung fu teacher's main goal is to show students how to fight well. **T F**
2. Kung fu films today are too violent and don't focus on the important things. **T F**
3. A kung fu master knows many different moves and why each is important. **T F**
4. The higher a student's kick or jump, the better at kung fu he or she is. **T F**
5. A lot of people today are studying kung fu for the wrong reasons. **T F**

Ask Answer Master Yang told Hu that "pride defeats man." What did he mean by this? How can learning this lesson help one practice kung fu more successfully? How can this advice help a person in life?

Extension

Have pairs of students role-play an interview with the director of a big, modern kung fu academy. Tell them to use the statements in Exercise **E** as a starting point to show the contrast between this kung fu teacher's point of view and Hu's perspective. Have pairs present their interviews to the class, and ask the class to vote for the most convincing one.

A Battle[1] for the Soul[2] of Kung Fu

The Shaolin temple in China.

Every year, thousands of tourists from all over the world visit the Shaolin Temple in China to see the birthplace of kung fu. It is here, says one popular story, that in the fifth century, a teacher from India taught a series of exercises to the monks at the temple. The monks adapted these moves for self-defense and over the next fourteen centuries used them in numerous battles.

Today, the Shaolin Temple is just a few kilometers from the city of Dengfeng, China's modern-day kung fu capital. In Dengfeng there are almost sixty martial arts academies with more than 50,000 students. These schools are attended by boys and girls from all over the country and every social class, ranging in age from 5 to their late 20s. Some arrive hoping to become movie stars or famous kickboxers. Others are motivated to learn skills that will get them good jobs in the military or police. A few are sent by their parents to learn discipline and hard work.

****

Hu Zhengsheng owns and runs a small school outside Dengfeng. At age 33, Hu has a handsome face and projects a confidence won through years of physical and mental testing. Unlike the big kung fu academies, which focus on acrobatics[3] and kickboxing, Hu teaches his 200 students the traditional Shaolin kung fu forms that his teacher, Yang Guiwu, passed on to him. Fighting is not the most important lesson of kung fu, Hu explains. He doesn't agree with how kung fu is often shown in the movies—a celebration of violence that ignores the more important teachings of respect for one's opponent. Instead, in his classes, Hu focuses on respect and responsibility. In each of his students he looks for a willingness to welcome adversity—getting up before sunrise, practicing in the rain—using it to control themselves and build character.

From his own experience Hu knows that one's idea of kung fu can change as a person matures. When he was young, he was obsessed with kung fu films and dreamed of using the moves to get revenge on bullies[4] in his village. At age 11 he entered the Shaolin Temple and was later introduced to his teacher Yang Guiwu. "When I met my master, I already had memorized many traditional moves," Hu says, "but he taught me the theory behind them—not just *how* to do something a certain way but *why*: He explained why I must move my arm a certain way. Why my weight must be on a certain part of my foot." Hu stands up to demonstrate. A strike[5] with your hand, he explains, is like a chess move. You hit the other person, but you are also prepared for how he will respond. Hu pauses. "Shaolin kung fu was not designed to entertain audiences or to attack schoolyard bullies." There are no high kicks or jumps, he explains. A kung fu master doesn't show off. Pride[6] defeats man and makes him weak, teacher Yang had told Hu as a boy. "It is hard for me to convince my students of this, though," he sighs. Today everyone studies kung fu to achieve something. Hu worries that the real meaning of studying this martial art, to learn about oneself, is being lost.

A Buddhist monk practices kung fu.

[1] **battle** a violent fight
[2] **soul** the spirit or most important part of something
[3] **acrobatics** difficult physical acts such as jumping high and balancing
[4] **bully** someone who uses their strength or power to hurt or scare others
[5] **strike** a hard hit using your hand
[6] **pride** a feeling that you are better or more important than others

Beyond the Reading

Have students research another martial art (karate, judo, taekwondo, or another one that interests them) and present it to the class. Have them consider these questions in their presentation: *What country is this martial art from? How and when did it originate? What are its important characteristics and philosophy? What qualities make someone good at this sport? How is it similar to and different than kung fu?*

Reading *continued*

D • Give students some common word partnerships with *adversity*: *faced with ~, overcome ~, endure ~, suffer ~*. Point out that these expressions are about the challenge of adversity, and that it is not common to talk about *welcoming adversity*, as in line 31. Ask students to explain why Hu thinks that this trait is important for students of kung fu.

• Point out the related word *adversary*. Explain that an adversary is an *opponent*, one of the vocabulary words they learned on page 134.

Answers: 1. difficult; 2. is; 3. hurt; 4. get attention

E Have pairs discuss the Ask and Answer questions. Then ask volunteers to share their answers and conclusions. Ask students to paraphrase the statement "pride defeats man" (e.g., *If a person is too proud, he / she is not strong.*).

Answers: 1. F; 2. T; 3. T; 4. F; 5. T

Purpose for Reading

In this article, students learn about the history of kung fu and about one kung fu teacher's perspective. This teacher explains how his own perceptions of kung fu have changed in his lifetime and how the public's perception has changed as well. Point out the title of the article, and have students take notes about the article in two columns: one for each side of the "battle."

Background Information

The Shaolin Temple is located on Mount Shaoshi in the Songshan mountain range of eastern China. Built in 495 C.E., it was founded as a Buddhist monastery by a monk from India named Batuo. About 30 years later, another Indian monk named Bodhidharma visited the temple and introduced the monks there to the art of kung fu. Shaolin has been destroyed and rebuilt many times throughout its history. In 2010, it was named a UNESCO World Heritage Site.

Video

10-15 min. **A**
10-15 min. **B**
10 min. **C**
10-15 min. **D**
Extension: 10-15 min.

A • Before showing the video, ask students what they know about the comic book character Spiderman. Then direct them to the photos on the page and guess why they think Alain Robert has this nickname.
- After students have watched the video with the sound off, have them write three questions about Alain Robert that they hope to have answered after watching the video again with sound.

Possible Answers: He climbs tall buildings. He appears to climb without ropes or other supports.

B Have students write two additional false statements based on the video. Then have them exchange papers with a partner and correct the other student's false statements.

Answers: 1. False. He has climbed over 100 buildings. 2. True. 3. False. He has had numerous arrests for climbing without a permit. 4. True. 5. False. He climbed mountains near his home on his own. 6. True.

C Have students work with a partner to discuss these sentences. Ask them to consider: *Are you afraid of heights? Would you risk your life for a sport? What safety precautions would you use if you were climbing? Do you do anything to try to overcome your fears? If so, what?*

Answers: 1. put yourself in danger; 2. deadly; 3. special equipment to prevent accidents; 4. beat

D After pairs have discussed their answers, poll the class to see how many students admire Alain Robert. Ask them to explain why someone might not admire him.

Video

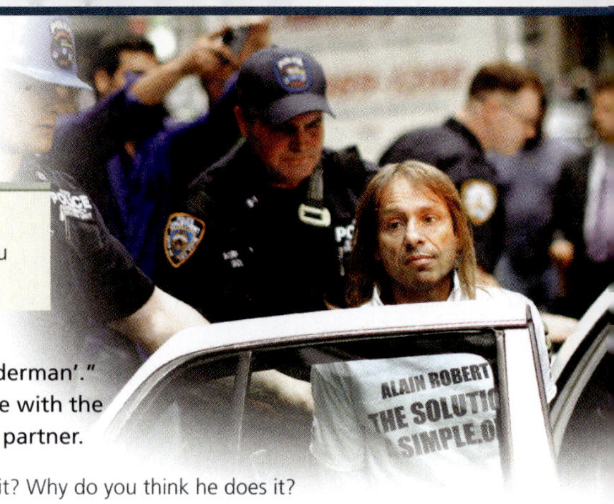

ascent a climb
ledge a narrow stand outside a window where you can put things

A Alain Robert is often called "the French 'Spiderman'." Look at the photos and watch the video once with the *sound off*. Then discuss the questions with a partner.

- What does Alain Robert do? How does he do it? Why do you think he does it?

B Read the statements. Then watch the video again with the *sound on* and mark the true statements. When you're done, correct the false ones so that they are true.

Alain Robert . . .	True	False
1. has climbed twenty buildings around the world.	☐	☐
2. normally uses no special equipment during a climb.	☐	☐
3. has never been arrested.	☐	☐
4. broke a world record.	☐	☐
5. has never rock climbed.	☐	☐
6. believes that climbing each building is a type of special test.	☐	☐

Alain Roberts climbing Tower One at Suntec City, Singapore.

C Read sentences 1–4 below and think about what you've seen and heard in the video already. Then choose the synonym that could replace the underlined word in each sentence.

1. Would you <u>risk your life</u> for a sport?
   a. pay money b. put yourself in danger c. quit your job
2. As he climbs, one wrong move could be <u>fatal</u>.
   a. deadly b. uncertain c. difficult
3. Most people use <u>safety precautions</u>.
   a. insurance policies b. special equipment to prevent accidents
   c. official permits
4. His goal is to <u>overcome</u> his fear.
   a. understand b. ignore c. beat

D Get together with a partner and explain . . .

- in detail who Alain Robert is, how he climbs, and why he does it. Use your own words.
- how you feel about Alain Robert. Do you admire him? Why or why not?

Extension

Write on the board these sentences from the video: "For Alain, each building is a personal challenge. His goal is not only to reach the top, but to face his fear of going higher ... and to overcome it." Have students write a paragraph about themselves in which they describe their own goals and challenges. Have them start their paragraphs with, "For me, ______ is a personal challenge. My goal is ________."

Writing

Explain Important Qualities

A Think about the people you learned about in this unit. What are the three most important qualities necessary to be good at kung fu? How about for an urban climber like Alain Robert? Select ideas from the list and then explain them to a partner.

commitment to hard work	modesty	responsibility	strategy
courage	patience	self-confidence	strength
determination	quick thinking	self-discipline	your idea: ______

B Read the short essay below by a student about her experience on a debate team. What does it take to be good at this activity? Complete the chart and then check your answers with a partner. You will complete a writing task on the next page.

What it takes to be a good debater		
What you have to do	**Reason**	**Qualities needed**
prepare by doing research	*so you can debate the issue from all sides*	*commitment to hard work*

> Notice the words in bold. The writer uses these to introduce and transition from one idea to the next.

The most important thing a good debater can do is prepare. Every debate focuses on a particular issue. In one debate I was in recently, we argued the pros and cons of playing video games. Whatever the issue, you must be ready to discuss it from your point of view and to respond to challenges from your opponents. Good debaters research the issue and study for hours before the debate so that they are ready. It's a lot of work and takes real commitment, but if you want to win you have to do it.

A good debater should also be able to speak persuasively. In addition to researching the issue, you must also be able to present and defend your ideas confidently and in a convincing way. This will score points for your team. Getting used to doing this in front of an audience takes a lot of practice—and courage. Good debaters are constantly working to perfect this skill.

Finally, a good debater stays focused even when things are difficult. During a debate, an opponent might say something unexpected or ask some hard questions. Some people get nervous when this happens, and this can cause a team to lose points. A good debater, though, stays calm and can think fast. Like speaking persuasively, this takes a lot of practice.

Rubric	Very Good	Satisfactory	Needs Improvement
Content			
Effective organization and pacing			
Use of grammar			
Organization			

Writing

5 min. **A**
5 min. **B**
35-45 min. **C**
5-10 min. **D**
Extension: 20 min.

A
- Point out that many of the qualities in this list have related adjectives. Encourage students to look up these adjectives: *committed, courageous, determined, enthusiastic, flexible, modest (humble), patient, responsible, self-confident, self-disciplined, strategic, strong.*
- Have students list the three qualities that best describe themselves.

Outcome: Upon completing this exercise, students will have met the Outcome ***evaluate the relationship between activities and personal qualities***.

B Draw students' attention to the bold words in the essay and explain how these phrases create a structure for the essay. As students prepare their timed writing pieces, encourage them to plan their transitions in their outlines.

Answers: Second row: *What you have to do*: speak persuasively, *Reason*: to present and defend ideas and win points, *Qualities needed*: confidence, courage; Third row: *What you have to do*: stay focused even when things are difficult, *Reason*: opponents ask hard questions, *Qualities needed*: ability to stay calm, think fast

C
- Distribute the list of sports, games, and activities provided on page 133 of this Teacher's Edition to help students pick an essay topic. Give students the option of writing about a non-sports activity. You might want to assign this task as homework.
- If your students are preparing for a specific test, confirm or adjust the pacing as appropriate. Note that for TOEFL, test-takers are given 20 minutes to write a response to an "independent writing task" prompt. For IELTS, pacing is between 20 and 40 minutes, depending on the task.

Outcome: Upon completing this exercise, students will have met the Outcome ***pace yourself as you write a timed essay.***

continued on page 142

Writing *continued*

Extension

Have students organize and write a timed compare-and-contrast essay about the competition of debating and that of kung fu. Explain that in a compare-and-contrast essay, they should explain how these activities are similar, explain how they are different, and draw a conclusion based on these similarities and differences. Give students twenty minutes to organize, write, and review their essays.

Speaking

20-25 min. A
20-30 min. B
Extension: 10-15 min.

A
- If you chose to skip the Writing activity, have students refer to Exercises **A, B**, and **C** on the Writing pages and have them create an outline.
- Consider introducing this exercise in class, and then assign students the task of practicing as homework so that they have enough time to prepare for their presentations.
- Encourage students to prepare notecards for their presentations. Tell them to use one notecard for each section of their outline.

B Encourage students to approach this activity as a formal presentation. Have them stand in front of their groups, speak clearly, and make eye contact. Remind the listeners to be respectful and pay close attention.

Outcome: Upon completing this exercise, students will have met the Outcome ***use an outline to support a presentation or essay***.

Extension

Have students think of someone famous or a person they know who has the qualities they described in their presentation. Encourage them to write notes in their outlines about how this person demonstrates each quality when they participate in the activity. Then have students present the person they chose to their groups from Exercise **B**.

C Read the Writing Strategy. Then do the following:

1. Think of an activity that you enjoy now or played in the past. What do you have to do to be good at it? Why? Outline two or three ideas. Use the chart in Exercise **B** as a model.
2. Use your outline to write your short essay. You will have forty-five minutes to do this. Remember to save five minutes at the end to review your work.

Writing Strategy

Pacing Yourself On many standardized English exams, test takers are often asked to write a timed essay in which they must give an opinion. Assuming that you have twenty-five minutes total, remember to pace yourself and allow time for . . .
- organizing and outlining your essay (about five minutes)
- writing the essay (about thirty-five minutes)
- checking your work (about five minutes)

D When time is up, exchange papers with a partner. Read your partner's writing and answer the questions in the Writing Checklist.

Writing Checklist

Does the essay . . .
- identify the activity clearly?
- explain what you have to do to be good at it?
- identify which qualities are necessary?

Speaking

A In the writing activity, you created an outline that described what you have to do to be good at an activity. You are going to use that outline to give a short (one- or two-minute) presentation. Do the following:

1. Read the Speaking Strategy.
2. Review your outline and, on your own, practice giving your presentation a few times.

Speaking Strategy

Speaking from an Outline

Getting Started: Preview the Topic *I'm on the debate team at my school, and today I'd like to talk about what it takes to be a good debater.*

During the Presentation

Use transition words (like those in the essay on page 141) to help your audience follow you.

Do not just read from your outline; remember to look up at your audience periodically.

Try not to speak too fast, but be sure to pace yourself: you have two minutes total.

Closing: Summarize and Take Questions

So, in conclusion, I think you have to do three important things to be a good debater. . . .

Thanks for your attention. Any questions?

B Get into a group of three or four people and do the following:

1. One person should give his or her presentation. It should last one or two minutes.
2. Those listening should take notes on a separate piece of paper using a chart like the one on page 141.
3. At the end of the person's presentation, those listening should review their notes and each person should ask the presenter one question.
4. Repeat steps 1–3 until everyone has presented.

You mentioned that good debaters need practice learning to speak persuasively. What kind of practice do they do exactly?

Rubric	Very Good	Satisfactory	Needs Improvement
Content			
Pacing and eye contact			
Use of grammar			
Organization			

Expanding Your Fluency

A Read the sayings below and then discuss the questions with a partner.

No pain, no gain.
You've got what it takes.
It's not whether you win or lose; it's how you play the game.
Practice makes perfect.
There's no *I* in *team*.
If at first you don't succeed, try, try again.
Run your own race.

1. What do you think each saying means?
2. Do you have a similar saying in your language? If so, what is it?
3. Do you agree with each saying? Why or why not?
4. Which of the sayings do you like the most and why?

B Choose one of the situations below. With a partner, create a two-minute role-play in which you use at least one of the expressions from Exercise **A**. Then do your role-play for another pair.

- You and a friend decided to take a yoga class together to get in shape. You thought the exercises would be easy, but after two weeks, you're still having a hard time getting used to them. You're feeling discouraged and are thinking about dropping the class.
- You applied for an internship with a video game company. You went on several interviews and everything went well, but the company chose someone else. You recently learned that a new position is available, but you're not sure whether to apply.
- You're working on a group project with two other people in your class. One of the people on the team is obsessed with perfection and insists on everything being done his/her way. It's driving you crazy and is making it hard for you to get motivated to do any work.

C Switch roles and repeat Exercise **B**, this time using a new scenario.

Check What You Know

Rate how well you can do the following tasks on a scale of 1–5 (5 being the best).

________ use reported speech to explain what someone else said
________ evaluate the relationship between activities and personal qualities
________ pace yourself as you write a timed essay
________ use an outline to support a presentation or essay

Extension

Have groups of four students play a game using the list of qualities in Exercise **A** on page 141. Groups should write the words on small pieces of paper and place them face down on the table. One student chooses a paper and describes the word to the group without using that word in the description. When another student guesses the word correctly, he / she gets to choose the next paper. Continue playing until all the words have been used (e.g., *patience*: This is when someone does not get angry if he / she has to wait a long time.).

Expanding Your Fluency

10-15 min. A
15-20 min. B
15-20 min. C
Extension: 10-15 min.

A
- *No pain, no gain* is often used to offer encouragement that hard work will lead to improvement.
- *You've got what it takes* expresses that someone has the qualities necessary for a certain activity.
- *It's not whether you win or lose…* is said to draw attention to good sportsmanship, as well as the importance of the quality of an experience instead of the outcome.
- *Practice makes perfect* expresses that people improve if they practice a lot.
- *There's no* I *in* team is a play on words to show that when you are part of a team, you should think about the team, not yourself.
- *If at first you don't succeed, try, try again* is used to encourage someone to be persistent, to not give up even if they fail.
- *Run your own race* is used to encourage someone not to rely on other people to determine his or her abilities and accomplishments.

C Give students this additional scenario as an option: *You and your friend have been taking tennis lessons together for several months. You stay late every week and do extra practice with the coach and your friend doesn't seem to make any effort, but she still beats you every time you play. You are tired of losing and are thinking about switching into a different sport so you won't lose to your friend again.*

Check What You Know

Refer students to the exercises in the unit where each Outcome is addressed.

- *use reported speech to explain what someone else said:* Grammar, Exercise **C**, page 135
- *evaluate the relationship between activities and personal qualities:* Writing, Exercise **A**, page 141
- *pace yourself as you write a timed essay:* Writing, Exercise **C**, page 142
- *use an outline to support a presentation or essay:* Speaking, Exercise **B**, page 142

Pronunciation

Rising and Falling Intonation

Intonation describes the changes in pitch in spoken language. Generally, the pitch of a sentence or group of words rises or falls. The intonation tells you what kind of sentence you are hearing.

Below are the most common uses of **rising intonation**. Listen carefully to the pitch in each example. Note that it *rises* at the end of the sentence because the emphasis is on the information in the question.

- Yes–no questions with question word order:
  - May I have a glass of milk?
  - Will you help me with my chores?
- Yes–no questions with statement word order:
  - The movie starts at noon?
  - The bus station is on the corner?

Below are the most common uses of **falling intonation**. Listen carefully to the pitch in each example. Note that it *falls* at the end of the sentence. In a statement, this indicates that the sentence has ended. In *wh*- questions, the pitch is high at the beginning to emphasize the *wh*- word and falls at the end.

- Declarative statements:
  - The snow is gone.
  - The bowl is full.
- *Wh*- questions:
  - What was that noise?
  - When is the movie?

Practice

A Read and listen to each sentence. Decide if the intonation is rising or falling. Then write *rising* or *falling* on the line.

1. You are still hungry after all that pizza? ____________
2. Where are the car keys? ____________
3. Do we have homework for English class tonight? ____________
4. Everyone was late for dinner. ____________
5. Do you think that painting is beautiful? ____________
6. Are there any rooms left at the hotel? ____________
7. The ball went over the fence. ____________
8. Who was at the door? ____________

B Write three sentences of your own with rising or falling intonation. Indicate which intonation your sentence has.

1. ____
____
2. ____
____
3. ____
____

Stress Changes with Prefixes and Suffixes

In English, adding prefixes and suffixes to words does not usually cause a change in stress. Here are some examples.

different	indifferent	differently
important	unimportant	importantly
arm	disarm	disarming

However, in some cases, adding a particular suffix will cause a shift in the syllable that is stressed.

picture picturesque

Practice

A **Listen to each word pair below. Mark the stressed syllable in each word to compare stress. The first one is done for you.**

1. photograph — photographic
2. public — publicity
3. anticipate — anticipation
4. care — caring
5. correlate — correlation
6. rhetoric — rhetorical
7. cheer — cheerful
8. stable — stability
9. energy — energetic
10. play — playing
11. library — librarian
12. philosophy — philosophical
13. immediate — immediately
14. electric — electrician
15. hero — heroic
16. eager — eagerly

B **Now, review the stressed syllables in each word pair. Which ones changed? Which ones did not? Write a rule about which suffixes cause a stress shift.**

____

____

____

Pronunciation

Heteronyms and Stress Shift

Words with the same spelling are called **homographs**. A subset of homographs are **heteronyms**: words that are spelled the same, but are a different part of speech and are often pronounced differently.

Word	Definition	Part of speech	Stress
project	A task or work that one plans to do	noun	PROject
project	To predict	verb	proJECT

You can often differentiate between heteronyms by identifying their part of speech. For most two-syllable heteronyms, the noun has the stress on the first syllable, while the verb has the stress on the second.

Word	Definition	Part of speech	Stress
digest	A collection of readings	noun	DIgest
digest	To take in or make use of, as in a meal	verb	diGEST
entrance	An opening through which to enter	noun	ENtrance
entrance	To fill with wonder	verb	enTRANCE

Note that you cannot apply this rule to all heteronyms. For example, the verb and noun *respect / respect* are pronounced the same. Also, some heteronyms have only one syllable, such as the noun and verb *row* (ROW) / *row* (ROH). Lastly, a few heteronyms, such as *invalid / invalid*, have more than two syllables.

Practice

A **For each form of the heteronym, write the part of speech and show which syllable is stressed. The first one is done for you. Then listen to confirm your answers.**

Heteronym pair	Part of speech	Stress
1. The police arrested the **suspect** late last night.	noun	SUSpect
2. I **suspect** that dinner is going to be late tonight.		
3. You will only **compound** the problem if you try to fix the sink yourself.		
4. The scientist invented a new **compound** that might help prevent allergies.		
5. We analyzed all the data from the latest **survey**.		
6. From the top of the mountain, I was able to **survey** the land for miles around.		
7. The lawyer did not **object** to the final ruling.		
8. The **object** in the sky last night was an airplane.		
9. My roommate will not **permit** me to use her computer.		
10. If we want to go fishing, we will need a **permit**.		
11. His **conduct** during the meeting was upsetting to everyone.		
12. Our director will **conduct** the orchestra during the festival.		

Linking Sounds

In spoken English, sounds in consecutive words are linked when the final consonant in one word is followed by an initial vowel in the next word.

- I've already made my bed.
- The dog tracked mud all over the kitchen.

They are also linked when the final consonant in one word is followed by the same initial consonant in the next word.

- His shirt tore when he did a flip.
- I made dinner last night.

Practice

A **Predict where sounds are linked in each of the following sentences. Underline your predicted linking sounds. Then listen to check your predictions. Circle the linking sounds to confirm or correct your work.**

1. There was music everywhere at the fair.
2. The bell rings at the end of each class.
3. Jamie said he was sorry for calling so late.
4. The sun rises each morning at 5:00 a.m.
5. Mary didn't have enough energy to finish raking the leaves.
6. Tina left the shower running this morning.
7. She thought the painting was outstanding.
8. When we got to the zoo, the lions were being fed.
9. My sister invited me to come, too.
10. Everyone thought the play was sort of funny.

Typical Stress Patterns in Three-Syllable Words

In English, many three-syllable words follow regular stress patterns. Listen to the pronunciation of these words, noting the rhythm of each pattern. (3 = the strongest stress; 1 = the weakest stress)

3-1-1 (stress on first syllable)	1-3-1 (stress on second syllable)	3-1-2 (stress on first syllable with minor stress on third syllable)
benefit	congested	simplify
terrible	inspection	manifest

Practice

A Listen to and then repeat aloud each three-syllable word. Then write the stress pattern you hear. You may want to mark the words as you listen and speak. The first one is done for you.

1.	magnify	3-1-2
2.	beloved	
3.	genuine	
4.	telephone	
5.	audience	
6.	penetrate	
7.	specify	
8.	bicycle	
9.	operate	
10.	manager	
11.	direction	
12.	excellent	
13.	triangle	
14.	fortunate	
15.	another	

Intonation Patterns and Relative Clauses

Many English sentences can be divided into chunks with internal intonation patterns. Some relative clauses provide additional, but not crucial, information about a noun or noun phrase. This type of clause is often signaled by the words *who*, *whom*, *whose*, or *which*. It is also separated from the main part of the sentence by commas to indicate a slight pause and has its own rising and falling intonation curve. In this case, the speaker mentions that the visiting sister is from Rio, but that detail is merely informative, not critical.

My sister,/ who lives in Rio,/ is coming to visit.

Other relative clauses provide important information about the noun or noun phrase. Without this information, the meaning of the sentence might be unclear. The intonation in this case does *not* fall after "My sister," but stays the same for the whole chunk, including the defining relative clause. In this case, the speaker must have more than one sister; the intonation and punctuation clarify which sister is visiting.

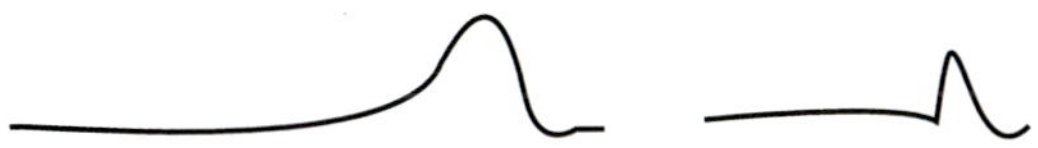

My sister who lives in Rio/ is coming to visit.

Listen to the difference between these two sentences.

- The shoes,/ which I bought yesterday,/ are the wrong color.
- The shoes that I bought yesterday/ are the wrong color.

Practice

A **Read each sentence aloud. Which segments have their own intonation curves? Separate each sentence into segments with a slash (/). Then listen to check your work. Revise your answers as necessary.**

1. Barry taught the puppy that he adopted to sit.
   Carol taught the toddler, whom she babysits, several new words.
2. The rake, which I loaned to my neighbor, broke.
   The tool that I borrowed from my father is missing.
3. Susan's new dress, which is red, is very pretty.
   The new coat that Hannah bought is beautiful.
4. Marco, who doesn't care about clothes, wears whatever fits.
   The woman who just walked by wears the coolest styles.
5. That boutique, which just opened last month, has high prices.
   The mall that opened recently is close to my house.
6. Cats that love water are very rare.
   Cats, who don't like water, are no fun to bathe.

Reduction in Perfect Modals

Reduction describes the process in spoken language when sounds are shortened and, often, changed slightly. Reduction occurs only in spoken language, not in formal writing (though you may sometimes see it written, for example, in dialogues).

Perfect modals in English include *must / should / would / could* + *have* + the past participle of a verb. When spoken, the *h* in *have* is usually dropped and the vowel sound is reduced to the schwa sound or *eh*.

- You must have left the gate unlocked; that is how the dog got out. ("mustehv," not "must have")
- We should have arrived earlier. ("shouldehv," not "should have")
- She could have gotten an A on the test if she had studied harder. ("couldehv," not "could have")
- If I had known you were going, I would have attended the party, too. ("wouldehv," not "would have")

TIP In very informal spoken English, perfect modals are often reduced even further to: *musteh*, *woulddeh*, *coulddeh*, and *shoulddeh*.

Note that when *must have* is not followed by a past participle, it does not get reduced. For example: Bella said that she must have a new dress for the dance.

Practice

A Say each sentence aloud, and then listen to the audio recording to check your pronunciation. Then say each sentence aloud again.

1. Jane would have gone to the movies with us, but she had to work.
2. I could have ordered pizza for lunch, but had a salad instead.
3. It must have snowed two feet last night!
4. I could have done my report on climate change, but someone else chose it first.
5. Juan thought he had his wallet with him, but he must have left it at home.
6. I'm so sorry; I should have remembered your birthday!
7. Pamela would have had ice cream, but there wasn't any.
8. I sent the package, but it must have been lost in the mail.
9. Danny did everything he could have done to win the contest.
10. Callie should have called Petra last night, but she came home too late.

Thought Groups

In spoken English, longer sentences can be divided into chunks, called **thought groups**. A thought group usually contains a major element, such as a prepositional phrase, a noun phrase, or a subject / verb. Also, it is signaled by a slight pause before and after it. Lastly, a thought group is just what its name implies: a phrase that coherently expresses a thought. Fluent speakers of English pace their speech to mark thought groups, which can in turn aid comprehension, add nuance, or emphasize or deemphasize certain details. Note: there is often more than one way to divide a sentence into thought groups.

Here are some examples of thought groups within longer sentences. The groups are separated by a slash (/).

- Scientists / are doing tests / to determine how humans decide / right from wrong.
- There are special areas / of the brain / that might control moral behavior.
- These areas / are associated with emotion / and what we call *social cognition*.

Practice

A **Read each sentence aloud and separate the thought groups with a slash (/). Then listen to check your work. Revise your answers as necessary.**

1. The sun was shining this morning, but then it started to rain.
2. Perry got up late and missed his train.
3. I hope to have my project done by the end of this week.
4. Everyone really enjoyed the movie yesterday.
5. By the end of the year, we should have finished redoing the spare bedroom.
6. The price of the washing machine was less than I remembered.
7. It was cold out, but I took the dog for a walk anyway.
8. The student won an award for her environmental work.
9. Susan sat by the phone, waiting to hear if she got the job.
10. Why didn't you come to the party last night?

Language Summary

Unit 1

adapt to change your ideas or behavior to suit a different situation **adaptation** (n.) **adaptive** (adj.)

ambitious needing exceptional effort and resources to be carried out successfully **ambitiously** (adv.) **ambition** (n.)

archaeologist a scientist who studies people and societies of the past **archaeology** (n.) **archaeological** (adj.)

average the normal amount or quality for a group of things or people **(to) average** (v., adj.)

buried under the ground and covered with earth **to bury** (v.) **burial** (n.)

come up with to suggest or think of an idea or plan

defeat to win a victory over someone in a battle or game **defeat** (n.)

determine to find out or to confirm certain information **determination** (n.) **indeterminate** (adj.)

generation the period of time (about 30 years) it takes for children to grow up and have their own families **generational** (adj.)

genetics the study of how certain characteristics (e.g., eye, hair, and skin color) are passed from one generation to the next by our genes **gene** (n.) **genetic** (adj.)

identical exactly the same **identically** (adv.)

invading entering a country by force with an army **invader** (n.) **invasion** (n.)

persuade to cause someone to do something by giving good reasons for doing it **persuasive** (adj.)

preserve to save or protect something for the future **preservation** (n.)

set out to start trying to do something

statistics numerical facts that are gathered through analyzing information **statistically** (adv.) **statistical** (adj.)

trait a particular characteristic a person has

typical showing the most usual characteristics of a person or thing **typically** (adv.)

Unit 2

accessible easy to reach or get into **(to) access** (v., n.) **accessibility** (n.)

adventurous willing to take risks and have new experiences **adventure** (n.)

atmosphere the character or feeling of a place **atmospheric** (adj.)

breathtaking very beautiful or amazing **breathless** (adj.)

charm the quality of being pleasant and attractive **to charm** (v.) **charming** (adj.)

convenience ease; suitability **convenient** (adj.) **inconvenient** (adj.)

destination the place you're going to (n)

diverse varied or different **diversity** (n.)

end up to arrive at a place or condition

get away to go away on vacation **getaway** (n.)

landmark well-known building or place

luxurious comfortable and expensive **luxury** (n.) **deluxe** (adj.)

outsider a stranger

particular someone difficult to please

perspective point of view

picturesque attractive, especially in an old-fashioned way **picture** (n.)

remote far away **remotely** (adv.)

rush to go rapidly **rush hour** (n.)

solitude the state of being or living alone **solo** (n.) **solitary** (adj.)

spontaneous coming from an impulse; unplanned **spontaneously** (adv.) **spontaneity** (n.)

spot place; location

timid someone who lacks confidence; shy

tranquil calm and peaceful **tranquility** (n.) **tranquilizer** (n.)

Unit 3

consume to use, especially in large amounts **consumer** (n.) **consumption** (n.) **consumerism** (n.)

contribute to be one of the causes of something **contribution** (n.) **contributor** (n.)

convert to change **conversion** (n.)

cut back on to reduce the amount of something **cutback** (n.)

cut down to decrease

eliminate to remove something entirely **elimination** (n.)

entire the whole of something **entirely** (adv.)

generate to make or produce

give up to quit doing something; to renounce

impact a strong effect **to impact** (v.)

injustice a lack of fairness in a situation **justice** (n.)

pollute to contaminate **pollution** (n.) **polluter** (n.) **unpolluted** (adj.)

prevent to keep from happening **prevention** (n.)

produce to generate **producer** (n.) **production** (n.)

project to predict

reduce to make smaller in amount or number **reduction** (n.)

rely on to depend on or use **reliable** (adj.) **unreliable** (adj.)

residents the people who live in a certain place (a house, neighborhood, city, country) **to reside** (v.) **residential** (adj.)

reverse to cause something to move in the opposite direction **reversal** (n.) **irreversible** (adj.)

roadblock a situation or condition that prevents further progress; an obstacle

run out to use something (up) completely

source the origin or starting place of something

supply to give an amount; provide **supplier** (n.) **supplies** (n.)

sustainable long-lasting or good for the environment **to sustain** (v.) **sustainability** (n.) **unsustainable** (adj.)

transmit send from one place to another place **transmission** (n.)

Unit 4

appearance, to make an to come out in public **to appear** (v.)

audience a group of people watching a performance **auditorium** (n.)

audition a short performance given by a person to demonstrate suitability for a show **to audition** (v.)

benefit a social event to raise funds for a person or cause **to benefit** (v.) **benefactor** (n.)

charity an organization that helps people in need **charitable** (adj.)

commercial related to the buying and selling of goods and services **commercially** (adv.) **commerce** (n.)

convince to persuade someone (to do something)

demo a brief recording illustrating the abilities of a musician

emerge to come out and be recognized or noticed

encounter to meet **encounter** (n.)

enthusiasm a feeling of energetic interest in something **enthusiast** (n.) **enthusiastic** (adj.)

fund-raising a way for schools and other organizations to raise money for a particular purpose **to fund-raise** (v.) **fund-raiser** (n.)

hardcore very committed (to something)

inspire encouraged (by) or motivated (by) **inspiration** (n.) **inspirational** (adj.)

launch to start **launch** (n.)

logo a special design used by a company or group

mainstream most typical or conventional

performance singing, dancing, or acting for an audience **to perform** (v.) **performer** (n.)

promote to encourage the popularity or sales of something **promoter** (n.) **promotional** (adj.)

realize to understand something, sometimes suddenly **realization** (n.)

Unit 5

altitude height off the ground

catch (someone) off guard to be surprised by someone or something

client someone who pays a person or company for a service; a customer

collapse to fall down suddenly **collapse** (n.) **collapsible** (adj.)

disorientation confusion **disoriented** (adj.)

encourage to give someone confidence or hope **discourage** (v.)

freak out to lose control and behave in an extremely emotional or excited way

freeze to be unable to move or think

handle to deal with a problem or situation successfully **to mishandle** (v.)

injure to damage a part of a person's body **injury** (n.)

intense very great or extreme **intensely** (adv.) **intensity** (n.)

monitor to follow or check something regularly

ordeal a very difficult, stressful situation

panic to feel very anxious or afraid all of a sudden **panic** (n.) **panicky** (adj.)

rescue to save someone from a dangerous situation **rescuer** (n.)

risk taker an adventurous person, unafraid of taking chances **risk** (v.) **risky** (adv.) dangerous

rival a person you compete with **rivalry** (n.) **(to) rival** (v., adj.)

set off (for a place): to start a trip

soak in to look at or enjoy a place as much as you can

summit top

trapped unable to escape from a place or situation because something is stopping you **(to) trap** (v., n.)

Unit 6

adventurous willing to take risks and have new experiences **adventure** (n.)

affordable reasonably priced, inexpensive **to afford** (v.)

authentic real, genuine **authenticity** (n.)

bargain to talk with someone to try to get a lower price on something **bargain** (n.)

brand a type of product made by a particular company

browse to look around casually

check (something) out to look at

daring ready to take risks; adventurous **to dare** (v.)

deal something good you buy, usually for a low price

dependable reliable

discount a reduction in the usual price of something **(to) discount** (v., adj.)

fake not real **(to) fake** (v., n.)

fashion-conscious someone interested in the latest trends, whatever the cost **fashionista** (n.)

goods products you buy

imitator someone who copies what someone else does **to imitate** (v.) **imitation** (n.)

outgoing friendly and sociable

practical someone inclined toward useful and functional things **impractical** (adj.)

purchase to buy something **purchase** (n.)

quality how good or bad something is

recommend to suggest to someone that a thing or person would be good or useful **recommendation** (n.)

rip off something overpriced **to rip off** (v.)

self-confident someone who trusts in his / her own abilities **self-confidence** (n.)

serious someone who gives a lot of importance to things **seriously** (adv.) **seriousness** (n.)

sophisticated someone cultivated and elegant **sophistication** (n.)

(be) worth it to be expensive because its quality is good **worthless** (adj.) **worthy** (adj.)

Unit 7

availability the fact that something can be used or reached **available** (adj.) **unavailable** (adj.)

bottom line the total amount of money a company has made or lost over a time

commute the daily journey you make between your home and place of work or school **to commute** (v.) **commuter** (n.)

cramped not big enough for the number of people or things in it **to cramp** (v.)

delay when you have to wait longer than expected for something to happen **to delay** (v.)

fit in to feel that you belong to a particular group and are accepted by them **misfit** (n.)

get in arrive

keep in mind to remember something important (often given as a warning/advice)

option something you can choose from a group of alternatives **to opt** (v.) **optional** (adj.)

overwhelming difficult to fight against

perfect match two things that go successfully together

pull in/pull out arrive/depart (especially used for vehicles such as trains, trucks, and cars)

punctual on time; not late **punctuality** (n.)

reliable trusted to work or behave well **to rely on** (v.) **unreliable** (adj.)

rush hour the times of day when most people are traveling to and from work

tend likely to behave in a particular way **tendency** (n.)

transfer to go or move something from one place to another

Unit 8

anonymous made or done by a person whose name is not known **anonymously** (adv.) **anonymity** (n.)

big deal something important

consequences results or effects (of an action)

criticize to express disapproval by saying what's wrong with something **critic** (n.) **criticism** (n.)

damage to harm something

discipline self-control; an action taken to correct inappropriate behavior **to discipline** (v.)

disruptive causing trouble and stopping something from continuing as usual **to disrupt** (v.) **disruption** (n.)

get away with to do something wrong or risky and not suffer any consequences

get into trouble to be in a position where you will be punished for something

get suspended temporarily not allowed to go to school or class because you've done something wrong **suspension** (n.)

goofy silly or ridiculous

illegal not allowed by law **illegally** (adv.) **legal** (adj.)

incident an event

invasion of privacy when your private life is disturbed in an unpleasant way **to invade** (v.) **invader** (n.)

private only for one person or group; not for everyone **privately** (adv.) **privacy** (n.)

punish to take action against someone for inappropriate behavior **punishment** (n.)

regulation an official rule (e.g., made by a government or school) **to regulate** (v.)

remove (a video) to delete or eliminate; **removal** (n.)

reputation the opinion that people have about someone or something; how much they respect or admire it **reputable** (adj.)

respectful to be polite and well-behaved towards someone (in authority) **(to) respect** (v., n.) **(to) disrespect** (v., n.)

responsibility something that is your job or duty to deal with **responsibly** (adv.) **responsible** (adj.)

restriction a limit on something **to restrict** (v.)

show up to appear

surveillance the careful watching of someone, especially by the police

sympathetic showing that you understand and care about someone's suffering **sympathy** (n.)

Unit 9

alert a warning, an alarm **(to) alert** (v., adj.)

attack to try to hurt someone with physical violence **attack** (n.) **attacker** (n.)

capture to catch a person or animal and confine it **capture** (n.) **captive** (adj.)

clone a genetic copy of an animal that has been made in a lab, using the DNA of another animal **to clone** (v.)

collar an item that an animal wears around its neck **to collar** (v.)

cruel very mean or unkind **cruelly** (adv.) **cruelty** (n.)

domesticated raised by people for agricultural purposes or living with people as household pets **domestication** (n.) **domestic** (adj.)

endangered in danger of dying out completely **to endanger** (v.)

evolve to slowly change and develop over time into a different form **evolution** (n.) **evolutionary** (adj.)

hunt to chase and kill an animal, usually for food **hunt** (n.) **hunter** (n.)

intercept to interrupt and stop something from happening **interception** (n.)

pesticide chemicals put on plants to kill insects

species a class of plants or animals that have the same characteristics

tag a device attached to someone or something that sounds an alarm **to tag** (v.)

train to teach a person or animal how to do something **trainee** (n.) **trainer** (n.)

treat to behave in a certain way toward someone **to mistreat** (v.) **treatment** (n.)

wild free, untamed, not taken care of by people **wildly** (adv.) **wilderness** (n.)

Unit 10

affect to influence or cause something to happen

appropriate the right or correct thing to do **appropriately** (adv.) **inappropriate** (adj.)

change (your) mind to change your decision or opinion about something

concentrate to pay close attention to something **concentration** (n.)

eager to really want to do something **eagerness** (n.)

effect the result or change that one thing causes in a second thing **side effect** (n.)

figure out to discover a solution to a problem

hesitate to not speak or act for a short time, usually because you are uncertain about something **hesitation** (n.)

impress to make someone admire you **impression** (n.) **impressive** (adj.)

intuition a feeling that something is true even when you have no proof of it **intuitively** (adv.) **intuitive** (adj.)

keep (something) in mind to remember

make up your mind to decide to do something

mature to develop **to mature** (v.)

peer someone who is your own age

process to review and consider information in order to understand it

rational logical, reasonable **rationalize** (v.) **rationally** (adv.) **irrational** (adj.)

react to respond or act in a certain way because of something that has happened **reaction** (n.)

regret to feel very sorry about the outcome of something **regret** (n.) **regretful** (adj.) **regrettable** (adj.)

speak your mind tell others honestly how you feel

Unit 11

assess to judge or decide the quality or amount of something **assessment** (n.)

batter to hit something with strong force

below freezing below the temperature at which a liquid becomes solid **to freeze** (v.) **freezing point** (n.)

boiling hot very hot **(to) boil** (v., n.)

bounce back to recover

break down to stop working properly **breakdown** (n.)

break through to emerge **breakthrough** (n.)

call off to cancel

chill out to relax

coastline the boundary between land and sea **coast** (n.) **coastal** (adj.)

cold spell when the weather suddenly gets cold and stays cold for a while **cold** (adj.)

come down to fall to the ground

come down with to get sick with a particular illness

consider to think about something carefully **consideration** (n.)

cut off to disconnect **cutoff** (n., adj.)

defend to protect someone or something against attack **defense** (n.) **defenseless** (adj.)

die down to become less

erosion the gradual removal of rock and dirt by the weather (wind, the sea, etc.) **to erode** (v.)

find out to discover

freeze up to become stuck; unable to move

frigid extremely cold

frostbite a medical condition resulting from overexposure to freezing temperatures

give up to part with; to let go of

heat stroke a medical condition resulting from overexposure to high temperatures

heatwave a period of unusually hot weather

hold off to delay, not happen immediately

ice cap a permanent covering of ice

intervene to become involved in a situation and try to change it **intervention** (n.)

look after to keep someone healthy or safe

mild moderately warm

pick up to increase

postpone to delay (an event)

put off to postpone

put up with to tolerate

recover to become well again **recovery** (n.)

refuse to decline something **refusal** (n.)

scattered showers irregular rain over an area

shrink to become smaller **shrinkage** (n.)

size up to assess

snow flurries brief, light snowfalls

step in to intervene

storm out to leave a place noisily because you're angry

take off to depart **takeoff** (n.)

think over to consider

tolerate to accept something that you may not like **tolerance** (n.) **tolerable** (adj.)

turn down to refuse

Unit 12

achieve to succeed in doing something after a lot of effort **achievement** (n.)

adjustment a change **to adjust** (v.)

beat to defeat someone in a competition **unbeatable** (adj.)

championship a competition to find the best player or team in a particular sport **champion** (n.)

coach a person who trains others to play a sport **to coach** (v.)

commitment dedication to doing something **to commit** (v.)

defend to protect from harm or injury **defense** (n.)

get used to to become accustomed to something

handful a small amount of something

in shape fit, healthy **out of shape** (adj.)

interpreter a person who translates what someone is saying into another language **to interpret** (v.) **to misinterpret** (v.)

motivation a strong desire or willingness to do something **to motivate** (v.) **motivational** (adj.)

NBA (National Basketball Association) the professional basketball organization in North America

obsessed constantly thinking about something **obsession** (n.)

opponent your rival, especially in a game **to oppose** (v.) **opposition** (n.)

physical education (PE) a school subject in which students exercise and play sports

recruit to choose and try to persuade someone to work for your organization **recruiter** (n.) **recruitment** (n.)

role model someone you admire and try to imitate

violence behavior that hurts, injures, or kills people **violently** (adv.) **violent** (adj.)

Grammar Summary

Unit 1

Review of Past Tenses	
simple past: Use for actions completed in the past at a specific time (sometimes inferred). Use time expressions like *a year ago, earlier today, last summer,* and *the other day*.	We **graduated** together. He **worked** there for a year.
past continuous: Use for ongoing past actions that may or may not be completed. Use with the simple past to describe what was going on when the action in the simple past occurred.	I **was working** all day yesterday. We **were studying** in college when we rented that apartment.
present perfect: Use for actions begun in the past and continuing up to now and for actions in the past that relate to the present. Use time expressions like *lately, recently, up to now, during the last two months,* and *this week*.	I**'ve worked** here for a year. **Have** you ever **studied** Portuguese?
present perfect continuous: Use to emphasize the length of an event. In spoken English the verb *to be* is almost always a contraction.	Recently, I**'ve been working** too much. She**'s been waiting** for an hour!

- Use *for* (+ a period of time) and *since* (+ a specific point in time) with the perfect tenses to describe "time up to now." Use *for* (but not *since*) with the simple past tense for a time period that has come to an end.

Unit 2

Uses of Infinitives and Gerunds	
1. purpose infinitive	*Last summer I went overseas **to study** English.*
2. *it* + *be* + adjective + infinitive	*It was great **to experience** life in a small town.*
3. *too* + adjective + infinitive	*At first, it was too hard **to communicate** in English.*
4. gerunds as subjects	***Learning** the language was essential.*
5. adjective + preposition + gerund	*The small town is famous for **skiing** in the winter and **hiking** in the summer.*
6. verb + preposition + gerund	*I look forward to **going back** next year!*

Unit 3

Review of Future Forms	
definite plans	**I'm going to take** the TOEFL next Saturday. **I'm taking** the TOEFL next Saturday.
predictions	By 2040, there **are going to be** over 8 billion people on Earth. By 2040, there **will be** over 8 billion people on Earth.
promises	**I'll call** you tonight after I get home. I **won't** forget.
ongoing future actions	Within ten years, Germany **will be using** less oil and more renewable sources.

Unit 4

- Note that the chart below is list of common patterns and tendencies. You may hear or see other uses, but learning these patterns will allow you to use infinitive complements in English correctly and naturally.

Infinitive Complements	
Infinitive complements that follow the pattern **verb + object + infinitive** fall into some common verb groups including ❶ *persuade* verbs (*advise, cause, convince*), ❷ *want* verbs (*expect, need*), ❸ *believe* verbs (*consider, recognize*), and ❹ *plan* verbs (*arrange*). Group ❺ verbs are *have, let*, and *make*.	
❶ Verb + object + infinitive	She **advised me to take** the job.
❷ Verb + (object) + infinitive	She **expects me to apply**. I **need to find** a job.
❸ Verb + object + infinitive of *be*	We **consider him to be** the best singer.
❹ Verb + *for* + object + infinitive	They **arranged for me to have** an interview.
❺ Verb + object + base form	His music **makes me feel** happy.
Group ❶: the object is required. Group ❷: the object is optional. Group ❸: follows the pattern **verb + object + infinitive**, and the infinitive is usually *to be*. Group ❹: follows the pattern **verb + *for* + object + infinitive**. Group ❺: follows the same basic pattern, but requires the base form of the verb rather than the full infinitive.	

- Note that the presence or absence of the object defines the meaning of the sentence.

  She expects for me to apply. (She thinks I will apply.)

  She expects to apply. (She is planning to apply herself.)

Grammar Summary

Unit 5

Adverbial Clauses	
Adverbial clauses explain when, why, where, or in what way something happened. Adverbial clauses begin with a *connecting word*. When the clause starts a sentence, it is followed by a comma.	
Time: *after, since, whenever, as soon as, until, while, before, when*	**After the mine collapsed**, the men were trapped. The men were trapped **after the mine collapsed**.
Reason: *because, since*	**Because the mine collapsed**, the men were trapped.
Contrast: *although, (even) though*	**Even though it was hard**, they survived for weeks.
Purpose: *so (that)*	They closed the mine **so (that) an accident doesn't happen again**.
Before, after, during, since, and *until* can also be followed by a noun phrase.	**Before** the collapse, the men heard a sound. **During** the collapse, one man was injured.

Unit 6

Adjective Clauses with Subject Relative Pronouns	
who = for people	❶ People **who visit Dubai during the shopping festival** can get some great deals.
which = for things	❷ The festival, **which gets over three million visitors**, lasts several weeks.
that = for people and things	❸ Nadia is someone **that spends a lot on clothes**. ❹ It's a festival **that takes place every year**.
subject-verb agreement	❺ It's a shop **that sells discount electronics**. ❻ They're shops **that sell designer handbags**.
Adjective clauses give more information about a noun and begin with a relative pronoun (*who, which, that*). In ❶, the adjective clause gives necessary information about the subject. It completes the meaning of the sentence. In ❷, the adjective clause gives extra information about the subject. You don't need it to complete the meaning of the sentence. It is separated from the main clause by commas.	

- When an adjective clause gives extra information, *that* cannot be used:
  The festival, ~~that~~ which gets over three million visitors . . .
- Don't repeat the subject after the relative pronoun:
  He's a person who ~~he~~ spends a lot on clothes.
- In everyday spoken English, *that* is used much more often than *which* to describe things.
  *Did you buy the jacket **that** was on sale?*

Unit 7

Comparative Forms			
	more than . . .	**less than . . .**	**equal to . . .**
Adjectives	Taking a taxi is **faster** and **more reliable than** taking the subway.	The subways are **less reliable than** they used to be. They are **not as nice as** they once were.	During rush hour, walking is **as fast as** taking the bus.
Adverbs	The trains run **faster** and **more frequently** than the bus.	The trains run **less frequently** on weekends than they do on weekdays.	The old trains run **as smoothly as** the new ones.
Noncount nouns	After I quit, I had **more time than** I used to.	As a new parent, I have **less time than** I used to.	I spend **as much** time working **as** (I did) before.
Count nouns	The local train makes **more stops than** the express (does).	The express train makes **fewer stops than** the local (does).	The Blue Line has **as many riders** as it did last year.
Irregular forms: good → better, bad → worse, far → further			

- We don't usually use *less* with one-syllable adjectives. We use *not as . . . as* instead.
  ~~*The bus is less fast than the train*~~.
  The bus is not as fast as the train.

- Here is an additional summary of comparative forms for review.

Single-syllable adjectives add *–er* (or just). If the adjective ends in a single vowel and a consonant, double the final consonant.	*clean → cleaner* *cute → cuter* *big → bigger*
Two-syllable adjectives ending in *–y, -le, and –ly* usually take *–er.*	*funny → funnier* *simple → simpler* *careful → careful*
Some adjectives can have two comparative forms.	*friendly → friendlier / more friendly* *happy → happier / more happy* *handsome → handsomer / more handsome*
Other adjectives with two syllables and adjectives with more than two syllables usually take *more.*	*complex → more complex* *intelligent → more intelligent* *beautiful → more beautiful*
Adverbs ending in *–ly* usually take *more.*	*softly → more softly* *quickly → more quickly* *regularly → more regularly*

Unit 8

Past Modals	
Use past modals with past participles to assess real or imaginary past actions.	
Disbelief / impossibility	Jen: Stella **couldn't have[1] been** texting. She lost her cell phone recently.
Possibility	Tom: She **might have[2] borrowed** a friend's phone to do it.
Logical conclusion	Amy: I heard she was texting her mother. It **must have been** something important.
Regret over an action that wasn't taken	Ed: Even so, she **should have waited** until after class to send a text.
Regret over an action that was taken	Mina: I agree. She **shouldn't have disrupted** the class.
[1]or *can't have*	[2]or *could have* or *may have*

- Note that while *mustn't have* is used in the context of a logical conclusion, the present/future *mustn't* is used to prohibit someone from doing something.

  You mustn't have parked on this street—I don't see you car anywhere. (logical conclusion)

  You mustn't park here because of street cleaning. (prohibition)

- As you see in the chart, *could have* is used with possibility. It can also be used in another, more subtle context: *a possibility that was not acted on* (a missed opportunity).

  Mina was late for class. She could have overslept. (It's possible the reason she was late is that she overslept; we don't know for sure).

  Mina was late for class. She could have asked me for a ride. (Mina had the option to ask for a ride, but she didn't, so she was late.)

Unit 9

Review of Passive Voice	
simple present	The animals **are** *kept* in tiny cages. It's cruel.
simple past	Dogs ______ ________ 15,000 years ago.
present perfect	They ______ ________ **trained** to do police and rescue work.
present continuous past continuous	The lost cat **is / was** ________ **cared for** by a volunteer at the animal shelter.
simple future	The cat ______ **be** ________ to its owner tomorrow.
with modals	Parrots **can** *be taught* to communicate with humans. Dogs **should** ______ ________ on a leash.

❶ Forming the passive: Use a form of *be* + the past participle. With modals: modal + *be* + past participle
❷ To show who does the action, use *by* + noun: *The lost cat* **was found** *by a neighbor*.
If it's clear who does the action, or if it's not important, don't use *by* + noun: *Parrots* **can be taught** *to speak.*
❸ You might use the passive if:
- It's obvious who did something or the doer of the action is a general group of people: *Parrots can be taught to speak.* (We know humans are the ones teaching.)
- The action is more important than who does it: *The boy was bitten by a spider.*

- Remember, when you change a sentence from active voice to passive voice, the pronoun changes from an object pronoun to a subject pronoun.

  My friends gave ***me*** *a puppy for my birthday.*

  I *was given a puppy for my birthday.*

Unit 10

The Conditional			
1. With possible (real) future events		**2. With imaginary (unreal) present situations**	
if *clause*	*result clause*	if *clause*	*result clause*
If I **do** that,	I'll **have** enough money	If you **had** a scholarship,	you **would have** enough money,

❶ This form of the conditional is used to make predictions and talk about possible future events.
The verb in the *if* clause is in the simple present. In the result clause, the verb is in the simple future.

❷ This form of the conditional is used to talk about imaginary present events. The information in the *if* clause is not true right now. The result clause describes an imagined result.
The verb in the *if* clause is in the simple past. In the result clause, *would(n't)* + verb is used.
Note: *be* → *were* for all subjects in the *if* clause: If I / you / he were the teacher . . .

Unit 11

Phrasal Verbs

A phrasal verb is a verb + preposition/particle. Some phrasal verbs are "separable;" the verb can be "separated" from the preposition/particle by an object (noun or a pronoun). Notice the placement of the pronoun in the separable verbs. Phrasal verbs have different meanings than the base verb on its own, as you will see in Activity **A**.

	With an object	Without an object
separable	She **gave up** her job. / She **gave** her job **up**. ~~She gave up it~~. / She **gave** it **up**. Other examples: *put off, size up, think over*	She **bounced back** (recovered) from her illness. The plane **took off** on a dangerous mission. Other examples: *die down, pick up, step in*
inseparable	She **looked after** her colleagues. The doctor **looked after** them. Other examples: *find out, put up with*	

Some phrasal verbs have three words. They are always inseparable: *How much longer do we have to* ***put up with*** *this rain? / Every winter I* ***come down with*** *a cold.*

- Phrasal verbs, like regular verbs can have more than one meaning. Some phrasal verbs can be used both transitively and intransitively.

  take off
  The plane eventually took off. (It left the ground.)
  Her career is really taking off. (It's going well.)
  He won't take his hat off. (He won't remove it.)
  I took three weeks off last summer. (I had a vacation.)

Unit 12

Reported Speech

Notice! Some verbs (*convince, remind, tell*) can follow more than one pattern.

Use reported speech to explain what someone else has said. The verb tense, certain time words (such as *now, last week*), and pronouns can shift in reported speech.

Patterns in reported speech:

❶ verb + (*that*) clause: Ana **said (that) she was taking a kickboxing class.**
use with verbs: *explain, insist, mention, say*

❷ verb + pronoun/noun + (*that*) clause: Derek **told me (that) he played rugby.**
use with verbs: *convince, promise, remind, tell*

❸ verb + pronoun/noun + infinitive: Derek **encouraged his team to practice** more.
use with verbs: *beg, convince, encourage, invite, remind, tell*

Notice! Pattern 3 verbs are often used to ask for something or to give advice or instructions.

Grammar Summary

Skills Index

Credits

Photo Credits

Unit 1 pp.x–1, top left: hfng/Shutterstock.com; top right: ©iStockphoto.com/Aldo Murillo; bottom left: Dynamic Graphics/Thinkstock; bottom right: ©iStockphoto.com/Daniel Laflor; **p.2**: Mike Theiss/National Geographic Stock; **p.3**: Yuri Arcurs/Shutterstock.com; **p.4**: Niagara705/Dreamstime.com; **p.5**: Bojana/Shutterstock.com; **p.6**: National Geographic Maps/National Geographic Image Collection; **p.6–7**: Kenneth Garrett/Getty Images; **p.9**: beltsazar/Shutterstock.com; **p.10**: Frans Lanting/National Geographic Stock

Unit 2 pp.12–13: Freesurf69/Dreamstime.com; **p.14**, left: ©iStockphoto.com/Gorfer; right (top): Frans Lanting/National Geographic Stock; right (bottom): Unfetteredmind/Dreamstime.com; **p.15**, left: Celsopupo/Dreamstime.com; right: Leire Unzueta/National Geographic Stock; **p.16**, top: zhangyang13576997233/Shutterstock.com; **p.17**: zimmytws/Shutterstock.com; **p.18**, top: Helga Esteb/Shutterstock.com; bottom: Panoramic Images/National Geographic Stock; **p.19**: Frans Lanting/National Geographic Stock; **p.20**: Kenneth Garrett/National Geographic Stock; **p.21**, top: Robodread/Dreamstime.com; **p.22**: Tupungato/Shutterstock.com

Unit 3 pp.24–25: Jim Richardson/National Geographic Stock; **p.26**: Andy Z./Shutterstock.com; **p.28**, left to right: Goodluz/Shutterstock.com; Blend Images/Alamy; Andresr/Shutterstock.com; **p.29**: Jim Richardson/National Geographic Stock; **pp.30–31**: Michael Melford/National Geographic Stock; **p.32**: Jim West/Alamy; **p.33**: Seif1958/Dreamstime.com; **p.34**: Radu Razvan/Shutterstock.com

Unit 4 pp.36–37: Hugh Sitton/Corbis; **p.38**, top: Getty Images; top inset: Roy van Ingen; bottom: Dwphotos/Dreamstime.com; **p.40**: Scott Mitchell/ZUMA Press/Corbis; **p.41**, top: Featureflash/Shutterstock.com; bottom: Jack.Q/Shutterstock.com; **p.42**, top: Kaarsten/Dreamstime.com; bottom, Hemis/Alamy; **p.43**: David Alan Harvey/National Geographic Stock; **p.44**, top: Arunas Gabalis/Shutterstock.com; middle: Lebrecht Music and Arts Photo Library/Alamy; bottom: Chris Hill/National Geographic Stock; **p.46**: Karramba Production/Shutterstock.com; **p.47**: Cristian Nitu/Dreamstime.com

Unit 5 pp.48–49: Joel Sartore/National Geographic Stock; **p.50**, left: Getty Images; right: AFP/Getty Images; **p.51**: StockShot/Alamy; **p.52**: Yuri Arcurs/Shutterstock.com; **p.53**: Konstantin Yolshin/Shutterstock.com; **p.55**: THP/Tim Hester Photography/Shutterstock.com; **p.56**: Bobby Model/National Geographic Stock; **p.57**: George F. Mobley/National Geographic Stock; **p.58**: Mike Parry/Minden Pictures; **p.59**: JG Photography/Alamy

Unit 6 pp.60-61: PictureNet/Corbis; **p.62**, top: MBI/Alamy; bottom: Art Kowalsky/Alamy; **p.64**, top: Mark Seberini/Dreamstime.com; bottom: Edwin Verin/Dreamstime.com; **p.65**: Camilla Watson/Getty Images; **p.66**: John Kasawa/Dreamstime.com; **p.67**, top: Andrey Burmakin/Shutterstock.com; bottom: Andresr/Shutterstock.com; **p.68**: VideojugBeauty/YouTube; **p.69**: conrado/Shutterstock.com; **pp.70-71**: Stephen Bisgrove/Alamy

Unit 7 pp.72–73: Tino Soriano/National Geographic Stock; **p.74**, top: Mika Heittola/Shutterstock.com; bottom: Ira Block/National Geographic Stock; **p.76**: Yusef El-Mansouri/Shutterstock.com; **p.78**, top: Rohan Van Twest/Alamy; bottom left: Supri Suharjoto/Shutterstock.com; bottom right: Kzenon/Shutterstock.com; **p.80**: ©iStockphoto.com/Henrik Jonsson; **p.81**: Morgan Lane Photography/Shutterstock.com; **p.82**: Katrina Brown/Dreamstime.com; **p.83**: David Cupp/National Geographic Stock

Unit 8 pp.84–85: Keith Barraclough/National Geographic Stock; **p.86**: Dirk Anschütz/Corbis; **p.87**: Mike Theiss/National Geographic Stock; **p.88**, top: William Weems/National Geographic Stock; bottom: Catalin Petolea/Shutterstock.com; **p.89**: Mika/Corbis; **p.93**, top: Image Source/Corbis; bottom: Dmytro Konstantynov/Dreamstime.com; **p. 94**, top: Cristi_m/Dreamstime.com; middle: Benoit Tessier/Reuters/Corbis; bottom: StockLite/Shutterstock.com; **p.95**, left: Caro/Alamy; right: Ianni Dimitrov/Alamy

Unit 9 pp.96–97: Patrick Shyu/National Geographic Stock; **p.98**: Jmiks/Shutterstock.com; **p.100**, top: Richard Laschon/Shutterstock.com; middle: donatas1205/Shutterstock.com; bottom: Vincent J. Musi/National Geographic Stock; **p.101**: John Elk III/Alamy; **p.102**: Gary Roberts/Alamy; **p.103**: Michael Nichols/National Geographic Stock; **p.105**, top: Konrad Wothe/Minden Pictures; middle: Medford Taylor/National Geographic Stock; bottom: Shawnjackson/Dreamstime.com; **p.106**: Renate Micallef/Dreamstime.com; **p.107**: Picsfive/Shutterstock.com

Unit 10 pp.108–109: Jim Richardson/National Geographic Stock; **p.110**, left (top): Gelpi/Shutterstock.com; (bottom): Chris Rout/Alamy; right: Peter Zoeller/Design Pics/Corbis; **p.111**: Sandra Eckhardt/Corbis; **p.113**: James Woodson/Thinkstock; **p.114**: takito/Shutterstock.com; **p.115**: Chris Crisman/Corbis; **p.116**: auremar/Shutterstock.com; **p.117**: MedusArt/Shutterstock.com; **p.118**: Nik Wheeler/Corbis

Unit 11 pp.120–121: Sigurdur Hrafn Stefnisson; **p.122**, top: Reuters/Corbis; bottom: George F. Mobley/National Geographic Stock; **p.123**: AFP/Getty Images; **p.124**: John Lund/Drew Kelly/Blend Images/Corbis; **p.125**, left to right: Jack Reynolds/Getty Images; Brian Thompson/National Geographic Stock; Mike Theiss/National Geographic Stock; **p.126**, top: Czacio/Dreamstime.com; bottom: John Wollwerth/Dreamstime.com; **p.127**: Chris Collins/Corbis; **p.128**: Kristina Afanasyeva/Dreamstime.com; **p.129**: Jim Reed/Jim Reed Photography - Severe & /Corbis; **p.130**: Sam Kittner/National Geographic Stock

Unit 12 pp.132–133: Chuck Pefley/Alamy; **p.134**, top: Jonathan Larsen/Diadem Images/Alamy; bottom: Jason Swalwell/Shutterstock.com; **p.135**: Shelly Castellano/Icon SMI/Corbis; **p.136**, top: Vico Collective/Alin Dragulin/Blend Images/Corbis; bottom: new vave/Shutterstock.com; **p.137**: Seandnad/Dreamstime.com; **pp.138–139**: Fritz Hoffmann/National Geographic Stock; **p.139**: John Warburton-Lee Photography/Alamy; **p.140**: Ang Wee Heng John/Dreamstime.com; **p.141**. Myrleen Pearson/Alamy; **p.143**: Ben Radford/Corbis

Text Credits

Readings from the following units were adapted from National Geographic.

Unit 1 Adapted from *Searching for Cleopatra* by various, National Geographic Extreme Explorer, January/February 2011. **Unit 2** Adapted from *Traveling Troubadour* by Keith Bellows, *National Geographic Traveler,* March 2011. **Unit 3** Adapted from *Plugging into the Sun* by George Johnson, National Geographic Magazine, September 2009. **Unit 4** Adapted from *Hip-Hop Planet* by James McBride, National Geographic Magazine, April 2007 **Unit 7** Adapted from *Changing America* by Joel L. Swerdlow, National Geographic Magazine, September 2001 **Unit 9** Adapted from *Orphans No More* by Charles Siebert, National Geographic Online, September 2011. **Unit 10** Adapted from *Beautiful Brains* by David Dobbs, National Geographic Magazine, October 2011. **Unit 12** Adapted from *Battle for the Soul of Kung Fu* by Peter Gwin, National Geographic Magazine, March 2011.

Unit 1

Listening

Exercise B, page 4

Announcer: Do you have boxes and boxes of family photos? What about all those videos that you shot while you were visiting Disneyland with your family? You've saved up all this stuff ... Now how are you going to pass on these memories to your children ... or your grandchildren?

You can do it in a fun and easy way. It's called "new family tree dot com" and it's brand new.

Our Web site is not like the other dry and boring Web sites on the market. They focus on statistics and research. They are places where you can store your life's memories ... and that's it. They focus on the past.

At new family tree dot com, we have an ambitious goal: we want this site to be a "place for the past ... and the present." A place where you can store your photo and video memories ... and tell your stories, but also a place where you can use your memories to connect with other family members ... *today.*

Listening

Exercises C and D, page 4

Announcer: What is something you always wanted to ask your mother, but never did? Maybe "How did you meet Dad?" or "Who was your best friend when you were growing up?"

And what do you want your relatives to know about you? Maybe you want to answer the question "What's your favorite subject in school?" or "Have you ever been in love?"

Here's how it works. Just log in to our Web site with your e-mail address. You'll see a list of different questions, under headings like "Childhood," "Hobbies," or even "Remember the time you did something fun." Choose one of our ideas or come up with a question of your own. Then write your answer and post it on the site.

While you're writing your answer, you can e-mail the same question to anyone in your family and ask them to answer it too! Then you can read what they've written and compare your answers to see how alike—or different—you really are.

Listen to what Rebecca had to say about her experience with new family tree dot com!

Woman: I chose to answer the question, "What is a memory from your childhood that makes you smile?" It's not something I would typically ask, but it's interesting to think about, isn't it? I answered it ... and I've sent the question to my sister too. I've been waiting for two days for her response—I hope she answers soon. *(laughs)* Anyway, with new family tree dot com, it feels like I'm reliving my favorite memories all over again ... with the people I love the most. It's really great!

Unit 2

Listening

Exercises B and C, page 16

Welcome to Beijing! Our walking tour today covers the old commercial heart of the city. All of the points on our tour are easily accessible on foot and you can complete this tour in one to two hours.

Our starting point, lying east of the Forbidden City, is the former home of a famous Chinese writer: Lao She. He was one of China's most famous novelists of the twentieth century. You can read about his life as well as view his study and library here.

Exiting his home, we next walk south on the street that is our second stop on this tour. This narrow street's name translates in English to "rich and powerful alley." Step into this tranquil alley to experience the charm of "old China": picturesque homes with beautifully decorated roofs and doors. These were the residences of some of the wealthiest residents of Beijing.

If you're feeling a little adventurous, check out our third destination, the Loving Life Massage Center. This center specializes in a kind of massage called Tui-na, which traditionally was performed by blind people. Treat yourself to a luxurious massage if you aren't in a hurry!

Continuing on to the fourth point, we find Dong Tang, or "East Church." This cathedral was built in the seventeenth century. It was destroyed at different times by a fire, an earthquake, and a war, and each time it was rebuilt. The area in front of the building is a popular spot with Beijing skateboarders.

Walking a bit further, we come to our fifth point on the tour: the foreign language bookstore. On the first and third floors, you can find Beijing's largest supply of foreign language materials. It's worth a look if you need a book or two.

It's easy to find our sixth stop on the tour. Just follow the crowds at any time of day to what's known as the "Snack Street." This pedestrian plaza features a diverse display of Chinese food from all corners of the country. The busy atmosphere and experience of eating here are unbeatable. Sit down for some noodles—they're tasty!

It's time to go shopping. Right down the street is point number seven on our tour, the Oriental Plaza, a huge indoor shopping mall. You can find both Chinese and foreign brands here. Downstairs is a large food court. If you're not too full, maybe you could grab something to drink.

For your convenience, the Oriental Plaza is connected to the Grand Hyatt Beijing, our final destination. Follow the signs and escalators to the lobby of the hotel. You can end your tour in front of the large hotel steps outside, where tourists are posing for photos. Why don't you join them and take a few photos of your own?

Unit 3

Listening

Exercise B, page 28

Welcome to Our Green Planet, the program that looks at planet Earth ... and how we can protect it. I'm George Ruiz, your host. Today we have a very special episode for you.

We all know that it's important to save energy and not pollute, right? But how exactly do we do that? Well, starting tonight, we're going to show you how. For the next twelve weeks, we're going to be following three different families—everyday people like you and me—as they attempt to "take our energy challenge" and lower their consumption as they save energy. And as you watch, we're hoping you can learn from each family's successes and failures. Maybe one day you'll want to join the energy challenge too!

Listening

Exercises C and D, page 28

Host: We're going to start out by checking in with three different families. Let's see how they are doing. First up is the Novak family in Slovenia. We're going to be speaking with Anica, the mother ... Hi, Anica, are you there?

Anica: Yes, it's me. Hello.

Host: So, how's it going so far?

Anica: Well, we've had some successes ... and some failures, I suppose.

Host: How have you been successful?

Anica: Well, we have cut back on our air travel. It was really easy to do. Slovenia is a small country. Most of the people travel by car anyway. Instead of taking a long trip every summer, we'll probably do it every other year.

Host: Sounds good. What's been difficult so far?

Anica: Hmm … I guess it's about bicycling. In my country, children have to pass an exam before they can ride a bicycle on public streets. Our children are too small to take the exam. So, we can't use bicycles for short trips. We have to take them everywhere by car.

Host: Anything else?

Anica: I have to admit … I hate gardening. When I was a teenager, we lived in the country and had a garden. It was so much work. Ugh. I don't like to get dirty … So we won't be growing our own food.

Host: Sounds like gardening isn't for you! *(laughs)*

Anica: No, definitely not. I'm a city girl!

(pause)

Host: Next up is Akira Noguchi from Japan. Hello, Akira.

Akira: Hello. Thanks for having me on the program.

Host: Our pleasure … How's it going? Are you cutting back on your energy consumption?

Akira: Yes, we are. It's funny … my wife and I realized something. We can save energy a couple of ways … without really trying. It's easy.

Host: For example?

Akira: Well, take our refrigerator. We changed the temperature to a mild setting. The food stays fresh and cold, but this refrigerator doesn't use much energy.

Host: Good for you!

Akira: And we have a dryer, but we rarely use it. We should probably get rid of it. Anyway, we almost always air dry our clothes. It takes longer, but it's worth it.

Host: What's been challenging so far?

Akira: Well, let me tell you something. I counted the number of appliances in our home—and we have 37!

Host: Wow. That's a lot.

Akira: I guess so … And I heard that it's important to unplug your electronic appliances when your not using them because they use too much energy … The problem is, I can't remember to unplug everything, especially in the morning when I'm in a hurry to get to work!

(pause)

Host: Finally, we'll speak to Dora Perez from Mexico. Hola, Dora.

Dora: Hi.

Host: I understand that you live in the country.

Dora: Yes, that's right. We live in a small city not far from San Miguel de Allende.

Host: Is it difficult to be energy efficient in the country?

Dora: In some ways, yes. My town is very small. When I go shopping, it's hard to find a lot of things. I buy a lot of things online. It's not good, I know. But I just can't give up online shopping.

Host: What about getting around? Do you travel by car usually?

Dora: Yes, we do. But recently, we've started sharing rides with our neighbors to the supermarket, to school, wherever. It's a nice way to catch up with your friends.

Host: Anything else you'd like to add?

Dora: I recently started using a solar cooker. We have a lot of sunny weather here, so it works well.

Host: How does it work?

Dora: You put the ingredients in the pot and leave it in a sunny place for four or five hours. It cooks everything perfectly and the best part is I'm also cutting down on my energy use!

Unit 4

Listening

Exercises B and C, page 40

Interviewer: How did you get interested in salsa music?

Carlos: Actually, I wasn't interested at first. I was more into skateboarding … and rock music. It's kind of funny to think about that now … But I guess I had a good voice … Anyway, there was this salsa band at my school and one day the singer—I think his name was Ben—quit the band. They asked me to sing with them that day. I didn't have to audition—it was my friend's band!

Interviewer: And then you joined their band?

Carlos: No, no … I was new to singing … I realized that I liked to sing, but I didn't know anything about music, really. It was at that time that my brother and I decided to study music—to learn about singing … and then later we formed a band. I finally got into salsa music then.

Interviewer: What changed for you?

Carlos: Well, the more I heard it, the more I liked the *energy* of salsa. It's such danceable music. Even though salsa music isn't native to my country, I still feel so much when I hear it or sing it. It makes me feel happy and inspires me.

Interviewer: What are you and your brother doing now?

Carlos: We're promoting our current album and writing music for a new one. A lot of the salsa bands out there just play covers—songs that are already well known—and we wanted to write our own music …

Interviewer: Tell me about your music.

Carlos: We're definitely a bit out of the mainstream. Now we play a kind of salsa that was popular in the 1970s. It's called *salsa dura.* It has a harder sound and features a lot of drums … in contrast to *salsa romantica*, which is softer and is more popular now.

Interviewer: Well still, your album is out now and it's been a huge commercial success.

Carlos: Yes, we've been lucky. We started out playing in small bars and saving money to record an album. It's been a long road … but our hard-core fans have stayed with us. They have always supported us and they inspire me every day.

Interviewer: You started out simply singing in your friends' band and look at you now. You have your own band and you're enjoying great success …

Carlos: Yes, I guess you could say we've "come of age." And I can't wait to see what's coming next!

Unit 5

Listening

Exercise B, page 52

Host: Welcome back to the show. We're talking with personal coach Greg Ravetti today. Great to have you with us today, Greg.

Greg Ravetti: Thanks; it's good be here.

Host: So, Greg, in a recent blog entry, you focused on the subject of panic. Why this topic?

Greg: Well, when most of us hear the word "panic," we think of a dangerous situation and people running around and screaming. But I wanted to look at some everyday things that cause anxiety—things that *most* people will experience in their lives. I also wanted to explain how to stay calm and handle those stressful situations.

Host: Can you give us an example?

Greg: Okay, well, for instance, I had a client who recently went on her first job interview …

Host: *(laughs)* That'll make a lot of people nervous.

Greg: Exactly. She was fine in the morning. But then, just before the interview, she got so anxious that she had trouble breathing. And then during the interview, she froze and had a really hard time answering questions.

Host: That happened to me once!

Greg: It happens to a lot of people. Your anxiety is so intense that you can't think or act normally.

Host: So what causes us to panic like this?

Greg: Good question. In most cases, people are worried about doing something poorly—making a mistake in the job interview, for example. And it's not just job interviews that are hard. For some people, taking a test at school can be an ordeal. And the greater the stress, the harder it is to think and act calmly.

Listening

Exercises C and D, page 52

Host: So, let's say you have to take a big test and you start to panic … what can you do?

Greg: In stressful situations like that, I encourage people to do three things. The first is to breathe slowly for a minute.

Host: How does that help?

Greg: Well, whenever you get anxious, you start breathing faster. That makes you feel *more* nervous.

Host: So you need to slow your breathing …

Greg: Right. Doing this will relax you so that you can think normally again.

Host: Okay, so after you've done that, what's the next step?

Greg: Next is to make a simple plan. For example, you're taking that test … and suddenly you freeze and forget everything. What can you do? One simple plan is to tell yourself: I'm going to answer the easy questions first. Then I'm going to do the harder ones. And I'm going to spend only two minutes on each question.

Host: Does making this kind of plan really help?

Greg: Definitely. Even though the plan is simple, it helps you feel more in control … This calms you so that you can think and go through the test step by step.

Host: How about planning ahead of time?

Greg: Absolutely. You don't have to wait for a stressful situation to happen. Try to imagine it *before* you're in it. Think about how you'll handle it—what you'll do or say. Have a plan ready.

Host: Good advice. And what about the third step?

Greg: The final step, of course, is to *follow* the plan you created … As with step two, following your plan will help you feel more in control and will reduce your anxiety …

Connections

Exercise A, page 53

(cell phone rings)

Fatima: Hello?

Amina: Hey Fatima. It's Amina.

Fatima *(sounding stressed)*: Oh hi, Amina. What's up?

Amina: Not much. Hey, you sound upset. Are you okay?

Fatima: No, I'm freaking out. You know that project for our English class that's due tomorrow? Well I haven't started it.

Amina: What?! Why not?

Fatima: Because I thought it was due *next* week! What am I going to do? This project is 50% of our grade.

Amina: Fatima, don't panic, okay? Have you done *any* work?

Fatima: Yeah, I've got an outline.

Amina: So even though you haven't started the project, you have some ideas.

Fatima: Yeah.

Amina: Okay, then; let me think for a minute …

Unit 6

Listening

Exercises B and C, page 64

Conversation 1

(on the street)

Mark: Where are we going? I thought you were finished shopping.

Lori: Yeah, but I just want to stop into this store for a minute. Their tablets are on sale and I need a new one.

(enter a store)

Mark: See anything you like?

Lori: Yeah, this one. It's just what I'm looking for and it's on sale for four hundred.

Mark: *Four hundred?* What a rip off! You can get that cheaper online.

Lori: Really? Where?

Mark: iGadget.

Lori: I don't know it.

Mark: Sure you do. It's that site that sells discount electronics.

Lori: Oh yeah … But isn't a lot of their stuff used?

Mark: Some of it is, but they sell lots of new stuff, too. I've gotten some really good deals. You should take a look their prices first.

Lori: Yeah, maybe you're right. Come on; let's go.

(pause)

Conversation 2

Alice: *(calling)* Mia?

Mia: I'm over here … in the shoe section.

Alice: You shopping for shoes?

Mia: Yeah, I need a new pair for work.

Alice: What are you looking for?

Mia: I don't know … something that's stylish but affordable.

Alice: Hey, check out this pair. They're kind of cute.

Mia: Let's see … Oh yeah, those *are* really nice. Let me try them on.

How do I look?

Alice: Great! Are you gonna get them?

Mia: Let's see how much they are … *A hundred and fifty dollars!?* There's no way I can afford that.

Alice: Hang on a minute. The sign says all shoes on this table are half off.

Mia: Yeah, but I've only got sixty.

Alice: I've got some cash. I can loan you the rest …

Mia: That'd be great! Come on; let's get'em.

Conversation 3

Clerk: Excuse me. Can I help you?

Thomas: Yeah, that'd be great. I'm shopping for a gift for my nephew who really loves biking.

Clerk: What kind of bike are you looking for?

Thomas: A road bike. He likes to go on long-distance rides with his friends …

Clerk: Okay … I've got several models I can show you … This one here, for example, is one of the best on the market.

Thomas: How much is it?

Clerk: Normally it sells for eight hundred, but it's been reduced to six forty.

Thomas: Whoa … that's more than I planned to spend.

Clerk: It is a little more expensive than the other bikes, but honestly, it's worth it. It's perfect for going on those longer rides … and we're selling it at a great price.

Thomas: Wouldya take five-fifty?

Clerk: Couldya do five ninety?

Thomas: All that I can afford is five sixty—max.

Clerk: That'll work.

Thomas: Great, then I'll take it.

Listening

Exercise C, page 64

(from Conversation 1)

Mark: See anything you like?

Lori: Yeah, this one. It's just what I'm looking for and it's on sale for four hundred.

Mark: *Four hundred?* What a rip off! You can get that cheaper online.

(from Conversation 2)

Alice: What are you looking for?

Mia: I don't know … something that's stylish but affordable.

Alice: Hey, check out this pair. They're kind of cute.

Mia: Let's see … Oh yeah, those *are* really nice. Let me try them on.

(from Conversation 3)

Thomas: How much is it?

Clerk: Normally it sells for eight hundred, but it's been reduced to six forty.

Thomas: Whoa … that's more than I planned to spend.

Clerk: It is a little more expensive than the other bikes, but honestly, it's worth it. It's perfect for going on those longer rides … and we're selling it at a great price.

Connections

Exercise A, page 65

(at an outdoor market)

Buyer: This is an interesting looking pen. How much do you want for it?

Seller: Twenty dollars.

Buyer: For this old pen?!

Seller: Ah, but it's not just *any* old pen. It's a pen that never runs out of ink.

Buyer: A pen that never runs out of ink? Really?

Seller: Yes. It's perfect for the person who never wants to buy another pen again! But I've only got three left. They're selling fast.

Buyer: Hmmm … Well, it *is* pretty … and you say it'll never run out of ink? I'll give you five dollars for it.

Seller: Ten. Come on; think of all the money you'll save. Ten is a great deal.

Buyer: Six. That's all I can afford.

Seller: Six it is!

Unit 7

Listening

Exercise B, page 76

Greta Fox: Good evening, I'm Greta Fox. Were you late to work this morning? Well, you're not alone. A recent transportation survey conducted in ten cities has found that the average morning commute time has increased to 47 minutes. That means that we're spending more time in cars, on trains, and on board buses these days as we head to work. So what's keeping us on the road longer? What better way to find out than to follow one of these brave commuters during rush hour? Jeremy Wexler reports.

(at a train station)

Jeremy: It's ten after eight, and I've arrived at Sullivan Station, where I always catch my regular 8:12 train to the city. Usually I … *(announcement)* wait a second … They just said that there's a delay. It's Friday, and this is the third time this week my train has been late. Many of the trains on this commuter line are old and need service. That means they break down often—usually at least once a week. When that happens, trains run less frequently and become more crowded. We'll see what the problem is today …

(on the train)

It's now 8:26 and I'm finally on board my train—we're pulling out 14 minutes late. It turns out that a train did break down a few stops back. As a result, it's very cramped here and impossible to find a seat. It looks like I'll be standing for the first part of my commute.

(at a train station)

OK, 8:42. I'm waiting on the platform for my connecting train to take me to Central Station. Once I get there, I have the option of walking to the studio or taking the number 3 bus. Because the bus is not very reliable, I usually walk. But if I catch it at just the right time, it saves me ten minutes. Nothing to do but wait and hope. I'm noticing that they've made improvements to this station. It's cleaner, they actually have benches to sit on and there's art on the walls. Because of that, this part of my trip has definitely become more pleasant. The trains might not be punctual, but the stations are looking better.

(walking)

Walking it is. The number 3 bus was nowhere in sight when I got to Central Station. I'm already six minutes late to work. Still, I have to say that trains and buses and walking are all better than driving. Traffic is getting worse every day, and parking is more expensive. If I can leave my car at home, I guess it's worth showing up to the studio a little late. But at least this time, I got to do some work on the way. This is Jeremy Wexler, reporting.

Listening

Exercise C, page 76

(at a train station)

Jeremy: It's ten after eight, and I've arrived at Sullivan Station, where I always catch my regular 8:12 train to the city. Usually I … *(announcement)* wait a second … They just said that there's a delay. It's Friday, and this is the third time this week my train has been late. Many of the trains on this commuter line are old and need service. That means they break down often—usually at least once a week. When that happens, trains run less frequently and become more crowded. We'll see what the problem is today …

(on the train)

It's now 8:26 and I'm finally on board my train—we're pulling out 14 minutes late. It turns out that a train did break down a few stops back. As a result, it's very cramped here and impossible to find a seat. It looks like I'll be standing for the first part of my commute.

(at a train station)

OK, 8:42. I'm waiting on the platform for my connecting train to take me to Central Station. Once I get there, I have the option of walking to the studio or taking the number 3 bus. Because the bus is not very reliable, I usually walk. But if I catch it at just the right time, it saves me ten minutes. Nothing to do but wait and hope. I'm noticing that they've made improvements to this station. It's cleaner, they actually have benches to sit on and there's art on the walls. Because of that, this part of my trip has definitely become more pleasant. The trains might not be punctual, but the stations are looking better.

(walking)

Walking it is. The number 3 bus was nowhere in sight when I got to Central Station. I'm already six minutes late to work. Still, I have to say that trains and buses and walking are all better than driving. Traffic is getting worse every day, and parking is more expensive. If I can leave my car at home, I guess it's worth showing up to the studio a little late. But at least this time, I got to do some work on the way. This is Jeremy Wexler, reporting.

Unit 8

Listening

Exercises B and C, page 89

Carly: Did you hear what happened? Micah got suspended from school. For five days!

Mark: You're kidding!

Carly: No, I'm not. He got in trouble for posting something online.

Mark: What exactly did he do?

Carly: Well, he criticized a teacher … Mr. Salazar.

Mark: Really? What did he say?

Carly: He wrote something like: "Mr Salazar is the worst math teacher I've ever had."

Mark: Wow. I don't think Mr. Salazar is a bad teacher. I mean, he *is* strict, but I kind of like his class …

Carly: Me too. Anyway, … Micah posted it on Saturday. Then he changed his mind and removed the post on Sunday but it was too late.

Mark: Everyone could see it?

Carly: Yeah. He didn't put any restrictions on the post, so the comment was public.

Mark: He should've kept it private.

Carly: Too late now.

Mark: Did Mr. Salazar see it?

Carly: I don't know, but someone must've told the school about it … because this morning the principal, Ms. Stevens, called Micah into her office. She said that his online posting was disruptive to school life. Then she called Micah's mom.

Mark: Gosh, they're really making a big deal out of this. Micah must feel terrible.

Carly: I know. Oh, and he has to write a letter of apology to Mr. Salazar.

Mark: How did his mom react?

Carly: I heard that she was pretty angry.

Mark: I feel bad for Micah … I can't imagine what he's going through.

Carly: Me neither. I hope things get better for him soon.

Mark: Yeah … I guess you really have to consider the consequences before you post something online.

Carly: No kidding! I was thinking the same thing.

Unit 9

Listening

Exercise B, page 100

Interviewer: So, Dr. Stern, you've been working with bonobos for several years …

Dr. Stern: Yes, that's right—both here in the States and in the Congo.

Interviewer: They're native to that country, correct?

Dr. Stern: Yes, in the wild they're found *only* in the Congo, though of course they can be seen in zoos and found in research centers like the Great Ape Trust all over the world.

Interviewer: Tell us a little about what got you interested in bonobos …

Dr. Stern: Well, genetically, they're very similar to humans—we've got 98% of the same DNA—so there's lots we can learn from them about how we evolved …

Interviewer: I've heard that bonobos tend to be very peaceful animals. That must make them easy to work with.

Dr. Stern: Well, the theory that bonobos are a peaceful species has never really been proven … although in the wild they do seem to be less aggressive and to attack each other less than some primates.

Interviewer: Speaking of the wild, what about threats from humans? Are bonobos endangered?

Dr. Stern: It's hard to say for sure, but we think they probably are. We do know that they're losing their natural habitat. Human populations are expanding into the bonobos' forest land—which can cause their numbers to decrease. We also know that bonobos are hunted for meat.

Listening

Exercise C, page 100

Interviewer: Okay … so let's talk a little about the recent work you've been doing with a bonobo named Kanzi. How long have you been studying him?

Dr. Stern: Since he was a baby. His mother was brought to the U.S. from the Congo, but Kanzi was born in the United States. He's interesting to scientists because of his advanced communication abilities. For example, when he was very young, Kanzi began learning human language on his own …

Interviewer: So scientists trained him to speak a language?

Dr. Stern: No, they didn't train him. *He learned it*—just by listening. He heard scientists talking to his mother. Later he tried using that same language on his own.

Interviewer: That's just how children learn language. They hear it and then they try to speak themselves.

Dr. Stern: Exactly.

Interviewer: Kanzi is one smart bonobo!

Dr. Stern: Yeah, he is. Kanzi was the first ape to learn a human language this way. He started out understanding and using single words and today he makes whole sentences. He's also able to understand thousands of spoken words in English and can communicate with us using a special keyboard. Oh … and there's one other thing …

Interviewer: What's that?

Dr. Stern: He also plays the piano. *(laughs)*

Interviewer: Wow … He sounds pretty special. I'd love to meet him someday.

Unit 10

Listening

Exercise A, page 112

Conversation 1

Eric: Hey Jane. Going to your cooking class?

Jane: Yeah, tonight's the fourth one. *(sarcastically)* I can't wait.

Eric: You don't sound too happy about it.

Jane: I'm actually thinking about dropping the class.

Eric: No way. Why?

Jane: Well, for the first three sessions, all we did was tour the kitchen and talk *about* food. I thought we were going to start cooking right away.

Eric: Hmmm. I know other people who've taken the same course and they loved it. You know, if I were you, I'd see how it goes tonight.

Jane: Yeah, I will. But if things don't change, I'm going to quit and take the painting course. I think there's still room in that one—it starts next week.

Conversation 2

Customer Service Rep: Thank you for calling InStar Wireless; this is Carmen. How can I help you?

Will: Yes, hi. About a month ago, I purchased a cell phone from one of your stores and I'd like to know what the return policy is.

CSR: Is there something wrong with the phone, sir?

Will: No, I've just changed my mind and would like to return it.

CSR: I see. Now, you say you bought the phone a month ago. Our policy states that you can return the phone within two weeks of purchase. If you return the phone later than that, you'll be charged a twenty-five dollar fee.

Will: Now … I don't have my receipt …

CSR: Well, if you had the receipt, we could refund your money—minus the fee—in the store. Without it, it'll take four weeks to process your request …

Will: *(sarcastically, annoyed)* Oh, that's great.

CSR: I'm sorry, sir, but that's our policy.

Will: Yeah, okay …

Conversation 3

(school bell)

Steven: So, do you have another class now?

Suzanne: Yeah, how about you?

Steven: I'm heading to the cafeteria for lunch.

Suzanne: So I guess I'll see you later so that we can go through our chemistry notes together?

Steven: Our notes?

Suzanne: Yeah, for the test tomorrow? Remember … we planned to study together this afternoon?

Steven: Oh yeah … um, what time were you thinking?

Suzanne: Well, I've got class until four, so how about 4:30 in the library?

Steven: *(hesitating)* Uh, yeah … maybe.

Suzanne: But … I thought we were going to study together today.

Steven: Well, it's just … um … my friend Sam texted me earlier. I, uh, said I'd meet him for coffee after my last class.

Suzanne: *(sarcastically)* Oh, well … have fun

Steven: Sorry for the last-minute change, but he's only in town for the day.

Suzanne: Okay, well … if you want to join me, I'll be in the library until 6:30.

Steven: Yeah, okay. I'll text you, all right?

Listening

Exercise B, page 112

(from Conversation 1)

Eric: Hey Jane. Going to your cooking class?

Jane: Yeah, tonight's the fourth one. *(sarcastically)* I can't wait.

Eric: You don't sound too happy about it.

(from Conversation 2)

Will: Now … I don't have my receipt …

CSR: Well, if you had the receipt, we could refund your money—minus the fee—in the store. Without it, it'll take four weeks to process your request …

Will: *(sarcastically, annoyed)* Oh, that's great.

CSR: I'm sorry, sir, but that's our policy.

(from Conversation 3)

Suzanne: Well, I've got class until four, so how about 4:30 in the library?

Steven: *(hesitating)* Uh, yeah … maybe.

Suzanne: But … I thought we were going to study together today.

Steven: Well, it's just … um … my friend Sam texted me earlier. I, uh, said I'd meet him for coffee after my last class.

Suzanne: *(sarcastically)* Oh, well … have fun.

Unit 11

Listening

Exercises B and C, page 124

Conversation 1

Carmen: Hey, Jill. How was your friend's party? Did you have a good time?

Jill: Yeah … I guess so.

Carmen: What do you mean? You didn't enjoy yourself?

Jill: I had a good time … in the beginning. But then there was an argument.

Carmen: Really? What happened?

Jill: I'm not sure exactly. These two guys started yelling in the other room. My friend tried to step in, but they couldn't be calmed down.

Carmen: So what happened?

Jill: Finally one guy said "I'm leaving then!" and he stormed out. He didn't even stay for the birthday cake!

Carmen: Wow. He must have been upset.

Conversation 2

Dan: You look worried, Bill.

Bill: I am, Dan … Over a hundred people are coming to the picnic today.

Dan: Yeah, I know. And everything looks great. You're really prepared. It's going to be fun.

Bill: I hope so. The weather report said it's supposed to rain, though. I don't want to call everything off, but if it starts to rain, I might have to cancel.

Dan: Don't worry. I really don't think it's going to rain until later tonight.

Bill: I hope you're right. If the rain can just hold off for a few more hours, everything will be fine.

Dan: Trust me. Just a few minutes ago the sun was trying to break through the clouds. In fact, I can see a bit of sunlight behind the clouds right now …

Conversation 3

Mom: Have you looked outside recently, Carrie? The weather!

Carrie: Yeah. It's really coming down out there. It's been snowing for hours.

Mom: I know … and it doesn't look like it will die down anytime soon … hey, wait a minute, young lady. What are you doing?

Carrie: Getting the car keys. I want to …

Mom: Carrie! Don't think you can just come in here and pick up the car keys without asking! Where are you going?

Carrie: Mom, chill out! Don't get so excited … I want to go to the movies. I'm meeting Deena there.

Mom: Are you kidding me? Look at all the snow! It's not safe.

Carrie: But Mom …

Mom: No buts. Listen. Why don't you text Deena? Instead of driving to the movie theater, she can walk over here … you can watch movies together here—in the family room. … OK?

Carrie: All right, Mom. I'll text Deena right now.

Conversation 4

Mr. Meyers: Hi, Andy … Hey, what's wrong?

Andy: Oh, nothing, Mr. Meyers … it's just …

Mr. Meyers: You can tell me.

Andy: Well, you know how I wanted to be in the school play … the one about the baseball player?

Mr. Meyers: Of course! It's the biggest play of the year … right before graduation.

Andy: That's the one.

Mr. Meyers: Did you audition for it?

Andy: I sure did. I prepared a couple of things to read and I practiced really hard. I was so excited about it. You know how much I love acting!

Mr. Meyers: I do. So … how did it go?

Andy: At first everything was going well. Then … I don't know what happened. I just froze up. It was like I could read the words on the paper, but my mouth wouldn't move.

Mr. Meyers: Oh no!

Andy: I don't think they're going to choose me. I was so terrible.

Mr. Meyers: Don't worry, Andy. They haven't made a decision yet

Unit 12

Listening

Exercise B, page 136

TV Anchor: In other sports news, a report is coming out of Beijing that basketball player Jason Jennings is not planning to stay on for a second year with the Tigers. The twenty-two-year-old first made news when he was recruited by the Chinese team—becoming one of a handful of American basketball players to leave the NBA to play in China.

For more on that story, we go to Kim Matthews who's live in our newsroom. Kim?

Reporter: Thanks Marc. I talked with Jason Jennings earlier today by phone about his decision not to play another season with the Tigers. Here's what he had to say … *(cut away)*

Reporter: Jason, you've played a strong season with the Tigers and helped lead your team to the national championship. A lot of people are surprised by your decision to retire from the team after only one season. Why now?

Listening

Exercises C and D, page 136

TV Anchor: In other sports news, a report is coming out of Beijing that basketball player Jason Jennings is not planning to stay on for a second year with the Tigers. The twenty-two-year-old first made news when he was recruited by the Chinese team—becoming one of a handful of American basketball players to leave the NBA to play in China.

For more on that story, we go to Kim Matthews who's live in our newsroom. Kim?

Reporter: Thanks Marc. I talked with Jason Jennings earlier today by phone about his decision not to play another season with the Tigers. Here's what he had to say … *(cut away)*

Reporter: Jason, you've played a strong season with the Tigers and helped lead your team to the national championship. A lot of people are surprised by your decision to retire from the team after only one season. Why now?

Jason Jennings: I've completed my contract for the year. I feel like I've achieved what I wanted to here and now it's time to move on …

Reporter: The last time we talked, you mentioned that you were having some difficulty getting used to life in China … How has that worked out for you?

Jason: Everyone told me the move would be fairly easy, but it's definitely been a bigger adjustment than I thought it was gonna be.

Reporter: In what way?

Jason: Well … I don't speak Chinese so I have to rely on interpreters for most things. It's been hard getting used to that. And, you know, not speaking the language has made it difficult sometimes to socialize with people outside the game. The constant media attention has also made it difficult to go out in public a lot of time, too. Reporters are always following me. I have no privacy.

Reporter: I read somewhere recently that you said you missed your mom's cooking.

Jason: *(laughs)* Yeah, it's weird. The food here in China is great, but there are times when I'll start missing certain foods from back home. It probably happens to everyone who lives abroad. You know, I remember back in the States, I was on a team with a player from Turkey. My experience here in China has taught me a lot about what he and other players go through when they move to the US to play in the NBA.

Reporter: Any chance the Tigers will be able to convince you to stay on for one more season?

Jason: I don't think so. Don't get me wrong … the fans here in China have been great, and so have my coaches and my teammates. Really, it's been a great experience … but I'm ready for my next move.

Reporter: Which is?

Jason: Well, I've got a couple options: I may be joining team USA to play in the summer Olympics. I'm also in talks now with a team in Barcelona to play there for a year …

Reporter: So you'd consider playing in another country again?

Jason: Possibly …

Unit 1
Who We Are

Vocabulary and Grammar

A

1. come up with
2. ambitious
3. statistics
4. typical
5. average
6. determine

B

1. has lived / has been living
2. has been working
3. determined
4. was waiting, arrived
5. has shown
6. has always wanted

D Answers will vary slightly.

1. How long have you been teaching piano?
2. Have you ever been to Japan?
3. Where did you and you husband celebrate your twentieth anniversary?
4. What were you doing when I called?
5. What did you do on Saturday night?

E Sample answers:

1. Recently I noticed that Jane has been drinking a lot of coffee.
2. Four years ago, I set out on an ambitious journey overseas.
3. Over time we were able to determine the average life span of a beetle.
4. Yesterday, I was driving to work when I heard the news.
5. My cousin's smile is his best trait.

Video

A

1. a 2. b 3. c 4. b

Writing

A hardworking, motivated, two years working at a small company promoting study abroad, ability to carry out several projects at once, advised students, helped prepare them, coordinated and problem-solved, worked with faculty, helped find host families, participating in a study abroad program, fluent in Spanish and Portuguese, love to encourage others to travel

Reading

A

1. False
2. False
3. True
4. False
5. True
6. False

B Answers will vary.

1. to inform the reader
2. to find out more about human genetic history through DNA
3. *Answers will vary.*
4. they carried the only missing lineage, which was also the oldest
5. because DNA has been shared, which makes it harder to find the histories

Unit 2
The World Awaits

Vocabulary and Grammar

A

(1) destination
(2) tranquil
(3) breathtaking
(4) adventurous
(5) remote
(6) accessible
(7) convenience
(8) get away

B

1. The picturesque town of Camden is famous for shopping and dining.
2. My cousin wants me to bring her a souvenir from Portland.
3. My parents plan on hiking at Acadia National Park.
4. My sister thinks that it is too cold to swim in the water.
5. Camping under the stars is breathtaking.

Video

A Answers will vary. Sample answers:

1. There is always something going on in Barcelona. / Barcelona is a very lively city.
2. He felt that it was more alive than Amsterdam.
3. Las Ramblas is lively at any time of day, morning, or night.
4. He mentioned countries all over the world, including Argentina, Spain, and Africa.
5. The flower shops are beautiful.

Reading

A

1. b
2. d
3. a
4. e
5. c
6. f

B

1. According to the author, you won't be able to keep your eyes on the road because of the clear blue sea and the charming villages on the coastline. It means that the Amalfi Coast is so beautiful and there are so many things to see that it would be hard to pay attention to the road.
2. The author believes that the village of Ravello inspired Richard Wagner to write his opera called *Parsifal*.
3. *Pay an arm and a leg* means that the prices are very high; it is meant to suggest that something is so expensive that getting it would involve a big sacrifice, like losing body parts.
4. The author thinks that taking a bus is the best way to see the Amalfi Coast because then visitors can focus on the sites and won't have to worry about the winding roads and steep cliffs.
5. *Answers will vary.*

Unit 3 The Great Energy Challenge

Vocabulary and Grammar

A

1. i
2. g
3. a
4. j
5. b
6. h
7. f
8. c
9. e
10. d

B

1. I'm going on
2. going to
3. will offer
4. I'll
5. will be
6. will
7. is going to be
8. will be

C Answers will vary. Sample answers:

1. Next weekend I'm visiting my brother.
2. By 2030, there will be no fossil fuels.
3. I'll send you an e-mail tonight.
4. Within fifteen years, they'll be living in the country.

Video

A

1. True.
2. False. Lauren grew up in a town that had clean air.
3. False. The coal plant has been contributing a significant amount of pollution.
4. True.
5. False. Lauren feels that we can call on our leaders for help and also be the leaders ourselves.

Writing

A

1. The committee thinks that the city's air quality is terrible.
2. The flyer mentions cars, buses, trucks, traffic, and factories as examples. It also talks about the short-term and long-term effects of air pollution.
3. The flyer suggests biking, walking, taking public transportation, and mowing lawns every two weeks instead of every week to make the city a healthy place to live.

Reading

A

1. b 2. c 3. a 4. a 5. c 6. b

B

	Pros	Cons
Coal	cheap, close by, jobs pay well, carries on a tradition	dangerous jobs
Natural gas	cleaner, gas taxes help small towns	disturbs wildlife, destroys land, angers ranchers and hunters
Solar power	renewable, more jobs	change is viewed as a threat

Review Units 1–3

Vocabulary Review

A

1. supply
2. noisy
3. nearby
4. unmotivated
5. unusual
6. consume
7. timid
8. incomplete
9. advance

B

1. breathtaking, picturesque
2. remote, tranquil
3. sustainable
4. ambitious
5. accommodations, resort

Grammar Review

A

1. 've / have been studying
2. was
3. decided
4. was reading called
5. have learned
6. 've / have wanted
7. have said
8. 've / have been working

B

1. Camping
2. to camp
3. been
4. diving, fishing, and swimming
5. sent
6. was
7. going to go
8. getting

Unit 4
The World's a Stage

Vocabulary and Grammar

A

1. emerged
2. convinced
3. performance
4. audience
5. launched
6. appearances
7. mainstream

B

1. to be
2. to study
3. to perform
4. have
5. to drop
6. feel
7. to find

C Answers will vary. Sample answers:

1. I'll advise him to take music lessons.
2. I consider her to be very talented.
3. I expect them to get dancing roles on TV.
4. I will arrange for them to audition for the show.
5. I will not let him go on any auditions.
6. I will convince him to work on the production side of television.

Video

A

1. a
2. b
3. b
4. c

Reading

A

1. In 2000, the band was formed.
2. In 2010, Grupo Fantasma won a Grammy.
3. When they found out they won the Grammy, they screamed on the bus.
4. This summer, they will go on tour all over North America and Europe.

C Answers will vary. Sample answers:

1. Two bands got together and formed one band in 2000.
2. It is the combination of different backgrounds that gives it a more widespread appeal.
3. They were shocked and excited.

Unit 5
No Need to Panic

Vocabulary and Grammar

A

1. trapped
2. panic
3. handle
4. rescue
5. ordeal
6. encouraging
7. intense

B

1. Marcos went to Japan so that he could visit a car factory. *purpose*
2. After his work was completed, he traveled around the country. *time*
3. Because a major earthquake hit Japan, he had to stay longer. *reason*
4. Many people were trapped since buildings collapsed. *reason*
5. Even though it was difficult, he helped many people. *contrast*
6. Marcos started a charity foundation to help victims as soon as he returned to the United States. *time*

C Answers will vary. Sample answers:

1. I went to Japan because I wanted to teach factory workers there about safety.
2. As soon as it was over, I ran outside to look for help.
3. I started a charity foundation so that victims would get the help they need.
4. Yes, even though I saw a lot of hardship there, I met so many great people.

D Answer will vary. Sample answer:

First, do not panic. Because the building collapsed, you are trapped. Stay calm. You will be rescued as soon as we can get to you. Make some noise so that we know where you are. Do not move.

Video

A Order from top to bottom:

2 – 5 – 10 – 7 – 1 – 8 – 3 – 6 – 4 – 9

Writing

A

1. Listen to the safety demonstration.
2. Fasten your seatbelt.
3. Remain calm.

Reading

A

1. True.
2. False: The woman did not panic and survived by jumping off the wing and into a ditch.
3. False: Most people ignore the safety lesson.
4. True.
5. False: The author believes people should plan ahead when flying.
6. False: The author suggests you count the number of rows to the nearest exit.

B Answers will vary. Sample answers:

BEFORE: Dress in comfortable clothes so you can move easily. Listen to the safety lesson. Count the number of rows to the nearest exit. Figure out how to open an exit door. DURING: Wear your seatbelt. Don't wander around the cabin. AFTER: Find the exit closest to you. Remember where the second exit is. Help others.

Unit 6 In Style

Vocabulary and Grammar

A

1. deals
2. recommend
3. goods
4. browsing
5. brand
6. affordable
7. discount
8. bargain

B

1. Yolanda, who cares about fashion, likes to browse through fashion magazines.
2. The store that Yolanda owns is busy all year.
3. People who come to shop after the holidays always get great deals.
4. Summer, which is always a busy season for shopping, is the best time to visit Yolanda's store.
5. Yolanda's brother Tyrone, who lives in London, also owns a discount store.
6. They both have popular stores that sell designer brands.

Video

A

1. Fake
2. Real
3. Real
4. Real
5. Fake
6. Fake

Writing

A Answers will vary. Sample answers:

Why Diego likes shopping online:

1. He can wear pajamas and stay on the couch.
2. He does not have to wait in line.
3. He can shop in the middle of the night.
4. He can search for deals without having to go to stores.

Why Charles likes shopping in stores:

1. He can shop with a friend.
2. He can browse in the store.
3. He can try on clothing.
4. He can check a product's quality in person.

Reading

A

1. a bee vase
2. a dog communicator
3. non-stop shoes
4. a victimless leather jacket
5. non-stop shoes

Review Units 4–6

Vocabulary Review

A

1. inspired
2. emerged
3. collapsed
4. injured
5. panicked
6. handled
7. convinced
8. audience
9. qualit

B Answers will vary.

1. A commercial success is a successful business like Starbucks coffee.
2. An ordeal is a difficult situation.
3. A performance is singing or acting in front of an audience.
4. To browse means to look around.
5. To rescue means to save someone from danger.

Grammar Review

A

1. c
2. f
3. d
4. a
5. e
6. g
7. b

B

1. who
2. because
3. to be
4. which
5. cry
6. who
7. so that
8. that
9. to take
10. that

Unit 7 On the Move

Vocabulary and Grammar

A

1. b
2. e
3. f
4. c
5. d
6. a

B Answers will vary. Sample answers:

1. Buses now are less reliable than they were in the past.
2. Cars in rush hour move as slowly as taxis.
3. The commuter train has fewer stops than the subway.
4. You need more time for walking than you do for riding a bicycle.
5. Buses during rush hour are as punctual as subways.
6. You are more cramped on a train than you are in a car.

C Answers will vary. Sample answers:

Lisa's commute is shorter than Katya's. It takes Katya more time to get to work. Lisa's commute is more expensive than Katya's. Katya's commute is better for the environment.

Video

A

1. ✓
2. Ø
3. ✓
4. Ø
5. ✓
6. ✓
7. Ø
8. *Answers will vary. Sample answers:* You don't get to choose the type of bike you ride. It's not as fast as a ten-speed. You don't own the bike.

B Answers will vary. Sample answers:

1. Using Capital Bikeshare to get to work is better for the environment than driving to work. Capital Bikeshare seems less convenient for commuting than driving to work.
2. Capital Bikeshare is as popular for getting to work as taking the subway. Capital Bikeshare seems more reliable than the subway for commuting to work.

Writing

A Answers will vary:

1. The bus is cheaper than the subway. / The subway is faster than the bus.
2. The subway is a better option than the expressway. / The expressway is cheaper than the subway.
3. Driving on the expressway is faster than taking the bus. / The bus system is less expensive than the expressway.

Reading

A Answers will vary:

1. you must pay fifty quetzales
2. a chicken was under the seat in front of him
3. they will eat them later
4. have been covered with bright colors, wild designs, and written messages
5. it was the same type of bus he rode as a child
6. each bus had a different destination

B

GUATEMALAN BUS:

1. It is an American school bus that has been painted with bright colors, wild designs, messages.
2. People bring chickens on the bus. / They are like moving towns.
3. Yes.
4. *Answers will vary.*
5. *Answers will vary.*

COLUMN 2: *Answers will vary.*

Unit 8 Think Twice

Vocabulary and Grammar

A

1. respectful
2. get into trouble
3. get away with
4. consequences
5. restrictions
6. regulations

B Answers will vary. Sample answers:

1. should have
2. shouldn't have
3. should have
4. shouldn't have
5. could have
6. couldn't have been

C Answers will vary. Sample answers:

1. He must have played really well in 2011.
2. He might have taken a performance-enhancing drug to help him play better.
3. Major League Baseball must have had problems in the past with players using PEDs.
4. He couldn't have taken PEDs if he says he's innocent.
5. Major League Baseball shouldn't have accused Ryan Braun until they had all the facts.

Video

A

1. embarrassing
2. Search
3. reputation
4. control
5. privately
6. name
7. responsibility
8. click

Writing

A

1. should've paid; must have been; could have prevented
2. Harry caused the fire. He lit a match and dropped it in a wastebasket.
3. The author would like to tell them how sorry he / she is for their loss.

Reading

A

1. many people died
2. caught fire
3. cruise companies trained the crew to ensure proper behavior
4. modern cruise ships now carry enough lifeboats for all passengers
5. it caused a shipwreck / it got stuck / it damaged the ship
6. he was accused of abandoning ship

B Answers will vary. Sample answers:

1. They could have performed lifeboat drills. / They could have had enough lifeboats for the passengers.
2. The crew must not have been disciplined very well.
3. He should have gone back. / He should have been the last man off the ship.

Unit 9 In the Wild

Vocabulary and Grammar

A Answers will vary. Sample answers:

1. The rider trained the horse to jump.
2. Someone captured the squirrel. / Capturing animals is cruel.
3. The cat is domesticated. / The cat is treated well.
4. One tiger is attacking another. / Tigers are an endangered species.

B

1. Sometimes he was attacked by other dogs.
2. He was captured by Animal Rescue and was brought to a shelter.
3. He will be trained by a dog trainer.
4. He is being taken care of by Jeff and Nancy.
5. He is being treated very well by their two daughters.

C

1. is held
2. was served
3. was being chased
4. left
5. was trapped
6. couldn't be captured
7. have been trained
8. will be caught
9. was injured
10. being taken care of

Video

A Order from top to bottom:

5 – 7 – 3 – 8 – 1 – 6 – 2 – 4

Writing

A Answers will vary. Sample answers:

IN FAVOR OF ZOOS: They help endangered animals reproduce and keep their species alive. They sometimes find injured or sick animals and help them get healthy. They keep animals safe that wouldn't have a chance of surviving in the wild.

AGAINST ZOOS: In zoos, some animals lose their natural instinct to hunt. Lots of zoos have trouble making money and can't take care of the animals properly. People who visit zoos don't always treat the animals kindly.

Reading

A

Paragraph 1: spirit / Kermode

A. North American black bear

B. Great Bear Rainforest / Canada / Canada's western coast

Paragraph 2:

A. bear meat

B. white bear was prohibited

Paragraph 3: environmental

A: speak about the bears / hunt the bears / speak about or hunt the bears

Paragraph 4:

A. industries

B. see bears / spot bears

Paragraph 5: safe

A. talk about the spirit bears / broadcast information about the spirit bears

B. spirit / Kermode bears

B

1. The wolves fish and the deer swim.
2. The black bears were hunted by First Nations hunters for their fur.
3. The Kermode bears are protected by the Gitga'at and other groups by not talking about them.

Review Units 7–9

Vocabulary Review

A

1. h
2. e
3. c
4. a
5. j
6. f
7. d
8. g
9. i
10. b

B

1. fit in
2. restriction
3. evolve
4. punctual
5. limit
6. disruptive

Grammar Review

A

1. must have
2. might have
3. should have
4. better
5. faster and more reliable
6. more
7. should be allowed
8. to be treated

B Answers will vary. Sample answers:

Sam weighs more than Chester. Sam is bigger than Chester. Chester is more social than Sam. Chester does not run as fast as the tiger. The tiger is a better swimmer than Chester.

Unit 10
Decisions, Decisions
Vocabulary and Grammar

A
1. change your mind
2. concentrate
3. regret
4. figure out
5. affect
6. hesitate

B
1. d
2. e
3. c
4. a
5. b

C Answers will vary. Sample answers:
1. I would try to get it back to its owner
2. let's see an action movie
3. I didn't go out to eat so much
4. I will go for a walk along the river
5. I'd like to go shopping with them

Video

A
True (✓): 1, 2, 6
False (no check):
3. Tyler makes a decision quickly.
4. Tyler's answer matches what most people who take the test say.
5. The majority of people say that it's not okay to leave her behind.
7. The scientists feel that Tyler's intuitive emotional response is what guided him in his decision.

Reading

A
1. e
2. c
3. a
4. f
5. d
6. b

B
1. They look for different options, encourage competition among ideas, and find a way to narrow choices.
2. It varies. Some people listen to different options. Others have their mind made up already and pressure people to conform.
3. *Answers will vary.*

Unit 11
Rain or Shine
Vocabulary and Grammar

A
1. postponed
2. take off
3. consider
4. cut off
5. mild
6. frigid *or* freezing
7. tolerate
8. refuse
9. freezing *or* frigid

B
1. c
2. g
3. a
4. e
5. h
6. b
7. d
8. f
9. g

Video

A
1. False
2. False
3. False
4. True
5. True
6. False

B Answers will vary. Sample answers:

1. John Rigby is in favor of defending the coastline. He says that they would lose lots of land if they didn't defend it.
2. He thinks it's a major problem in Essex because they've lost more than half of the marsh in just 30 years.

Writing

A

Phrasal verbs: go out, looked out, stuck in, run back, cut off / got cut off, knocked down, get back.

Similes:

1. March goes in like a lion and out like a lamb.
2. The wind was howling like a wolf.
3. she was as snug as a bug in a rug
4. The weather was as mild as a lamb!

B Answers will vary. Sample answers:

I am as angry as a lion. The rainstorm was as mild as a bunny. My friend Ted is like a happy puppy. The tornado was as wild as a bull.

Reading

A

1. a
2. b
3. b
4. a
5. c

B Answers will vary. Sample answers:

1. A "rule of thumb" is an idea that is generally believed to be true without having to be proven.
2. Cyprus must be located between 0 and 30 degrees north latitude.
3. People know how to conserve water.
4. The American Southwest will become even drier than it is now.

Unit 12 What's Your Game?

Vocabulary and Grammar

A

1. c 2. d 3. b 4. a 5. e 6. f

B Answers will vary. Sample answers:

1. obsessed; Isla said that she is obsessed with professional tennis.
2. championship; Charlotte asked if Isla could get her tickets to the tennis match this year.
3. in shape; Jae asked if that was how Isla stayed in shape.
4. Isla said that she and Charlotte did play tennis together often.
5. opponents; Jae asked if Isla would want to play doubles against him and Ramon. He said that they were strong opponents.
6. beat; Isla answered definitely and said that with Charlotte as her partner, they would surely beat them.

D

1. Jia explained that training for a marathon is a big commitment.
2. Marcos promised that he would teach Samuel how to fish this weekend.
3. Ray begged me to let him watch another hour of television.
4. Amelia said that her biggest motivation for cycling was to seek adventure.

Video

A

1. a 2. b 3. a 4. c

B Answers will vary. Sample answers:

1. Alain said that even when you were facing a problem where your life was in danger, there was only one option.
2. He means the only option is to keep climbing; otherwise he'll fall.
3. He is adventurous, strong, and daring. He is passionate about climbing.
4. *Answers will vary.*

Reading

A

1. Jamie Mitchell is an athlete who has won the Rainbow Sands Molokai to Oahu Paddleboard Race eight times. He is strong and dedicated to his sport.
2. Paddleboard racing combines surfing and rowing. You paddle using your arms for long distances in the ocean.
3. It is difficult because of the rough waves, wind, and currents.
5. No, he can't support himself on the money so he has to work other jobs.

6–10. *Answers will vary.*

Review Units 10–12

Vocabulary Review

A

1. h	2. d	3. e	4. j	5. b
6. g	7. i	8. c	9. a	10. f

B

1. assess, consider
2. frigid, mild
3. postpone
4. championship
5. mind

C Answers will vary. Sample answers:

(1) We came in second place last year.
(2) The team trains every day for two to three hours. It's difficult, but worth the effort.
(3) I told them not to give up. They worked very hard to beat our opponents.
(4) Not at all! We have a commitment to work hard and try our best.

Grammar Review

A

1. gets, will ride
2. lived, would walk
3. had, would go
4. could swim, would join
5. finish, will cook

B Answers will vary:

1. Kal encouraged me to study on Saturday instead of tonight.
2. Kal begged me to change my mind and come to the movies with them.
3. Kal said that they were going to see the new Brad Pitt movie. He said that it was supposed to be great.
4. Kal asked if I knew that the actor had to train four hours a day for the role.

C

1. found out
2. woke up
3. picked up
4. take off
5. look into
6. check in

Review Puzzle

Units 1–3

ACROSS:

1. atmosphere; **4.** accessible; **7.** has lived; **10.** statistics; **11.** luxurious; **13.** trait; **14.** eliminate; **15.** waiting; **17.** sustainable; **20.** generate; **23.** source; **24.** breathtaking; **25.** project; **26.** worked

DOWN:

1. adventurous; **2.** determine; **3.** will call; **5.** will be; **6.** going; **8.** destination; **9.** dancing; **10.** spot; **12.** consume; **16.** to visit; **18.** entire; **19.** ambitious; **21.** remote; **22.** starting

Review Puzzle

Units 4–6

ACROSS:

2. convince; 5. who; 6. purchase; 7. for; 10. that; 11. emerge; 13. affordable; 17. trapped; 19. rescue; 20. handle; 22. hardcore; 23. quality; 24. bargain; 25. which; 27. injured

DOWN:

1. so that; 3. discount; 4. ordeal; 8. recommend; 9. brand; 10. to apply; 12. mainstream; 14. even though; 15. after; 16. performance; 18. audience; 21. as soon as; 26. collapse

Review Puzzle

Units 7–9

ACROSS:

3. rush hour; 6. should not; 11. criticize; 12. consequences; 14. was found; 18. reliable; 19. are kept; 22. respectful; 23. endangered; 25. capture; 26. might; 27. disruptive

DOWN:

1. faster; 2. punish; 4. option; 5. punctually; 7. overwhelming; 8. transfer; 9. wild ;10. fit in; 11. cruel; 13. commute; 15. as fast as; 16. fewer; 17. cramped; 20. attack; 21. hunt; 22. restrictions; 24. trained

Review Puzzle

Units 10–12

ACROSS:

5. tolerate; 7. die down; 11. coach; 14. will walk; 15. if; 17. obsessed; 20. defend; 21. frigid; 22. regret; 24. process; 26. effect; 27. cut off; 28. postponed

DOWN:

1. intervene; 2. begged; 3. mild; 4. rational; 6. opponent; 8. would go; 9. look after; 10. give up; 12. mind ;13. told; 16. figure out; 18. beat; 19. were; 23. assess; 25. refuse

Unit 1
The Human Family Tree

Spencer Wells: It is basically a quest to understand,. you know, where we all came from. That's one of those key human questions that everybody is kind of searching for the answer to. And, you know, who am I? Who are my ancestors? And we're using the tools of science to get the answers to that.

Woman 1: Oh, I like that. I like that. That's great.

Man 1: Cause when I was born, my mother told me I had like some blonde hair on my back. I don't know where that came from. *(laughter)* It's not there now!

Narrator: Now, hundreds of New Yorkers are lining up to get these questions answered too, and learn about their own ancient pasts.

Man 2: It's… it's who I am. The more I know about my past, the more I can understand myself.

Man 3: Well I think we were looking for something unexpected, you know. We sort of know where we're from but, you know, we don't really know where we're from.

Woman 2: He's very excited about it, and he thinks that he's gonna change his life.

Narrator: Genealogy allows most of us to trace our ancestors back about four or five generations, to a great-great grandparent, perhaps.

Man 4: I probably can go as far as probably 100 years.

Woman 3: This is your deep, deep ancestry, so we're not necessarily thinking your grandparents… *(fade)*

Narrator: If we're lucky, we'd know where these ancestors lived.

Man 5: Well I certainly don't know much about my background. Uh…

Woman 4: I know that, you know, I'm from Madras, the southern part of India. My parents lived there, and my grandparents lived there. So, beyond them I have no clue at all.

Woman 5: My mom's from South Korea, and on my father's side, um, I am German, Irish, English, and I think a little bit of Native American. But that part I'm not sure.

Spencer Wells: So what do you know about your ancestry?

Man 6: New York. That's about it.

Narrator: These DNA tests tell a deeper story. Rather than taking us back just a handful of generations, they take us back many thousands.

Man 7: Ready for it now? She can't talk now, so I can abuse her (tease her).

Spencer Wells: The cheek swab is basically a way of getting at the DNA history book that we're carrying inside of ourselves. All of that information has to be copied in every generation to pass on to kids and grandkids and great-grandkids. So we're carrying this continuous kind of genetic historic document that goes back through the generations. Since, you know, tens, hundreds, thousands of years ago.

Narrator: No matter where we're from, how different we appear, if we look back through the generations at the roots of the human family tree, we find we are all related.

…

Narrator: Our ancient connections may not be obvious to this group. Our ancestors adapted to different climates, and as a result, humans are now among the most physically varied looking species on the planet. But looks can be deceiving.

Spencer Wells: We're basically identical at the genetic level. I mean, if you look at the average person's DNA sequence and compare the same region to another person they're unrelated to, you now, they're 99.9 percent identical.

Unit 2
Barcelona's Street Life

Speaker 1: Oh there's something very special about Barcelona. Like, anytime you go out of your house, there's always something going on. You'll always find a friend on the streets. It's where living is. You're not in your place; you're on the streets.

Speaker 2: Yeah, that you can go out into the street at night, and… it's always lively. There's never… nobody in the *Ramblas*, for example. There always… every hour a day, there's life. I came here, I felt somehow better than in Amsterdam. More… more alive, more vital, you understand? Vital? That's uh… yeah, that makes it very enjoyable, at least for me. And inspiring too.

Speaker 3: It's a very nice place, because in the *Ramblas* you can find… I don't know… theatre, music from Argentina, from Spain, from Africa, from all the world.

Speaker 4: Things that on the street happen, never will happen in a theatre. For example, we play and like, ten, fifteen people start to dance at one time, for example, then you think like, yeah, this is… this is beautiful, you know. The *Ramblas* is *the* street in Barcelona, and I think in Europe, and maybe in the world, that like, you're gonna be entertained. No matter how. I mean, if you walk past by the flower shops, I mean the way they build it up is beautiful. Even the street is decorated. I mean, you get entertained. It's worth coming to Barcelona.

Speaker 5: It's a way of life. *Ramblas* is… you have everything. You have traffic of people, you have tourists, you have thieves, you have performers. *Ramblas* is everything. It's a vibrant of life. Yeah, it's a way of life. It's really really a way of life. I love it.

Unit 3
We Need to Be Leaders Ourselves

Voiceover: Greenpeace activists are out here today in Bridgeport, Connecticut. We've been out here for a couple hours now. Things are going quite well. The, uh… *(fade)*

My name is Lauren, and I'm an activist with Greenpeace.

I'm out here today because dirty coal energy is something that our country has been relying on for way too long.

Well I'm deeply concerned about coal and its impacts on our climate and on our local communities.

I've had the luxury of growing up in a town where I didn't have to worry about whether my air was clean enough to breathe. That should be a basic human right.

This plant here in Bridgeport that has been running for over fifty years and has been contributing a significant amount of pollution to this community is an injustice.

We are working here with the community that wants to see this coal plant shut down.

We don't need coal to power our country anymore. Right now, they're the biggest roadblock to renewable energy coming in to our country and providing new jobs. And we can call on our leaders to shut them down, but sometimes we need to be the leaders ourselves.

Unit 4
Songs Under a Big Sky

Iarla: My name is Iarla Ó Lionáird and I'm an Irishman. I come from Cork, West Cork, and I'm a person who sings.

Narrator: Iarla was the eighth of twelve children born to an Irish-speaking family famous for generations of singers. He was five years old before he learned English.

Iarla grew up singing Sean-nós in Gaelic, the old way, a dark passionate style that melds song and oral history.

Iarla: I remember my first day in school Mrs. MacSweeney, Mrs. Mac was my teacher. I remember she lifted me up and she stood me on a desk—first day I was ever in school, I was about five—and she said "Sing." It was almost as if there was—there were kind of shoes (and) they were waiting for me to put my feet into it.

Narrator: All through his youth, Iarla sang the old way but as he *came of age*, his enthusiasm flagged.

Iarla: I felt a little bit like a museum piece, really. Oh I had spent like twenty years of my life perfecting as best I could this way of singing… to find out that nobody was interested, except the people I grew up with. And that was a horrible *realization*. That was like the coldest breakfast you ever had to eat.

Narrator: Frustrated, despairing, Iarla found himself on a dead-end street. He quit singing entirely until fortune revealed a path. Without so much as an *audition*, he was invited to work with the Afro-Celt Sound System.

Iarla: I'd been so fortunate that I had the real experience of being there with these people when they sing and make music. And in a way, they're Irish, to some extent. The brevity of everything they do, and the levity of everything they do… so there's a genuineness and a largeness of heart that I experienced in African music, that I suppose it just shook me to the foundations, you know. I never really experienced it before.

Narrator: *Inspired* by his encounter with the African artists, Iarla reclaimed his sound and began bringing it to *audiences* again.

Iarla: Thank you. Thank you very much for listening to me. I really appreciate it. Thank you very much. Thank you. Thanks a lot. Thank you.

Unit 5
Surviving Deadly Everest

Narrator: Mount Everest. At more than 29,000 feet, it towers over everything else on Earth, making it the ultimate challenge for mountain climbers. But with extreme challenge comes extreme risk, and Everest is no exception. To date, the mountain has claimed the lives of some 200 climbers, about one for every eight who have reached the top.

The most notorious tragedy occurred in May of 1996, when a blizzard trapped and killed eight climbers in a single day. The New Zealand-based guide company, Adventure Consultants, had a team on the summit that day. Half of them perished. Including the company's president and cofounder, Rob Hall. Guy Cotter was in base camp that day and assisted with the rescue of fifteen climbers. Now Cotter runs Adventure Consultants and continues to guide groups to the top of Everest.

Guy Cotter: A lot of soul-searching was done, from ourselves and people in the industry as a whole about what happened in '96.

Narrator: On a mountain that has claimed as many lives as this one, Cotter has learned that safety must come first.

Guy Cotter: Naturally, you know, we are operating in a very dangerous environment. Climbing the highest mountains in the world is not a safe occupation even for very experienced people. So, we have to apply an additional level of safety and resources to try and minimize risk.

Narrator: It's April in Nepal, and Adventure Consultants is organizing an expedition up Everest for a group of climbers nicknamed "Team Canada." They will be led by experienced climbing guides Luis Benitez and Steve Moffat. Together with nearly a dozen Sherpas, they will begin the long journey to the summit. But first, every bit of gear that goes up the mountain is checked and rechecked by the guides. While most of their equipment travels ahead with the Sherpas, the team sets out on foot to allow their bodies to gradually adjust to the altitude.

Man: There she is. Big E. The pointy one right in the back.

Guy Cotter: Yeah, yeah. A few days to travel yet.

Narrator: A week later, the team approaches base camp. At more than 17,000 feet above sea level, this'll be their home for the next month and a half.

In 1996, the team was caught off guard by a sudden storm. Today computers and satellite phones allow the guides to monitor the latest weather conditions and communicate with the outside world.

The climbers take part in a *puja* ceremony to ask permission to set foot on the mountain.

Guy Cotter: They say prayers to ask forgiveness of the gods for us to enter into the mountain environment of mother goddess of the Earth. So this process can go on for several hours. We have to go through this before any of us can go onto the mountain.

Narrator: Over the next few weeks, Team Canada travels back and forth between four camps at various altitudes to prepare themselves for the final summit push. By mid-May, conditions are perfect for a summit attempt. The team is ready. Cotter and the guides carefully prepare the supplemental oxygen supply.

Man 2: So these are as important for saving your life as shoes are.

Narrator: There's about one-third the amount of oxygen at the summit as there is at sea level. While some have completed the climb without oxygen, it's an important safety tool used by most climbers today. Without it, a climber's body can become starved of oxygen, causing sickness, disorientation, and even death.

Man 3: Vic, I have to tell you, you kind of look like an aardvark I once knew.

Narrator: As the team pushes higher on the mountain, each step becomes a challenge, the lack of oxygen slowing their pace to a crawl. Sometimes they look more like zombies than climbers. While the team rests at the fourth and final camp, the weather report comes in from base camp. There are no storms in sight. In 1996, advanced warning of the oncoming storm could have prevented disaster. Team Canada's fortunate to have access to the latest weather information, and the clear forecast means they're headed to the top. The team sets off in darkness. After hours of trudging, day breaks, and the summit of Everest appears in the near distance.

Woman: We're just about to climb the last step. We're very close to the summit now. It's such a dream come true. The sun is coming up. It's beautiful.

Narrator: After nearly two months of work, Team Canada reaches the top. There's time for a few photos and a break to soak in the view and to appreciate the accomplishment, one that has taken lives of so many others.

Back at camp, the team is welcomed with a celebration put on by the Sherpas.

Ten years after the worst disaster in climbing history, another team summits Everest and returns safely. But while Team Canada was successful, the season was not without its share of tragedy. Eleven climbers from other expedition groups died on the mountain, the highest number since 1996. But for these climbers and many like them, the risk is worth the reward, a chance to stand on top of the world.

Unit 6
How to Spot a Fake Louis Vuitton Bag

Narrator: How to spot a fake Louis Vuitton bag.

Step one. The price is wrong. Louis Vuitton monogrammed canvas bags run from $375 and up, with most bags selling for over $1,000. If you're buying a brand-new Louis Vuitton bag for less than $300, you're not getting a deal; you're getting a fake.

Step two. What's in a name? Jess Zaino of the Style Network knows some secrets in telling a real from a fake Louis Vuitton.

Jess Zaino: It's easy to tell the difference between a real Louis and a fake Louis Vuitton. Which is, usually, the LV's are crooked. If you have any "LV" that is in a crease or in a stitch, it is *not* the real thing.

Narrator: Step three. Material matters. The Louis Vuitton monogrammed bags are made of canvas, but the handles and piping are natural cowhide leather. The color of the leather should be a light tan with the edge dyed red and the stitching in yellow. After a few weeks of handling your bag, the leather handles will oxidize and fade to a darker brown. If your leather handles don't change colors, it's a fake.

Step four. Location. Louis Vuitton doesn't have any authorized street resellers. So if you buy your bag from a street dealer, it's not the genuine article. Also be careful buying bags online. You can find authentic Louis Vuitton bags, but there are also a plethora of fakes. Pay attention to the seller feedback, and ask about buyer protection and the return policy. One Web site that is authorized to sell Louis Vuitton bags is www.eluxury.com.

Step five. Trust your instinct. When it comes down to it, go with your gut. If you feel funny about where or how much you're paying, walk away. For more information about how to tell the authenticity of a Louis Vuitton bag, visit a Louis Vuitton retailer or call the headquarters at 212-758-8877. Remember, if you do spring for the real thing, Louis Vuitton guarantees a perfect product. Done.

Unit 7
Capital Bikeshare

Man, dark hair with collared shirt: Well, it's so easy to use. You come up to a bike, you make your adjustments, you stick in your key card and you ride away. And it's great.

Woman with glasses: Instead of taking the metro and then transferring to another metro line, I'll take bikeshare to the red line and eliminate the metro transfer. Kind of makes the commute a little easier.

Young couple, woman speaking: It's a good way to see DC instead of walking around.

Young couple, man speaking: And it saves your leg muscles and energy for the actual museums and stuff to see.

Josh Stevens: Once I got into the swing of it, in about a month, I just found that I was riding absolutely everywhere.

Chris Holbern, project manager: Bikesharing seemed like a perfect match for DC: a dense, urban area, a lot of people like to bike and we want to get more people out biking. We have a hundred and fourteen stations with about eleven hundred bikes. People join bikeshare for a year, a month, or a day, and they receive a key in the mail for a year member or they use their credit card to go off or if you're a tourist user. You can use any of the bikes from any of the stations and return it to any other station.

Matthew Klein, businessman: We understood that the bikeshare program was going to come to Washington in a big way and so we wanted to be an early adopter—it's been well executed in the way that D-DOT has approached it, so we couldn't be more happy with the program.

Matt Pearson, downtown business district: We like street life. We like people out on the streets. It's great for business to have people in cafes, people riding bikes down the street, more people walking from place to place during the work hour. It just means that many more people circulating through the downtown area in an easy, healthy, and affordable way.

Meleah Geertsma: DC is very much a professional biking city. Everyone bikes around in their suits and their work clothes, and I've used it a number of times when I'm dressed up to go straight into work.

Shinpei Tsay: I started to use it because I live in New York City and I come down to DC for work. And because I can't keep a bike in the office and I go straight to the office from the train station, I actually use bikeshare to get around town. I've been using it for meetings and getting around late at night. It's just been really convenient.

Josh Stevens: I know at any given time I can get to pretty much anywhere I'm going which is in about a three-, four-mile radius in about fifteen minutes.

Chris Holbern, project manager: It's a simple easy bike. It's three speeds. It's got a basket and a bell, a built-in light so you can use it at night.

Matt Pearson, downtown business district: They're safe, they're solid, they've got a nice style to them. They're safe for young people and old people and they're kind of cool too.

Meleah Geertsma: It's good to adjust the seat first and put your bag into the front. You know, it's very easy to just start up within a minute or so of getting to the station. It really doesn't take much time at all.

Man in T-shirt on bike: I walk out my door, I get on the bike, I drop it off here, and then I go. My favorite part is that I don't have to worry about my bike getting stolen.

Older couple, woman with headband speaking: After work I'll take it to go to the gym or if I have to pick up my son at school, I'll cycle. There's a bikeshare right outside his school so I'll drop the bike off there and then we can metro it home on the bus.

Chris Holbern, project manager: Part of our system is to keep the system clean and operating, whether it's oil and change, fixing brake cables. And then another major part of our contractor job is to redistribute bikes so if a station is full like it typically is downtown in the morning, the van comes by, picks up ten or fifteen bikes, and takes them back uptown.

Man, dark hair with collared shirt: The spotcycle app is great because you can check how many bikes are there, you can see how many docks are there. Sometimes it's frustrating if you get to a bike station, you arrive at your destination, and there are no bikes left. You can alleviate all that by just checking out the availability of the open docks.

Matthew Klein, businessman: Any new tools, any new choices that we can bring into the transportation equation that people have, it's going to improve mobility for everybody in Washington. So it's a constructive thing for the economic health of Washington in general.

Man, dark hair with collared shirt: I kept seeing all these red bikes zooming past me when I was walking to work and it just sort of hit me on the head, why haven't I signed up for bikeshare yet?

Chris Holbern, project manager: Right now we have about 14,000 annual members, the majority of those live in DC and Arlington. And then we've had about 40,000 day users since we launched. And those numbers are increasing.

Josh Stevens: Without really changing anything else in my lifestyle, since I've started I've dropped about 25 pounds.

Matt Pearson, downtown business district: If you're close to bikeshare now, you have access to a whole 'nother group of people that you didn't have access to before. The downtown business community and also the business communities all around our neighborhoods in DC really believe that having sustainable forms of transportation in their areas improve their bottom line.

Unit 8
Protecting Reputations Online

In the past, doing something embarrassing wasn't a big deal. It happened, and then people moved on. But now that things can be shared on the Web immediately, those embarrassing moments can last forever and impact your reputation and those of your friends. This is "Protecting Reputations Online—in Plain English."

Let's talk about what happens on the Web: Search engines are constantly scanning it. Their goal is to take a snapshot of every word, picture, and video on the Web and save it for search results. This means that once a page has been scanned, it may be there forever. Even if the image is deleted from a site, it may still be found in the future, which is when problems can occur.

Think about it this way: if you share videos of yourself or others doing illegal things or photos that make people look bad, it could seriously harm their reputations and sometimes it's hard to tell. What seems like a funny photo today ("Yay!") may look very different to someone who finds it in the future ("Boo!").

By understanding a few things now, you can help avoid problems later. It starts with what you choose to put on Web sites. Sharing on the Web can be fun and productive, but it can also cause problems so it's up to you to think about the people in the photo or story—including yourself—before you share it. Would you want your grandfather to see this photo? Or a future boss? Once you click, you lose control of who can see the photo on the Web... and no one wants to lose control. This means your friends have to depend on you to take responsibility for the images, stories, and videos you share on the Web.

Luckily, you don't have to share everything publicly. Find ways to share your life privately, without having it scanned by search engines. And be careful using people's names. Names are easy for search engines to scan. Another step is asking your friends to think about what they share on the Web. Let them know, that, from now on, you're going to take responsibility. Talk about the risks and what impact photos could have in the future. Agree to think before you click. This way, you can act goofy today and still have the respect you deserve tomorrow.

Of course, you can't control everything on the Web. If you feel a photo, story, or video could put your reputation at risk, you can take action. Contact the person who posted it and ask them to remove it. Taking action today can make it harder to find in the future. So the point is, sharing your life online can be fun and productive, but it can also mean losing control. You have a responsibility to help protect your reputation and the reputations of those around you. Think before you click. I'm Lee LeFever of Common Craft and this has been "Protecting Reputations Online—in Plain English."

Unit 9
Great Migrations (excerpt)

Narrator: Today, the team is collaring an elephant with a state-of-the-art device that might save its life: a tag that sends an alert when the animal nears a farm.

Iain: Many elephants across Africa get shot because they cause damage to human property, to crops, to livelihoods, and indeed they kill people. You want every hi-tech option that you can deploy.

Narrator: Iain Douglas Hamilton searches for a herd, scanning the landscape by air, while researcher David Daballen's team is on the ground.

Iain: David? David?

David: Ah, sorry Iain?

Iain: Where I'm circling, there are two groups of elephants tightly under the trees.

David: *(over radio)* OK, copy Iain. *(live)* He's found them in a perfect place. We don't want to lose them, because, you know, they're not quite often at the moment around. So we want to take the opportunity to tag them, put a collar. Because we know them from our past experience, they will defend so much. And if we have four cars, we can position ourselves in different positions to make sure that the females would not see the female that has gone down.

Narrator: They identify the female to be collared.

David: That's it.

Iain: OK, she's down.

David: Yeah, OK, rush, rush, rush. Let's get a good position. Drive.

Narrator: Once she's unconscious, Daballen has only twenty minutes to attach the collar. The anesthesia makes the trunk muscles go slack. A stick will keep her airway open. This particular collar will do what Douglas Hamilton once only dreamed of. It will allow an elephant to communicate with him. The collar sends its alert to a cell phone via text message. This high-tech innovation is called "geo-fencing." When an elephant crosses a virtual fence line, the GPS unit in the collar sends an SMS, or text message, to a server in Nairobi. The server then sends text alerts to a list of recipients who can quickly intercept the herd before it reaches a farm or human settlement.

Unit 10 Moral Dilemma (excerpt)

Jonathan Cohen: Neuroscience is the study of the brain and, in particular, how the brain gives rise to the mind. That is, how is it that the physical mechanisms of the brain lead us to do the sorts of things that we think of the mind as doing.

Narrator: Can we see these physical mechanisms at work? In the FMRI scanner at Princeton, research subject Tyler faces a rudimentary dilemma designed to show increased activity in parts of the brain associated with emotion.

Voice: You're walking along a country road, when you hear a plea for help coming from some roadside bushes. You encounter a woman who is covered with blood. The woman explains that she was attacked while hiking, and asks you to take her to a nearby hospital. Your initial inclination is to help this woman, who will probably die if she does not get to the hospital soon. However, if you help this woman, her blood will ruin your designer suit. Is it appropriate for you to leave this woman by the side of the road?

Narrator: No, it's not appropriate. Tyler's answer comes quickly and is consistent with the majority of Greene and Cohen's data.

Joshua Greene: Most people say, "No, that's not okay." Well, my theory, developed with Jon Cohen and other people, is that, on the one hand, we have an intuitive emotional response that makes us say, "No, terrible, don't do that." And if you look at the brain data that is lots of people answering lots of questions like this and averaging it all together, what you see ... you see increased activity in the parts of the brain that are associated with emotion and what we call social cognition.

Narrator: Greene and Cohen's findings suggest that if the woman were a faceless person on the other side of the world—dying in the Congo, for example—Tyler might have felt okay leaving her by the side of the road. But, because she's right there in front of him, he has an intuitive emotional response that tells him to help her and stops him from committing what many would call "evil."

Unit 11 Sinking England

Narrator: All may seem calm along these beautiful stretches of British coastline, but there is a battle being fought on the beaches of Britain. It's a fight for survival against the mighty force of the North Sea. Erosion of this coastline has been going on for thousands of years, but things have gotten much worse. Now, tough decisions are being made: spend millions on defending the battered coastline or abandon huge areas of Britain to the sea. Here in North Yorkshire, the local and central government has spent a lot of money to defend this battered coastline.

Man 1: If we didn't defend, well nature would take its course and we would invariably lose significant amounts of land. Great Britain is a shrinking asset.

Narrator: Many seaside towns have to be protected. Cliffs are held in place by rock bolts and new sand added to receding beaches. But the majority of the money goes to building new sea walls and repairing the Victorian and even older ones.

Man 1: The sea defenses themselves are in a very sorry state. We simply can't continue to paper over the cracks.

Narrator: One reason Britain is in such a bad way is its geology. Due to the Earth movements after the last ice age, the country is gradually tilting, so while Scotland rises, the south of England falls. On top of that, global warming is set to really stir things up. Sea levels in the southern UK are expected to rise about one to three feet by the end of the century. These are the salt marshes of Essex, just outside of London.

Man 2: Well here at Essex the problem simply couldn't be worse because we are in the front line and that we know that we've lost more than 50% of our salt marsh in just 30 years.

Narrator: Salt marshes help to defend the coastline by absorbing the energy of the waves. In addition to human development and other processes that have reduced the size of salt marshes, flood defenses are preventing them from spreading naturally inland, so instead of building more sea walls, in some places farm land is flooded and salt marshes recreated, giving natural protection to the coast. Whether the choice is to battle against nature or work with it, the long-term outcome remains unchanged. Britain is an ever-shrinking island.

Unit 12 Alain Robert: The French Spiderman

Are you afraid of heights? Would you ever risk your life for a sport? Alain Robert would.

Known as the French "Spiderman," this fearless, adventure-seeking athlete has climbed over 100 skyscrapers... including the seven tallest towers in the world. As he sometimes climbs without permits, police are often waiting for him at the top.

Alain climbs without ropes, meaning every climb he completes is extremely dangerous. One wrong move or stroke of bad luck could be fatal. But neither fear of heights, personal injury, or the law can stop Alain. For him, the only option is to keep climbing... all the way to the top.

Alain's passion for his sport has brought him a lot of attention, and even some world records. People are amazed to see him take on such impressive ascents with nothing more than climbing shoes and a bag of chalk. Crowds gather to cheer him on, and Alain gives them quite a show.

A typical climb for Alain takes place in a busy, high-profile urban area, such as today's climb in the La Défense neighborhood of Paris. A trace of chalk on a window marks his ascent.

Alain climbs by holding on to small spaces or by pulling himself up onto window ledges. Over the years, he's spent so many hours holding on tightly to the sides of buildings that he's injured his fingers and can no longer straighten them normally.

With such a dangerous profession, it's no wonder he has had some bad luck.

He has had numerous arrests for climbing without a permit, and he's also been in two major climbing accidents. Doctors tell Alain that his injuries make climbing more dangerous and have advised him to stop, but he can't. He loves it too much.

Today in La Défense, a crowd gathers steadily as news spreads that Alain is climbing the Suez Tower. That tiny speck on the side of the building is actually a man determined to reach the top. For Alain, each building is a personal challenge. His goal is not only to reach the top, but to face his fear of going higher ... and to overcome it—a lesson that he believes we can apply to our everyday lives. "We set ourselves limits," he says, "but we are all strong enough to aim higher, to achieve our goals. All we have to do is find strength within ourselves."

Alain first found that strength climbing rocks, not buildings, in the mountains around his home. Of course rock climbing is a popular sport around the world, but most people still use safety precautions like ropes. Not Alain! Whether he is on a mountain or on a building, even if he thinks he might fall, he carries on, because, as he says, "when you are facing a problem where your life is in danger, there is only one option." And the view from the top is worth it!